The Search For King

SOLOMON'S TREASURE

The Search For King

SOLOMON'S TREASURE

the lost isles of gold & the garden of eden

TIMOTHY SCHWAB
ANNA ZAMORANOS

A Collaborative Effort From
The TGC Research Team & Viewer Contributions

Foreward by Dr. Grepor "Butch" Belgica, M. Div., D. Min.

To order additional copies of this book, contact:

Ophir Institute
OphirInstitute@gmail.com
Facebook: The God Culture - Original
www.OphirInstitute.com

Table of Contents

Almost 6,000 attended the Restore Philippines Conference by The God Culture in collaboration with Love Philippines Movement at University of Southeastern Philippines Sports Dome, Davao, in October 2019. Photo By Idelle Ison.

"Thoroughly researched, well supported with Biblical truths, strongly convicted."

This revolutionary book is an eye-opener as it challenges what is now accepted as truth by probing history with unquestionable pieces of evidence. It is high-time for this book to spread like wildfire as it answers one of the most important issues in the Bible – the origin of the Kingdom. Tim is a shouting voice whose only agenda is to seek the truth and expose it to the world. His study unearthed the true identity of the Filipinos as Ophirians. I highly recommend this book for it will be an important key to bringing revival to this nation and generation, it is a piece of the puzzle that will complete the bigger picture in this end times."

– Bishops Rod and Ruth Cubos, Christ The Healer International Missions Movement Mindanao–Visayas–Luzon–Thailand–Singapore–Dubai and Beyond

Dedication

**In loving memory of
Pastor Ian V. Calo
Surviving Spouse Ate Hannah A. Dionen**

Approximately one year before he passed, Pastor Ian discovered "Solomon's Gold Series" by The God Culture on YouTube where we systematically prove the Philippines is the ancient land of gold – Ophir and the Garden of Eden.

Though we never had the pleasure of meeting, Pastor Ian began to teach and show our videos to his congregation weekly in order to educate Filipinos. When his health deteriorated, this man of God continued in good spirits educating his fellow Kababayan all the way up until his last days. Even when in the hospital in Manila, he commanded an audience of doctors, nurses and anyone he could captivating them with this knowledge that was not new after all but restored from ancient times.

In our visit to his congregation in Butuan, we found a group who was ignited for God and well-educated not just in this renewed history but in the Bible generally. That is a legacy.

ENJOY OUR
COFFEE TABLE BOOK:

A high quality pictorial view touring the
Philippines with an abbreviated case as the
ancient land of gold. Available for purchase at:
www.OphirInstitute.com.

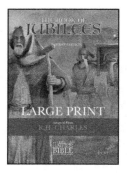

TEST THE BOOK OF JUBILEES:

Apply the Torah Test to this book found in the
Dead Sea Scrolls and viewed as scripture since
at least 150 B.C. by Levite Temple Priests.
Includes 50 Chapters, Full-color Maps,
Torah Calendar, Cross-references, etc.
Available for purchase at :
www.OphirInstitute.com.

www.thegodculture.com
Facebook: The God Culture - Original
YouTube: The God Culture or Solomon's Gold Series
Email: thegodculture@gmail.com

REVIEW OUR SOURCES:
WHILE READING

Our complete, comprehensive
Sourcebook of our sources includes
copy of the origin source document
with link in most cases, additional
commentary, maps, complete
attribution, etc.
Available for free download
as an electronic file at:
www.OphirInstitute.com.

Foreward
By Dr. Grepor "Butch" Belgica, M. Div., D. Min.

The Philippines is in the ancient land of Havilah, the land described in ancient writings as encompassed by the Pishon River (Gen 2:11 The name of the first is the Pishon. It is the one that flowed around the whole land of Havilah, where there is gold. 12 And the gold of that land is good; bdellium and onyx stone are there). Amazingly, the land of creation, named Elda, could likewise be traced in Havilah, described also as the land of Eve, the mother of all human beings after them.

Interestingly, the Filipino are Shemites, basically descendants of the eldest son of Noah – Shem, who begat Arphaxad, the grandfather of Eber (of Hebrews), who fathered Joktan.

Two of the 13 sons of Joktan, Ophir and Havilah, were apparently named after the land of their inheritance, when Noah divided the entire earth unto his sons by their clans, their languages, their lands, and their nations. And from these the nations spread abroad on the earth after the flood.

The accepted scientific way of determining the land of creation is biodiversity. Southeast Asia, as declared by science journals and hundreds of scientists, is the world center of biodiversity -- marine, mammals, plants and animals -- with the Philippines as the epicenter in all.

Having been educated in schools founded by Western colonizers and taught by Filipino teachers as gullible as I was, I grew up believing that Portuguese navigator, Ferdinand Magellan, a mercenary for the monarchy of Spain, discovered Las Islas Filipinas (Philippine Islands). He did not! I soon found out. To insist on such historical narrative, loaded with colonialist's bias, is to perpetuate a prevarication.

The Italian explorer, Antonio Pigafetta who served as Magellan's assistant, kept an accurate chronicle of their journey. He reported that Magellan accomplished his contract to locate the land of Solomon's source of gold, Ophir.

Now it can be told that the end of the dark ages (when the bible was translated from a prohibitive language – Latin, and became more accessible), came a mad rush from nations in the cold West, in search for Solomon's lands of gold, precious stones and spices. And the peace-loving, contented peoples from the warm, fertile lands of the East were invaded and plundered.

Historical evidence would confirm that the gems and jewelleries adorning the kings and nobles of the West were worn by ordinary subjects of the royalties in the East, particularly in the South and Far East. Whereas the royalties of the West had colourful delicate sash across their body, the nobles of the ancient Philippines wore skilfully minted sash of pure gold at least 20 kilos in weight, not to mention the gold trinkets and necklaces.

These and much, much more can be extracted from these monumental literary works: for precious knowledge, and facts to cherish in a lifetime.

The authors, Timothy and Anna, have done a magnificent work in this research and study of ancient writings and Scriptures. "In my radar" did I have them so to speak, since 2016; meticulously following their videos in The God Culture Channel in YouTube. And I had cultivated a strong, covenantal bond with them as kinsmen in Yeshua the Messiah, and fellow bondservants of the Almighty Creator, YHWH our Elohim! Their indefatigable energy to seek "Truth" and "prove all things" are remarkable indeed!

1734 MAP PROVES OWNERSHIP IN THE SOUTH CHINA SEA

Carta hydrographica y chorographica de las Yslas Filipinas : dedicada al Rey Nuestro Señor por el Mariscal d. Campo D. Fernando Valdes Tamon Cavallo del Orden de Santiago de Govor. Y Capn. Contributor Names: Murillo Velarde, Pedro, 1696-1753. Bagay, Nicolás de la Cruz, 1701-. Published Manila, 1734. US Library of Congress. Public Domain. Special permission to publish from Mel Velarde, owner of the original in the Philippines.

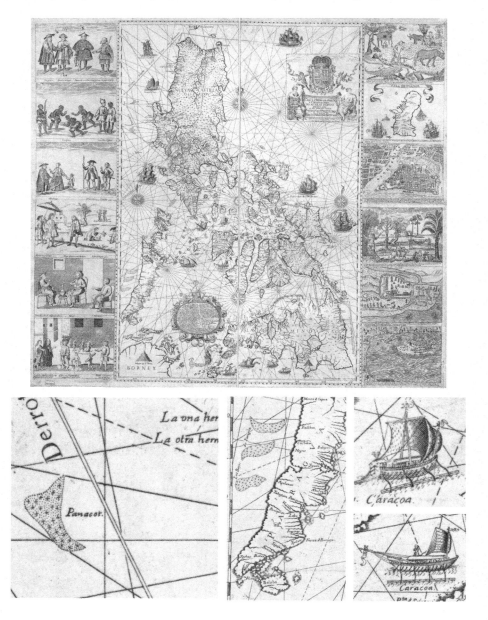

When Philippine businessman Mel Velarde was fortunate enough to secure the original publishing of this 1734 map from a London auction, he likely had no idea just how important this would become. In modern times, specifically since 1947, China has attempted to claim land it never claimed in any Chinese document, government decree nor map previously. In other words, their own history proves this claim exaggerated. With a decimated Philippines, it attempted to exploit and encroach on Philippine territory in the West Philippine Sea. If China had a true claim and case, they would have presented such at the United Nations but they failed to present anything intelligible.

This map is one of the proofs which manifest the shoals in question are historic territory of the Philippines long before the attempted land grab. Above, the Panacot shoals, modern Scarborough Shoals are clearly labeled in Filipino even as territory of the Philippines. There is little to discuss which is likely why China did not even attend the hearing thus failing to exercise it's claim and losing the ruling. In addition, this 1734 map demonstrates the shoals off the coast of Palawan named for Palawan even as Philippine territory. Whether this included all such shoals in that area or not, certainly China has no such claim. In a nation where honor is paramount, one would think the Chinese government would admit their shortcoming and withdraw from land not theirs by law. There is no actual dispute these islands belong to the Philippines as a 1947 unsupported claim after WWII certainly does not qualify as historic in any sense especially when China's history records they did not include these lands prior and Philippine history makes ownership clear. Also, a Buddhist monk finally crossing the sea for China in 671 A.D. proves China is nothing but far behind in the arena of exploration. Even Chinese records show nations like the Philippines arriving in Canton in 990 B.C. in which taxes were documented and in the third century A.D. thus China has no position in any sense. The Hague already ruled China is illegally occupying such land and if they continue to do so, they only prove to be yet another colonial mindset.

The Philippines had large ships long before the Chinese and again this 1734 map documents the Caracoa in that era as a large ship as well twice.

The enigmatic Queen of Sheba – one of the world's first female billionaires.

Filipina illustrated in the Boxer Codex, 1590. Public Domain. [299]

Introduction

The resplendent sun glistened bright on a midsummer-morning on the ancient, narrow, stone streets of Jerusalem and the City of David. In the distance, the smell of anticipation was in the air. It was about 970 B.C. and the unimaginable was under way. An ominous expectation loomed as the First Temple of God was being erected along with King Solomon's Palace. Crowds began to converge along the thoroughfare as a very great train of camels paraded through the city gates inspiring awe and wonder into the hearts of the Israelites. The spectators peered at what appeared to be an extreme abundance of spices including frankincense, myrrh and cinnamon of such considerable store, the land of the tabernacle of God had never seen such prosperity before.

This was followed by a large troop of exotic golden-skinned peoples draped in blue and purple luxury linens and silks and decked with fine gold and precious stones. The women displayed Egyptian-style shebyu collars of gold and earrings and bracelets of pure gold bedazzled with baguettes. The men radiated with pride boasting their ancestral Sacred Thread, a heavy cord of finely woven solid gold swathed across their shoulders, breasts and adjoining in a knot at their waists, with belts intricately meshed of very fine gold, earrings, necklaces, gold and jewel embellished dagger handle, arm and leg bands all of authentic gold of Ophir. The yellow Gold of Sheba followed in the next progression as the dromedaries conveyed 4.5 tons of unblemished gold in wedges succeeded by a colorful rainbow of precious gemstones.

For this was an oblation to the Temple project commenced at the time of the enigmatic Queen of Sheba, one of the world's very first female billionaires and likely one of the wealthiest, if not the wealthiest matron in all of history. Trailing behind, The Queen of Sheba was chauffeured upon a regal, illustrious carriage bejeweled with gemstones and gilded golden posts bestride atop 4 camels. The empress is obscured by opulent cobalt and indigo textiles adorned in fringes of gold and silver from her native archipelago but the thronging congregation could only distinguish her arms of flawless golden skin and her sleeves of silk garment encrusted with gold. The elegant entourage sashays to King Solomon's new Palace being erected back-dropped by an unadorned Temple which lay incomplete.

The concentration of the crowd was suddenly frenzied by the triumphal sounding of an orchestra of ram's horns as an even weightier caravan entered the city corridor. It was Hiram, King of Tyre, who was delegated Admiral of King Solomon's recent navy to go to Ophir from the Red Sea port newly fabricated 344 km South of Jerusalem. Hiram, a blended Hebrew, part Phoenician man of stature, led the next divisions of even-toed ungulates from his return trek from Ophir. He and his navy of diverse, tall, bearded and white-skinned Phoenician sailors and dark-skinned Israelites arrived to a hero's ovation as they escorted a royal fortune of the gold of Ophir valued at $588 million today weighing over 13,000 kilograms (15 tons).

They conducted a plenitude of metals as silver, lead, iron and tin as the troupes of camel-powered wagons ensued. Coaches of ivory from Ophir supplanted in bulk along with a massive volume of the exotic, foreign red sandalwood never seen in Israel until that day. These prized, foreign timbers spanned 100-feet long boasting a rich red hue. The parade ended with a horde of friendly long-tailed monkeys performing to admirers as they run, vault and scale their Phoenician handlers culminating in a fireworks display of color as alluring peacocks thrill all in assembly with their exquisite glamour. It was greater than a Barnum and Bailey Circus act as the crowd palpably acknowledge each stage of bounty as they had never experienced an event like this nor would they ever again.

These were the gifts from the very first journey from Ophir and they fully identify only one land on all of Earth as this ancient land of Gold, we will authenticate as the modern Philippines. Why is the Queen of Sheba in the middle of this narrative? Most scholars fail to look at the

Table of Nations in Genesis 10 to notice that not only are there two Shebas listed, one is the very brother of Ophir to which her story cannot be separated. The Queen of Sheba descended from the Brother of Ophir not the wrong Sheba in Ethiopia which we will substantiate does not fit any of these anecdotes.

In this book, we will thoroughly test the origin of these elements, dig deeply into practically every scripture on the topic and offer a history that is little known about the only land which qualifies as Ophir and was recorded as such as fact not speculatively. We will explore ancient maps and geographical markers, offer observable science and dissect the language of this very land of antiquity to uncover Hebrew roots in many words which linguists agree. We do not offer a claim but we will demonstrate indisputably that this ancient land of gold is none other than the Philippines and just to make sure, we will test the other claims around the world as well. You will likely find as we have, in comparison to the abundant, overwhelming evidence in the Philippines, there is no other narrative one could remotely consider as the ancient isles, and they must be islands, of gold in any sense.

As the history of the Philippines is restored in Ophir, this will bear out that Sheba and Tarshish are also found in this same region within the modern Philippine archipelago. Once we have accomplished this task, we will tackle one of the largest enigmas known to man – locating the region of the Garden of Eden, the Land of Creation and the Rivers from Eden. That sounds like an impossible challenge yet review the results for yourself. We include this not because we chose to head in such direction but as a perk, this deposition just so happens to lead there and again, there is no other coherent defense anywhere else on earth once one objectively reviews this substantiation.

Once again, we will prove and we will not stake a petition nor does this truth require any scholarly consensus which is an impertinent paradigm of control already guilty of losing the isles of gold. It stands as truth or it does not. Test it for yourself and forego the many agendas that have obscured what was known for thousands of years and then, somehow lost. How exactly did the rabbis and church lose the land of gold? Peter calls it "willing ignorance" in 2 Peter 3.

We find these lands in the Philippines as well, as this gold region transcends all of history as it is first recorded in Genesis 2 and leads to the Philippines in definition even in that passage as you will find. Along this journey, we will locate all of these elusive traditions even positing and testing our strong theory locating the Rivers from Eden – all 5 of them. This theory is actually the first to fit the Biblical descriptions of these rivers and we challenge anyone to find another that does. Though we do not require one's belief in that theory to prove our case, however, it becomes further entrenched as a result of this entire position and very difficult to dismiss nor disprove.

We are The God Culture, a group of independent researchers who set out in search of the sector of King Solomon's resources – Ophir. Over the past three years, we have been able to produce over fifty YouTube videos which document our journey through these facets which lead to the Philippines. Many have asked why a group of Americans would take interest in this topic. We do not care about gold except it is the resource which defines the ancient realm in which prophecy tells us much of it's role in the last days. Every scholar should be seeking this but few even know what Ophir represents.

Even King Solomon realized later in his life as he wrote Ecclesiastes, that all the gold was meaningless without a relationship with Yahuah God. The true value of these areas of antiquity has nothing to do with it's gold but it's people who are called by His name. Though our leader who is of mixed Native American and European descent, is married to a Filipina, our aim all along has been to find these true locations regardless of where they may abide as reconstructing this archaic geography, restores prophecy which is where this writing will ultimately lead and that will astound indeed. This is one of the greatest revelations of our age and we encourage everyone to do as we have, just as 1 Thessalonians 5:21 admonishes us, "Prove all things, hold fast that which is good."

If you have arrived on this page a skeptic, you are a welcomed guest as we began there too. As you prove all things, we believe you will find this is not a theory nor a journey of speculation but one which follows the facts and they are abundant – far more than we have been taught. If you are Muslim, Catholic, Christian, Atheist or seeking, we encourage you to review these evidences because even if you do not believe the Bible, no rational human could possibly deny there are pieces of history within. Since it is the origin of this entire historical narrative of Ophir, you will never be able to prove this out without it. Even Indiana Jones does so. We make no apologies that we build our foundation on the Bible. We challenge academics, scholars, government officials and all regular folk, to execute a trial of this data even in attempt to disprove. This expedition will change your perspective and life. Selah.

King Solomon's Temple, Jerusalem.

Solomon's navy returning from Ophir with almug wood.

Chapter 1 | Evidence Ophir Existed

In 1946, archaeologists representing the Israel Exploration Society and the municipality of Tel-Aviv in Tell Qasile (modern Tel-Aviv, Israel) excavated two Hebrew ostraca – an inscribed pottery shard. [1] [2] Tell Qasile is positioned on the northern bank of the Yarqon River likely where Hiram, King of Tyre once conveyed timber down from Lebanon (ancient Tyre/Phoenicia). This fragment, dated around the eighth century B.C., transcribes as:

> *"Gold of Ophir to(for) Beth Horon*
> *30 Shekels..." – Kitchen[3][4]*

Tell Qasile pottery shard. [3][4]

This attested fragment confirms the existence of the land of gold from which King Solomon's navy imported resources. [4] It also demonstrates Ophir is a legitimate, physical land of Gold and no legend. This is in no way similar to the South American legend of El Dorado which if one researched, initiated with a "Golden Man" who dives into gold dust coating himself not a city nor an empire which it later morphed into and no trace has ever been found. That's a fairy tale. Ophir is not as it has now been found and the resources are still there but no golden man, golden temples nor great architecture are ever recorded in any narrative of Ophir. Finally, this ostraca substantiates King Solomon existed as he sent a navy to Ophir and that gold ends up in Israel as an offering and not just to any project but a city which King Solomon built – Beth Horon.

Any scholar claiming there is no proof of King Solomon's existence is ignoring this very obvious find which confirms his presence at least three ways. It was King Solomon who erected not only the Temple of Yahuah God but one of the cities he is recorded to have constructed in 2 Chronicles 8:5 is Beth-Horon. Here, we have a settled reference that truly cannot be discredited. Ophir was an authentic seat of gold and resources. We recognize they returned with that gold because there is an archaeological record which is well-established by history demonstrating that specific gold migrating into ancient Israel in Solomon's era in circulation even in Solomon's construction project and labeled so. Based on this alone, historians should adjust their mapping of the ancient Phoenician shipping routes to include not only the Mediterranean Sea but the Red Sea port King Solomon built in Eziongeber which most ignore even after evidence was unearthed.

Additionally, a shekel on average weighed about 10 grams or 0.4 ounces. Thus, this inscribed 30 shekels is about 12 ounces in weight. As of the writing of this book, gold is valued at approximately $1,334.79 per ounce. Therefore, this is about a $16,000 likely personal contribution which is very significant for an individual donation to an extraneous development venture when the Temple was already functioning.

Solomon's existence is also further supported in archaeology yet there are those who continue to this day to claim none has ever been produced to determine the Biblical King Solomon nor King David existed. We already showed you evidence in archaeology but they neglect it because it does not reinforce their world-view fundamentally. It's time we shatter such dubious archetypes or we will never get to the truth. King Solomon and King David's existence as well as a kingdom of Israel are supplementally affirmed in excavations in Jerusalem by Israeli archaeologist Eilat Mazar and reputed in international news especially in a report from National Geographic.

"A 3,000-year-old defensive wall possibly built by King Solomon has been unearthed in Jerusalem, according to the Israeli archaeologist [Eilat Mazar] who led the excavation. The discovery appears to validate a Bible passage, she says. Ancient artifacts found in and around the complex pointed Mazar to the tenth-century B.C. date. Ceramics found near the

wall helped narrow the date down, being of a level of sophistication common to the second half of the tenth century B.C.— King Solomon's time, according to Mazar." "We don't have many kings during the tenth century that could have built such a structure, basically just David and Solomon," she said." –National Geographic [5]

Not only does this serve as evidence that King Solomon and King David's kingdom existed, it emerges more deeply entrenched in light of the ostraca identifying King Solomon's land of Ophir, King Solomon's city of Beth-Horon and King Solomon's literal gold of Ophir in actual use in significance. We can accentuate this with the writings which record the history of David and Solomon. David is mentioned over 1,000 times in the Bible by name in the Books of Ruth, 1 and 2 Samuel, 1 Kings, 1 and 2 Chronicles, Ezra, Nehemiah, Psalm, Proverbs, Ecclesiastes, Isaiah, Jeremiah, Ezekiel, Hosea, Amos, and Zechariah in the Old Testament and then, Matthew, Mark, Luke, John, Acts, Romans, 2 Timothy, Hebrews and Revelation in the New Testament even by Messiah who sprang from David's lineage. In fact, apply the dates of these accounts and you will find King David is recorded from childhood to death to the time of the writing of Revelation in the First Century A.D. as he was real. No one can honestly ignore all this historical evidence and call that position scholarly. Is it not uniquely ignorant to include a pagan writing of a king declaring victory as archaeology while discounting one of the very oldest, best documented books in all of history?

King Solomon is recorded in 2 Samuel, 1 and 2 Kings, 1 and 2 Chronicles, Nehemiah, Psalm, Proverbs, Song of Songs, Ecclesiastes and Jeremiah in the Old Testament and in Matthew, Luke and Acts in the New Testament even by Messiah Himself.

We, then, have their writings in concurrent employment attributed to King David as the Book of Psalm and multiple writings of King Solomon in Proverbs, Ecclesiastes and Song of Songs without mentioning other extra-biblical writings. Also, sources from Israel's enemies such as the Mesha Stele in the Louvre Museum dated 840 B.C. and the Tell Dan Stele from the 9th century B.C. housed in The Israel Museum mention David and his lineage contemporaneously. As foes, there is no purpose in their recording King David other than as fact.

Additionally, debated finds include "Solomonic Gates" found dating to the 10th century B.C. in Hazor, Megiddo and Gezer just as scripture defines. It is the dating that is debated based largely on the mixture used. However, could not Solomon have been the origin of such technique? Of course he could and he is recorded as building all three of those cities in 1 Kings 9:15. Even pottery affirms this dating but why not ignore that and contest it? Only willing ignorance would cause one to dismiss the obvious. However, even without that, David and Solomon were real.

In the same vein, there are those who will examine this staggering abundance of documentation we are about to delineate and attempt to dismiss it for a number of reasons perhaps. This is why we demand they prosecute the sweeping conclusions not just one tertiary side note as that will not unravel this multifaceted and comprehensive position. We are haggard of this generation who does not prove anything anymore but wishes to grab a sound-bite as if that is a remote representation of grounds of affidavit. Most, today, do not believe in anything because few are verifying anymore and that is a sad state leaving us vulnerable to propaganda. Selah.

3000-year-old defense wall found in the City of David. [5]

Tell Dan Stele. [388]

"Solomonic Gate" in Megiddo. [415]

Mesha Stele. [33]

Chapter 2 | Biblical Foundation of Ophir

Hebrew: **Ôwphîyr:** אופיר*: o-feer': reducing to ashes, fine gold. of uncertain derivation; Ophir, the name of a son of Joktan, and of a gold region in the East: −Ophir. [6]*
Ancient Hebrew: (א)A, (ו)U, (פ)P, (י)Y, (ר)R.

The shroud of confusion regarding ancient Ophir begins with it's name rendered from the Hebrew in all modern Bibles and Bible dictionaries, we have reviewed, improperly. It begins with an Hebrew "A" or Aleph (א), not an "O." This letter is always "A" in sound and translation. It is never "O" nor "U." In fact, the second letter is an Ancient Hebrew WAW or U (ו) though "W" is also correct as a "W" is simply "UU" or "Double U." Thus, you are looking at the actual origin of the chemical symbol for gold in this word as it begins with "AU" not "OW." It should be rendered in Ancient Hebrew to English as AUPYR, AUPIR, AUPHYR or similar. They certainly did attempt to reduce Ophir to ashes but this meaning is erroneous and appears spurious perhaps exposing their intent.

The origin of the chemical symbol for gold, AU, is said to be the Latin Aurum or Aurea which we will determine in the next chapter is the equivalent of Ophir. This is the kingdom of gold for the Greeks which carried over into Latin but AUPYR is the origin of that reference as you will find thus the true origin of the chemical symbol for gold − AU. It is used twelve times in the Bible and with brilliance. The Bible offers markers along the way which lead us to the isles of the East in the Philippines and nowhere else. Scholars have been confused about the origin of this word but when you truly look at the Ancient Hebrew, you find the word for light as used in Genesis when God said let there be light. We will prove this is the same land.

Genesis 1:3 KJV
And God said, Let there be light: and there was light.
Hebrew: Ôwr: אוֹר: light. [7] (א is ALWAYS "A" not "O")

Isaiah 24:15 KJV
Wherefore glorify ye the LORD in the fires, even the name of the LORD
God of Israel in the isles of the sea. (LORD is YHWH, Yahuah)
Hebrew: ûwr: אור: fires, light. [8] (א is ALWAYS "A" not "U")

Contrast this to another use of the same Hebrew word in Isaiah. Understand that there were no vowel points as the dots you see that supposedly differentiate these two words, the exact same otherwise, were inserted around 1000 A.D. or so by the Masoretes. They are the same word in Ancient Hebrew. As much as we appreciate the Textus Receptus and you will note we use the King James Version principally in our teachings which was translated from that manuscript, we also remain aware these vowel points did not exist for thousands of years prior and somehow these words could be read and understood without vowel points that entire time. Thus, we still do not actually need them much of the time or should test them often. This is redefined as a different word that is obviously the same use in this passage not fires but light and it is rendered in Isaiah as now beginning with an "U" in Strong's Concordance and others but it's an Aleph (א) which is always "A" not "U" nor "O."

This verse even identifies the isles of the sea which we will later prove is Ophir even tying Ophir to this same word for light which is it's true origin etymologically. AUR(אור) is "light" and insert PY(פי) for AUPYR and it renders "Mouth of Light." [122] This is a direct identification in Hebrew of the land where Yahuah God said "Let there be light." This is because this word in Hebrew is really AUR not OWR nor UWR which are truly ludicrous renderings especially when the first letter ALEPH (א) which is always "A," could not be mistaken by a Hebrew scholar. As you can see, we have gone extremely deep into this topic even assessing the

Hebrew word for word and letter for letter in this pursuit. We find Ophir to be the region of light known as the Land of Creation which you will find proves out completely as the Philippines.

We have what would be one of the largest oversights in Hebrew translation – one in which no actual Hebrew scholar could possibly err. We point this out early because we wish to establish a pattern you will identify in this story which has not only been suppressed in history but in Bible interpretation really working hand-in-hand. We are all to prove all things (1Thess. 5:21) lest we be deceived and the delusion in which we live, we were warned, is strong. Also, you will find we restore the name of God recorded over 6,800 times in the Hebrew Bible as YHWH never as Lord which taken back into Hebrew is the word Ba'al. We will provide charts with explanation in the back of this book because we pronounce this phonetically and you will find us using Yahuah in place of LORD in narration. Feel free to review that now if you feel the need. Let us commence with the Bible narrative.

> *1 Kings 9:26-28 KJV*
> *And king Solomon made a navy of ships in Eziongeber, which is beside Eloth, on the shore of the Red sea, in the land of Edom. And Hiram sent in the navy his servants, shipmen that had knowledge of the sea, with the servants of Solomon. And they came to Ophir, and fetched from thence gold, four hundred and twenty talents, and brought it to king Solomon.*

King Solomon was following the edict of his father, King David, to build a temple which would house the very presence of Yahuah God. However, there is something very conspicuous about this measure on the part of Solomon. His father David had already placed the essential stock such as gold, wood, etc. into the treasury before he died and Solomon already had the necessities to build the Temple. However, he fabricates state-of-the-art, merchant marine vessels and a new seaport on the Red Sea to fetch gold and resources he already retained from his father. It does not seem to make rational sense until you understand what gold and what district this is.

As we said, this work is not about gold as capital or currency but as a means to identify the most extraordinary province in all of antiquity.

This is not an exploration for opulence, it is a divine campaign for Yahuah's gold that Adam used in the first sacrifice which we will test. This was not just any region simply yielding this mineral, but they had to have been prospecting gold in colossal bounty for Solomon's navy fetched such fortune on the inaugural expedition. Four hundred and twenty talents of gold is $588 million in today's market value. Low-end estimates of a Biblical talent of gold reveal a weight of 33 kilograms (75 lbs.), so we use the conservative measure for calculations though it could be considerably greater to almost double. This is 13,860 kg. (15.75 tons) of gold on one foray also requiring very large ships to transport such substantial cargo which we will check as well. This acquisition continued every 3 years for Solomon's 40-year reign. This thereupon certifies Ophir as not just some arbitrary ground or island that materialized grains of gold but the greatest expanse of gold in history would be found there. We should find remnants of this in some form still today and we do. Many are simply unaware.

Remember, this was about 970 B.C. and mining equipment at that time was minimal. This rules out even South Africa which requires bulky modern equipment to extract gold which is why South Africa's gold rush did not even boom until around 1884 and they did not even discover gold panning in history until 1000 A.D. according to their own history. [9] One would think this ancient land would be far better documented and that is because it actually is. As this geographical knowledge has been obscured in the past century since the 1890s especially, it is not actually hard to find when we inspect the original, authoritative sources. It has been inhumed but not expunged and no longer shall it be concealed. After reading this repository we have curated, you will have to interrogate this intelligence. We hope you will thoroughly examine this yourself as our sources are among the most credible (see Sourcebook) and this exhibition of research, well-supported and vetted. We do not require nor expect scholarly consensus however on a topic scholars have remained ignorant for centuries.

One of the largest questions that should nag at academics, is why would Solomon build a new port and navy on the Red Sea to fetch more resources for the temple? We find his father David had already acquired and placed all the resources needed to build the temple in the treasury. What did the wise Solomon know that we do not? Well, much, but especially the full narrative for one, as he understood Genesis and knew exactly where the Garden of Eden, Rivers from Eden, Havilah as well as Ophir were located in region. After reading this edition, you too will discover these and though we have compiled this information, it was really already available to all of us. We are not proclaiming anything unfamiliar to true testimony but restoring a truth that the world once knew.

King Solomon was cognizant the land in which his fleet would sojourn would net the same offerings that Adam used in the first sacrifice of atonement – gold, frankincense and myrrh. Before one applies backwards reasoning using these spice commodities to pinpoint Ophir, how about we conduct comprehensive research unearthing Ophir and then identify these Biblical spices especially because they originate there as they must and we will explore that too. He sought the wood that Noah used to build the ark. They did not have more value for being of superior quality necessarily but he was erecting Yahuah's temple and he wanted elements of more reverence to Him replacing those that did not have that fundamental nostalgia. This story is far more precious than we had ever imagined and far more significant as is this land.

Some scholars have actually attempted to deduce that Ophir and Tarshish are located in Britain or Spain or even the Americas but again, why would King Solomon build a port on the Red Sea to circumnavigate Africa extending the campaign by four times in duration? He certainly would not need to go to Spain for instance, when his admiral, Hiram, already had established trade routes with Spain with one of the largest fleets of ships on the Mediterranean just North of Israel in Phoenicia (Tyre). Logic does not progress in that direction especially when one finds the King of Spain named Ophir and Tarshish in the Far East in the Philippines many times over for many centuries and the British attempted to counter though they lost the debate but they won the war so they were able to effectively suppress Spain's find.

However, the British went to Malaysia and named a mountain there in 1801 as Mt. Ophir so they too, knew they were not Ophir and Tarshish. Of course, the Malays knew better and rejected that name and continue to use their local name Gunung Ledang to this day. When we first began this journey, we were told by a friend that Britain had already settled this debate. Look back in history and you will find Spain lost it's power but this narrative has never been disproven nor is it a new one. The world knew where Ophir was all the way up until Spain was defeated in the 1890s. There was no mystery and there should not be one today. Solomon built on the Red Sea to head East not West nor to places very close to him but to a very foreign land of foreign resources he did not have access until that time and he already traded with both Ethiopia and Yemen who are far too close. We test the ships and calculate this.

Take a look at the modern Bible maps for this era and they are clueless on this topic such as the Holman Bible Atlas, those in the back of the King James Bible and those most popular on the internet. First, many of them show Sheba from Cush/Ethiopia/Ham living in the same place as Sheba from Joktan/Shem which would mean one of them would be cursed as they cannot live in the same territory since Noah divided the Earth into three separate parts for his three sons. They do the same with Havilah and many of them place Ophir in Saudi Arabia or sometimes Africa, sometimes the Persian Gulf and sometimes all three. All are wrong on this topic as we will prove overwhelmingly. These cartographers have no idea where Ophir is and most do not claim to even invoking question marks and multiple locations in speculation.

Over time, those question marks disappeared without satisfying the actual query. In fact, on many maps, scholars attempt to claim Ophir in Saudi Arabia because of the name Ophira found in Saudi Arabia. The problem is they have not bothered to read the definition of Ophira [15] which means "towards Ophir" or "to Ophir" or better termed, not Ophir or on the way to Ophir. These are weak guesses based on etymologies and wordplay which do not even connect. Ophir is not just a nation, he is a person for which that nation is named because he migrated there after the Tower of Babel dispersion. Many miss the Table of Nations in Genesis 10 thinking it to be a bore yet, it is brilliant as it reveals exactly where Ophir lived and to where he migrated after Babel fell. We have derived much revelation from Genesis 10.

Genesis 10:26-30 KJV
And Joktan begat Almodad, and Sheleph, and Hazarmaveth, and Jerah,

And Hadoram, and Uzal, and Diklah, And Obal, and Abimael, and **Sheba***, And* **Ophir***, and* **Havilah***, and Jobab: all these were the sons of Joktan. And their dwelling was from Mesha, as thou goest unto Sephar a mount of the east.*

Notice Joktan had thirteen sons but among them are Ophir and his brothers Sheba and Havilah. Sheba being the older of the three and the accurate Sheba from which the Queen of Sheba descended, is from Shem not Ham as her story falls right in the middle of the trip to Ophir (Ch. 7). Those are the younger sons along with Jobab. However, the Bible does not leave their geography to chance but defines it specifically as at the time of the Tower of Babel, their families lived right next to Shinar (modern Iraq) in modern day Mesha or Meshad, Iran. In the next chapter, we will fully vet this. Then, they migrated all the way to the Far East to Sephar, the Mount of the East. These are two very specific references and historic markers that one cannot mistake. Ophir, Sheba and Havilah pioneered the lands which would bear their names returning to the ancient homeland of Noah and Adam.

The gold of Ophir was renowned in scripture even before the days of Solomon as Job first writes of it.

Job 22:24 KJV
Then shalt thou lay up gold as dust, and the **gold of Ophir** *as the stones of the brooks.*

Job 28:16 KJV
It cannot be valued with the **gold of Ophir***, with the* **precious onyx***, or the sapphire.*

Many scholars agree the Book of Job was written before the days of Moses and is the oldest book of the Bible. Here Job is aware of Ophir even in his time as having the most valuable gold and he even ties in onyx just like Genesis 2 which is no coincidence. Job knew what this region represented and likely, where it was at least generally in direction as Noah and his sons were conscious because they once flourished there and cherished the memory of Ancient Havilah.

King David, Solomon's father clearly was aware of Ophir even acquiring a bit of gold from there somehow. He describes the gold of Ophir as royal gold of queens and equates that to the gold of Sheba given to the ultimate royalty, Messiah, by the Wise Kings whom we have an entire chapter forthcoming.

> *Psalm 45:9 KJV*
> **Kings' daughters** *were among thy honourable women: upon thy right hand did stand the* **queen in gold of Ophir.**

> *Psalm 72:15 KJV*
> *...to him shall be given of the* **gold of Sheba***...*

> *Isaiah 13:12 KJV*
> *Then I will make a man* **more precious than fine gold***; even a man than the* **golden wedge of Ophir.**

The writers of the Bible even extra-biblical texts such as Tobit, knew what Ophir represented. The Book of Tobit 13:17 (KJVA) places the gold of Ophir as the gold used to pave the streets of New Jerusalem. This gold is not just important, it is renowned and sacred from the time of Creation to the Final Day of Judgment. It mattered to Yahuah in the beginning, remains notable today and will always be precious.

However, in addition to the migration of Ophir and Sheba which we will track next, Chronicles begins elaborating on specifics that assist in narrowing this.

> *2 Chronicles 9:21 KJV*
> *For the king's ships (Solomon's) went to Tarshish (Ophir) with the servants of Huram (Hiram King of Tyre)* **every 3 years***, once came the ships of Tarshish bringing* **gold***,* **silver***,* **ivory** *and* **apes** *and* **peacocks.**

This is a literal gold mine in scripture. We now have a distance we can test as well as resources which we will classify in the next chapters. Note, too, Tarshish is a place and it is in the same region as Ophir according to this passage and others we will review later. There is no placing one in India and one in Britain thousands of miles apart according to the origin of this narrative. They are in the same region and they are both isles. We already know Solomon was headed East from the Red Sea because West would be ridiculously redundant to the point of increasing the journey by a factor of four.

How far would the ships of that era travel on a 3-year journey? Some question this saying Solomon did not proceed that far but instead just waited to traverse wherever every three years. Many of those types will also tell you the Bible is allegory so they can change it to say whatever they want. It says what it says. One channel on YouTube even attempts to move Israel, Assyria, Babylon and even Rome into Africa which is illiterate Biblically and historically. They ignore many passages such as Abraham travelling South to Egypt (Gen. 12:10) and from Egypt, North to return to Canaan (Gen. 13:1). However, this accuses King Solomon of being complacent. This entire case proves this a 3-year round trip journey from multiple angles especially when we test Isaiah's isles of the East at the ends of the earth. Africa is not East and not Shem's territory either but Ham's and wrong. We can locate this gold republic many ways and we shall.

Journey from the Red Sea Port to Ophir in the Far East on Shem's border.

*Acropolis ruins in Fortune island of
Nasugbu, Batangas, Philippines.*

Chapter 3 | Greek, Indian, Chinese Ancient Source of Gold

Malaka! That is not Greece but the Acropolis ruins in Fortune Island of Nagsugbu, Batangas, Philippines. This word "malaka" in Greek is an exclamation of surprise. However, it reminds us of the Tagalog word "malakas" meaning strong. One must love the Greeks not for their esoteric philosophy and certainly not for their conquering empire but for their anecdotes in which some prove to be founded in truth. This is one of those accounts and it leads to Ophir.

Remember, King Solomon partnered with Hiram, King of Tyre – the Phoenician. In the era of Solomon, the Phoenicians ruled the seas in the Mediterranean but few historians even recognize that they had a whole new route now thanks to Solomon as of 970 B.C. into the Indian Ocean. The Phoenician language is the origin of the Greek language and it's influences in culture and mariner history are significant as it was absorbed into Greece in part. In doing so, the Greeks acquired the knowledge of the shipping routes of the Phoenicians including the route to Ophir for Gold and Tarshish for Silver. In the Greek language, these two areas would be rebranded in name in Greek. As the Romans did not continue these routes, this would be lost and rediscovered but records and maps exist from early in the Roman period. Note they did not typically reflect Malaysia nor Indochina and the Ganges empties into the South China Sea on most maps.

Many have chronicled about the reputed Greek isle of gold called Chryse and their isle of silver known as Argyre. However, until Magellan, the West did not actually rediscover them yet but they would narrow in on it over time. This has been misconstrued though.

"Pliny also alludes to a Southeast Asian peninsula. Noting that the Seres (Chinese) wait for trade to come to them, he lists three rivers of China, which are followed by the "promontory of Chryse", and then a bay. Elsewhere in his Natural History, however, Pliny referred to Chryse as an island... It was more often mapped as an island in medieval mappaemundi." – Thomas Suarez [16]

We find many authors who provide good facts and then, very poor interpretation such as Suarez. Pliny never alludes to Chryse as a peninsula. He firmly identifies it as an island several times and to claim this noted geographer was confused about the difference is illogical. Ptolemy makes that error but his map is no where near credible regarding Southeast Asian geography which is practically non-existent. Pliny mentions directions from three rivers in China, a bay and the "promontory of Chryse." A promontory can be a peninsula but is merely a rocky point also found on islands many times. It is unscholarly to overrule Pliny's references to Chryse as an island to then, claim he meant a peninsula this one time in confusion. A true geographer would not. We also find Suarez then misleading in British propaganda even ignorning portions of The Periplus and Pomponius Mela even though he quotes them.

However, in that era of Messiah, they did not rediscover Chryse and neither had been there. Josephus makes a further connection. This is no new land but simply the Greek name for the Biblical Ophir. We will review the Bible equates Tarshish in the same area as Ophir as the source of silver. He renders it in Latin as Aurea Chersonesus in which Aurea or Aurum is the origin of the chemical symbol "AU" for gold and Chersonesus is the word for peninsula. It is an island.

"...to whom Solomon gave this command, that they should go along with his own stewards to the land that was of old called Ophir, but now the Aurea Chersonesus: which belongs to India: to fetch him gold." – Flavius Josephus, 93 A.D. [19]

Aurea in Latin is Chryse in Greek which is Ophir in Hebrew. He also ties this as the Indian land of gold in antiquity and remember, India was vast in interpretation in those days from Afghanistan to the Indies including the Philippines. In the first century A.D., a Greek writing titled "The Periplus of the Erythaean Sea" housed in the British Museum (Add. ms. 19391, ff 9-12) [17] closes in on this antique land of gold with incredible accuracy and it is reaffirmed many times. It locates Chryse.

> *"...the last part of the inhabited world toward the east, under the rising sun itself"* – *The Periplus of the Erythaean Sea, 60 A.D.* [17]

What is the last part of the inhabited world to the East under the rising sun? The Philippines is called "Land of the Morning" in it's National Anthem "Lupang Hinirang" just as Japan refers to itself as "Land of the Rising Sun." These are lands to the East of China not on the mainland of Malaysia. However, though many authors ignore this, The Periplus scores far more specific and we are astonished how many scholars seem to read and then ignore what it says including Suarez.

> *"After this region under the very north, the sea outside ending in a land called This."* [China] – *The Periplus of the Erythaean Sea* [17]

"After this region" means beyond it. One passes it. "Under the very North" of what? This(China) and the Tropic of Cancer(Taiwan). This is an island Southeast of China. "The sea outside ending in... This [China]" is obvious but completely overlooked. It says what it says and the writer of the Periplus was recording directions dictated to him from the Indians and those of Sri Lanka as to the location of their land of gold which is also Chryse. He was not mapping a journey he took. This means in antiquity, India had a gold source to the East and does not represent the land of gold. His directions are accurate and when the world learned the geography of Southeast Asia, the location became obvious which is how Magellan found it.

One attempted to say these are not continued directions but just identifying China yet they did not bother to read. China is not in the sea beyond China nor under the Tropic of Cancer. Is there a sea within the mainland of China? No. The China Sea is beyond it, East, just as the directions tell us. They also tell us South of China thus this island is in the South China Sea. It further identifies that "This" is China, the land from where they brought "silk" to India. The marker here is China though it has no identification as Ophir or Chryse. One then, heads beyond China to it's sea to the South below Cancer. This has always identified the area of the Philippines and never Malaysia. Taiwan is an island not isles, not below Cancer and we now know the Philippines is the second most abundant land of untapped gold reserves on the planet [11][12][13] not Taiwan nor does it have such history as the Philippines which is overwhelming. It has no claim of being ancient Ophir.

Again, in all fairness to Josephus, Ptolemy and others, they did not physically go there 2,000 years ago and you can see from the maps of that era, the Philippines is essentially ignored or wrapped into the Malay archipelago in the Western mindset. That becomes antiquated thinking. Obviously, they had no idea of it's exact geography until Magellan's era. Their maps draw India due South of China ignoring the Malay Peninsula and Indochina but they illustrate islands. Why? They are following the facts they knew as best they could. However, this is the course of knowledge as it unfolds. No one should fault those cartographers and historians but we also should not treat them as if they knew an area where they had never been. Again, Magellan is the key here as he found Ophir and Chryse. Ptolemy did not.

We are accused of taking the facts such as the Periplus and interpreting them for ourselves ignoring what an author or scholar concluded. However, that is called thinking. None of us should ever blindly accept what any author says without testing it. Forming a paradigm solely around what scholars who never found Ophir and Chryse interpreted leads to the ignorance of that era. "Prove all things..." (1 Thess. 5:21)

In those days, the locations of Chryse and Argyre were known generally in the Far East beyond India and Southeast of China but not specifically though thought progressed as men physically arrived in the East Indies. Author Thomas Suarez guesses "Chryse most likely represented Malaya while Argyre was probably Burma." [16] Even his language is tentative and not firm because he did not find Ophir and never went there. Portuguese and Spanish explorers did not find Ophir nor Chryse in Malaysia as Magellan and Barbosa planned their next voyage around Ophir being islands East of Malaysia in a progressing view. For Magellan knew where it was – the Philippines. Barbosa accompanied the circumnavigation where both would find their deaths in the Philippines.

Exploring Malaysia, the Portuguese Duarte Barbosa observed a people known as the "Lequios" or "Lequii" or in some sources, "Lucoes." This people is later specified even by Pigafetta as originating in the Philippines as we will cover in the history chapter. The Lequios were described as:

> *"From Malaca they take the same goods as the Chins [Chinese] take. These islands are called Lequios [in one version 'Liquii']. The Malaca people say that they are better men, and richer and more eminent merchants than the Chins." –Duarte Barbosa, 1516 [148]*

Magellan, who also explored under Portugal in Malaysia before embarking on his voyage to return to Southeast Asia for the Spanish crown, is recorded by author Charles E. Nowell as rewriting a portion of his copy of Barbosa's journal. In regards to the inhabitants of the Philippines, the Lequios, he substitutes "Tarsis" and "Ofir" or Tarshish and Ophir. He knew where he was headed and he knew Malaysia did not meet the criteria for Ophir or Chryse though close in proximity, it was East of the Malay Peninsula which he found in the Philippines.

> *"Magellan's version substitutes for Barbosa's "Lequios" the words "Tarsis" and "Ofir" "…the Biblical Tarshish and Ophir associated with Solomon…" – Charles E. Nowell [148]*

Just after Magellan's voyage, explorer Sebastian Cabot, was hired by the King of Spain to follow a Western route to Southeast Asia. In his contract, the king of Spain appears to identify the region of Tarshish and Ophir as this is in a South to North progression in areas. The Portuguese already conquered Malaysia at that point. This was the Spanish voyage. The contract lists Moluccas or essentially Indonesia/Malaysia and heads North in progression to the Philippines as Tarsis and Ophir. Then, it heads further northward to Japan and China. We will cover more on this.

> *"On March 4, 1525, less than 6 years after Magellan's voyage, former*

British explorer Sebastian Cabot signed a contract with Spain which did have as one of its objectives "to discover Moluccas, Tarsis, Ophir, Cipango and Cathay." –Nowell [150]

They were islands yet some confused the Malay Peninsula because Ptolemy believed it to be we are told. However, Ptolemy never used the Malay Peninsula, he was describing Burma instead and this becomes evident on later maps. He was wrong and knew nothing of Far East geography which is non-existent on his mapping but an enclosed Indian Ocean in ignorance. However, the Western thought did not know about the Philippines as a separate entity mostly yet until Barbosa, Pinto and Magellan largely. The Bible also says they are isles and you will find that in Chapter 8 (Ps. 72:10, Is. 23:6, Is. 60:9, 1 Ki. 22:48, 2 Chr. 20:36). They identified the Philippines and returned there to the isles of gold.

Author Nowell provides the context of the progression in thinking from the age of Josephus forward.

"Later Christian writers for centuries associated the gold of Ophir with East Africa, but at the time of the Portuguese discoveries Ophir was thought of as the Aurea Chersonnesus (Golden Peninsula) of Ptolemy, in which that Greek geographer also placed Cattigara, mentioned by Pigafetta as the immediate transpacific goal of Magellan. But Magellan connected Solomon's treasure with something else he had read in Barbosa: Facing this great land of China there are many islands in the sea, beyond which [on the other side of the sea] there's a very large land which they say is mainland, from which there come to Malacca every year three or four ships, like those of the Chins, belonging to white men who are said to be great and rich merchants: they bring much gold, and silver in bars, silk, rich cloth, and much very good wheat, beautiful porcelains, and many other merchandises." – Charles E. Nowell [150]

The Malay Peninsula is not facing China nor is Ethiopia, Yemen, Britain, Spain, India, etc. The world especially those in the know among the Colonial powers in that age were gunning for Ophir, the isles of gold and honing in. They guessed it in East Africa to start but they wanted the real land of gold and they did not find it there. The thought at the time of Magellan and Barbosa's excursions to Malaysia, it was believed to be there but again, that is antiquated thought after they went there and did not find it. Magellan connected it to the Philippines as a result of that trip. The Lequios were the key and they were not Malays. All that time, scholarly thought progressed until Magellan found Ophir.

If you read his writing further, author Charles E. Nowell continues to do the same in making assumptions based on Ophir or Chryse being North of the equator in Southeast Asia as it is Southeast of China. However, he leaps over the Philippines which is just North of the equator and what one would think the first choice to test. The Philippines is typically ignored especially by the British in their claims.

A reconstruction of Pomponius Mela's 43 A.D. mapping [below], demonstrates from the "olden writers," Chryse and Argyre as isles to the Southeast of China. In his writings, he places this between the Malay Peninsula (Colis) and China (Tamus) as isles thus in the South China Sea not Malaysia nor India. [16] His map omits the entire Malay Peninsula and Indochina but includes what is obviously the islands Southeast of China which we know as the Philippines as Chryse and Argyre.

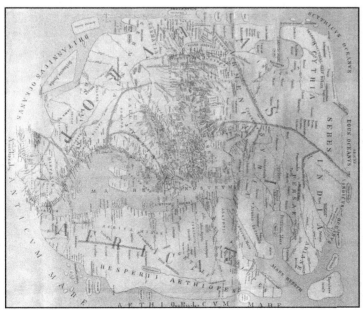
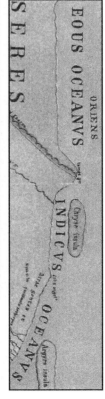

World Map of Pomponius Mela, 43 A.D. rotated north up.
Reconstruction by Dr. Konrad Miller (reconstructed 1898). [18]
Inset right. As below, one turns the corner when reaching the
South China Sea to the East and heads North to the Philippines.

There are other editions but Mela's directions place these islands in the South China Sea as Argyre is placed beyond the Ganges which is rendered in Indochina wrong to India but in the perspective of the ancient world accurate to the Philippines. That was the thought at that time which progressed.

Notice this map is a reconstruction in 1898 by Dr. Konrad Miller who is a well-respected cartographer especially in reconstruction of ancient maps. He published these over a century ago very widely and this is vetted. Anyone can look at this map and see it is not identifying Malaysia but the Philippines though Mela was not aware of all Southeast Asian geography in it's entirety or he would not have left out so much. China is to the North right where it should be affirming the Periplus. This shows the isle of Chryse as essentially Luzon Island, Philippines. It skips a pace and illustrates Argyre, land of silver, as basically modern Mindanao obviously not matching geographic shapes to no surprise. This is not Malaysia nor Taiwan nor Indonesia. It is the Philippines. Even some editions of Eratosthenes' 194 B.C. map render these same two islands though not named. [50]

19th-century reconstruction of Eratosthenes' map of the (for the Greeks) known world, c. 194 BC. Public Domain. [50] Inset upper right.

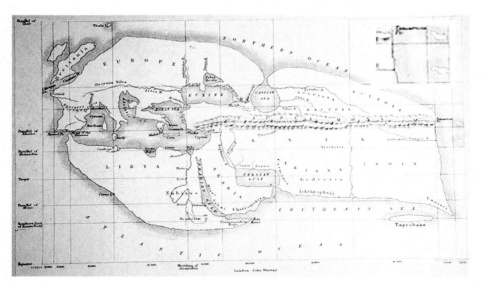

This is the preservation of the location of Chryse (Ophir) in the Philippines. This is not Ethiopia, Yemen, Britain, Spain, India, Malaysia, Indonesia, New Zealand, Peru nor anyone making such claims. As we test their resources, most of these fail fifty percent of the test from the start. This is no mystery and by the end of this book you will know.

This is confirmed in other maps from that era. Dionysius Periegetes [the Tourist], offers directions from a Northern perspective.

"But not farre from this Islande there lyeth an other, whiche is called the farthest Tile, where as when the hote somers Sun approcheth to the northern Pole, their nyghtes be like vnto perpetuall daye, in fairenesse and brightnesse, vntill he returns agayne to the South. From thence if a man sayling towards Scythia turne his shippe to the East, he shall fynde Chrysia, whiche is an other Ilande of the Ocean, in the whiche also the Sunne shyneth very clearly: then if he returne him contrarie to the south, immediatly he shall discouer Taprobana..." "They lye directely vnder the lyne of Cancer..."
– Dionysius Periegetes [The Tourist], 124 A.D. [154]

The Scythian Main has always been a well-noted area of the North in the Russian Steppes as far as Mongolia. There are two maps on the next page which fully identify this reconstructing the original directions of Dionysius. From the area of the Sacae or Scythians [151] also identified the same on Pomponius Mela's map, one journeys to the Eastern Ocean likely from the North Sea. This really affirms the Periplus from a different perspective from the North heading South and East into the South China Sea. Chryse near Taprobane is consistent with the rendering of maps of that age which skipped Indochina and Malaysia. Chryse is mapped Southeast of Seres(China) directly under the Tropic(lyne) of Cancer which parallels Taiwan. That is not the Malay Peninsula but the Philippines. Dionysius identifies Chryse as an island Southeast of China in the ocean not a peninsula and firmly.

There are only reconstructions for this map but we use two very reputable, published ones. They are similar and compare to Mela's map and these all align in that era as well as with the Periplus. [20] They did not realize what they were mapping as they obviously do not represent

Note: Seres is China. Southeast of China in the sea is Chryse. That is the Philippines.

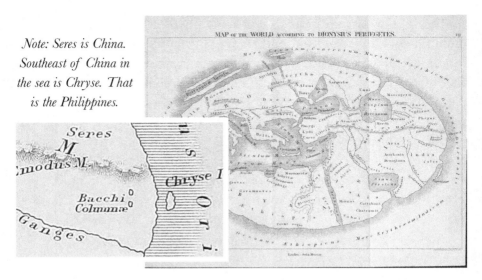

"The World According to Dionysius Periegetes, from Bunbury's A History of Ancient Geography Among the Greeks and Romans, From the Earliest Ages Till the Fall of the Roman Empire." 1879. Public Domain. [20]

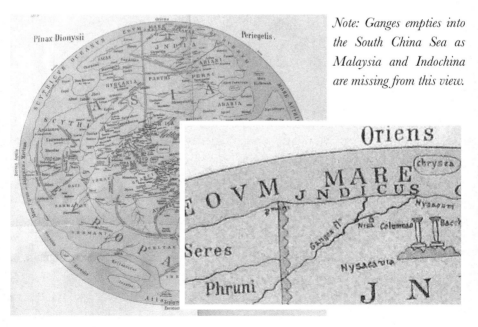

Note: Ganges empties into the South China Sea as Malaysia and Indochina are missing from this view.

"Weltkarte des Dionysios Periegetis." 1898 Reconstruction by Dr. Konrad Miller. Mappae Mundi Bd. Vi. "Rekonstruierte Karten." Public Domain. [20]

the entire geography of the Far East but that is the Philippines not Malaysia. The island of Chryse which Josephus told us is Biblical Ophir also equated to Cattigara, is not a legend, it is real. They were hunting, Magellan found it and it took less than a century for a movement sparked by the British to begin suppressing this truth. This debate lasted until Spain succumbed to a U.S. takeover of the Philippines about 1900 and it has since been obscured. Is there really a question as to why the usurper of the land of gold would desire to keep it quiet? Granted that is evil but no surprise.

The Greeks traded with the Philippines for gold and silver from roughly around 800-150 B.C. and Mela retained this from the "olden writers" of Greece. This further affirms the claim that the Philippines was mining gold in 1000 B.C. as the Encyclopedic Dictionary of Archaeology alludes and author, researcher and historian Paul Kekai Manansala, author Scott Walker, Wikipedia and others stake. [10] The Greeks were merely continuing the Phoenician routes of Solomon's navy. One cannot ignore the origin of the Greek language and marine acumen being Phoenicia who were Solomon's navy.

There is history which demonstrates chronological large-scale gold mining and trade in the Philippines from before 1000 B.C. to present. Today, the Philippines is reported by Forbes Magazine, NY Times and others remaining number two on all of earth in untapped gold deposits in the ground [11][12] even after mining gold for over 3000 years. This is not based on mining production nor investment as the Philippines ranks much lower on those modern reports as The Frasier Institute especially cites past corruption, lack of security and many other factors as deterrents to investors placing the Philippines near the bottom. Even in 1941, the Philippines was the world's fifth largest gold producer though conditions changed but the gold did not. [23] Yet, in a true assessment of size from a publishing by Bangko Sentral in 2004, the Philippines was estimated as number 2 in gold production per square kilometer. [116]

The number one today in untapped gold reserves, South Africa, has only had it's gold rush for a little over 100 years. [9] In 300,000 square kilometers, the Philippines has more gold in the ground than China who is over thirty times larger in area and even known for gold output. Also, that report took place before the Benham Rise was recognized as territory of the Philippines by the United Nations.

Throughout history, the Philippines was recorded as the Land of Gold by other nations. The Greeks named it Chryse, "The Golden One." [17][18][20] Indian history called it Suvarnadwipa or "Island of Gold" [17][19] as the Periplus is the record of those directions. The Chinese log the Philippines as Lusong Dao "Isles of Gold" in 200 A.D. [23]. Buddhist i-Tsing named it Chin-Chou, "Isle of Gold" and Chin-lin, "Golden Neighbor" in 671 A.D. which is Suvarnadwipa [22]. Finally, the Chinese characterize the Philippines as Chin-san, "Mountain of Gold." [23] [See Sourcebook]

Certainly, the West lost the route but it was never lost to the world. When the Muslims arrived around 1200 A.D., they had pursued their legends of gold like Waqwaq in the Philippines. [22] Then, we have the Spanish which we will cover in an entire chapter, who record repeatedly that the Philippines was the most abundant land of gold and in some accounts more gold than they had ever encountered in all of antiquity. Is this even debatable? Not really.

Trade with the Philippines continued as far as Egypt and West Asia in the first millennium as Laszlo Legeza as well as a book published by Bangko Sentral suggest Philippine gold ending up in Egypt.

> *"Hellenistic trade beads of West Asiatic and Egyptian origins found in early burials in many places in the Philippines, prove that such early trade contacts, no matter how irregular, existed between the Philippine archipelago and West Asia by the first centuries of the first millennium A.D." –Laszlo Legeza [21]*

> *"Apart from India and China, Butuan is known to have had extensive trading connections with Arabia and in all probability with Sumatra and Java. The locally produced gold necklaces comprising of dentate interlocking beads seem to have reached Egypt, later to be mistakenly identified by European collectors as Egyptian." –Laszlo Legeza [21]*

> *"Some of the non-Indian borrowed designs found only in their original sources and in the Philippine area suggest direct linkages with other cultural currents from the Indian Ocean. Among these are kamagi*

necklaces(Aldred 1978: 105) and penannular, barter rings which both
show Egyptian influence(Aldred 1978: 20, 94). The earliest insular
Southeast Asian products reached the Mediterranean through a port on
the Arabian Gulf, which were transported overland to the headwaters of
the Nile, then shipped down to Alexandria. Austronesian traders are also
known to have reached Madagascar(Miller 1969; Taylor 1976), so the
African connection is an established fact."
−Villegas, Bangko Sentral [21]

Professor Adrian Horridge believed by 200 B.C., this trade existed
between Philippines and India, Sri Lanka and Africa. [27] [407] The
Philippines led the seas trading as far as Africa as "established fact,"
"proven" before China was even a marine power.

"A Chinese manuscript of the third century A.D. records that there were
ships arriving in China from different foreign ports. These ships were
believed to be Southeast Asian and sailed by Southeast Asian seaman.
It is asserted that by the third century Filipinos were sailing to Funan
on the southern tip of Indochina. The Chinese did not have ocean-going
ships until after the eighth century. By the year 982, Philippine ships
were repeatedly calling on ports in southern China. It is presumed that the
initial contact with China was with Filipino seamen sailing a Filipino
ship and not an Arab vessel as was previously claimed..."
−William Larousse [25]

Philippine Supreme Court Justice Antonio T. Carpio, also records trade
with ancient China in which Filipinos are documented as arriving in
China first.

"Chinese Yuan Dynasty scholar Ma Tuan-lin wrote that in 982 AD,
Austronesian traders from the Philippines, whom the Chinese at that time
called Mo-yi or Ma-I, were already traveling to Canton to trade."
−Supreme Court Justice Carpio [27]

Filipinos, or rather, Ophirians travelled to Canton and other parts of
China to trade centuries before China was crossing the ocean to the

Philippines. Theirs is a rich shipping history which archaeology affirms and we will cover. Let's firm this up with girth.

In 1492, Columbus sailed the ocean blue... According to his journals and notes, he was not seeking the Americas but intended to locate Ophir (Chryse) and Tarshish (Argyre). [144-147] In that year, the first globe [below] was released by Martin Behaim employed by Portugal. [394] He accurately depicts portions that on other maps up until that time were not precisely represented. Notice, India and Taprobana(Sri Lanka) are close to where they actually are on today's maps. China(Cathaia), Burma, Malay Peninsula (Coilur), Java Major and Minor, Indochina(represented as another India) are all placed true to their positions in geography but Japan is too far South and obviously not to be used as a marker here in the face of all the others. This is not a surprise as that is the area in which was not yet explored in detail along with the Philippines especially. He adds the Malay Peninsula but that is not Chryse. The world well knew this. In the South China Sea, Southeast of China and North of the equator is Chryse which bears the shape of Luzon Island especially at the top and South, Argyre which matches the shape of Mindanao especially at the top. Columbus was operating with this mindset as well. He believed he would find Ophir there in the area of the Philippines just above the equator. He did not find Chryse. However, Behaim's map does and so does Magellan in three decades. It is the Philippines.

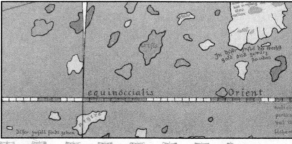

A modern facsimile of Martin Behaim's 1492 Erdapfel map. Behaim Globe (1492–1493) Ernst Ravenstein: Martin Behaim. His Life and his Globe. London 1908. Public Domain. [394] Inset right.

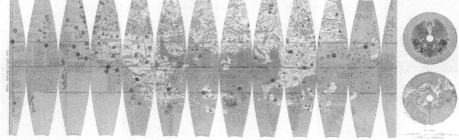

Chapter 4 | From Mesha to Sephar, Mount of the East

Genesis 10:26-30 KJV

*And Joktan begat Almodad, and Sheleph, and Hazarmaveth, and Jerah, And Hadoram, and Uzal, and Diklah, 28 And Obal, and Abimael, and **Sheba**, And **Ophir**, and **Havilah**, and Jobab: all these were the sons of Joktan. And their **dwelling** was **from Mesha**, as thou **goest unto Sephar** a **mount of the east**.*

Ophir is an authentic descendent of Noah, Shem, Arphaxad all the way to his grandfather Eber. There is only one Ophir in Genesis 10 and all of scripture for that matter. We do not have to guess where Ophir nor his brother Sheba originated as at the time of the Tower of Babel, Ophir lived in Mesha and then, he and his brothers migrated to Sephar, the Mount of the East. These are three distinct places we can pinpoint even today.

Mesha is their initial homeland and it is an extremely ancient Hebrew word not Persian in origin. It should be in the near vicinity of the land of Shinar where the Tower of Babel was built as the whole earth population lived within that area at that time but would disperse after Babel was destroyed. Mesha cannot be assumed to be on the Red Sea either in Saudi Arabia nor Ethiopia according to the Bible. That is a 3-4 month round trip journey not three years.

Genesis 11:1-4 KJV

*And the whole earth was of one language, and of one speech. And it came to pass, as **they journeyed from the east**, that they found a plain in the **land of Shinar**; and they dwelt there. And they said one*

to another, Go to, let us make brick, and burn them throughly. And they
had brick for stone, and slime had they for morter. And they said, Go to,
let us build us a city and a tower, whose top may reach unto heaven; and
let us make us a name, lest we be scattered abroad upon the face of the
whole earth.

Many are familiar with the end times uniting of the peoples of the
earth. This is not a new concept as in Babel, the Book of Jubilees 8
records Kainam found stone tablets which caused him to sin owning
to them. He hid them from Noah fearing his wrath. This same religion
from Babel will be the One World Religion which once again coalesces
to fight Yahuah in vanity. This is man's religion which is never a Biblical
concept as Yahuah only established covenant relationship with man.
These are Noah's descendants and notice as well, they migrated from
the East not the Northwest from Turkey. Therefore, the Bible says the
ark could not have landed there (Map in Ch. 18). It also describes the
ark landing at Flood peak on Day 150 meaning it landed on the tallest
mountain (See Ch. 18).

We find Mesha in Iran by similar name today as "Mashhad" or
"Meshad" which is the beginning of the Silk Road to the Orient. We
would agree with anyone saying that within itself is not enough to make
such connection. However, follow this through. In Hebrew, Mesha
means "to depart or remove" or "retreat" [29] because it is where
Joktan departed from the caravan with Peleg as they were the two sons
of Eber (or Hebrew). As the Biblical Mesha is that place of separation
and migration origin, Peleg and Joktan would eventually establish the
boundaries of Shem's territory. Peleg's generations drifted more slowly
to the West as even by Abraham's era, they lived in Ur, or Iraq today,
and it was Abraham who left his family there and migrated to Canaan
or what would become Israel which is the Western border of Shem.
Joktan and sons would immigrate more directly as they journeyed right
to the Eastern-most frontier of Shem to the islands in Southeast Asia.

In understanding Biblical geography, we have sought additional
assistance from the very historical and accurate Book of Jubilees, though
in our series on YouTube, we proved the Philippines was Ophir without
one extra-biblical text. Jubilees was found in the Dead Sea Scrolls and

dated to about 150 B.C. but of course, that dating is from a copy not an original. We have no original manuscripts of the Bible nor are they required. It has been in constant circulation and it was the tradition of the scribe to copy these over to preserve the original text. The same is true of the Book of Jubilees as it has always been in constant circulation even as scripture in fact. We have a chapter near the end of this book (Ch. 20) which vets this where we find the Qumran community used it as Torah. Jesus, John, Peter, Luke and Paul quote the Book of Jubilees for significant doctrine which does not derive anywhere else in the Old Testament and the early church quoted it as scripture as well. Regardless, we will use it in this book as history as it is accurately dated to at least 150 B.C., thus history.

The Book of Jubilees defines Noah's division of the earth between his three sons – Shem, Ham and Japheth. Then, it renders the first initial distribution of Shem to his sons. Arphaxad, the ancestor of Joktan and Ophir was only given 2 territories in the days before the Tower of Babel meaning Ophir and his brothers could have only lived in one of these 2 regions. Neither is in Ham's territory of Africa thus Ethiopia is out nor are they in Saudi Arabia/Yemen.

> *Jubilees 9:4a (R.H. Charles, 1903)*
> *And for Arpachshad came forth the third portion, all the land of the region of the Chaldees to the east of the Euphrates…*

This first territory was located in Iran/Media/Persia and Flavius Josephus renders this the same as "Arphaxad named the Arphaxadites, are now called Chaldeans." [30] We see these Chaldeans separate in Mesha where Joktan's family migrated East to a territory called Sephar, a mount of the East. His brother Peleg, the other son of Eber who is the ancestor of Abraham can also be tracked beginning to migrate to the West ending up in Ur which is why we find Chaldea or the Chaldeans in more modern history as Southern Iraq though they did not begin there. However, that territory did not belong to Arphaxad thus they were actually out of territory and seemed comfortable there until Abraham who finished the migration into Canaan (Israel). Arphaxad's second territory was essentially what we call Israel or formerly Canaan.

Jubilees 9:4b (R.H. Charles, 1903)
...bordering on the Red Sea, and all the waters of the desert close to the
tongue of the sea which looks towards Egypt, all the land of Lebanon
and Sanir and 'Amana to the border of the Euphrates.

However, this second inheritance was stolen from Arphaxad and his descendants by Canaan, son of Ham. This is why even in the days that Israel entered the land after the Exodus from Egypt it was still named for Canaan, son of Ham. Of course, Canaan received a second curse for this behavior, this time from his father Ham and brothers. This is why that land was called the Promised Land. It was not promised to Abraham initially, it was promised to his ancestor Arphaxad, son of Shem and restored to Abraham's lineage, the Israelites.

Jubilees 10:29 (R.H. Charles, 1903)
And Canaan saw the land of Lebanon to the river of Egypt, that it was
very good, and he went not into the land of his inheritance to the west...

On our YouTube Channel, The God Culture, we receive many comments, Messenger Messages and emails daily. Sometimes we will field challenges and this is a healthy process because over the years, we have been able to prove out virtually every aspect of this topic. Of course, there are those who take it a bit far especially trolls but that is life. One challenge appears credible on the surface and actually gains support from Bible dictionaries whom have done little to no actual research on this topic. It derives from a search through the scriptures for people named Mesha in English only and a connection is attempted which almost seems reasonable until you test it and it quickly unravels.

Genesis 10:30 KJV
*...And their dwelling was from **Mesha**, as thou goest unto Sephar a*
mount of the east.
Hebrew: Mesha: מֵשָׁא *: [31]*

Some attempt an argument that a king named Mesha, King of Moab must be this same Mesha and the origin of the Genesis 10 Mesha.

2 Kings 3:4 KJV

*And **Mesha king of Moab** was a sheepmaster, and rendered unto the king of Israel an hundred thousand lambs, and an hundred thousand rams, with the wool.*

Hebrew: Mesha, King of Moab: מישׁיע *: [32]*
Hebrew: Mesha region, Gen. 10: משׁא *: [31]*

Do you notice these two words are not the same in Hebrew? They are even two different words in Strong's Concordance by number. Mesha, King of Moab is not Mesha, the territory of Genesis 10. However, where is Mesha the king's territory? Not Mesha. He is Mesha, King of Moab. Did Moses know where Moab was? Of course he did as he writes about Moab which is just East of the Dead Sea which is the territory that was given to one of the sons of Lot named Moab and his brother Ammon, the name of the capitol of Jordan to this day even.

This was not the King of a territory called Mesha but a man named such and not even after the Genesis 10 land which is a different Hebrew word. There is no relation and that is not scholarship.

However, this becomes a further disaster for such scholars as they seem to forget that Joktan and sons migrated from Mesha to Sephar, the Mount of the East in about 2200 B.C. However, we have a carving, The Mesha Stele or Moabite Stone on display at the Louvre Museum in Paris, France. Mesha, King of the land of Moab reigned in about 840 B.C. [33] Follow the logic here. Is a King who lived in 840 B.C. the origin of the name of a land from 2200 B.C., 1,400 years prior? Of course not. It is a ludicrous assumption not based on any Biblical aptitude. No Bible dictionary should ever render such as that is an illiterate stance.

We would also note there are two more Mesha's listed in scripture in 1 Chronicles 2:42 and 1 Chronicles 8:9 even later than the King of Moab and they are that same Hebrew word as the King of Moab not the one from Genesis 10 which only appears once in actuality. Neither is the same Hebrew word nor era as Mesha where Joktan lived. There is nothing wrong with taking this direction in research but one must test it in approaching that reasoning. When it is 1,400 years later, a different Hebrew word and associated with a territory known by a different name around the era of the narrative, they are backing the wrong horse.

However, once again, Flavius Josephus in Antiquities of the Jews explains this geography. He renders the names in the passage in Latin but this will bring full clarity to the location of Mesha which is not in Moab, nor in Yemen/Saudi Arabia nor Ethiopia. Also, as one ignorant gnostic proposed, it is not in the bottom of the Indian Ocean fitting a forced occult Atlantis.

> *Genesis 10:26-30: MESHA: (According to Josephus)*
> *Now Joctan, one of the sons of Heber, had these sons, Elmodad, Saleph,*
> *Asermoth, Jera, Adoram, Aizel, Decla, Ebal, Abimael, **Sabeus***
> ***(Sheba), Ophir, Euilat (Havilah)**, and Jobab. These inhabited*
> *from **Cophen**, an Indian river, **and** in part of **Aria** adjoining to it.*
> *—Flavius Josephus, Antiquities, 93 A.D. [34]*

Josephus is only dealing with Mesha in this rendering not Sephar and he is narrowing down the area very specifically based on references that we can connect even today in modern history. Ophir and family lived initially in the border region of what we would identify today as Iran and Afghanistan. The Cophen River is acknowledged as the modern Kabul River in Afghanistan. Notice then Josephus connects this with "and" meaning this is a border region. The second region is "part of Aria adjoining to it." Aria is very easy to identify as Arya is the Old Persian name of what we call Iran today and it's etymology still originates in Aryan. Therefore, Josephus is locating Mesha on the border of Iran and Afghanistan. Meshad, Iran accordingly materializes to be positioned on the Northeastern border of Iran right next to Afghanistan exactly where he placed it. Mesha is Meshad, Iran.

Josephus locates Mesha on the border of Iran and Afghanistan – Meshad, Iran.

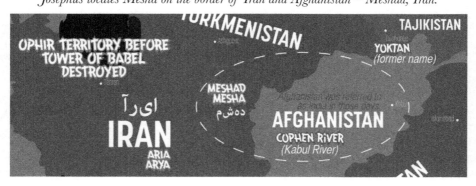

Ophir never lived near Saudi Arabia, Yemen nor Ethiopia. It is the place of "departure" by Hebrew definition and Joktan's sons migrated from there in Iran. However, we can also firmly locate Sephar, the Mount of the East to which they migrated as well. It also is not Yemen, Saudi Arabia nor Ethiopia which are all horrible guesses in the wrong direction and fit no narrative of Ophir we have ever tested. On this topic, we find the scholarship sorely lacking.

Sephar

> *Genesis 10:30 KJV*
> *…And their dwelling was from Mesha, as thou **goest unto Sephar** a **mount of the east**.*

When one researches Sephar in Bible Dictionaries, they receive a whole lot of guessing based on etymologies and once again, these scholars do not prove out their own thinking in the slightest. We should require much more of them than to have initials after their name. In fact, that should require even more detail not this kind of discreditable banter. No wonder modern science has a field day with many Bible scholars. Easton's and Smith's Bible Dictionary for instance, enter complete guess mode when they define this as:

> *"**supposed by some** to be the ancient Himyaritic capital, "Shaphar," **Zaphar**, on the Indian Ocean, between the Persian Gulf and the Red Sea." [35]*

Just a quick review of the history of this land in Yemen, quickly dismisses this as a failure. Zaphar, Yemen was not even founded until the second century B.C. which is 2000 years too late to be the origin of the base to where Joktan and sons migrated. Add to that "Zaphar" is NOT Sephar nor is it Hebrew in origin. Admittedly, it looks close but the dilemma for many scholars is that is the sole logic they use at times and certainly that is all they are showing in these dictionaries on this topic. Let us understand though that these dictionaries do not actually have an answer as to where Sephar is as they even use tentative language like "supposed by some." They do not know. The good news is we can know.

International Standard Bible Dictionary [35] does the same but picks a different word, "Qafar," which sounds similar again but still in Saudi Arabia which we already proved, Joktan and his sons never lived near there. Again, they disclaim their own reference as they first use the language "it cannot be doubted" yet then, they doubt their own reference when they tell us it possesses a discrepancy but of course, they ignore the largest flaw, Joktan never lived there and the word Qafar is not the word Sephar in any sense. They are manufacturing a giant leap against logic using an Arabic word to try to force it into a Hebrew narrative of similar sound.

The true flaw that breeds this kind of thinking out of necessity to understand is an erroneous assumption that Noah's generations did not know how to travel especially by boat thus stayed close to the Middle East because they were not capable of sojourning further. It is amazing how scholars review passages after the Tower of Babel demonstrating all peoples spread all over the entire Earth and yet still maintain such limited thinking. Perhaps they do not actually believe the Bible. Imagine, Noah and his sons built such a sophisticated supertanker that man has been unable to match it until recent times but with steel ships still not wood and especially not without nails. The ark was a masterpiece but to think that after the Flood with the new World Ocean now formed, that Noah's sons would develop amnesia and completely forget how to make wood float and build ships is simply a false paradigm not rooted in reason.

In Parts 3 and 4 of our Flood Series, we map out the territories of Noah's division of the earth between his three sons from the Book of Jubilees 8 and it is far more vast than just the Middle East. He mentions areas to Russia which cannot be anywhere else, East of India, the North Pole, Europe, Asia, Africa and even includes the Americas in his division all the way to Alaska and across the Pacific even to Australia. Noah knew the entire Earth because he had writings from his ancestors such as Enoch where Enoch was taken on a tour of the entire Earth by Angels. We assume so many things that are just plain wrong unfortunately. This is why we must all "prove all things" lest we be deceived. Here is how we discovered Sephar and we didn't even have a fancy hat and whip.

One definition of the Hebrew word Sephar is:
SEPHARÀH: ספר: "Towards a Numerous Population." [36]

Even today, sixty percent of the entire world population would still be defined as inhabiting the Orient or Far East region including China and India. Therefore, simply put, Joktan's family migrated to the East of Meshad, Iran based on this definition. This immediately discounts any claim from Ethiopia, Yemen, Britain, Spain and even the Americas but we will deal with each head on in this exhibition. [37]

However, this word Sephar begins to journey down a path in definition that we even remained hesitant at first. Filipinos were responding in great number early in this series that not only was the Philippines Ophir, but they would continually remind us, it was also the location of the Garden of Eden. Now, that is an amazing thought but not something we thought we could ever prove. In latter chapters, however, you will find there is a very good reason why these references begin to lead down this path of logic.

This word Sephar certainly commences in this progression as for one, it is a Hebrew reference to the Tree of Life especially among Kabbalists whom we do not embrace but the Hebrew is applicable none-the-less. The Tree of Life remains in the midst of the Garden of Eden and always has been located there. You will never find a Bible passage which indicates it was destroyed by the Flood but instead it even appears in prophecy in the last days. (Rev. 22:14) You also will not find the Kabbalistic Tree of Life which is supposedly on another plane of existence which is the root of that doctrine not Bible yet taught in many denominations.

Hebrew: sephar: רפס: Tree of Life
Sefirot (ספירות), singular sefirah, "counting"/"enumeration"
Similar to the first definition towards a numerous population, the Sefirot
is the name of the Tree of Life in Kabbalah.
Etymological possibilities from the same Hebrew root include:
sefer ("text" - ספר), sfar ("boundary" - ספר)
sippur ("recounting a story" - סיפור)
sappir ("sapphire" - ספיר, "brilliance", "luminary")
sofer, or safra ("scribe" - סופר, ספרא). [38]

Upon further examination, every one of these definitions makes sense in the ancient context of the Tree of Life in the Garden of Eden. We will cover Jubilees where Enoch was taken into the Garden of Eden as a "scribe" "recording the deeds of men until the Day of Final Judgment" as a "text" "recounting a story" in the presence of "brilliant light and luminary" Angels on, we will prove, Shem's Eastern "boundary." Just as many ancient Hebrew words from early Genesis, we often find that all the definitions fit the ancient concept not just one. We will drill into this word further when we find Sephar is one of the names of the Biblical land of Gold known as Parvaim or Sephar-vaim which is the same as Ophir in application and etymologically.

Therefore, Sephar is not an abstract concept. It is a specific place where the Tree of Life exists in the Garden of Eden and it will become known as Ophir. When one finds this land, they do in fact locate the Garden of Eden but we will prove that from multiple angles before finalizing in conclusion. We did not expect this. However, as you follow the evidence trail, the bread crumbs lead there and to not continue such path would be a shortcoming in logic. Sephar will lead to the Philippines.

Mount of the East

> *Genesis 10:30 KJV*
> *And their dwelling was from Mesha, as thou goest unto Sephar a **mount of the east (qedem:** קדם**).** [39]*

This is the same Hebrew word used to describe the region of the Garden of Eden in fact.

> *Genesis 2:8 KJV [39]*
> *And the Lord God planted a garden **eastward (qedem:** קדם**)** in Eden;*

The word used here is another very ancient Hebrew word which bears all of it's meanings at once. This vets out and we will unravel it completely by the end of this book.

qedem: קדם: *[39]*
east, antiquity, front, that which is before, aforetime, ancient time, of old,
earliest time, beginning, mount of the east, mount of the orient, eastward,
to or toward the east.

What land is from antiquity, that which is before, aforetime, ancient, from of old, earliest time, beginning? Only the Land of Creation but that is not a conclusion we can draw yet but we will address this. A land on the front or border, eastward, to or toward the east? We will show you this is language that becomes obvious once we have mapped the Garden of Eden, the land of Adam and Eve which is the Land of Gold and the Land of Creation.

We know media mogul, Oprah, would like to disparage Yahuah because He supposedly told Adam where the gold was which is complete ignorance as He never had to tell Adam where the gold was because Adam was created in the Land of Gold. It is the marker resource in identifying this region which is preserved to this day. Let us not pretend Oprah, as a billionaire is not serving Mammon (god of money) herself thus this was a very hypocritical statement from her. Even this word Qedem begins to head in the ZIP code of the Garden of Eden and we keep observing this pattern with the narratives of Ophir, the Temple and Biblical gold and the Garden of Eden which we will not ignore.

Many read this passage in Genesis 10 as "a mount of the East" as if it is indistinct and impossible to identify and if that were the case, that may be true. However, the Book of Jubilees tells us there is a Holy Mountain of Yahuah God literally named the "Mount of the East." This is not some random mountain, it is one specific locality of only four holy places on Earth.

First, let us begin with the story of Enoch, the great prophet who was seventh from Adam not to be confused with Cain's evil son named Enoch. He was righteous and walked so closely with Yahuah that Yahuah took Him but where? Genesis does not say, it just says he was not. The assumption is Heaven.

Genesis 5:24 KJV
And Enoch walked with God: and he was not; for God took him.

The Book of Jubilees sheds light on this topic as it recounts Enoch was taken from among men and conducted into the Garden of Eden. We found Ophir without using this book but it is integral in realizing the Garden of Eden as it gives exact directions.

> *Book of Jubilees 4:23-24 (R.H. Charles. 1903)*
> *And he (Enoch) was taken from amongst the children of men, and we conducted him into the Garden of Eden in majesty and honor, and behold there he writes down the condemnation and judgment of the world, and all the wickedness of the children of men. And on account of it YAHUAH brought the waters of the flood upon all the land of Eden; for there he was set as a sign and that he should testify against all the children of men, that he should recount all the deeds of the generations until the day of condemnation.*

Notice Eden which is not the location of the Garden of Eden which is planted in the East or to the East of Eden was flooded but the Garden of Eden was not. It survived the Flood. Enoch will be there in the Garden until the Day of Judgment, thus, he is still there today.

> *Book of Jubilees 4:25-26 (R.H. Charles. 1903)*
> *And he (Enoch in the Garden) burnt the incense of the sanctuary, (even) sweet spices acceptable before YHWH on the Mount. For YHWH has four places on the earth, the Garden of Eden, and the Mount of the East, and this mountain on which you are this day, Mount Sinai, and Mount Zion (which) will be sanctified in the new creation for a sanctification of the earth; through it will the earth be sanctified from all (its) guilt and its uncleanness throughout the generations of the world.*

When Enoch was escorted into the Garden, he replaced Adam as High Priest essentially. He offered sacrifices on the Mount of the East which is located there and we will later find Adam, after exile, sacrificed gold, frankincense and myrrh on the same mountain which also protrudes out of the Garden. The garden was planted in the East and this is why this is called the Mount of the East. We will test these spices as well which do not originate in Ethiopia and Yemen which requires a complete ignoring of history and science as well as modern business for that matter. Once again, we have a reference identifying the Garden. When Moses wrote Joktan's sons departed from Meshad, Iran to Sephar, Mount of the East, he was being very explicit that they returned to the land of the Garden of Eden as both references lead there in the Hebrew language.

According to Rabi-Kohan Shalomim Y. Halahawi, PHD, DD, ORT, Enoch burned this incense specifically on the Mount of the East which conveys the Hebrew name "Mount Qatar" or "Keter." [40] We will identify this mountain in the Philippines later in Chapter 19. When we enter that line of reasoning we are further proving things out but we can not be as certain as what we can attest we prove that the Philippines is the land of Ophir, Sheba and Tarshish as well as we discover the Garden of Eden, Rivers From Eden, the Land of Creation and Ancient Havilah (Land of Eve) along the way. That journey begins already in the next chapter and we have not proven our position yet but we will as you continue. This becomes more and more evident as it unfolds and each chapter essentially builds upon the previous until the evidence mounts to an irrefutable, overwhelming status. See if you agree by the end of this book. Please allow this chapter to serve as foundation for coming chapters which we will greatly expound upon and thoroughly test this track in progressive fashion.

Ophir and his brothers, lived with the two sons of Eber (Hebrews), their father Joktan and their uncle Peleg in Meshad, Iran at the time of the Tower of Babel. They separated there and "departed" migrating to the East (qedem: קדם) [39] to Sephar or the land of the Garden of Eden. The account then reinforces they went to the Mount of the East also located in the Garden of Eden. These are not coincidences and when you see how all the evidence piles up, this becomes more than compelling but proven. This is foundation so far and we have only begun to embark on our expedition.

Finally, Elath(Eziongeber) on the Red Sea was a real port. Strabo mentions the port of Aila(Elath) 1,260 stadia from Gaza where camels converged to trade, the Ptolemies of Egypt established a port not far from Aelana(Elath) confirmed by Pliny the Elder and Ptolemy mentions Aelana(Elath) as part of the Nabateans. [409] This entire narrative is based in historical fact.

Chapter 5 | Havilah, Land of Eve, Land of Creation

The ancient land of Adam and Eve is designated as Havilah in Genesis 2 and it is represented by three resources which lead to only one nation even today. The Bible is proficient. This reminisces of the Rivers from Eden which we will test in Chapter 17. We truly attempt to leave no stone unturned in this expedition.

> *Genesis 2:10-12 KJV*
> *And a river went out of Eden to water the garden; and from thence it was parted, and became into four heads. The name of the first is Pison: that is it which compasseth the whole land of Havilah, where there is gold; And the gold of that land is good: there is bdellium and the onyx stone.*

When studying this passage, most scholars read it, even cite it and deviate from it to dock on assumptions which they do not return and validate with scripture. We will. However, this island (not India, Ethiopia nor Yemen) surrounded by the Pison River from Eden is named Havilah in antiquity. It's interpretation divulges much more than solely some incidental estate.

הוילה: *havilah: that suffers pain; that brings forth, circle. [41]*

"That suffers pain, that brings forth" refers to childbirth – Eve's curse from the Garden of Eden. What many miss is this word Havilah is a direct Hebrew variant of Eve's Hebrew name as it is a reference not just to Eve's curse but to Eve's land named after her because Eve was not named until after the exile from the Garden. Notice also, this word

Havilah means "circle" which is doubtlessly an allusion to the basis that it is encompassed by the Pison River. We will demonstrate the Pison is still there and still functions. We will also locate Havilah.

Genesis 3:20 KJV
And Adam called his wife's name Eve; because she was the mother of all living.

חוה: *chavvah: life-giver; Chavvah (or Eve), the first woman:—Eve. [42]*

Eve is the life giver. Compare the two words and they are the same Hebrew letters. Havilah as a variant adds an "YL" or in Hebrew, a "Y," YAD and an "L," LAMED. Interestingly, "IY" is the Hebrew word for isle even and perhaps this is a prophetic forerunner to the Philippines, Havilah which will become over 7,000 islands after the Flood. Before the Flood, the Philippines was known as the Mountains of Eden but was one isle. Therefore, if one can locate this ancient land of Havilah, you have found the land of Adam and Eve as it is named for Eve. Let us unearth it now.

Genesis 2:11-12 KJV
*The name of the first is Pison: that is it which compasseth the whole land of Havilah, where there is **gold**; And the gold of that land is **good**: there is **bdellium** and the **onyx stone**.*

Three resources define this nation so now we assess. First, there is gold but not just some gold. The gold of this land is towb: טוב or abundant as in wealthy, prosperous or bountiful especially. [405] In other words, this is not just any land of gold, it is the land of gold defined by having the most gold. Where is that? We already demonstrated the Philippines is the leader in all of history in gold. [10] [11] [12]

Next, we have bdellium which some scholars argue over yet it is a very simple topic to resolve. They generally claim it is either pearl or African resin. Please note the resin they mention as African is also found in the Philippines thus not specifically African even. This is an attempt to stretch the scripture for Africa to fit yet it cannot on many levels especially since it's in the wrong direction, far too close and in Ham's territory. The Hebrew word bdellium is only used twice in scripture. The second time does remedy.

> *Numbers 11:7 KJV*
> *And the **manna** was as coriander seed, and the colour thereof as the **colour of bdellium**.*

Would it make sense that the Israelites ate manna the color of nasty, gritty, dirty looking blackish-brown resin, or pearly white? The entire Old Testament never mentions the word pearl in Hebrew except these two times but has a name for every sacred resin or spice used and none known as bdellium ever. It's pearl and there really is no question. The largest pearls on all of earth indisputably are found in the Philippines. The very largest pearl to date which has been found on all of earth is the 34-kilogram "Puerto Princessa Pearl" found in the Palawan Sea in 2006. This is the largest on record. [43] There are several found near that size including a 28-kilogram pearl also found in the Palawan Sea owned by a family from Canada who thought they had a stone until it was examined. [44] Also, the aforementioned 1492 globe map of Behaim pinpoints one of the islands next to Chryse (Luzon) in the Philippines as "Thilis" which is known historically as the "Isle of Pearl." [394] That is far more likely Palawan and again, legendary from ancient times.

"Puerto Princess Pearl" found in 2006 is the largest pearl in recorded history at 34 kg (75 lb.).
—Forbes Magazine [43]

The Guinness Book of World Records began registering the largest pearl in the 1930s. At that time, the largest was 15 kilograms also found in the Palawan Sea. From that time until today, every pearl who has set this record has originated in the Philippines and no other nation even makes the cut. There is a reason why the Philippines is called "The Pearl of the Orient" as Dr. Jose Rizal coined though not new in his time. There is no other land on Earth which could compete.

Let's examine the third element – the onyx stone. Many think jewelry but this instead is the onyx stone used in construction, a cousin to marble. Even in ancient history, Egypt used onyx in construction. Many called it alabaster but it tests often times as brown or yellow onyx. [395] The very strongest marble and onyx stone on earth is found in Romblon, Philippines – the strongest, not Italy. [45][46] Therefore the Philippines is Number 1 in onyx stone as well. No wonder Job 28:16 ties in onyx with Ophir because he knew Havilah was Ophir.

We just broke down an ancient verse from Genesis 2, from thousands of years ago and the Philippines leads the world not in just one resource but all three and we will continue to prove this out. The Philippines is the ancient land of Havilah, the land of Adam and Eve, surrounded by the ancient Pison River from Eden which we will vet further and it matches as well. The Book of Jubilees defines this land even more.

> *Jubilees 3:32 (R.H. Charles, 1903)*
> *And on the new moon of the fourth month, Adam and his wife went forth from the Garden of Eden, and they dwelt in the land of **Elda, in the land of their creation.***

> *Jubilees 4:29 (R.H. Charles, 1903)*
> *And at the close of the nineteenth jubilee, in the seventh week in the sixth year [930 A.M.] thereof, Adam died, and all his sons buried him in the **land of his creation**, and he was the first to be buried in the earth.*

> *Genesis 3:23 KJV*
> *Therefore the Lord God sent him forth from the garden of Eden, to till the **ground from whence he was taken**. (land of creation)*

Adam and Eve's land of exile in Genesis 2 is called Havilah and we have located it in the Philippines. The Book of Jubilees now equates this same land in which they were exiled to Elda, the Land of their Creation twice which we now realize Genesis 3 identified all along as it is literal. Odd, Elda even sounds Filipino. The Philippines is the Land of Creation as it is Havilah.

However, we can test this further scientifically. We are certain most have heard of the "Out of Africa Theory" based largely on the dating of old bones of pre-flood man of which science does not remotely understand today. We will cover that deeper in the Rivers From Eden chapter. However, there was a world-wide Flood event.

On top of every mountain range on the earth, marine fossils have been unearthed. How did they get there? The earth was flooded to 15 cubits above the tallest mountain. However, many in modern science would answer with yet another theory unproven. The mountains rose up out of the seas they would explain. Understand, even the Himalayas and Mt. Everest have marine fossils. What sea did the Himalayas ascend from? This mountain range is massive in scope and in the middle of a continent not by a sea. Even worse, if there was such extreme, abrupt plate movement at the time of the Flood that would cause the Himalayas to rise as much as over five miles into the sky, then you are not reading this book and we are not writing it. We are all dead already. Little life, if any, could survive the earthquake that would ensue.

There was a global flood as recorded in over 300 flood accounts in credible, valid history that science ignores because that is not their discipline. Some attempt to use the one that they claim does not represent a global event yet it actually does as the ark in that story landed on a mountain thus the volume of water necessary would require a world-wide Flood. 2 Peter 3 is very clear in warning about this "willing ignorance" in our era and we are there.

Mankind and land animals rebooted during the Flood and are no firm scientific measure to determine the origin of species. However, marine life was not wiped out by the deluge as such. Therefore, we have a credible measure by which to allocate the root of life in region. If we can locate the most bio-diverse marine population on earth, we would have actually found the Land of Creation scientifically. In the past twenty or so years, marine biologists have now determined that this center of life, without even realizing what they have actually found, is the measure of the origin of species. Sorry Charlie, Darwin that is.

"Philippines is not only part of the center but is, in fact, the epicenter of marine biodiversity, with the richest concentration of marine life on the entire planet." –Carpenter Report, 2005 [351]

"The Philippines sits at the heart of the Coral Triangle, the global center of marine biodiversity. About halfway between the provinces of Batangas and Mindoro, the Verde Island Passage boasts the highest concentration of marine species in the planet." –CNN, 2012 [352]

"Some 100 scientists have declared the Philippines as the world's "center of marine biodiversity" — not the Great Reef Barrier off east Australia — because of its vast species of marine and coastal resources, according to the World Bank." –The Philippine Star, 2006 [353]

What none of these sources realize is that their efforts to report and applaud "the Center of the Center of Marine Biodiversity on Earth" as they should, serves as scientific evidence for the very land of Creation. Not only is this the Philippines but the Verde Island Passage between Mindoro and Batangas "boasts the highest concentration of marine species on the planet." We had always thought this was the Great Barrier Reef but the Philippines eclipses that by a large margin. Also, consider that the Coral Triangle area in which the Philippines is the Epicenter offers broader evidence that the origin of species occurred there as it is not merely a tiny pocket, though the Philippines is the Epicenter, it is a vast area as would be expected for thousands of years of marine species population.

The Land of Creation is the Philippines and Moses knew it thousands of years ago and defined it in a clever way that could not be mistaken today. For the Philippines leads globally in gold, pearl and the onyx stone as well as marine biodiversity. It is the only land who could even fit this ancient writing of perhaps 1700 B.C. The world has forgotten much. How exactly has this even become a mystery?

Though marine life is certainly the best way to track the Creation event, we find two biodiversity studies that further support this track.

The first was released in 1998 by Conservation International and results are published through World Atlas, RedRank and others which ranks the Philippines as #5 in overall biodiversity internationally including plants and animals. [389] Remember, this study predates the marine discoveries we just covered. However, the Philippines ranks fifth among nations that are 4-32 times it's size in area thus this is really not a comparison. In fact, when you add the areas of Southeast Asia together including Papua New Guinea #6, Malaysia #7, Australia #9, Indonesia #10, China #11 and India # 16, this ranking of 17 countries clearly points to the Orient area around the Philippines with the Philippines as it's leading epicenter yet again.

However, in recent years, The Field Museum in Chicago in conjunction with the Philippines, conducted a study on Luzon Island especially which offers major support for this vein of thought. It boasts the "World's greatest concentration of unique mammal species is on Philippine island." The Field Museum circulated a Press Release with this title with these findings in July 2016 and published them.

"Where is the world's greatest concentration of unique species of mammals? A team of American and Filipino authors have concluded that it is Luzon Island, in the Philippines. Their 15-year project, summarized in a paper published in the scientific journal Frontiers of Biogeography, has shown that out of 56 species of non-flying mammal species that are now known to live on the island, 52 live nowhere else in the world. Of those 56 species, 28 were discovered during the course of the project. Nineteen of the species have been formally described in scientific journals, and nine are currently "in the works."

"We started our study on Luzon in 2000 because we knew at the time that most of the native mammal species on the island were unique to the island, and we wanted to understand why that is the case. We did not expect that we would double the number already known," said Lawrence Heaney, the project's leader, who is the Negaunee Curator of Mammals at The Field Museum in Chicago." "All 28 of the species we discovered during the project are members of two branches on the tree of life that are confined to the Philippines," according to Eric Rickart, a team member who is based at the Natural History Museum of Utah." "There are

individual mountains on Luzon that have five species of mammals that live nowhere else. That's more unique species on one mountain than live in any country in continental Europe. The concentration of unique biodiversity in the Philippines is really staggering." – The Field Museum, Chicago, 2016 [390]

This is an interesting and indeed staggering find. The thing is how can there be so many unique species on one island? Even this article from scientists discounts the landbridge theory of the Philippines being connected to mainland Asia at one time as does this find really. Additionally, we will cover, chicken migration patterns even demonstrate the Philippines as the place of origin in populating the Polynesian islands as does a DNA study we will review. [391][123] Is this confirmation bias or confirmation that leads to a conclusion one may call bias once they conclude such? Critics have only that allegation but cannot deny Genesis 2. The Philippines is indeed the Land of Eve, Havilah and the Land of Creation supported by science and this is only the beginning.

The reef spreads color and life. Tubbataha Reef, Philippines.

Chapter 6 | Biblical Gold Leads to Ophir, Philippines

Parvaim Ties Ophir and the Garden of Eden

1 Chronicles 29:4 KJV
*Even three thousand talents of gold, of the **gold of Ophir**, and seven*
thousand talents of refined silver, to overlay the walls of the houses withal:

There are several references to gold in scripture. King Solomon used many tons of gold to build the temple. Sadly, some academics especially will form false narratives demanding for archaeology that the temple existed. However, the story is clear the temple was utterly destroyed and who would think logically that those walls overlaid with gold and refined silver would be left there in tact as a museum. Babylon took all of it. Why do you think Daniel identifies that empire as the head of gold? They had lots of it and much of it was taken from Judaea especially the Temple and Solomon's Palace. Nothing was left and the second temple was the same as even Messiah prophesied not one stone would be left upon another and it was not. This project embodied billions of dollars of gold. However, the Bible reveals much more about this than identifying it as the gold of Ophir solely. Why? You will find it is providing clues to preserve this knowledge. For instance, later in 2 Chronicles, the author discusses this same gold he just referenced as originating in Ophir which was used to overlay the walls but this time by a different name.

2 Chronicles 3:6-7 KJV
Further, he adorned the house (Temple of Solomon) with precious stones;
*and the gold was **gold from Parvaim**. He also overlaid the house*
*with gold—the beams, the thresholds and its **walls** and its doors; and*
he carved cherubim on the walls.

Why use Ophir the first time and then, Parvaim introducing a new word to describe the same gold? This is a clue which preserves this history in such a brilliant way, even manipulators do not see it. This Hebrew word Parvaim opens this topic greatly in fact.

> *Hebrew: Parvaim: Parvayim:* פרוים: *Oriental regions; Orient or eastern and is a general term for the east. Probably Ophir. Shortened form of* **Cepharvayim** *which occurs in the Syriac and Targum Jonathan for the "***Sephar***" of Genesis 10:30. Only used 1X. [47]*

This is a bridge that binds much of this anecdote together and really offers insight. This use of Parvaim equates it to Ophir and the Bible Dictionaries and Concordances pick up on that. It first serves to give us a regional location of Ophir as it is equated in the Orient or Far East which would not include Saudi Arabia, Yemen nor Ethiopia. Let us not forget the Bible was written by Israelites who never viewed Israel nor the Middle East as the Orient – East. That's a new Western mindset that cannot be applied to the writers of the Bible. However, this meaning is even more profound. Probably Ophir? No, definitely Ophir, they are equated by scripture in the same application. However, this next tie is the glue that we never expected. Shortened form of Cephar-vayim. In other words, Sephar, the mount of the East where Ophir, Sheba and Tarshish migrated is Cephar-vaim or Par-vaim. Though we do not consider the Pharisee Bibles scripture, it is telling when the Syriac and Targum of Jonathan both render this word Sephar in Genesis 10 as Cepharvaim or Parvaim equating these words. Sephar is made plural essentially. The place where Ophir migrated. We also know Sephar is a Hebrew word in which one of it's meanings is the Tree of Life which is also in the Garden of Eden. Observe how the Dead Sea Scrolls really shed light on this connection.

In the Dead Sea Scrolls there is even further support for this and a deeper association in Genesis Apocryphon. This is the narrative of Noah's birth in which his father Lamech was very worried by his appearance of milky white skin which seemed more like the Nephilim who were the offspring of Fallen Angels and human women. He inquires of his father, Methuselah who encourages him Noah is fully human. Many wonder about this but we feel strongly this is setting up the Flood as Noah was to preserve all races thus he was likely given Albino-like genes of sort that could allow all races to continue. This is a fragment and we are not making a case for it being included in the Canon of scripture but it is history and it expounds upon this geographic word Parvaim or similar as an historic source of affirmation.

> *Genesis Apocryphon Fragment. 1QapGen, 1Q20. Column II.*
> *This fruit was planted by you and by no stranger or Watcher or Son of Heaven… [Why] is your countenance thus changed and dismayed, and why is your spirit thus distressed… I speak to you truthfully.' Then I, Lamech, ran to Methuselah my father, and I told him all these things. [And I asked him to go to Enoch] his father for he would surely learn all things from him. For he was beloved, and he shared the lot [of the angels], who taught him all things. And when Methuselah heard Enoch his father to learn all things truthfully from him… his will. He went at once to Parwain and he found him there… [and] he said to Enoch his father, 'O my father, O my lord, to whom I… And I say to you, lest you be angry with me because I come here… [48]*

In the previous chapter, we revealed that Enoch was not taken to Heaven but into the Garden of Eden. However, here we have a reference that Parvaim which is equated as Ophir and Sephar where Ophir immigrated, is the place where Enoch lived. Where did Enoch live? In the Garden of Eden as High Priest even performing sacrifices. We know also the Garden is protected by at least two terrible angels with a flaming sword that turns in every direction. Enoch would have had to exit the Garden and Methusaleh would not have been allowed inside. It is incorruptible with the Holy of Holies of Yahuah which just as with the Temple, only the High Priest may enter. This is not the only gold which leads in this same zip code. We're guessing that might be 7777.

Gold of Uphaz, Ophir, Havilah and Land of Creation

> *Jeremiah 10:9 KJV*
> *Silver spread into plates is brought from Tarshish, and gold from*

Uphaz, *the work of the workman, and of the hands of the founder: blue and purple is their clothing: they are all the work of cunning men.*

Daniel 10:5 KJV
*Then I lifted up mine eyes, and looked, and behold a certain man clothed in linen, whose loins were girded with **fine gold of Uphaz**:*

Uphaz is another gold which is Ophir by definition but yet another clue as to the dynamic of the symbiotic relationship between Ophir and the land of Adam and Eve, Havilah.

UPHAZ: Hebrew: אופז: *'Uwphaz: Fine Gold, **gold of Phasis or Pison**. Perhaps a corruption, Probably another name for* אופיר: *'Owphiyr:* **Ophir**. *[49]*

Uphaz is the fine gold of the Pison River. As we already proved out, this river surrounds the land of Adam and Eve named Havilah after Havah's or Eve's curse of childbirth. It is not a corruption as this word is perfect and it is not probably but definitely the same as Ophir as the two are the same word with different endings because Uphaz is the gold of Ophir which is Havilah surrounded by the Pison River. This is the Genesis 2 gold Adam used in the first sacrifice of atonement when exiled from the Garden. It is precious to Yahuah and this is why Solomon knew to fetch it for the Temple project from this primordial estate.

A deeper look at this Hebrew word reveals even more. Somehow translators who render Hebrew words really made a huge error with both Uphaz and Ophir and it is not one any Hebrew scholar could mistake. Uphaz does not start with an "U" and Ophir does not begin with an "O." These are very poor renderings as everyone knows that the Hebrew letter Aleph is always an "A" never "U" nor "O." Then, the second letter is the Hebrew WAW or "U" or "W." It's an "U." Ophir and Uphaz are the original land of the gold of Creation and Havilah. We are told the Chemical Symbol for gold, which is AU, originates in Latin but we showed you Josephus says that is the Latin name for Ophir. Ophir and Uphaz begin with AU because they are the complete origin of that emblem as the land of gold.

אופז: *Uphaz: A U P A Z   [49]*
אופיר: *Ophir: A U P I R   [6]*

The difference between these two words is Uphaz has a Z on the end which in Ancient Hebrew Pictograph form is represented by a pick-axe used to mine gold of course. Literally, PAZ is a Hebrew word for gold and AU is the Chemical Symbol for gold. That is no coincidence. It is a name for the gold of Ophir. They are otherwise the same first three letters. When we look deeper into the Pictographs for these letters, we render the following ancient meanings embedded into these very ancient words (our interpretation):

> *AUPAZ: Inhabiting & Mining Gold At the Ends of the Earth Where Elohim Is*
>
> *AUPYR: The Beginning, First Man Exiled to Inhabit & Till the Ground & Worship Elohim At the Ends of the Earth*

The ancients knew where this Land of Eve survived as they knew where the Garden and the Land of Creation existed whether they were able to get there or not. These were not mysteries and they certainly knew it was East of Iran. Both Parvaim and Uphaz serve to deepen our position that the Philippines is Ophir and they begin to unveil the similarities in geography between Ophir, Havilah, Land of Creation and Garden of Eden. Some will ask, why do all these things have to be in the Philippines? They do not have to and frankly, it would not matter to us if the Garden was in Africa or elsewhere. We would be happy to locate it regardless. However, the evidence leads where it leads. There must be more to Ophir than just possessing gold or Solomon's journey makes no sense. When the Bible defines a land of gold since Genesis 2, what would make us think that man is even capable of depleting it's resource? After all, these thousands of years, we have not and it still remains number 2 in untapped gold reserves on the planet. [11][12]

Chapter 7 | Queen of Sheba Revisited

In our introduction, we provide a visual presentation of the enigmatic Queen of Sheba's triumphal entry into Jerusalem when she offered her gifts to the Temple project. This truly must have been one of the most monumental displays in history. This sovereign forged an impression on antiquity and yet, after this event, she disappears back into her own land never to be heard from again until the Last Days. It is this expanse which has caused much speculation in which some cultures have attempted to fill in blanks but we will demonstrate, they have formed occult narratives against scripture to justify their claims. We will restore this understanding and clarify whom the Queen of Sheba was, how she would have conducted herself and from where she commenced her notable voyage which has captured the hearts and minds of so many. We assure you the Hollywood narrative of this Queen arriving as a pagan harlot is utterly false. This was a true, authentic lady by every measure within this story.

This narrative has sadly been greatly distorted in modern thinking even in most seminaries. The main reason is scholarship is incorporating legends that the Talmud has picked up from occult sources and when you learn their claims and origins, you will be very disappointed. One only has to read the Table of Nations in Genesis 10 to notice that there are two Sheba's listed in that era not just one. Many commentaries just overlook the second Sheba completely yet that is the actual brother of Ophir in which this Queen's adventure cannot be separated.

In Psalm 72, David equates the correct Sheba with Tarshish, the isles (Ophir) and Seba.

Psalm 72:10 KJV
*The kings of **Tarshish** and of **the isles (Ophir)** shall bring presents: the kings of **Sheba** and **Seba** shall offer gifts.*

You will note that Ophir and Tarshish are the same land. However, now we see Sheba and Seba together with them. Seba is the origin of the word Saba or Sabah and denotes a territory of Sheba [61] which is why they are mentioned together like this. This is practically the sole position for Yemen which was formerly Saba or the Sabaeans whom even from the days of Job were known in scripture thus, not a new people as described in these passages. This is because Saba is not Sheba, it's Seba and the Philippines has an ancient territory called Sabah all the same not to mention one of it's most abundant fruits is also the "saba" or banana. Therefore, there is no position based on this etymology from Yemen as Saba and Sabah are well-recorded in the Philippines.

Jeremiah 6:20 KJV
*To what purpose cometh there to me **incense (frankincense) from Sheba**, and the **sweet cane** from a far country? your burnt offerings are not acceptable, nor your sacrifices sweet unto me.*

Is Ethiopia located just down the Red Sea really considered a far country? Not logically. What sweet cane is this referring? Scholars simply aren't testing. This reveals Ethiopia is the wrong Sheba.

Sugarcane

If this sweet cane is sugarcane, then, Ethiopia is the wrong Sheba for this passage. Not only is it really not a far country but it has no ancient application of sugarcane which was introduced there in the 1500s according to an African science journal.

*"Sugarcane has been cultivated by smallholder farmers **since 16th century in Ethiopia** and preceded the commercial production."*
–Hindawi Advances In Agriculture, 2018 [369]

However, the Philippines matches this perfectly cultivating sugarcane even 1000 or more years before the era of Solomon.

> *"The sugar industry of the Philippines has had a colorful and dramatic history. The industry started some **two to four thousand years before the Christian era** where vessels from the Celebes brought sugarcane cuttings to Mindanao. Eventually, these plants spread further north to the Visayan islands and Luzon."*
> *–Republic of the Philippines, Dept. of Agriculture [368]*

In addition, Chinese history records the Philippines trading wine made of sugarcane in 982 A.D. before the Muslims nor Spanish arrived and such tradition continues today. [27] Thus, it was already growing there natively. This fits the Bible, Ethiopia does not.

In Hebrew incense is frankincense which in this passage, is combined with sugarcane both from Sheba, a far country. That is a clue. Lebownah is typically translated as frankincense. However, some translations differ on sweet cane but the case becomes even more impossible for Ethiopia as this Sheba. Scholars assume that frankincense which is invoked here by Jeremiah must mean Ethiopia and that is another false paradigm we will address in coming chapters. This proves that Ethiopia is also not the right frankincense in fact.

Sweet Calamus/ Sweet Flag

If this is "sweet calamus" as rendered by the NIV, NLT and other versions, Ethiopia is even more so the wrong Sheba. This is not a native plant to Ethiopia but was introduced very recently in history to Africa but in South Africa especially originating from the Orient.

> *"Acorus calamus L.: Common names: sweet-flag (Eng.); makkalmoes (Afr.); ikalamuzi (Zulu): **This plant originated from Asia** but has been cultivated in **South Africa since early colonial times** along stream banks and in wetlands. It is now distributed countrywide and has become naturalized."*
> *–South African National Biodiversity Institute [370]*

However, in the Philippines "sweet calamus," called Lubigan, is native likely from very ancient times. Unlike Ethiopia, we find no evidence this plant was introduced and this society traded with China before Solomon. Many overlook the fact that the Philippines has a different climate in the mountains.

> *"Along streams in mountains, creeks other moist places with running water, on boulders, etc., at low and medium altitude in Luzon (Laguna). Also found in Bontoc and Benguet provinces in swamps, at an altitude of about 1,300 meters, as a naturalized element. Also occurs in the temperate to sub-temperate regions of Eurasia and the Americas."*
> *– Godofredo U. Stuart Jr., M.D. [371]*

Therefore, the Sheba referred to in Jeremiah 6:20 is the one from the brother of Ophir from Joktan from Shem not the one from Ham's lineage in Ethiopia(Cush). You will notice scholars simply ignore Ophir's brother Sheba's descendants due to ignorance on this topic. This also means frankincense must come from the Philippines as well and it most certainly does. It is called "poor man's frankincense."[270] Ethiopia is the wrong Sheba for the Queen of Sheba.

> *Matthew 12:42 KJV (Parallel In Luke 11:31)*
> *The queen of the south shall rise up in the judgment with this generation, and shall condemn it: for she came from the uttermost parts of the earth to hear the wisdom of Solomon; and, behold, a greater than Solomon is here.*

Messiah places the Queen of Sheba's location at the "uttermost parts of the Earth" as well. Even before His time in 194 B.C., Eratosthenes' maps represent the known world. At the ends of the earth to the East were islands East of China. We already showed you the 43 A.D. map of Pomponius Mela and 124 A.D. map of Dionysius showing the same. [50, 18, 20–Ch. 3] Of course, He also happened to have participated in Creation (John 1) thus He would have foreknowledge as well as viewing the Earth from Heaven. The challenge with this though is this Sheba cannot be Ethiopia who is not in the uttermost parts of the Earth. Then, we have Ezekiel also equating Tarshish and Sheba. Dedan is there too but understand Tarshish also has a brother Dodan and both are rendered DDN in Ancient Hebrew in which the Bible was written and he too followed Tarshish into the Land of Adam and Eve. Tarshish never ties with Ethiopia but the isles of the East.

> *Ezekiel 38:13 KJV*
> **Sheba**, and **Dedan**, and the merchants of **Tarshish**, with all the
> *young lions thereof, shall say unto thee, Art thou come to take a spoil? hast*
> *thou gathered thy company to take a prey? to carry away* **silver** *and*
> **gold**, *to take away cattle and goods, to take a great spoil?*

Some focus on the young lions in this passage. The word כפיר: kephîyr [51] is also defined "village (as covered by walls)" which the Philippines has walls or concrete especially fences everywhere. It is one of the first icons one notices when they visit there.

David equates the gold of Ophir and Sheba as well as the gold of royalty and that of Messiah. He is equating that Sheba as Brother of Ophir not Ethiopia.

> *Psalm 45:9 KJV*
> *Kings' daughters were among thy honorable women: upon thy right hand*
> *did stand the queen in* **gold of Ophir**.

> *Psalm 72:15 KJV*
> *And he shall live, and to him shall be given of the* **gold of Sheba**:
> *prayer also shall be made for him continually; and daily shall he be*
> *praised.*

This begins to lead to the right Sheba as there are two to choose from in Genesis 10. Ophir especially has a brother named Sheba and they migrated to Sephar, the Mount of the East, ancient Havilah in about 2200 B.C. The Queen of Sheba descended from this Sheba and was Queen of the territory named after her ancestor, a male. We do not know her name but only the territory for which she is Queen – her family. How can we be sure though this Queen is associated with Ophir and not Ham's lineage? There is only one Ophir in all of scripture and he is from Shem and just so happens to have a brother named Sheba.

> *Genesis 10:26-30 KJV*
> *And Joktan begat Almodad, and Sheleph, and Hazarmaveth, and Jerah,*
> *And Hadoram, and Uzal, and Diklah, 28 And Obal, and Abimael,*
> *and **Sheba**, And **Ophir**, and Havilah, and Jobab: all these were the*
> *sons of Joktan. And their dwelling was from Mesha, as thou goest unto*
> *Sephar a mount of the east.*

> *Genesis 10:7 KJV : SONS OF CUSH/ LINE OF HAM*
> *And the sons of Cush; **Seba**, and Havilah, and **Sabtah**, and Raamah,*
> *and **Sabtecha**: and the sons of Raamah; **Sheba**, and Dedan.*

Not only did Cush have Seba but Sabtah and Sabtecha thus his lineage
is riddled with possibilities for the origin of Sabaens in Yemen. They
have to focus on just Sheba ignoring such and it is the wrong Sheba. The
source of the Queen of Sheba story in scripture makes this crystal clear.
The beginning of her story starts with "And."

> *1 Kings 9:26-10:1 KJV*
> *And king Solomon made a navy of ships in Eziongeber, which is beside*
> *Eloth, on the shore of the Red Sea, in the land of Edom. And Hiram*
> *sent in the navy his servants, shipmen that had knowledge of the sea, with*
> *the servants of Solomon. And they came to Ophir, and fetched from thence*
> *gold, four hundred and twenty talents, and brought it to king Solomon.*
> ***10:1 AND** when the **queen of Sheba heard** of the fame of*
> *Solomon concerning the name of the Lord, she came to prove him with*
> *hard questions.*

    Hers is a continuation of the previous story which this falls right at
the midpoint and is completely bookended on both sides. This is a
progressive story of Solomon building a navy and port on the Red Sea.
They go to Ophir... They fetch gold in Ophir... They are in Ophir...
They are not in Ethiopia... AND when the Queen of Sheba heard of
the fame of Solomon concerning the name of Yahuah... From whom?
Solomon's navy. There is no forcing this any other way. Ophir had a

brother named Sheba and this Sheba had a descendant ruling his region in 970 B.C. who was visited by Solomon's navy in her land of Sheba which is in Ophir as they are the same land in the same nation just as Tarshish and Ophir are equated and used interchangeably in scripture. The Queen of Sheba affirms this when she tells Solomon she heard of him in her own land. From whom? Solomon's navy. Where were they at this point in this very chronological story? In Ophir.

> *1 Kings 10:6 KJV*
> *It was a true report that **I heard in mine own land**...*

There are even historic sources claiming these brothers, Ophir, Sheba and Havilah settled and lived together once they migrated. This Sheba from which the Queen originated is her ancestor, brother of Ophir not the wrong Sheba from Ham's lineage.

> *"Kitab al-Magall (Clementine literature) and the Cave of Treasures hold that in the early days after the Tower of Babylon, the children of Havilah, son of Joktan built a city and kingdom, which was near to those of his brothers, Sheba and Ophir." [52] [156]*

Because an occult narrative was inserted into this in modern thinking falsely, this gets changed to a point that it no longer even looks like the same story and that is because it is not.

> *1 Kings 10:1 KJV*
> *And when the queen of Sheba heard of the fame of Solomon **concerning the name of the Lord (YHWH, Yahuah)**, she came to prove him with hard questions.*

Notice the Queen of Sheba was not interested in Solomon's fame or wealth. She had plenty of her own. She had heard about his God and she knew their families were cousins. This says the fame of Solomon concerning the name of the Lord (YHWH, Yahuah). That is quite a distinction from what most of us have been told. It is assumed the Queen was a pagan yet why would she care about the name of Solomon's God?

Why come to prove him with hard questions and give to the Temple Biblically? It is the story of one who knew the history of her people who were also Hebrews from Eber just as Solomon's people were. They were separated back in Iran and Joktan's sons including Ophir, Sheba and Havilah headed East to Sephar, the Mount of the East in Havilah, Philippines. She was not an Israelite Hebrew but a Hebrew from Eber.

This region would be renamed Ophir, Sheba and an area for Tarshish who was from Japheth but it was his ships which transported them there as they had none seaworthy in Northeast Iran. This Queen was not there to pay tribute to Solomon nor does it ever say such. She brought gifts of incredible wealth not for Solomon though but for the Temple project as she was bringing an offering from her people which would match the first sacrifice of Adam in her land – gold, frankincense and myrrh. This would be repeated 1000 years later when her ancestors would arrive in Jerusalem again with the same gifts as an offering to the Messiah as a toddler. We will get to that too.

> *I Kings 10:2 KJV (Parallel in II Chronicles 9)*
> *And she came to Jerusalem with a very great train, with camels that bare spices, and very much gold, and precious stones: and when she was come to Solomon, she communed with him of all that was in her heart.*

Some hyper-focus on the word camels in this passage and assume this means the Queen must have come from the Middle East. However, she is not gifting camels, she is riding them for transportation. How else did people get around back then especially with the kind of gifts she brought. The gold alone weighed about 4,000 kilograms (4.5 tons). She would have come with Solomon's navy as you will see, this is consistent with this narrative landing at the Red Sea Port of Eziongeber. From there, she would have a 344-kilometer (215-mile) journey to enter Jerusalem. She would need camels for that and she did not have to bring them with her on the ship because they were already there. Why would anyone bring camels for transportation to the Middle East when they were the abundant transport of those days?

Along with the gold, she brought spices and precious stones and likely a large entourage. However, this is a precious story as when she met

Solomon, she communed with him all that was in her heart. Frankly, that even fits the Filipino culture to this day. However, this was no pagan. This was a sincere believer already. She brought the ancient gifts from the estate of Adam to the Temple which denotes one who knew the covenant and was exercising it. She knew exactly what she was doing and so did Solomon. Can you imagine finding a long lost cousin and your families used to live together many years ago yet you were thousands of miles apart now. There would be so many questions indeed but she had tough ones and that is key. Then, the Queen offers her gifts.

> *I Kings 10:10 KJV*
> *And she gave the king an **hundred and twenty talents of gold**, and of **spices** very great store, and **precious stones**: there came **no more such abundance of spices as these** which the queen of Sheba gave to king Solomon.*

Many do not realize this may well be the wealthiest woman in all of history. If not, she is among them. The Queen gave 120 talents of gold. A conservative estimate in today's value places this at $168 million just in gold. She, then, donated spices of very great store but check out this language. The land of the Tabernacle and Temple offering daily spice sacrifices had never seen such "abundance of spices as these." There is a strong possibility, that is another equal gifting as the gold in value and then precious stones which we have no measure.

However, consider this. This would be the Queen of Sheba's First Fruit Offering some would call a tithe to the Temple Project meaning this would represent 10%. If just the gold is 10% of her gold, that is $1.68 billion in net worth just in gold and the spices were likely of equal value. This was among the first female billionaires in history. Sorry again, Oprah. However, notice what happens next in the story because at the same time she gives her gifts, so does Solomon's navy and the same gifts essentially because they arrived from the same land with the same resources at the same time.

> *I Kings 10:11-12 KJV*
> *And the navy also of Hiram, that brought **gold from Ophir**, brought*

*in from Ophir great plenty of **almug trees**, and **precious stones**.
And the king made of the almug trees pillars for the house of the Lord,
and for the king's house, harps also and psalteries for singers: there came
no such almug trees, nor were seen unto this day.*

Hiram, King of Tyre and admiral of Solomon's fleet, brings gold from
Ophir as the Queen brought the gold of Sheba. They are the same. He
brought precious stones just as the Queen did and her third gift of spices
actually matches the almug wood which has incense resin. The same
gifts at the same time. We will break down these resources in Chapter 9.
However, here is the end of the story.

I Kings 10:13 KJV
*And king Solomon gave unto the queen of Sheba all her desire, whatsoever she asked, beside
that which Solomon gave her of his royal bounty. So **she turned and went to her
own country**, she and her servants.*

Solomon offered gifts to the Queen as well. We have no idea if she even
accepted anything. Perhaps he gave her one of his ships to return home.
One of the things you may have heard at this point, is that Solomon and
the Queen of Sheba had an affair. Does the Bible say that? No. It says
she turned and went to her own country, she and her servants. Does it
say Solomon fathered a child with her? No. Would a Filipina especially
a Queen really participate in such without marriage in that age and with
a married man? We do not believe so. Even Solomon is still known as
righteous at this point though he enters a dark spiral downward after
the Temple. In fact, there is no knowing exactly what age she was as the
Queen of Sheba may have been a child even. Where does this thinking
come from if not from the Bible? This is really poor. The origin of
this claim and the expanded story is an occult writing in Ethiopia also
translating into the Quran and Talmud in which the Queen has the
...hairy legs and hoof of a goat. Really?

*[Islam] "She picked up her skirt to walk over the flood and so revealed her
legs, which were **covered with hair, like a goat's**. (A later Arabic
tale tells of how the Queen of Sheba came to have a **goat's hoof as
a foot**...)" [Ethiopia] "The stories are immortalised in the Ethiopian*

*holy book - the Kebra Nagast - where we find accounts of the **queen's hairy hoof**...* " *"As for the queen herself, her history remains an enigma. She was a woman of power, an adoring mother and a mysterious lover - also a founder of nations and **a demon with a cloven hoof.***" —BBC [53]

We do not believe the Queen of Sheba nor any Ethiopian Queen either was a Goat Lady and neither should any scholar. We reject that as illogical and unbiblical as David spent most of his years ridding the Kingdom of Israel of Nephilim hybrids and now his wise son, still righteous at the time, not only entertains a Nephilim hybrid in his court but the story continues.

"Here, the queen returns to her capital, Aksum, in northern Ethiopia, and months later gives birth to Solomon's son, who is named Menelik, meaning 'Son of the Wise'." —BBC [53]

This is disgusting. However, Ethiopia has only this to support it's claim of the wrong Sheba. Scripture certainly does not agree nor does real history. This has the Queen having an affair which the Bible does not record and then, a child the Bible does not cite. If Solomon had a son it would be there especially with this Queen. And the Goat Lady?... That's ba-a-a-a-d! This is also the root of the Ethiopian claim to house the Ark of the Covenant. Of course, they call it credible yet it was not even published until the 14th century, 2400 years after the Queen of Sheba. Before teaching something in the Bible, we should know the origin of those doctrines. Unfortunately, many just accept what seminaries dispense assuming they have done their due diligence. They have not in this case nor on this entire topic which you have already witnessed multiple times. Test everything.

You will then see stories of archaeology in Ethiopia by British archaeologist Louise Schofield claiming she may have found the gold of Sheba's wealth except she did not actually find gold. She found a temple dated one thousand years later and a possible gold mine which she did not enter as the entrance was impeded nor was there gold there that she proved. This did not stop her from making the claim that she found Sheba's wealth in fraud really. There are articles in The Guardian on her supposed finds. We encourage you to read them and test them. [54]

Schofield assumes the Queen of Sheba worshipped the symbol of the sun and crescent moon. That is the ancient goddess who is the Harlot of Babylon. Where did we read that in the Bible? Nowhere. Did she find one shred of evidence the Queen of Sheba from scripture originated in Ethiopia? None. She is following an occult fraudulent claim of no value from the Kebra Nagast in circular reasoning yet again.

As of the writing of this book, it has been 7 years and still no follow up on this story of Britain's find in Ethiopia that we can find. It was another fake news story which made it's assertions and then withdrew into the shadows leaving a wake of deception. That's standard occult news reporting. [54]

In fact, go to the British Museum and they well-document what has been found in Ethiopia. The oldest artifact even found there in all their digs has been dated to 275 A.D. [55] That's 1200 years after the Queen of Sheba. There is no support nor news there. Let's restore the Bible.

Now that we know who is not the Queen of Sheba is there a way to pinpoint where she originated? We believe this can be accomplished by using the Hebrew language in her island. For Sheba is in fact Cebu.

In looking at ancient maps of the Philippines, we find a consistent theme. There is no Cebu on the maps – not with a C. This makes sense as there is no C in ancient Philippine languages. Instead we see the island labeled as ZEBU in 1855 (right) which is the same in the 1906 Map by Justus Perthes, and SEBOE in 1893 (right). In 1521, Antonio Pigafetta recorded it as Zubu or ZZubu. [67] We have never found an ancient map which renders Sugbu however and etymologically, we find that to be quite a stretch and completely unmerited and illogical. Then, back in 1765, we found "A New Map of the Philippine Islands" by Thomas Kitchin (next page). [58] It renders Cebu as SEBU. Generally, these all lead to Sebu which is close to the modern name.

This is very interesting as when you look at the Hebrew, there is a word which ties yet none of the dialogues regarding the origin of Cebu from linguists fit. They do not know it's etymology.

SHEBU'AH: SHEBU: SHEBA: שבועה: and שבע: an oath: week: seven: the First Sabbath. [59]

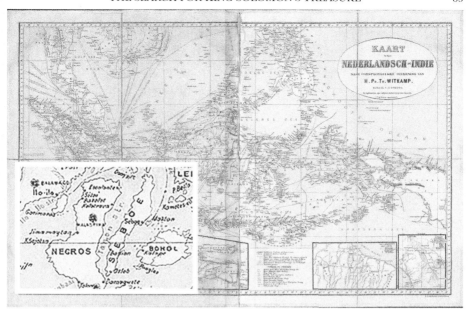

Netherlands Map. 1893 Nederlandsch Indie Map. Public Domain. [56]

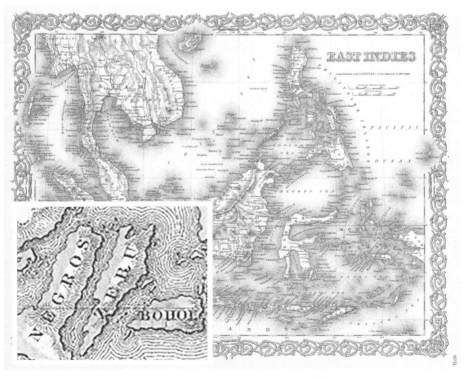

J. H. Colton, 1855. Issued as page no. 31 in volume 2 of the first edition of George Washington Colton's 1855 Atlas of the World. Public Domain. [57]

Some may be familiar with the plural of this Hebrew word – Shavuot, the Feast of Weeks or even more so, in Greek as Pentecost. This is one of seven Biblical Feast Days which takes place in early June or so. Shebu and Sebu are variants of the same word as it is S-B-U in Hebrew.

> *SEBU:* צבו: *tsebu: properly, will; concretely, an affair (as a matter of determination):—purpose. [60] SEBU:* שבו: *take captive. [60]*

In Daniel 6:17, sebu is applied as sealed with a "purpose." This word Sebu can also mean "take captive" in other forms which is similar to will and an affair. It fits right into the same genre of sheba and shebua as it is in the same family of derivatives as oath requires a sealing with a purpose, will and an affair in the sense of we are His bride and even take captive as we submit as His servants. Notice this is rendered as "S," shin and "TS," tsad which could be where the "Z" sound originates in Zebu. Sebu is also equated to Sebu'ot or Shavuot/Shebu'a and Sheba.

> *SHEBA:* שבא: *and* שבע: *oath, seven. [61]*

These words all linger around the first Sabbath or Shabbat also known as Shebat or Sebat. It is the seventh day and a day of oath.

This is where this really begins to raise the hairs on one's neck. Just as this word Sebu leads to Shebu'ah or Shebat or Sebat. We literally find a 1646 map by Dudley's Dell Arcano de Mare which renders Cebu as "Isle of Sebat." (right) How is this possible? Cebu is Sheba, the land of the Sebat/Shabbat or Sabbath and not just any Sabbath but the very first one on Day 7 of Creation – Shebu'a or Shavuot. It is the Feast Day which commemorates the first Sabbath/Shabbat. This took place in Sheba which means 7 as well as oath because shebu'a is also the Day of Covenant Renewal. The first Sabbath written and recorded on an island in the Philippines which still bares such name in Hebrew. No one can satisfy where this etymology came from because it is Hebrew.

Where was the first Sebat or Sabbath? In the Land of Creation as Adam was not taken into the Garden yet but still in the land where he was created on the seventh (Sheba) day. That land would be renamed as Havilah by Adam and then Sheba, Ophir and Tarshish. We know this

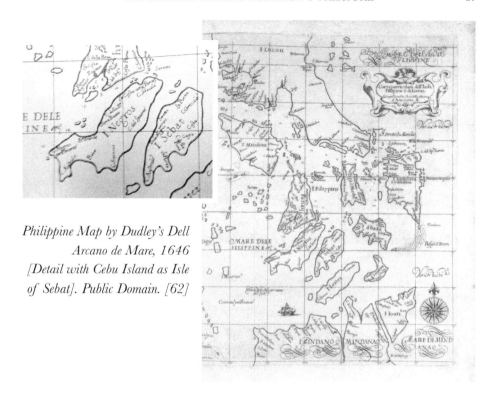

Philippine Map by Dudley's Dell Arcano de Mare, 1646 [Detail with Cebu Island as Isle of Sebat]. Public Domain. [62]

land today as the Philippines and would it not be appropriate for the Philippines to restore this original Feast Day of Shavuot/Shebu'a? In addition to Cebu/Sebu Island, Mindanao also has a large Lake Sebu for that matter. From a Bible perspective, this certainly appears to be why Sheba was named so prophetically as he would return to the Land of Creation. His brother Havilah obviously was named after the same land of Adam and Eve(Havah).

Finally, Ophir, which begins with AUR or "light" in Hebrew and PY or "mouth" denoting the Genesis 1 region, is equally prophetic. These three sons of Joktan were named for their future purpose to return to the Land of Creation. Sheba is Cebu, a direct variant in Hebrew of the same word. Is this perhaps the reason the island of Cebu appears to be shaped like a rib as in Eve was created from Adam's rib, and even placed in the right position geographically in the form of the archipelago?

Let's expand this a little further into what some would call coincidences. Cebu City today is still known as the "Queen City of the South" and no one seems to coherently know where that identifier originated. Iloilo, Panay, also in Visayas near Cebu, has the same nomenclature. It likely originated in Matthew 12:42 as Messiah called Sheba the "Queen of the South" which is the same connotation of Cebu and Iloilo today (Matt. 12:42, Luke 11:30). Along the same vein, Sheba means 7 [61] and Cebu just by chance happens to be in Region 7. Additionally, is it not fascinating that Lake Sebu in Mindanao has Seven Falls or Sheba Falls?

In fact, as a side note, the Philippines was to include 7,107 islands but that number has been updated recently to 7,641 according to the recent data from National Mapping and Resource Information. [63] We wonder if this number will not eventually be fully identified as 7,700 or 7,777 as the land of 7 or Yahuah's number of completion otherwise known in Hebrew as Sheba/Sebu/Shebu'a. Even in a list ranking the numerations of islands around the world, the Philippines actually ranks 7th. [376] Of course, these kinds of things can be dismissed as mere coincidence but when you pile them on top of all of the firm, indisputable evidence, they begin to seem not so coincidental anymore. The extent of challenges to these findings over the past 3 years, are debates based on these types of side notes. Yet, we are researchers and we will continue to note such but one cannot unravel our findings by straining gnats. You do not have to accept that line of reasoning as proven nor do we say it is but this case overall, most certainly is proven and this secondary supporting evidence has merit as well in thought.

Is it a coincidence that oil deposits were first discovered in the Philippines in Cebu in 1896? [64] Magellan and Barbosa landed in Cebu where they both also met their ends. The Battle of Leyte next to Cebu also remains the largest naval battle in history to most scholars. Why there? The significance of this land transcends back to Creation perhaps. You decide. Much more evidence to weigh.

Chapter 8 | The Isles in the East
At the Ends of the Earth

It is not too difficult to figure out whom Isaiah especially refers to when he continually prophesies of the isles in the East in the last days. We can all reason this out pretty simply yet one must really wonder when some out there attempt to identify these prophesies with places West of Israel when they must be East. Some even propagate lands not known for isles when they must be isles. Even more mediocre, some apply known locations close to Israel in Isaiah's time when he tells us they are located at the ends of the earth. It's almost as if they are not even reading the Bible.

We will offer those scriptures, but follow the logic. Isaiah refers to the Isles in the East at the ends of the earth many times. So let's go to Israel on a map in our minds and take King Solomon's journey. There are no isles in the Red Sea of significance. Saudi Arabia has what they call rocks in that region mostly not pronounced islands. As we head East of Israel and the Red Sea, we have to travel to India to find the sizable island of Sri Lanka but that's an isle not isles. We have to continue to the East Indies to arrive at significant isles. The explorers knew this.

Understand Indonesia is in Ham's territory not Shem's. Taiwan is an isle not isles. All that is left is a piece of Malaysia not mainland and the Philippines who, by the way, had historical ownership of Sabah which state accounts for half of Malaysia's isles. Other than misleading claims usually from the British, we have never found a coherent claim from Malaysia nor are they nor Indonesia known for worshipping the Creator of the Bible. It is not difficult to ascertain, Isaiah is referring to the Philippines. We are not the first to figure this out as there is a very large church out there who takes these prophesies of the Isles of the East and attempts to ascribe them all to one man at the top. We believe this is the usurping of prophesies of the Philippines as a people by one man for personal gain and we reject that. This matches 2 Chronicles perfectly.

> *2 Chronicles 9:21 KJV*
> *For the king's ships (Solomon's) went to Tarshish with the servants of Huram (Hiram): EVERY THREE YEARS once came the ships of Tarshish bringing gold, and silver, ivory, and apes and peacocks.*

We will prove in the next chapter, every one of these resources is not only native to but points to the Philippine region. One would think scholars would focus on the entire list but they rarely do. We will also test the ships of Solomon's era and you will see this also firmly identifies the region of the Philippines. Solomon's navy was navigating to the isles of the East that Isaiah would later predict in an end times context as would Ezekiel and even Messiah Himself. We will get to prophecy as well. This also coincides with the sons of Joktan who in Genesis 10 migrated from Iran to the Far East to the isles. This just keeps coming into focus more and more and by the end of this book, you will see clearly. We are not covering the scriptures in content in this chapter but simply looking for geographic markers which will help us to locate these isles of the East as Isaiah actually does so. We will cover prophetic significance later (Ch.16).

> *Isaiah 41 KJV*
> *1-2 Keep silence before me, O **islands**; and let the people renew their strength: let them come near; then let them speak: let us come near together to judgment. Who raised up the **righteous man from the east**...*
> *3 ...he had not gone with his feet...*
> *5 **The isles** saw it, and feared; **the ends of the earth** were afraid, drew near, and came...*

Just look for the clues and we will cover these in detail in a later chapter. These are islands who will come to judgment, righteous men. The word in Hebrew could be man or men and in looking at all of these in context, it's men not man. The isles at the ends of the earth. See for yourself if these do not lead to the Philippines. They certainly do not lead to

Africa, Yemen, India, Britain, Peru, nor Spain. In this promise to the Lost Tribes of Israel, Isaiah becomes specific.

> *Isaiah 60:9 KJV*
> *Surely **the isles** shall **wait** for me, and the **ships of Tarshish** first, to bring thy sons from far, their **silver** and their **gold** with them, unto the name of the Lord thy God, and to the Holy One of Israel, because he hath glorified thee.*

Where is Tarshish? Mindanao, Philippines. This is the Philippines. The isles of silver, Tarshish and gold, Ophir even. Isaiah is clear.

> *Isaiah 42:4 KJV*
> *He shall not fail nor be discouraged, till he have set judgment in the earth: and **the isles shall wait for his law**.*

These isles await the restoration of His law and again, they will come to judge. We see this as a recurring theme. Without this restored geography, we are massively missing the proper context by which to interpret prophecies like this.

> *Isaiah 42:10 KJV*
> ***Sing** unto the Lord a new song, and his praise from **the ends of the earth**, ye that go **down** (South) to the sea, and all that is therein; **the isles**, and the inhabitants thereof.*

These isles who sing are again at the ends of the earth, south and really, East from Israel and not just one but all the inhabitants generally like to sing. That is a real tough one.

> *Isaiah 24:15*
> *KJV: Wherefore glorify ye the LORD in the fires ('owr: רוא: actually AUR), [8] even the name of the LORD God of Israel in the **isles of the sea**.*
> *NIV: Therefore in the **east** give glory to the LORD; exalt the name of the LORD, the God of Israel, in the **islands of the sea**.*

Isaiah uses the Hebrew word for light here which is oddly interpreted fires. In fact, a strong look at this word leads to the three letters of Ophir (really AUPYR) in fact demonstrating that this is Ophir's origin. The NIV renders this as East but again it is AUR or AUPYR, Ophir. That is the isles of the East.

> *Isaiah 46:11 KJV*
> *Calling a **ravenous bird** from the **east**, the man that executeth my counsel from a **far country**:*
> *`ayit:* עַיִט*: Bird of Prey. `iysh:* אִישׁ*: Man, Men, Great men. [65]*

What would be the far country from the East with the greatest bird of prey? The Philippines has the largest eagle on Earth. However, this is far and to the East of Israel. We cover the eagle later too.

> *Isaiah 41:3-5 KJV*
> *He pursued them, and passed safely; even by the way that he had not gone with his feet. Who hath wrought and done it, calling the generations* ***from the beginning?*** *I the Lord, the first, and with the last; I am he.* ***The isles*** *saw it, and feared;* ***the ends of the earth*** *were afraid, drew near, and came.*

The isles at the ends of the earth who draw near to him and fear Him. They are the same who are waiting for His law to be restored. The same who have the ships of Tarshish.

> *Isaiah 41:9 KJV*
> *Thou whom I have taken from **the ends of the earth**, and called thee from the **chief men** thereof, and said unto thee, Thou art my servant; I have chosen thee, and not cast thee away.*

Chief men from the ends of the earth who will come on...? The ships of Tarshish, Philippines. Let's bring in other prophets who were also aware of these isles of the East and their role. This was known in ancient times and really up until the late 1800s.

Ezekiel 27:3 KJV
And say unto **Tyrus**, *O thou that art situate at the* **entry of the sea**, *which are the merchant of the people for* **many isles**...

Jeremiah 25:22-23 KJV
And all the kings of **Tyrus**, *and all the kings of Zidon, and the kings of* **the isles which are beyond the sea**, *Dedan, and Tema, and Buz, and all that are in the* **utmost corners**...

Jeremiah 31:10 KJV
Hear the word of the Lord, O ye nations, and declare it in **the isles afar off**...

These are rebukes of Tyre, Solomon's navy and deal with the many isles of the Philippines. Ezekiel speaks of "many isles" at the "entry of the sea." Could this be the entry of the East Indian Ocean? Likely. Jeremiah affirms this and proclaims these isles are "beyond the sea." Which sea? The Erythaean Sea as recorded in Jeremiah's time by Heroditus also known as the Indian Ocean as it is called today. We covered maps that pinpoint Chryse (Ophir) and Argyre (Tarshish) there as well. He, then, talks of isles declaring the word of Yahuah "afar off." He is not nor is anyone talking about Greece, Britain nor Canada. These isles are East at the ends of the Earth and they are identified as Tarshish, Ophir and Sheba.

Matthew 12:42 KJV (PARALLEL IN LUKE 11:31)
The **queen of the south** *shall rise up in the judgment with this generation, and shall condemn it: for she came from the* **uttermost** *(utmost)* **parts of the earth** *to hear the wisdom of Solomon*...

This is the Queen of Sheba who came from the uttermost parts of the earth to hear the wisdom of Solomon. Where were the uttermost extremities of the earth in Messiah's day? Even in 194 B.C., some versions of Eratosthenes mapped the isles of the East in the area of the Philippines as the uttermost parts. [50] Additionally, so did Pomponius Mela in 43 A.D., Dionysius the Tourist in 124 A.D. and even, Behaim in

1492, the year Columbus set sail to go to Ophir and Tarshish though he never made it that far. [18] The prophets are not foretelling of Ethiopia which is not nor has ever been known as isles nor Yemen nor even India as India's isles are the East Indies which included the Philippines. Put it all together and this spells out exact directions to the region of Philippines.

First, these are isles not an isle and not mainland nor a peninsula and a multitude or entire archipelago. They must be East of Israel, East of the Red Sea and really, East of Iran. These are in Shem's territory not Ham's nor Japheth's. They are known as the isles of Gold and Silver and even named as Tarshish and we know scripture equates that as the Biblical silver and Ophir next to it as the Biblical gold. This land is afar off, a far country to the East in the uttermost parts of the earth, a three-year round trip journey. This nation must identify with the greatest bird of prey and the Philippines does as well. Then, it must be located beyond the Indian Ocean to the East.

Look at a map. What did Isaiah and the other prophets just do here? They gave us detailed directions leading to the Philippines region. It cannot be Sri Lanka as that is not beyond the Indian Ocean nor isles. Taiwan is only an isle. The other archipelagos are Indonesia in Ham's territory and Malaysia with no supporting true history other than being mistaken by some and part of it belonged to the Philippines in ancient times. The Philippines appears on multiple maps as the ancient land of gold and when we get to the abundant history, was called Ophir and Tarshish by historic precedence. No other nation can compete in claim. This is the Philippines and no where else on Earth and an examination of the resources listed in these narratives affirms this.

"Most of the gold in the prehistoric and early historic periods would, however, undoubtedly have been extracted by panning alluvial sediments, a technique requiring little capital investment in equipment and no specialist technology, but unfortunately leaving no discernable archaeological signature."
– Anna T. N. Bennett, ArcheoSciences, 33 | 2009, 99-107. [417]

Chapter 9 | Testing All the Resources of Ophir, Sheba and Tarshish

2 Chronicles 9:21 KJV
For the king's ships went to Tarshish with the servants of Huram: ***every three years*** *once came the ships of* ***Tarshish*** *bringing* ***gold****, and* ***silver****,* ***ivory****, and* ***apes*** *and* ***peacocks****.*

We will now thoroughly test each of these resources in which Solomon's navy fetched from Ophir, Tarshish and Sheba. Tarshish is Ophir in area as they are equated several times in scripture and Sheba, Ophir's brother is equated to both lands as well.

1 Kings 22:48 KJV
Jehoshaphat made ships of ***Tharshish*** *to* ***go to Ophir for gold****: but they went not; for the ships were broken at Eziongeber.*

Also, Tarshish is a location not wood nor just a name for the ships. They physically went to a tangible place called Tarshish which is in the same region as Ophir and Sheba. This notable expedition was altered in this passage as the Red Sea port was destroyed.

2 Chronicles 20:36 KJV
And he joined himself with him to make ***ships to go to Tarshish****: and they made the ships in* ***Eziongeber****.*

Gold

> *"In the island (Mindanao) belonging to the king (Butuan) who came to the ship there are mines of gold, which they find in pieces as big as a walnut or an egg, by seeking in the ground."* [67]

> *"Pieces of gold, the size of walnuts and eggs are found by sifting the earth in the island (Mindanao) of that king (Butuan) who came to our ships."* —Pigafetta, 1521 [68]

Above Pigafetta describes from two different translations, though pretty much the same, that the King of Butuan was able to secure a gold nugget the size of a chicken egg or walnut by simply sifting through the earth or seeking in the ground. This actually fits what would have to be the case in the ancient land of gold from at least 1000 B.C. as there was no major mining equipment in that era. The Philippines not only matches this but we offer two additional legends which affirm this point that the gold in the Philippines was available by picking it up from the shallows of rivers and even the ground. Granted these are oral legends in which the story may change some depending on whom you talk but these affirm this position. Silver, we will withhold for Tarshish. However, please allow us to use this opportunity to expand on the gold narrative a little as we have already proven the Philippines leads.

> *"In addition, a much recent assessment reveals that the Philippines is second to South Africa in gold production per square kilometres."* — Villegas, Bangko Sentral (2004) [116]

Again, even in production, an apples-to-apples comparison in size by Bangko Sentral showed the Philippines as second in gold output as well in 2004. We have already covered just how prevalent and abundant the gold of the Philippines is as fact. However, there are even more archaeology finds of gold dated as early as 400 B.C. and 500 B.C.

> *"Based on archaeological evidence, gold artifacts appear as early as 400 to 250 BC in the Philippines. The earliest site with gold artifacts*

is in Luzon where burials with gold earrings are associated with the
Novaliches Pottery Complex. Beyer dates this complex from 250 BC
to the 4th century AD, while Solheim dates this complex from 400 BC
to 250 AD. (Solheim 1964: 173, 210; Beyer 1947; 234; 1936;
1948: 5; Scott 1968:38). Other excavations like the ones at Guri Cave,
Palawan have a jar burial assemblage that date between 300 and 500
BC. Among the artifacts recovered were gold beads." [402]

No one can date gold directly but only based on items with which it is found. This gold was not likely created in the year it was buried but passed down from antiquity according to history we will cover. Those demanding someone date gold, which cannot be dated, to 1000 B.C. are simply creating a false paradigm in thinking. It's still there in the ground formed before 1000 B.C. and still number 2 on all of earth in untapped gold deposits. That's archaeology and science. The King of Butuan acquired his large gold nugget without mining and ancient Philippine legends affirm Pigafetta's account.

Excerpts from *The Datu Who Became A Tortoise [69]*
"During that time, gold can be seen on shallow areas..."
"Buyung Abaw often went to collect gold in the shallow areas of the
sea... Buyong Abaw will go collect gold from the shallow waters with
Matang Ayaon..."
Excerpt from *Pearls of Mindanao [70]*
"The young man was a fisherman and he also collected gold from the
shallows. He was saving what he got for their marriage."

Finally, there is a book called the Cave of Treasures that we do not use as and reject as scripture but we glean a fact from it. It actually makes the claim that upon leaving the Garden of Eden which means Adam was in Havilah, Philippines, he was able to find gold on the sides of the Mount of the East where he then made the first sacrifice of atonement. There is no mention of excavating.

"Now Adam and Eve were virgins, and Adam wished to know Eve his
wife. And Adam took from the skirts of the mountain of Paradise, gold,

and myrrh, and frankincense, and he placed them in the cave, and he
blessed the cave, and consecrated it that it might be the house of prayer for
himself and his sons. And he called the cave "ME`ARATH GAZZE"
(i.e. "CAVE OF TREASURES")" [71]

Regardless of whether one views this as scripture, notice the pattern especially of gifts. This means Adam offered gold, frankincense and myrrh and also at his death. The Queen of Sheba would later bring the same gifts to the Temple project and the Wise Men brought the exact same gifts to Messiah.

SECOND BOOK OF ADAM AND EVE 8:16-19 [397]
"Then Adam let his blessing descend upon Seth, and upon his children,
and upon all his children's children. He then turned to his son Seth, and
to Eve his wife, and, said to them, "Preserve this gold, this incense, and
this myrrh, that God has given us for a sign; for in days that are coming,
a flood will overwhelm the whole creation. But those who shall go into
the ark shall take with them the gold, the incense, and the myrrh, together
with my body; and will lay the gold, the incense, and the myrrh, with my
body in the midst of the earth."

Ivory

Many have attempted to debate that the Philippines does not have elephants and look around today and this is a true point but not in antiquity. Unfortunately, some in the academic community have really obscured this even since we began our research years ago and the extremely odd thing is they should know better because there is abundant archaeology to support this.

In fact, search the internet or news outlets in recent times in the Philippines and you will see an ivory source identified since prehistoric times. Even international media such as Smithsonian Magazine and National Geographic have picked up on the "700,000-year-old Butchered Rhino Pushes Back Ancient Human Arrival in the Philippines." [72] The rhino horn is a great source of ivory. However, we can determine this fully even without the rhino and prove that elephants did once roam the Philippines natively.

When we began this research, the Wikipedia article for elephants in the Philippines clarified this as it rendered that elephants were once native to the Philippines but went extinct between the 1300s – 1600s. Of course, it is not quite that simple as someone has now changed that Wikipedia article to read:

> *"The Asian elephant was introduced to the Philippines, originally transported to the Sultanate of Sulu and Maguindanao, but became extinct on those areas or were transported back to Sabah for unknown reasons sometime during the 13th to 16th(?) century."* [73]

It is true in the 1300's the Sultanate of Sulu brought something like 600 elephants to the island of Jolo. It is outright wrong to say those were the only elephants who ever lived in the Philippines. The source for this Wikipedia article is FilipiKNOW.net by the way but we have heard from many who are hearing this narrative in academia today. It is not credible as it ignores much archaeology.

Our research has seen other online sources repeating this same narrative over and over as if it is fact but it is merely a parsing of fact. This is dangerous. For instance, Pinoy-Culture.com, likely just repurposing the same line they had been taught which is common, had an article published February 11, 2015, which told this same story but omitted the many evidences that demonstrate elephants were already in the Philippines all along. [74] We use the word "had" because since releasing our video on ivory where we cite their article with a screen shot, the link now leads to "suspended page." To their credit, perhaps they further researched the topic and found as we have that elephants are native to the Philippines. However, we continue to see this but we view this as very positive that outlets would remove things that are proven to be wrong.

We even see Lonely Planet attempt to chime in but perhaps after their article which they had to take down claiming the Chinese built the Banaue Rice Terraces, we should all be sure to test everything that comes from that source. We bump into such China propaganda often in fact especially from several other YouTube channels who attempt to appear like they are covering the same material we cover. We have found them illiterate when it comes to the Bible, history, geography and science and usually with a bent towards China supremacy. We are not interested in propping up government of other countries which we have never done, we are just searching for the truth here.

The Philippine Daily Inquirer's writer, Ambeth Ocampo, however, really conducted his research. In an article dated June 4, 2014, he documents elephants, stegodon, buffalo and rhinoceros as all native to the Philippines. These are all great sources for ivory and even without elephants, the Philippines has been documented to have ivory as far back as history goes in the Philippines. [75]

However, one must overlook tons of archaeology in order to conclude elephants were not native to the Philippines including the very latin identification of species which is specific to the Philippines such as Rhinoceros philippinensis unearthed in Fort Bonifacio along with Stegodon luzonensis, Bubalus cebuensis, a dwarf buffalo found in Cebu and Elephas Beyeri named after anthropologist H. Otley Beyer who found these bones on Cabarruyan Island in Luzon. These predate the Sultanate of Sulu's introduction of elephants. Elephants were still roaming the Philippines in the 17th century according to Jesuit Ignacio Francisco Alcino in his multivolume "Historia de las islas e indios de Bisayas" (1668) in which their "ivory was used for bracelets, ear pendants, daggers and sword hilts, and even jewelry boxes" at that time. [75]

However, please indulge us as we delve deeper into academia on this one to further support this because it is so abundant, we could literally write an entire book on how elephants are native to the Philippines since very prehistoric times. When we witness academics lining up in step with such a mantra as this has become, one can see this is a control narrative.

> *"Elephas Beyeri is an extinct species of dwarf elephant belonging to the Elephantidae family. It was named after the anthropologist H. Otley Beyer. The type specimen was discovered on Cabarruyan Island in The Philippines but has since been lost. Further fossils were found in Visayas and at a number of sites in Luzon. It is unclear if these belonged to Elephas beyeri or Elephas namadicus due to their fragmented nature and the missing holotype."* – Evolution of Island Mammals [76]

Elephant remains were also found in Cagayan, Kalinga and Apayao in Northern Luzon. Again, these predate the Sultanate of Sulu so drop the control line.

> *"The significance of the Cagayan Valley as an archaeological area was first reported by H. Otley Beyer in 1947, when the presence of fossilized remains of elephants were found during a mining prospecting activity. In the early 1970s, the Cagayan Valley Archaeological Project was launched by the National Museum, resulting in the discovery and recording of over 100 sites in the anticlines and synclines at Cagayan, Kalinga and Apayao Provinces."* – Ronquillo [77]

In fact, when one breaks down the story of the Sultanate of Sulu in history, they will find his elephants were eventually taken to Borneo where some still survive and not throughout the Philippines though since the bones predate him, that would not matter.

> *"The sultan of Java gifted a few hundred elephants native to the island of Java (now part of Indonesia) to the sultan of Sulu more than 600 years ago. The sultan of Sulu kept the Javan elephants on Jolo island, the capital of Sulu, which is an archipelago that is now part of the Philippines. The elephants were presumed extinct on Java by the end of the 18th century, but the small population sent to Sulu ended up in Borneo, and the six- to seven-foot-tall animals persist there today."*
> *–The Scientist [78]*

To recap a map we created based on the findings of National Geographic, Smithsonian Magazine, Philippine Daily Inquirer, Evolution of Island Mammals 2011, FilipiKNOW, Philippine E-Journals 2000, the-scientist. com and others, elephant bones have been found in archaeology predating the Sultanate of Sulu in Kalinga, Apayao, Cagayan, Pangasinan, Panay and Palawan. That is not a little discrepancy as these virtually all date prior to the Sultanate of Sulu. Then, pre-historic Rhino remains were found in Fort Bonafacio and Kalinga, Buffalo were found in Mindoro and Cebu and finally, Stegodon unearthed in Fort Bonafacio and Davao. In other words, ivory is found native all over the Philippines previously.

Even history agrees as in 1521, Pigafetta witnessed elephants as he mentioned them multiple times especially in Palawan.

"When we arrived at the city (Palawan), we were obliged to wait about two hours in the prahu, until there came thither two elephants covered with silk..." –Pigafetta, 1521 [79]

Antonio de Morga mentions another application for ivory derived from buffalo horn in which Dr. Jose Rizal responds documenting that weapon has been erased from history. This sad history has been the plight of the Philippines but this is coming to an end.

"At the waist they carry a dagger four fingers in breadth, the blade pointed, and a third of a vara in length; the hilt is of gold or ivory. The pommel is open and has two cross bars or projections, without any other guard. They are called bararaos. They have two cutting edges, and are kept in wooden scabbards, or those of buffalo-horn, admirably wrought."
–Antonio de Morga, 1609 [80]

"This weapon has been lost, and even its name is gone. A proof of the decline into which the present Filipinos have fallen is the comparison of the weapons that they manufacture now, with those described to us by the historians. The hilts of the talibones now are not of gold or ivory, nor are their scabbards of horn, nor are they admirably wrought."
–Rizal Note to de Morga, 1890 [81]

Ivory was native to the Philippines since pre-history, in the days of King Solomon and the Queen of Sheba, long before the time of the Sultanate of Sulu, in the era of the Spanish and all the way up until they went extinct in the 1600s or so.

Apes

Unfortunately, some things get rather lost in translation when one only examines the English version of the Bible. We find a plethora of revelation and understanding in the original Hebrew and Greek languages as you have likely observed by now. Solomon's navy returned with apes and we cannot begin to tell you how many demanded we produce a large, hairy Africa-type ape in order to prove this position. The problem is they are inserting their own modern thinking and not looking at the origin of the word which is not African-style large apes nor would they have had the technology to handle such primates in that era. They also would not need them as Solomon is not known for building a zoo and they serve no other purpose. Instead, this word simply means monkey and specifically a monkey with a tail or long-tailed.

apes: Hebrew: qôwph: קוֹף*: Probably of foreign origin,* **a monkey:** — *ape... **especially monkeys with tails**. [82]*

We would agree the Philippines is not known for African-style apes but those seeking such are not following the Bible. We are pursuing monkeys with long tails and yes, they are abundant in the Philippines. However, we can get more definitive on this one because in this case, we actually have archaeology of a relief from the walls of the palace of Assyria which illustrates Phoenician sailors (Solomon's navy) arriving with long-tailed monkeys not big African-style apes.

This relief tells us much as it is just after Solomon's time in 865 B.C. and the Phoenicians brought apes, or really long-tailed monkeys, from Ophir according to the Bible account. However, what is astonishing about this carving is that you can identify these monkeys as a match to the Philippine Long-Tailed Macaque. [pictured next page] The face, hands, feet, size, structure and tail all appear to be a match. Of course, there are other macaques around the world but we are not testing the world, we are testing whether the Philippines has the apes of the Bible and they have what appears to be a precise harmony.

The Philippine Long-Tailed Macaque not only exists today all over the archipelago but fossils have been excavated in Palawan which were identified as being that of the Philippine Long-Tailed Macaque from prehistoric times. [84] The apes of 2 Chronicles are definitely found native in the Philippines now and even before the time of Solomon and they also bear the same image as the relief in Assyria as yet another full circle proof.

*Left: PHILIPPINE LONG-TAILED MACAQUE   (Macaca fascicularis philippensis)
Right: Phoenician Sailors Bringing Monkeys (right) from Ophir. From court D, panel 7,
the north-west palace of the Assyrian king Ashurnasirpal II at Nimrud (ancient Kalhu;
Biblical Calah). From Mesopotamia, modern-day Iraq. Neo-Assyrian period, 865-860
BCE. The British Museum, London. [83]*

Peacocks

Some modern translations render this word baboons instead of
peacocks. However, that's new theology and there is not a single
precedence which they are following with that. However, search Google
for Philippines Baboon and the first result is the Philippine Long-Tailed
Macaque we just covered. Thus, it is still found in the Philippines but
we have never seen any kind of credible logic to change the Bible word
for peacock to baboon and these new translations should be required to
prove any changes like that. After all they are changing the Word and
that is a serious endeavor with very dire consequences. This is why you
will find us referencing back to the original Hebrew and Greek rather
than looking at multiple new translations.

Research Westcott and Hort who wrote new manuscripts by which
most modern translations originate. That manuscript is not the Bible

and read their letters where they specifically intended to attack the deity of Messiah and change the Word. There is little to be learned from their manuscript nor any translation which originates from it including some you may not be aware. This word remains peacock however and never changed.

The Philippines has a native peacock named the Palawan Peacock.

> *"Endemic to the Philippines, the Palawan peacock-pheasant is found in the humid forests of Palawan Island in the southern part of the Philippine archipelago."* [86]

We find references to this peacock in Pigafetta's Journal twice.

> *"The next day the king of that island sent a prahu to the ships; it was very handsome, with its prow and stern ornamented with gold; on the bow fluttered a white and blue flag, with a tuft of peacock's feathers at the top of the staff"* –Pigafetta, 1521 [85]

> *"Afterwards there came nine men to the governor's house, sent by the king, with as many large wooden trays, in each of which were ten or twelve china dishes, with the flesh of various animals, such as veal, capons, fowls, peacocks, and others, with various sorts of fish, so that only of flesh there were thirty or thirty-two different viands."*
> –Pigafetta, 1521 [85]

Just from this single passage in 2 Chronicles which identifies resources of Ophir and Tarshish, this allows us to narrow this down already. Solomon's navy returned with gold, and silver, ivory, and apes and peacocks. There are no other stops on the list and this was the very first journey to Ophir and Tarshish. There is no record of their establishing trading posts along the way nor was that their purpose. They were building the Temple and to complete the project, Solomon wanted specific resources such as the gold Adam used in the first sacrifice which only comes from one place, the wood of Noah which was used to build the ark from this same land and all the resources of ancient Havilah, the land of his ancient ancestors – Adam and Eve.

However, the Bible is far more brilliant than given credit even by scholars, many of which do not actually believe the Bible unfortunately. It just knocked out any claim of Ophir coming from Ethiopia who not only is in the wrong territory but has no peacocks, almug trees (we will cover) and was not located in the uttermost parts of the earth. Yemen has no ivory, peacocks, almug nor is it in the uttermost parts of the earth. Both fail miserably the resource test and every test we have attempted. Nothing can replace the actual land of gold in history – the Philippines.

The Bible lists more resources though than just this one passage which come from Tarshish especially as well as Sheba which is further defined. We will test all of them and you will continually notice the others making assertions, deteriorate under examination.

Resources of Tarshish

> *Ezekiel 27:12 KJV*
> **Tarshish** *was thy merchant by reason of the multitude of all kind of riches; with* **silver**, **iron**, **tin**, *and* **lead**, *they traded in thy fairs.*

> *Jeremiah 10:9 KJV*
> **Silver** *spread into plates is* **brought from Tarshish**…

Tarshish is a place next to Ophir. They are in the same direction and region in destination. Now, we have yet more resources we can test and narrow this down beginning with silver as promised. Tarshish is the Biblical land of silver equated to the Greek Argyre which we saw is mapped by Pomponius Mela, Dionysius The Tourist and Behaim as Mindanao, Philippines. By rare occurrence, it just happens that Mindanao is the only place in the Philippines which can fully fit this part of the list for Tarshish especially tin.

Silver

> *"Nickel mines are located in Zambales, Palawan, Agusan del Sur, Surigao del Norte and Surigao del Sur, while the gold with silver mines are in Benguet, Masbate, Camarines Norte, Davao del Norte and Agusan*

del Sur. The copper with gold and silver mines are located in Benguet,
Cebu and Zamboanga del Norte. The copper mine with gold, silver and
zinc is in Albay..." —Philippine Daily Inquirer *[87]*

Notice some attempt to hyper-focus on King Solomon's copper mines yet no Biblical narrative mentions copper but there is also copper in the Philippines. It even fits narratives outside the Bible. Much of this silver is found with gold thus it has always been abundant in the Philippines and all over the archipelago.

> *"Of the total of sixteen lode and placer mines which were producing gold*
> *and silver bullion in appreciable quantities at the close of 1935, nine are*
> *situated in the Benguet mining district."*
> *—Port of Manila and Other Philippine Ports Year Book. (1936) [88]*

Iron

Peruse the many mining reports and you will find the Philippines is not mining iron at present. Does this mean they do not qualify? Iron is one of the largest mineral deposits in the Philippines, even gifted to President Quirino, and the government has shut down the last operation due to environmental infractions. Therefore, you will not see it on reports but it is definitely there and in abundance though few seem to have ever researched.

> *"Iron ore, one of the Philippines' largest mineral deposits, is not being*
> *extracted at present."* —Philippine Statistics Authority *[89]*

> *"The Philippines has suspended the operations of the country's only iron ore*
> *miner due to environmental infractions."* —ABS-CBN, Reuters 2016 *[90]*

Philippine Iron Ore given as a gift to President Quirino. Exhibit in Syquia Mansion Museum, Vigan, Philippines. Photo By The God Culture.

Iron ore is found all over the archipelago as well and was referenced in the early 1900s by an American scientist as well as history to 200 A.D.

> *"There are numerous veins of iron that will well repay working." –* *James Walsh, Ih.D, M.D. 1865-1942 [91]*

> *"Even as early as the third century, the Chinese reported that* *gold was mined in Luzon, and it was a principal medium of exchange* *with Chinese traders. Iron, copper, coal and other minerals were also* *discovered, but little effort was made to mine them." –Port of Manila* *and Other Philippine Ports Year Book. (1936) [88]*

Tin

This is one of the largest assumptions that we often see. Some will claim Tin does not originate in the Philippines. However, once again, this thinking is based on distribution maps out there for countries who are mining tin and the Philippines has not been friendly for mining companies who do not take care of their environment. Having said that, even in our travels around the Philippines, in Mindanao, we have had active miners confirm there is definitely tin in Mindanao. However, remember in ancient times, tin mining was akin to gold mining in process.

> *"Tin is an essential metal in the creation of tin bronzes, and its acquisition* *was an important part of ancient cultures from the Bronze Age onward. Its* *use began in the Middle East and the Balkans around 3000 BC. Ancient* *sources of tin were therefore rare, and the metal usually had to be traded over* *very long distances to meet demand in areas which lacked tin deposits. It is* *likely that the earliest deposits were alluvial and perhaps exploited by the* *same methods used for panning gold in placer deposits." [92]*

Many of the modern sources of tin would not even qualify in ancient times but the Philippines had gold panning operations since the most ancient of times. However, we do not need to rely on just that logic as the Philippines has tin indisputably.

"The economy is primarily agricultural. Tin mining takes place around Mindanao."
—World Encyclopedia 2005 by Oxford University Press [93]

"Tin is not so abundant."
—James J. Walsh, , Ih.D., M.D. 1865-1942. [91]

Dr. Walsh notes tin is not so abundant in the early 1900s yet it is there but we only affirm Mindanao. In 2005, World Encyclopedia by Oxford University Press and The American Desk Encyclopedia thought it noteworthy enough to mention that Mindanao was mining tin. Although we do not find it on modern mining lists for the Philippines which is no surprise, we have had first hand accounts from miners especially on Mindanao who note that tin is still there though not a focus.

Lead

lead: `owphereth: עפרת *[95]*

Before we delve into lead, take a look at the Hebrew name for lead, owphereth. Is it possible this element may come from Ophir? The Philippines also has lead.

"Although the Philippines is rich in mineral resources, mining activities constitute only a small portion of GDP and employ an even smaller fraction of the population. Most of the country's metallic minerals, including gold, iron ore, lead, zinc, chromite, and copper, are drawn from major deposits on the islands of Luzon and Mindanao." —Encyclopaedia Britannica 2019 [96]

"An FTAA may be entered into for the exploration, development and utilization of gold, copper, nickel, chromite, lead, zinc and other minerals." —Primer on the Philippine Minerals Industry [97]

Once again, you will not find this resource on mining lists because it is not currently being mined but that does not mean it is not there. In fact, Encyclopaedia Britannica which updated this reference recently, affirms both lead and even iron ore again on Luzon and Mindanao. The resources of Tarshish are all found natively in the Philippines and specifically on Mindanao as Tarshish. This is after we already found all the Biblical resources of Ophir. Ethiopia and Yemen are already out of the running. Britain is not East of the Red Sea and does not have native peacocks nor almug wood. Spain is also not East and does not have indigenous ivory, apes, peacocks nor almug trees. Even Peru cannot fit the journey timewise and is missing ivory, peacocks and almug wood natively. These aren't mere misses, they are ludicrous propositions and anyone calling themselves a scholar who did not begin with a resource test, is no scholar on this topic. The only other coherent claim as far as resources are concerned is India yet it's own history says it had a source of ancient gold and silver, isles to the East thus none of these make any sense except the Philippines. Chapter 3 addressed Malaysia. However, we have one more list to test for the gifts of Sheba and Solomon's navy.

Offerings of the Queen of Sheba and Solomon's Navy Returning from Ophir

> *I Kings 10:10-12 KJV*
> *And she gave the king an hundred and twenty talents of **gold**, and of **spices** very great store, and **precious stones**: there came no more such abundance of spices as these which the queen of Sheba gave to king Solomon. And the navy also of Hiram, that brought **gold from Ophir**, brought in from Ophir great plenty of **almug trees**, and **precious stones**. And the king made of the almug trees pillars for the house of the Lord, and for the king's house, harps also and psalteries for singers: there came no such almug trees, nor were seen unto this day.*

First, notice again how the offerings the Queen of Sheba brought essentially match those of Hiram, King of Tyre, admiral of Solomon's returning navy from Ophir. They arrive and offer their gifts at the same time. The Queen of Sheba came from Ophir which is why her land too is known for gold. She donated gold to the Temple project yet Solomon already had all he needed even before his trip to Ophir. He was replacing what was in the treasury with the gold of Ophir yet she gives her gold to the Temple project as well? This was acceptable because her gold is the gold of Ophir. Even King David equated the gold of Ophir with Sheba. We have well-covered the abundant gold of the Philippines at this point so we already know for both gold is a check.

Spices

The Hebrew word used here for spices is usually interpreted as frankincense. We are well aware we are all told by the Rabbis that Ethiopia has the only tree on earth which produces frankincense. However, yet again, this is not accurate by any reasonable logic. The Philippines has a frankincense. It's called "Poor Man's Frankincense" [96] which we will cover in Chapter 15 in detail not because it is of lesser quality but since it is not designated by the Rabbis as the Biblical Frankincense, it has a lower perceived value. This is why many perfume companies from the U.S. and Europe are buying frankincense from the Philippines. It originates from the Pili Tree as Manila elemi. [98] In fact, in Part 12C of Solomon's Gold Series, we test every Biblical spice we can find and every one of them is native to the Philippines except one which is unidentified as a lost reference as no one is sure what the plant is. Regardless, the Philippines has frankincense and as a tropical rain forest, most spices and all Biblical ones.

Precious Stones

There are some who claim the Philippines does not have precious stones but to say so is to ignore history which we have already covered multiple observations of gemstones in the Philippines. Resource lists and even the United Nations for that matter, record the Philippines as a source for precious stones.

> "Aside from gold deposits, the Philippines is also rich in gemstones such as opal, jasper, quartz, tektite, Zambales and Mindoro jade, garnet, epidote, jadeite, and blue and green schist."
> –Board of Investments, DTI Business Development Manager for Fashion and Jewelry [94]

"Agate, Amethyst, Calcite, Garnet, Hematite, Jade, Pearl, Pyrite, Quartz, Sphalerite" —OKD2 [99]

"Chinese silk, porcelain, jars, gold, ivory, and beads were traded for wax, bird's nest, teakwood, rattan, pearls, precious stones and other marine and forest products [from Philippines]." —United Nations, 2019 [100]

The Philippines has every one of these resources natively – gold, spices and precious stones. However, we can also narrow down this lost reference of wood.

Almug Wood

The Bible does not tell us what this almug or algum wood is as these are the only times it is used without much description. We know it is a foreign wood "never seen in Israel" before which tells us it does not originate from any of it's normal trading partners which would include Ethiopia and Yemen thus neither are Ophir. Many scholars believe it is a red sandalwood based on descriptions of the Temple from other sources describing pillars in appearance as red sandalwood. [377] Look up the distribution list for red sandalwood and once again, the Philippines does not make it onto some maps. It comes from India but not the Philippines according to some.

There is only one massive problem with this thinking. The national tree of the Philippines, the Narra, is a red sandalwood with incense resin or spices matching the Queen of Sheba's offering. Why is this the national tree of the Philippines? We do not believe that to be coincidence. We believe Narra is the perfect fit for this narrative as this word also likely has Hebrew origins connected to the Queen of Sheba.

Hebrew: na'ara: נַעֲרָה *: girl, young woman, respectful.*
"She who must be admired." *[101]*

The Hebrew word na'ara is used twenty-four times in scripture such as referring to Dinah the daughter of Jacob and usually associated with a young woman or girl of purity – a virgin. When we see a tie like this as na'ara in Hebrew and the national tree Narra which fits the wood used in the Temple and then, bearing such meaning as "She who must be admired," we strongly believe this is not chance. This red sandalwood ties to the Temple and to the Queen of Sheba, the wealthiest woman possibly of all time who must be admired indeed. Additionally, we believe this leads even deeper as Noah lived in ancient Havilah, land of Adam and Eve (Havah) and would have used this same wood to build the ark. This is the reason King Solomon sought it out.

Narra has an incense resin or spice and is a preferred wood for boat-building according to The Wood Database and Stuart Xchange. [102]

"Yields "kino," (incense resin) containing kinotannic acid." [102]

"Old narra is a much sought-after wood for its durability and use in floorings, cabinetry, construction, furniture making, decorative carvings, and musical instruments. A preferred wood for boat-making because of resistance to seawater." –Stuart, M.D. [102]

Everything Solomon used almug wood to build, Narra is well-suited in those applications. However, we believe this leads us to the wood used to build the ark which is why Solomon sought it as well as the gold used in Adam's first sacrifice. These resources were not about monetary value but sentimental value to Yahuah God as this was His Temple which would house His Ark of the Covenant with His presence. Remember, David was called a man after Yahuah's own heart. He and Solomon knew that Yahuah would prefer items that had more precious meaning to Him. That is why this is no ordinary journey and it appears to defy reason because it was not about man's gain but about Him. It is also why we see the rebuke of Tyre so strong as it defiled the use of these resources.

Genesis 6:14 KJV
*Make thee an ark of **gopher wood**; rooms shalt thou make in the ark, and shalt **pitch** it within and without with **pitch**.*

Anyone know what gopher wood is? It's ok, neither does any scholar.

It is considered to be a lost reference. Some attempt to claim the word refers to pitch but read the scripture, the Hebrew word for pitch is already in there in that same sentence twice so it is not pitch in meaning but a different word. They then guess it is cypress but there is a Hebrew word for cypress (tirzah, תרזה) [103] which is no where near the word gopher (גפר) not even a single letter. They are just guessing with no basis. Cypress is a good wood for building ships but understand Noah was not actually building what we would call a ship for efficiency, he was building a vessel of survival which would withstand tsunamis without flipping, a ship so durable it could plow through major debris without damage, among other things. We wonder if scholars are looking at this wrongly. Our concordances are of little use on this.

> *Hebrew:* גפר *: gopher wood: A kind of tree or wood. Word Origin: of* **uncertain derivation**. *The word Gopher is not Hebrew and only appears in the bible one time. [104]*

We are greatly confused that a Hebrew scholar would suggest an ancient word in Genesis 6 was not of Hebrew origin especially since it has no track to any other language of congruence really. Something may be somehow corrupted and we understand, there is no track today but they have no evidence of that. The original language of Creation according to the Book of Jubilees was Hebrew thus in Genesis 6 before the Flood, gopher wood should be Hebrew. What are we missing on this? Perhaps the word itself has been slightly corrupted of sort. In our research, we found two instances from the 1800's that make one wonder if this word gopher is not being rendered correctly. Here is a reference from studylight.org which claims Webster's Dictionary 1828 defined:

> *"***Opher Wood***: A species of wood used in the construction of Noah's ark." –studylight.org on 1828 Webster's Dictionary [105]*

Opher is obviously a variant spelling of Ophir. Is it possible this word was rendered in the Bible at one time as Opher instead referencing it's origin from the land of Ophir? Did Noah build the ark of the wood from Ophir? Unfortunately, we were unable to reproduce this definition in the 1828 dictionary claimed by styudylight. However, it got us searching for an affirming reference and oddly we found one also from the 1800's which has also now been removed from Google books. In 1816, we were shocked to find Rev. Joseph Thomas wrote a book called "The Pilgrim's Muse" in which he renders Genesis 6:14 in poetry as:

> *"Make thee an asylum of* **Opher wood.***"*
> *–Rev. Joseph Thomas, 1816 [106 - See Sourcebook]*

However, we were able to secure this page from the rare book itself for our Sourcebook, though Google has now deleted it since our video. We will let you determine what that means. This shows the wood of Ophir with the word Opher even capitalized as if it were a place? It sure appears likely. However, we can not prove this out any further at this time. It is an interesting thought that Noah built the ark of the same wood as the Temple which is why Solomon desired it for the Temple project. Narra named for the Queen of Sheba – Opher wood perhaps.

Every resource of Solomon tests as native to the Philippines and all other claims fail in this chapter except India whose claim already failed the test of it's own history. We offer a full test of each of the major claims and they are merely fallacious overtures in almost all cases as only the Far East could even fit Ophir on any level. Most fail more than 50 percent of the criteria. India fails it's own history and Malaysia and Indonesia both were never seriously considered as possibilities after Magellan found Ophir. He was in Malaysia and Indonesia prior and ruled them out as the Portuguese certainly knew they were not Ophir and so did the locals. The British propagate such unsubstantiated myth but that does not make it worthy of review as it fails very quickly and these are not applying scholarship but propaganda. We will demonstrate the British East Indies Company has been paying to suppress this narrative for centuries. The Philippines is Ophir, Sheba, Tarshish, Ancient Havilah and the Land of Creation not because it has to be to fit our narrative but because this is where the evidence leads as these are all the same land in scripture and history and there is no debating that. No one has successfully in three years. Test for yourself.

Ophir–Tarshish Resource Test Survey of Native Elements and Orientation.	History As Ophir (Documented Beyond Claims.)	East of Meshad, Iran (Ophir Migration) [34]	Gold & Silver	Ivory	Apes (Monkeys)
Ethiopia *Fail!*	✗	✗	✓	✓	✓
Yemen *Fail!*	✗	✗	✓	✗	✓
India *Fail!*	✗	✓	✓	✓	✓
Britain *Fail!*	✗	✗	✓	✗	✓
Spain *Fail!*	✗	✗	✓	✗	✗
Peru *Fail!*	✗	✗	✓	✗	✓
Malay Peninsula *Claim specific to the Peninsula *Fail!*	✗	✓	✓	✓	✓
Indonesia *Even Britain abandoned this claim. *Fail!*	✗	✓	✓	✓	✓
Philippines *Pass!*	✓	✓	✓	✓	✓
	*See Timeline Ch. 12	*See Timeline Ch. 12	[75–81]	[82–94]

©2020 Timothy Schwab.

Ophir & Tarshish: 2 Chr. 9:21
Tarshish: Ez. 27:12
Ophir & Sheba: 1 Ki. 10:10-12
Directions: Gen. 10:26-30,
Jub. 8
Isles: Ps. 72:10, Is. 23:6,
Is. 60:9, 1 Ki. 22:48,
2 Chr. 20:36

None of these claims has the history of Ophir Except Philippines

5 of the 9 Claims aren't even East of Mesha, Iran

The Philippines is #1 In Gold. None of these others compare

Peacocks (Never Parrots nor Baboons in Bible)	Iron	Tin	Lead	Almug wood (Red Sandalwood) [377]	Isles (Never Mainland nor Peninsula) [16][17][18][20][154][50]	3-Year Journey (From Red Sea Round Trip With Trade) *Estimates in Ch. 10	Shem's Territory (Ophir is from Shem) *Map in Ch. 18
X	✓	X	✓	X	X	Missing 8 of 13 / X	X *Ham's Area.
X	✓	X	✓	X	X	Missing 8 of 13 / X	✓ *Saba derives from Seba from Ham though.
✓	✓	✓	✓	✓	X *Claim is mainland India.	Missing 3 of 13 / X	✓
X	✓	✓	✓	X	✓	Missing 6 of 13 / ✓ *Wrong direction.	X *Japheth's Area.
X	✓	✓	✓	X	X	Missing 8 of 13 / X *Wrong direction.	X *Japheth's Area
X	✓	✓	✓	X	X	Missing 8 of 13 / X *Over 5 years.	X *Ham's Area.
✓	✓	✓	✓	✓	X *Peninsula is not an island.	Missing 2 of 13 / ✓	✓
✓	✓	✓	✓	✓	✓	Missing 2 of 13 / ✓	X *Ham's Area.
✓ [85-86]	✓ [88-91]	✓ [91-93]	✓ [95-97]	✓ [101-102]	✓	Meets ALL Criteria! / ✓	✓

©2020 Timothy Schwab

5 of the 9 Claims don't even have native Peacocks

Only the Orient has Red Sandalwood

6 of the 9 Claims aren't even Isles

4 of the 9 Claims aren't even 3 Years Journey. 2 others in Wrong Direction

5 of the 9 Claims aren't even Shem's. Though Shem's, Saba was taken by Seba from Ham

NOTE: Assessment based on internet searches except the Philippines which is far more vetted. Not intended to represent comprehensive science for all countries. If a resource somehow turns up native in one of these lands upon deeper research, it does not change the fact that most of these fail half or more of the resources test and all fail in the end except the Philippines.

Chapter 10 | Restoring Tarshish and Jonah's Journey

2 Chronicles 9:21 KJV
For the king's ships (Solomon's) **went to Tarshish** *(Ophir) with the servants of Huram (Hiram King of Tyre) EVERY 3 YEARS, once came the ships of Tarshish bringing gold, silver, Ivory and apes and peacocks.*

Solomon's navy traversed far to reach these precious isles of gold – Ophir. One of the other names for this same region of Ophir is Tarshish which is fully and indisputably equated with Ophir in many passages. Is this because the writers of Kings and Chronicles disagree with each other? Not at all for they are the same place generally. In addition to 2 Chronicles 9, there are several scriptures which identify Tarshish especially the ships of Tarshish and they equate it to Ophir. The ships of Tarshish go to Ophir for gold and Tarshish for silver but both in the same area.

1 Kings 22:48 KJV
Jehoshaphat made ships of **Tharshish** *to go to Ophir for gold: but they* **went not**; *for the* **ships were broken** *at Eziongeber.*

Jeremiah 10:9 KJV
Silver spread into plates is brought from **Tarshish**…

Ezekiel 27:12 KJV
Tarshish *was* **thy merchant** *by reason of the* **multitude** *of all kind of* **riches**; *with silver, iron, tin, and lead, they traded in thy fairs.*

2 Chronicles 20:36 KJV
*And he joined himself with him to make **ships to go to Tarshish**:*
and they made the ships in Eziongeber.

Tarshish like Ophir is an isle and part of an archipelago of isles. Thus, any theory which places Tarshish anywhere but isles is ignorant of scripture.

Psalm 72:10 KJV
*The kings of **Tarshish and of the isles** shall bring presents: the kings of **Sheba** and **Seba** shall offer gifts.*

Isaiah 23:6 KJV
*Pass ye over to **Tarshish**; howl, ye **inhabitants of the isle**.*

Isaiah 60:9 KJV
*Surely **the isles** shall wait for me, and the **ships of Tarshish** first, to bring thy sons from far, their **silver** and their **gold** with them, unto the name of the LORD thy God, and to the Holy One of Israel, because he hath glorified thee.*

Notice, Tarshish is known for ships. Some scholars estimate that it may be a wood but in reading 2 Chronicles 9:21 and Jeremiah 10:9 especially, this cannot be the case and we are sure they regret making such an uneducated guess. The ships of Tarshish or Solomon's navy go to Ophir and Tarshish which you will find is equated by history as well. Tarshish is in the region of Ophir, it is a place known for silver and other resources which we have tested. It is associated with isles just as Ophir and Sheba are. We covered Sheba (Ch. 7) but you can already see the equation with Ophir and Tarshish in these scriptures. However, the largest misunderstanding we read and hear is that of the story of Jonah which in modern theology is absolutely wrong to the Bible geographically.

Correcting the Journey of Jonah

One of the first objections we hear from Pastors and scholars is that

Jonah travelled West to go to Tarshish. However, they are lacking the full context of the time. The Red Sea port was broken by Yahuah just before Jonah's time in the days of King Jehoshaphat who attempted to replicate Solomon's trip to Ophir. No such trip occurred and with the port destroyed by Yahuah, there was only one route left for the Ships of Tarshish to return to Ophir from Israel – through the Mediterranean Sea. A much longer journey indeed, they were there and not Eziongeber none-the-less according to Jonah.

> *1 Kings 22:48 KJV*
> *Jehoshaphat made **ships of Tharshish** to go to Ophir for gold: but they **went not**; for the **ships were broken** at Eziongeber.*

> *Psalm 48:7 KJV*
> ***Thou breakest** the **ships of Tarshish** with an east wind.*

Now with proper context we can read the story of Jonah and understand it. Jonah is very direct in supporting that Tarshish is in the East ultimately certainly not in Spain nor Britain which do not fit Tarshish on many levels. Tarshish is in the same place as Ophir, a 3-year round trip journey from the Red Sea to the East and they would both have to prove they are Ophir as well. Notice how deliberate Jonah is in this account. It will make one realize just how brilliantly the Bible is written in fact and how foolish man's attempts at interpretation can be at times.

> *Jonah 1:1-3 KJV*
> *Now the word of the Lord came unto **Jonah** the son of Amittai, saying, Arise, go to Nineveh, that great city, and cry against it; for their wickedness is come up before me. But Jonah rose up to flee unto Tarshish from the presence of the Lord, and went down to **Joppa**; and he found a **ship going to Tarshish**: so he paid the fare thereof, and went down into it, to go with them **unto Tarshish** from the presence of the Lord.*

It is true Joppa is on the West Coast of Israel on the Mediterranean Sea and Jonah boarded a ship there which was headed to the Biblical Tarshish. However, since when does the Bible ever disagree with itself? We have found never. All such supposed contradictions are from those who are challenged in their understanding so let us not blame that on the Bible. They are all easily explained. This is one of those cases. Was Jonah seeking the most efficient route here? Was he a merchant? No. Jonah was running from Yahuah and he wanted to go as far as possible. So, he chose a ship heading to the Far East. Notice, he is going to a physical Tarshish as well and also remember, there is no Red Sea Port option in this era as it was destroyed. Well, fortunately for Jonah, he was stopped in his tracks soon after.

Jonah 1:17 KJV
*Now the Lord had prepared a **great fish** to swallow up Jonah. And Jonah was in the **belly** of the fish **three days and three nights**.*

We know in Sunday school we are told this was a whale. However, it says simply great fish. Whatever it was Jonah survived in it's belly for three days and nights. We have no hesitation in positing a thought on this however. Science has proven a man could not likely survive in a whale's stomach and it leaves scholars with no answer. So consider this as a theory on this side note. This would have to be a sea creature with the capacity for Jonah to breath while inside it's inners and large enough to support a man. This stumps the best of scholars if they are honest about it. Our theory is this may have been, and we cannot prove this, Leviathan, the great sea creature recorded in the Book of Job as living at the bottom of the sea but also breathing fire. This requires oxygen within his apparatus and he was massive in size thus it would make sense that Yahuah sent Leviathan over to swallow Jonah. Again, we cannot prove that as we have yet to see Leviathan but it does make sense. No, he is not a spirit nor demon and Yahuah created him according to scripture.

Jonah 2:10-3:3 KJV
*And the Lord spake unto the fish, and it **vomited out Jonah** upon the dry land. And the word of the Lord came unto Jonah the second time, saying, Arise, go unto Nineveh, that great city, and preach unto it the preaching that I bid thee. So Jonah arose, and went unto Nineveh, according to the word of the Lord. Now **Nineveh** was an exceeding great city of **three days' journey**.*

Photo: 1532 Grynaeus's Novus Orbis Regionum Map with our Jonah additions. Jonah must travel around Africa to fit his story. Public Domain.

What many scholars are missing here is that there are two separated three-day periods in the narrative. Jonah survived in the belly of the creature for three days and nights but then once spit up on shore, Jonah preserves this location. Some read this very backwards when they claim that this passage documents the city of Nineveh as being so large that it represented a three-day journey from one end to the other. The challenge with that kind of thinking is it defies the archaeology we have which demonstrates Nineveh as a large city for that day but no where near that size. It was "within an area of 750 hectares (1,900 acres) circumscribed by a 12-kilometre (7.5 mi) brick rampart." [396] That is not even a day journey whether alone three. It's walled in so this measure is pretty accurate. What Jonah exacts in this passage with sagacity preserves the path of his voyage and the location of Tarshish.

This is noting a three-day journey from that drop-off point to Nineveh and that perfectly fits only one place on earth. Jonah was ejected on the shores of the Persian Gulf by the Tigris/Euphrates mouth which dumps into the Gulf. If one were to test this, it actually proves itself out quickly. If Jonah was only headed to Spain or Britain, then he would have been swallowed in the Mediterranean Sea which is certainly not known for the severe tempests over the ocean like this. Then, he would be delivered back to somewhere on the East Coast of the Mediterranean. We challenge everyone to review this on a map and you will find there are no great water routes unless you get to the Euphrates but then you still have to get over to the Tigris and the distance is far. To get to the water, one would likely use the camel, which is capable of travelling an average of 30-40 km (18-25 miles) per day. To journey the 191 miles just to get to the Euphrates River, that's already 7.5 days and you have hardly begun the excursion. Go ahead and triple the speed of the camel and it still cannot work. Once on the river, things would go smoother with 2 days to travel the 424 miles to get to the Tigris River and then another day to travel up the Tigris to Nineveh. That is 10.5 days if all goes smoothly and go ahead and cut it in half assuming our estimate is conservative and still it does not work.

Some attempt to inject a sort of transfiguration here in this case and when one does so, they abandon logic burdening a narrative with a massive miracle requirement which Jonah would have no issue mentioning another if it occurred as he was swallowed by a fish and a storm calmed. What's a little transfiguration? One might as well inject, what if a space ship landed?

The reason this does not work is because Jonah wanted us all to know Tarshish is not near the Mediterranean. The ship to Tarshish would have exited the Mediterranean, curved around the coast of Africa all the way into the Indian Ocean and there Jonah would be swallowed. He would be deposited on the banks of the Tigris and Euphrates mouth at the Persian Gulf, which is exactly a 3-day journey up the Tigris to Nineveh. How did we miss this for so many years? No matter. Let us restore His Word. As we do, we will all find we can believe it – all of it.

Who is Tarshish?

> *Genesis 10:2 KJV*
> *The sons of **Japheth**; Gomer, and Magog, and Madai, and **Javan**,*
> *and Tubal, and Meshech, and Tiras.*

The sons of Joktan – Ophir, Sheba and Havilah are all from Noah's son Shem. However, Tarshish is from Japheth. How does he enter this narrative of the journey to Ophir? The only Tarshish mentioned in Genesis 10 is this one.

> *Genesis 10:4-5 KJV*
> *And the sons of **Javan**; Elishah, and **Tarshish**, Kittim, and*
> *Dodanim. By these were the isles of the Gentiles divided in their lands;*
> *every one after his tongue, after their families, in their nations.*

Tarshish is the son of Javan, the father of Greece according to history and the Book of Jubilees. Along with his brothers, he inherited the Greek isles very accurately termed the isles of the Gentiles in Genesis 10. However, if we are to follow the supposed history which ignores the Bible and makes unsupported assumptions often times, we would believe no one had ships back in 2200 B.C. We have not found any ships that would credibly date back that far indeed. However, the thinking it would be preserved that long is not reasonable except in extremely rare cases.

However, what good would inheriting isles be if you could not travel there. They got to their inheritance somehow and they were not that great of swimmers. We are actually expected to believe that Noah and his sons construct a ship of supertanker complex construction years before this and yet, they all forgot how to build a ship after the Flood especially with a large world ocean to cross now. Of course, they boated and had ships. Tarshish especially found a way to build something to get to his inheritance and this is how he enters the Ophir migration. We are certainly not the first to make such connection.

> *"And that this was really so, and that the **principal settler of these***
> ***archipelagoes** [**Philippines**] was **Tharsis**, son of **Javan**,*

together with his brothers, as were Ophir and Hevilath of India, we see in
the tenth chapter of Genesis..." —Father Francisco Colin, 1663 [156]

With Tarshish arrived his brothers, the sons of Javan, the mariner family from Japheth as they were all returning to the land of Noah. The territory was given to the sons of Shem in Noah's division of the Earth which Ophir, Sheba and Havilah were the ones to claim it but they needed ships to get there.

Ophir, Sheba and Havilah lived in Meshad, Iran which in 1663, was a territory right adjacent to what was referred to as India (Afghanistan) still by many so it is not inconsistent for Father Colin to identify them so as they did originate in that region. This was not exactly a yachting area and certainly not one possessing vessels which could cross the sea but Tarshish and his brothers had ships. Therefore, Ophir and Sheba needed ships and Tarshish provided them. His payment for this endeavor carrying them back to their homeland would be to inherit a piece of that land logically as he certainly did according to scripture in order to have land in that region especially since Tarshish's territory is no where near there otherwise but the Greek isles. David mentions ships and kings of Tarshish two times before Solomon's reign before his navy even began construction (Ps. 48:7, 72:10). Both are prophesies that Tarshish will bring gifts to Messiah with Ophir and Sheba and it's ships destroyed.

Rome did not benefit from this knowledge so easily as this was established by Israel with Phoenicia managing the route. Greece inherited this and, as they represent Tarshish's family. That makes sense.

Tarshish is Mindanao, Philippines as it is mapped as the Greek land of silver, Argyre (The Hebrew Tarshish) especially on the 1492 Portuguese globe of Behaim just South of Luzon/Chryse. Mindanao also tests as the only place in the Philippines which fully aligns with Tarshish in resources especially due to tin.

Chapter 11 | Ancient Ships: King Solomon and Ophir

Quinquireme of Nineveh from distant Ophir,
Rowing home to haven in sunny Palestine,
With a cargo of ivory,
And apes and peacocks,
Sandalwood, cedarwood, and sweet white wine.

Stately Spanish galleon coming from the Isthmus,
Dipping through the Tropics by the palm-green shores,
With a cargo of diamonds,
Emeralds, amethysts,
Topazes, and cinnamon, and gold moidores.

Dirty British coaster with a salt-caked smoke stack
Butting through the Channel in the mad March days,
With a cargo of Tyne coal,
Road-rail, pig-lead,
Firewood, iron-ware, and cheap tin trays.

– "CARGOES" BY JOHN MASEFIELD, 1903 [107]

The fascination with the ancient land of gold has always captivated the minds of many. Over a century ago, the famous Poet Laureate, John Edward Masefield composed a poem in seaman's terms. He equates the ancient Ophir with the era of the Spanish who certainly did travel to Ophir and then, with the British who do not actually belong in the narrative but no surprise since he was English. The odd thing he does here is connect the ships of Tarshish though as the Ships of Nineveh. If you have researched the migrations of the Northern Kingdom of Israel as we have, you will likely find as we, that they were taken captive into Assyria and upon their release once Babylon conquered Assyria, they were given their freedom by the Babylonian King.

Some remained in Assyria or Nineveh, which we know today as Kurdistan and others migrated in fact, to the Philippines, the isles of the sea of Isaiah 11. Masefield takes license and adds "sweet white wine" from Ophir which many have mentioned may be a reference to palm wine, Tuba or sugarcane wine, Basi from the Philippines. Ophir also had a shipping history which rivaled the Spanish when they visited.

> *2 Esdras 13:39-49 KJVA*
>
> *And whereas thou sawest that he gathered another peaceable multitude unto him; Those are the ten tribes, which were carried away prisoners out of their own land in the time of Osea the king, whom Salmanasar the king of Assyria led away captive, and he carried them over the waters, and so came they into another land. But they took this counsel among themselves, that they would leave the multitude of the heathen, and go forth into a further country, where never mankind dwelt, That they might there keep their statutes, which they never kept in their own land. And they entered into Euphrates by the narrow places of the river. For the most High then shewed signs for them, and held still the flood, till they were passed over. For through that country there was a great way to go, namely, of **a year and a half**: and the same region is called **Arsareth.** Then **dwelt they there until the latter time**; and now when they shall begin to come, The Highest shall stay the springs of the stream again, that they may go through: therefore sawest thou the multitude with peace. But those that be left behind of thy people are they that are found within my borders. Now when he destroyeth the multitude of the nations that are gathered together, he shall defend his people that remain.*

The second Exodus of the Lost Tribes of Northern Israel leads them to Arsareth on a year and a half journey from Assyria. We map this out in detail in our Lost Tribes Series. However, we are not the first to do so. In his research, detailed in his margin notes and journals, Columbus, too, believed that Ophir, Tarshish, the Garden of Eden and Arsareth were the islands just North of the equator in the Far East now known as the Philippines. We already discussed Behaim's globe of the same year 1492 which demonstrates Chryse/Ophir as exactly there in the Philippines. Their contemporary, Italian Jewish scholar, R. Abraham Peristol, (Farissol, 1451-1526), believed the same as Behaim and Columbus. His writings are preserved in the 1846 work of Rev. Thomas Stackhouse and the Jews do not like Farrisol's conclusions as they hid Ophir and the Lost Tribes pretty well and continue to obscure.

> *"Another Jewish author, in his description of the world, has found out very commodious habitations for the **ten tribes**, and in many places has given them a glorious establishment. In a country which he calls Perricha, inclosed by unknown mountains, and bounded by Assyria, he has settled some, and made them a flourishing populous kingdom. Others he places in the desert of Chabor, which, according to him, lies upon the Indian sea, where they live, in the manner of the ancient Rechabites, without houses, sowing, or the use of wine. Nay, he enters the Indies, the isles of Bengala, **the Philippines**, and several other places..."* −The Rev. Thomas Stackhouse, M.A. (1846) Quoting Farissol (1500) [108]

In fully researching this topic, you will find the isles of Bengala may relate to Visayas and he spells out the Philippines very specifically of course the name is modernized to the time of Stackhouse as Philippines. In fact, there is only one desert in the Philippines which is the Paoay-LaPaz Sand Dunes in Laoag on Luzon and that is *"a further country, where never mankind dwelt."* He is describing multiple landing sites based on what he had learned but Farrisol never travelled there and did not know the exact geography of the area already proven in 1500 but they were getting warmer back then until Magellan found it. This also explains why even when the Spanish arrived, although they describe a society who was literate, sophisticated in shipbuilding, well-dressed in some cases wearing an astonishing amount of gold, they never describe great architecture. Many seek this architecture in demand to prove this narrative and they are stuck in a false paradigm. There is none to be expected nor has any other nation on earth produced such nor will they.

Ancient Ophir is never described as having temples at all whether alone ones of gold, it is never recorded to have great infrastructure in any sense just a mega-abundance of resources. The humble lifestyle of the Filipino even fits the oath of a Rechabite as Farrisol said. We have already demonstrated these resources, every one of them, exist in the Philippines natively and it leads in gold in all of history. However, when it comes to ships, the history of the Philippines has been obscured.

Masefield likens these ancient ships of Tarshish to the Quinquireme, a large ancient Roman galley with 5 banks of oars on each side. [109] That is a very large ship to attribute to Solomon's era. However, one would be surprised to learn of the ancient Phoenician technology even in the 900 B.C. era when the Temple was constructed. Though excessive, he is not far off.

Ancient boating is so misunderstood. It is odd that the trireme is even mentioned in Plato's account of ancient Atlantis from before the Flood yet no one seems to question that but they cannot seem to believe Noah built an ark though he received the specifications from Yahuah God Himself. Furthermore, some claim Solomon's navy may not have had the technology to travel as far as the Philippines.

In 900 B.C., the Phoenicians had advanced to a ship similar to a bireme for Greece and Rome which would have had two banks of oars rowing and large sails to power it with wind as well. The Phoenicians included King Hiram of Tyre who was hired as Solomon's Admiral to lead this new navy and port on the Red Sea including the construction of the ships which would have been Phoenician-designed. Both Ezekiel 27:25-26 and the story of Jonah 1:13 concur the ships of Tarshish were powered by rowers and into the seas. There is credible history to affirm this position from Heroditus, Josephus and Thucydides.

"Heroditus and Thucydides record these ancient ships could journey an average speed of **6 miles per hour.**" *[Trade ships] "Their cargo capacity was somewhere in the region of* **450 tons.** *A fleet might consist of up to* **50 cargo vessels...**" *—Ancient History Encyclopedia [110] "Moreover the King built* **many ships** *in the Egyptian bay of the Red Sea; in a certain place called Ezion-geber."* *—Josephus [111]*

A Phoenician Galley Illustration from
Sea Pictures by James Macaulay
Religious Tract Society c 1880.

King Solomon built many ships, a navy or fleet of likely 50. Based on Phoenician merchant ships of that time, they were large with at least two rows of rowers carrying 450 tons of cargo and travelling at 6 miles per hour. Let us understand a little context about the habits of these Phoenician Merchant Ships and we can calculate this journey based on these capabilities. The Phoenician merchants were very conservative which is why they were the best in their era. They did not wreck often because they hugged the coasts and only sailed in the daytime avoiding obstacles hard to see at night.

> *"The navigation of the Phoenicians, in early times, was no doubt cautious and timid. So far from venturing out of sight of land, they usually hugged the coast, ready at any moment, if the sea or sky threatened, to change their course and steer directly for the shore. On a shelving coast they were not at all afraid to run their ships aground, since, like the Greek vessels, they could be easily pulled up out of reach of the waves, and again pulled down and launched, when the storm was over and the sea calm once more. At first they sailed, we may be sure, only in the daytime, casting anchor at nightfall, or else dragging their ships up upon the beach, and so awaiting the dawn. But after a time they grew more bold."*
> *–George Rawlinson [112]*

In addition, on extremely long explorations in this era, it was customary to purchase land upon arrival in order to plant one's own crops for the return trip. Along with trading, timbering, mining and other preparations for the return, we have calculated in one year for this. Most all the claims of Ophir are far closer than the Philippines and with this in mind, they are far too close. Let us remember, the Bible story lays out the very first journey thus this was not intended on the initial journey to establish other trade routes but to go to Ophir for a very special gold. Let us crunch some numbers assuming an average distance of 20 nautical miles per day based on these accounts.

Eziongeber to **YEMEN** = *991 Nautical Miles (50 days one way)* *ROUND TRIP:* **3 MONTHS** *(too close)*

Eziongeber to **ETHIOPIA** = *1,131 Nautical Miles (57 days one way) ROUND TRIP:* **4 MONTHS** *(too close)*

Eziongeber to **INDIA** = *3,086 Nautical Miles (154 days one way) ROUND TRIP:* **1 YEAR** *(too close)*

Eziongeber to **PHILIPPINES** = *6,824 Nautical Miles (342 days one way) ROUND TRIP: 2 YEARS AT SEA PLUS 1 YEAR TO PLANT, HARVEST AND TRADE =* **3 YEARS**

Only the region of the Philippines harmonizes with this 3-year round trip excursion. Yemen would be three months round trip down the Red Sea and back. Consider that even in the days of Job long before Solomon, the Sabaeans of Yemen were well-known and recorded in scripture all along. They are never called Ophir, Tarshish nor even Sheba once. They are Sabaeans. King Solomon already not only traded with Yemen in his era but they are among the Kings of Arabia who paid him tribute regularly so that was his territory of rule even – "all the kings of Arabia" (1 Kings 10:15). There is no fitting that square peg into this round hole no matter how one crams it.

Ethiopia is equally as poor of a guess as not only is it in Ham's territory rather than Shem's which it has to be to concur but this would be four months at sea which leaves two years and eight months of doing what? King Solomon was not so haphazard. This was a trip that took place every three years because it is three years distance with all included.

Even India is far too short as it is only a one year outing round trip leaving two years to trade, plant and harvest. Of course, we already covered their own history says Ophir is an island to the East of India not mainland India anyway. Only the area of the Philippines fits as it is a two-year expedition at sea round trip with 1 year to trade, plant and harvest. However, that only identifies a region.

One has to read further in this book to narrow this down as Taiwan is an island not isles thus it does not work. Indonesia is in Ham's territory as is Australia and everything in between thus cannot work. Anything to the East of the Philippines is no longer Shem's territory either thus we eliminate even Solomon Islands which were named inappropriately by an explorer who even knew he missed Ophir or he would have named it Ophir. Of course, there is little gold there as well, no history and no actual claim really. Japan is too far North. China, India and Mainland Asia are not isles. Essentially, just by applying logic, we already find this is the Philippines but we, of course, are proving this entire case here.

If they travelled faster even knowing there are storms and the conservative nature of the Phoenicians, that would be even worse for all those making claims to be Ophir as they are too close to fit already. Also, there still would not be enough to make up the extra 6,000 nautical miles distance across the Pacific and back added to the trip somehow to get to the Americas. You will notice, at this point, after three years publicly and several million views on YouTube, we have just about heard it all and this is very healthy. Not only does our research stand this test, it has been fully vetted from virtually every angle possible. This is why no one has been able to disprove our conclusions but we welcome anyone to try.

For those requiring these ships from almost 1000 B.C. be found in order to believe the route, consider the oldest Phoenician ship found to date in archaeology is from the seventh century B.C. at Playa de la Isla in Puerto de Mazarrón, Spain thus no Phoenician ship from Solomon's era has ever been found anywhere on earth yet. [113] To then assume the Phoenicians never existed in that era which is the exact logic used to discount the existence of ancient Israel in fact, would be ignorance.

You can never prove something did not exist because you did not find especially a wooden ship that not only survived in tact without deteriorating over that period of time but underwater even. Then, knowing the Phoenicians were cautious, there may not actually be any ships of Tarshish on the bottom of the ocean to find and since 95% of the ocean floor remains unexplored, those who require such may wish to rethink their position or perhaps think period rather than creating false paradigms by which to test setting up failure from the beginning. [114] Beyond this, we have coins from the Phoenicians illustrating their shipping prowess as far back as the fourth century B.C. [115] The second oldest Phoenician ship found in archaeology is dated to the third century B.C. The Philippines is recorded crossing the Indian Ocean in their own ships about that time. [120]

Ancient Philippine Ships: Balangay

One challenge we received often in the beginning was if the Philippines is Ophir and Ophir was so wealthy, why doesn't the Philippines have a great shipping history. However, the fact is this is completely untrue. Most of us are just not aware of the rich shipping history abundant in the Philippines. Antonio Pigafetta, the Italian historian travelling with Magellan, was laughed at for centuries as he had written the following upon first contact with the ancient Philippines. The first ship is called the balangay.

> *After Zzubu (Cebu):*
> *"After midday, as I wished to return to the ships, the king, with the other chief men of the island, desired to accompany me in the same **balangai**, going by the same river" –Antonio Pigafetta, 1521 [117]*
> *March 28, 1521:*
> *"…we saw come two long boats, which they call **Ballanghai**, full of men." – Antonio Pigafetta, 1521 [117]*
> *March 29, 1521:*
> *"…and led us under a place covered with canes, where there was a **ballanghai**, that is to say, a boat, **eighty feet long** or thereabouts, **resembling a fusta**." – Antonio Pigafetta, 1521 [117]*
> *At Zubu (Cebu):*
> *"We set out from Zubu at midnight, we were sixty men armed with corslets and helmets; there were with us the Christian king, the prince,*

*and some of the chief men, and many others divided among **twenty or thirty balangai.**"* – Antonio Pigafetta, 1521 [117]

Note, these were built and functional before the Spanish. We know some are already snickering. How could the Philippines build a ship that was 80-feet long in ancient times? And it resembled a Portuguese fusta? And the Philippines had several of them? For centuries even some historians scoffed at this assertion of Pigafetta's. Perhaps this first sailing historian to circumnavigate the globe sniffed a few too many herbs along the way. We assure you he was not embellishing but precise in estimation.

*"To date, **nine ancient wooden boats** have been discovered by locals searching for alluvial gold on land near the Masao River, west of Butuan City, Libertad District, Mindanao. The vessels have been called variously the Butuan Boats, **balangay** or balanhay..."*
–The International Journal of Nautical Archaeology [118]

Replica of an ancient Balangay ship sets sail.

It's sails made of buri or nipa fiber, nine Balangay were found and documented by the Philippine government. [27] One was over 80-feet in length [27] proving Pigafetta was exact in his estimation. The others were about 50-feet in length. [27] The capacity of these ships could hold about 60-90 people. [27] However, the dating really flabbergasted many as one was estimated to be as early as 320 A.D. and others 1250 A.D. [118][27] 1,200 years before Spain, the Philippines already had a robust maritime history. Also, of note, ancient gold was found in these digs.

> "...metal artifacts **gold**... worked stone and clay artifacts in the form of **gold** melting slag... **gold** fragments (worked and unworked)" were found among these Balangay." –Ronquillo [404]

This is the first wooden watercraft excavated in Southeast Asia obliterating that nine-dash line and proving the Philippines as the epicenter of yet another category including the oldest bones and biodiversity leader.

> "The Balangay was the first-ever and the **oldest wooden watercraft** excavated in Southeast Asia demonstrating early Filipinos' boatbuilding genius and seafaring expertise in the pre-colonial times." –Republic of the Philippines [119]

Their design in construction is in fact, similar to a Portuguese fusta but this is long before the Portuguese or Spanish ever stepped foot in the Indies nor were even powers. These were Philippine built. How did the Philippines acquire such shipbuilding skills? They are Ophir. This suggests the Philippines was a power at sea long before the Spanish and long before the Chinese who did not have an ocean-going vessel for about 500 years after this period of this one find. No wonder their history says Filipinos showed up in their ports first before they had crossed the ocean. That 9-dash line keeps losing dashes as they have no credible history to support their claim of obvious Philippine territory.

Supreme Court Justice Antonio T. Carpio sheds light on this in his position prosecuting the case for the Philippine jurisdiction in the South China Sea or really, West Philippine Sea.

*"Professor Adrian Horridge believes that by **200 BC**, **Austronesian** sailors were regularly carrying cloves and cinnamon **to India** and **Sri Lanka**, and perhaps even as far as the coast of **Africa** in sailboats with outriggers."* —Supreme Court Justice Antonio T. Carpio [27] [407]

As early as 200 B.C., the Philippines was sailing likely in these balangay to India, Sri Lanka and Africa. This explains how trade with first century Egypt and West Asia was possible as well and it was two-way not just one. [21] However, they are working towards this history already defined in the Bible as prior to Solomon, King David already acquired significant quantities of gold and silver of Ophir yet had no navy yet (1 Ch. 29:4). Before Israel had a Red Sea port to go there, Ophir's goods arrived there somehow. Then, David further mentions the gold of Ophir in the context as that worn by royalty in his day indicating trade not just with Israel but at least the greater Middle East likely including Egypt (Ps. 45:9). Furthermore, the gold of Sheba would be brought to the Messiah (Ps. 72:15) meaning David knew what Sheba represented as well as Ophir equating them and both in Israel long ago.

In his early work not long after the Flood, Job already knew the value of the gold of Ophir in his era yet had no ships (Job 28:16, 24). Even after Solomon, King Jehoshaphat attempted to rebuild and re-establish this trade with Ophir yet the ships were destroyed by Yahuah (1Ki. 22:48). Understand that is very close to the era in which the Northern Kingdom was about to be taken captive into the very land Jonah was preaching repentance and salvation. Therefore, Ophir had to bring goods to Israel instead which we see in Jonah's story. The ships of Tarshish were certainly trading in Israel again travelling the long way around Africa to the port at Joppa (Jn. 1:1-3) as did the Three Kings after Messiah's birth in about 6 B.C. or so.

If only historians realized the historical characters of the Bible record history whether they enjoy the theology or not. Clearly, Professor Adrian Horridge, Legeza and Bangko Sentral's Villegas share similar views of ancient Austronesians arriving in the West before the West journeyed to them. He explains further in the context of the 200 B.C to 200 A.D. era really.

*"Theories that Austronesian rigs were derived from those of the Indian Ocean, or even from Egypt, are mistaken because the **Austronesians** had **left Mainland Asia long before** contacts spread eastwards."*
–Professor Adrian Horridge [407]

We had one question the "belief" of Adrian Horridge yet his "belief" is clear here and Justice Carpio was accurate in his rendering of such. In our Sourcebook we offer that detail for your review.

According to Sir Robert Douglas in 1904 and since forgotten, the Philippines was arriving in China as early as around 990 B.C. That is not Israel nor Egypt but the fact they were already out trading in their ships speaks volumes. Understand, China had no ocean-going trade vessels in 990 B.C. for almost 2000 more years thus these traders arrived there. That is King David's era in which products of the Philippines were already being exchanged internationally. Therefore, the Philippines is the likely embodiment of the active trade of Ophir resources documented predating the West to East trade routes even that of Solomon's navy, and before the Chinese were crossing the ocean to trade as this trade occurred in Canton.

*"The British Museum's oriental scholar (Douglas: Europe and the Far East, Cambridge, 1904) states that by the beginning of the Chou dynasty (B. C. 1122-255) intercourse had been established at Canton with eight foreign nations. Duties as early as **990 B.C.** were levied, and among the imports figure birds, pearls and tortoise shell, products of **the Philippines**..."* –Dr. Austin Craig, 1914 [403]

In his original work "Europe and the Far East, 1506-1912," Sir Douglas, whom Dr. Austin Craig is citing, notes this trade took place in Canton in 990 B.C. thus Filipinos and others travelled there. [403] Dr. Craig (1914) concluded these products originated in the Philippines. Additionally, he says Former Prime Minister Paterno believed the Philippines as Ophir. [403] This dating is consistent with archaeology which demonstrates the Philippines was trading cross-regionally with Vietnam and Taiwan as early as 1500 B.C. with increasing continuity and reach. [408]

After these balangay ships were unearthed in Butuan, Art Valdez and his team who were the first all-filipino team to scale Mt. Everest, decided to build replicas and sail them to prove the design sea worthy. They first crossed the South China Sea to China. [121] The second leg navigated throughout Southeast Asia and then, in 2010 to Micronesia and Madagascar. [121] Finally, they are reported to have ventured even further. [121] These were not sailors yet perhaps it was in their DNA.

The balangay is now proven not only that it is capable of sailing the seas even to Egypt as history records but beyond. We were able to visit these sites and especially the oldest and largest ship. The Balangay Site Museum in Butuan houses the excavated balangay dated 320 A.D. [27] We would encourage every Filipino to visit and restore your heritage. We find it extremely odd that this has not received international news coverage to a larger degree as this single find changes the course of what we thought was history. It also just so happens to further prove out the Bible narrative on Ophir.

It is no surprise one could locate a source which may dispute one of these points. However, this is not a case of nor does it hinge on one source. One would have to disprove our conclusions and no one has in over 3 years now. Test this for yourself.

These balangay replicas will sail again in 2020-2021. [120] In the Philippines, many are still unaware of the gravity of this find. Outside the country, very few even have this knowledge especially scholars attempting to interpret Ophir's location omitting the actual isles of Ophir from consideration.

However, the balangay was not the largest ship.

Ancient Philippine Ships: Junks

> *"Towards the North-west is the island of **Lozon (Luzon)**, which is at two days' distance; a large island, to which come to trade every year **six or eight junks** of the people called **Lequii."***
> *–Antonio Pigafetta, 1521 [117]*

The lequii or lequios or lucoes of Luzon are none other than Iloconos of Ilocos as we prove in the next chapter. They had six to eight ships Pigafetta called junks. You may have heard of the large Chinese junk ships. These are similar and likely their origin as the Philippines leads in shipping history not China. Just in Pigafetta's account alone, we count about 20 Philippine junks. This is significant as these ships are massive even larger than the 80-foot long balangay. These are from Luzon, the next he encounters is from Palawan.

> "...*we met a **junk** which was coming from Borneo. We made signals to it to strike its sails; but as it would not obey we overtook it, captured and pillaged it. It had on board the Governor of **Pulaoan**, with a son and a brother of his. We made them all prisoners, and put them to ransom....*"
> – Antonio Pigafetta, 1521 [117]

You will find this pattern of behavior on the part of the Spanish as if they were pirates and thugs but let us be clear, this is their account. It was likely even worse. No wonder Magellan, then Barbosa and much of Magellan's crew were killed in the Philippines. They certainly did not come in peace. How exactly could any man justify coming into another's country and capturing their people, even Governors, putting them to ransom, demanding tribute and allegiance to a king the people had never met nor heard anything about and to the point of the sword even burning villages? Anyone who would even attempt to justify such behavior is placating evil. This should be condemned yet it was not even by the Pope who happened to be the ruler ultimately of the Holy Roman Empire in which Spain served. Think about it. However, Pigafetta does not leave this to our imagination as he describes these junk ships in detail.

> "*The **junks** mentioned several times above are their **largest** vessels, and they are constructed in this manner. The lower part of the ships and the sides to a height of **two spans above water-line** are built of planks joined together with wooden bolts, and they are well enough put together. The upper works are made of very large canes for a counterpoise. One of these junks carries as much cargo as our ships. The masts are of bamboo, and the sails of bark of trees.*" –Antonio Pigafetta, 1521 [117]

If these ships could carry as much cargo as the Spanish ships, they must be approximately the same size as the Spanish ships. Pigafetta was impressed with these junks as large as the Spanish to the height of two spans or two stories above the water-line. Seeing and hearing of as many as 20 of them in a foreign land one expected to just take over must have been alarming in a sense especially once Magellan was killed, then, in a separate event, his replacement Barbosa, also Magellan's brother-in-law, was killed with other leaders and then, July 29, 1521 happened.

> *"On Monday, the 29th of July, we saw coming towards us more than* **a hundred prahus,** *divided into three squadrons, and* **as many tungulis,** *which are their smaller kind of boats. At this sight, and fearing treachery, we hurriedly set sail, and left behind an anchor in the sea. Our suspicions increased when we observed that behind us were certain* **junks** *which had come the day before. Our first operation was to free ourselves from the* **junks,** *against which we fired,* **capturing four** *and killing many people:* **three or four other junks** *went aground in escaping. In one of those which we captured was a* **son** *of the* **king** *of the isle of* **Luzon...**"*
> – Antonio Pigafetta, 1521 [117]

Imagine, an entire armada of over two hundred ships coming from the Philippines to attack? Until we know our history, that would seem impossible but the ancient Philippines had an array of ships. Over one hundred prahus alone, one hundred tungulis, which we had not mentioned before is a smaller craft, and between seven to eight junks as large as the Spanish ships. It does appear from this narrative that Luzon or Ophir is responding to the Spanish at this point. If you read the narrative further, you will see Pigafetta downplaying this crediting Sabah (still Philippines) yet it seems improbable to us that the son of the King of Luzon was employed by the Raja of Sulu.

However, one will also note, the Spanish do not return to Visayas after this and never head North to Luzon on this first voyage even though they had heard of the gold there. Credit is given that all two hundred plus ships belong to the Raja of Sabah, which at that time was actually still the Philippines but even so, we question that portion of the narrative. Pigafetta was paid by Spain to tell their version of history. He was to assist them in justifying the theft of a people thus, he was under pressure to characterize the Filipino as a lesser species of savage and pagans. He did, yet even in the midst of this, the things he records do not tell the same story which would evolve from the Jesuit education establishment writings one hundred years later. We are all still victim to this error today.

Ferdinand Mendez Pinto, a Portuguese explorer, wrote of his exploration to the Orient in the 1550s as did De Morga in 1609. They knew what a junk was as did Pigafetta and they describe these junks in detail. Then, they were illustrated and they were very large ships.

> "…*we discovered a good haven eastward where in the Island of Camboia, distant some six leagues from the firm land, we met a* **junk of Lequois***, that was going to the kingdom of Siam, with an ambassador from the Nautauquim of Lindau…*" *—Ferdinand Pinto, 1546 [124]*

> "*These vessels have been used commonly through the islands since olden times. They have other larger vessels called 'lapis,' and 'tapaques,' which are used to carry their merchandise, and which are very suitable, as they are roomy and draw but little water. They generally drag them ashore every night, at the mouths of rivers and creeks, among which they always navigate without going into the open sea or leaving the shore. All the natives can row and manage these boats. Some are so long that they can carry one hundred rowers on a side and thirty soldiers above to fight. The boats commonly used are barangays and vireys, which carry a less crew and fighting force. Now they put many of them together with iron nails instead of the wooden pegs and the joints in the planks, while the helms and bows have beaks like Castilian boats.*" *—Antonio de Morga, 1609 [125]*

What happened to these junk ships and marine acumen of the Filipino? Dr. Jose Rizal records the ships were made to vanish and skill retrograded.

> "*The Filipinos, like the inhabitants of the Marianas, who are no less skillful and dexterous in navigation, far from progressing, have retrograded; since, although boats are now built in the islands, we might assert that they are all after European models. The boats that held one hundred rowers to a side and thirty soldiers have disappeared. The country that once, with primitive methods, built ships of about 2,000 toneladas, today (1890)*

has to go to foreign ports, as Hongkong, to give the gold wrenched from the poor, in exchange for unserviceable cruisers. The rivers are blocked up, and navigation in the interior of the islands is perishing, thanks to the obstacles created by a timid and mistrusting system of government; and there scarcely remains in the memory anything but the name of all that naval architecture. It has vanished, without modern, improvements having come to replace it in such proportion as during the past centuries has occurred in adjacent countries." –Rizal's Note to de Morga, 1890 [126]

Finally, one other Philippine-designed ship was a terror to Spain on the seas in the seventeenth century as recorded by William Henry Scott. These large outrigger warships were called the Karakoa (not to be confused with Karaoke). These appear to be uniquely different from the junks mentioned by Pigafetta as these were so fast they impressed Spanish priest Francisco Combés who in 1667 wrote of these ships which were estimated to travel 12 to 15 knots. [128]

*Karakoa can be "as long as **25 metres (82 ft)** in length." "The Karakoa could mount **forty** of them **on a side**, and its **speed was proverbial**." –William Henry Scott [128]*

"The care and technique with which they build them makes their ships sail like birds, while ours are like lead in comparison."
– Francisco Combes, 1667 [128]

Though difficult to find archaeology on these ships as they were decommissioned by the Spanish for obvious reasons and there is no reason to believe the Spanish kept any portions for museum preservation as Dr. Rizal alluded as well – they "disappeared."

"By the end of the 16th century, the Spanish denounced karakoa shipbuilding and its usage. It later led to a total ban of the ship and the traditions assigned to it." [130]

However, there is a shipwreck of what appears to be a returning Philippine-built junk dating prior to the Spanish.

"Due to the extent of the vessel's preservation, the archaeologists have also been able to understand how the ship was loaded and what kind of goods were stored in its different compartments."

"...clear evidence that this ship was built in the Philippines."

– Marine Archaeologist Franck Goddio [412]

The renown French archaeologist says the evidence is clear this was built in the Philippines even according to the way the ship was loaded. Unfortunately, The National Museum of the Philippines suggested this as a Thai ship based largely on Thai artifacts found in the lower cargo holds and the construction both speculation easily challenged. However, that is the published consensus in "suggestion." The Santa Cruz Junk discovered in 2001 off of Zambales is documented to the 1400s. [412]

Ophir was a power at sea as fact so much so that they banished Spain in the first naval battle and the Portuguese conquered Malaysia and Indonesia but chose not to attempt such with Ophir. This is likely why the Muslims did not conquer the Philippines but lived among them as businessmen and why China never conquered the Philippines either.

One of the most interesting testaments to the shipping abilities inherent in the DNA of the Filipino is the fact that the Philippines is the world's main supplier of seamen today with over 229,000 Filipino seaman serving on board merchant shipping vessels around the world at any given time. [131]

In fact, Filipino seamen comprise more than 25 percent of 1.5 million mariners worldwide, the "single biggest nationality bloc" in the shipping industry. [132] Even today, the call of ancient Ophir beckons the modern Filipino and most do not even realize this was the course of their ancestors. In the next chapter, we will prove the aforementioned Lequios are in fact Filipinos and they were known historically to trade gold in several, large junk ships. Ophir ruled the seas which the Spanish and 9-dash line cannot erase.

17th-century Karakoa, Historia de las islas e indios de Bisayas (1668), Francisco Ignacio Alcina.[127]

Chapter 12 | Little Known History of Ophir, Philippines

*"About their necks they wear **gold necklaces**, wrought like spun wax, and with links in our fashion, some larger than others. On their arms they wear **armlets of wrought gold**, which they call calombigas, and which are very large and made in different patterns. Some wear strings of **precious stones**—cornelians and agates; and other blue and white stones, which they esteem highly. They wear around the **legs** some **strings** of these **stones**, and **certain cords**, covered with black pitch in many foldings, as garters."* –Antonio de Morga, 1609 [134]

Who are these people and why does it appear they have been erased from history? Here they were in 1609 almost a century after Magellan's initial visit and this group is not described as natives in loin clothes. We recognize there certainly were some such tribes but this people has been obliterated from taught history largely and we are taught the ancient Filipinos were principally tribal natives. However, we will show you they existed, in great number and all over. Everything expressed from the mega-abundance of gold and precious stones to the cord or perhaps, "sacred thread" as de Morga describes are not fiction but found in archaeology even.

Some ask if we have physical evidence which proves the Philippines as Ophir and in this chapter, we will cover very substantial tangible testimony and archaeology no one can refute and no other country making claims of Ophir has. It is important to note, all other petitions hang on a couple of small threads, basic etymologies of massive expansion in order to reach such conclusions yet the Philippines is packaged, fully accessorized, wrapped and tied with a bow in examination.

De Morga is not alone in his representation of the amount of gold in the Philippines even owned by the average person. Guido de Lavezaris categorizes the Philippines into three distinct classes of citizens and they all owned gold. Analogous to this, the Boxer Codex illustrated Filipinos in 1590 or so which validates these depictions. Many have attempted to scoff at these but wait til you see the actual archaeology which proves these to be truth.

In 1574, Guido de Lavezaris, second Spanish Governor General of the Philippines, responds to a Jesuit-style attempt to marginalize the Philippines as you will find becomes the narrative a hundred years later unfortunately. That is what we are taught today and it is erroneous. Fray Martin de Rada of the order of St. Augustine attempts to mischaracterize Filipinos so blatantly and drastically, it yielded a strong response from Lavezaris and others when they consider his writings "harsh, harmful to this whole community, and very prejudicial" as Rada is "misled," "ill informed" and "erroneous" in their words. [135] Lavezaris describes the ancient social structure and the wealth of the Philippines specifically on Luzon Island in the same manner which agrees with the Boxer Codex of 1590, de Morga in 1609 and Riquel in 1574 of the same era. In time, this narrative will be wiped out but no one can discard this history.

The Upper Class:

> *"There are some* **chiefs** *in this island who have* **on their persons ten or twelve thousand ducats'** *worth of* **gold** *in* **jewels** *-- to say nothing of the lands, slaves, and mines that they own. There are so many of these chiefs that they are* **innumerable.***"*
> *–Guido de Lavezaris, 1574 [135]*

Not only does this describe a people that is extremely prosperous but it classifies the form of government as flat-level similar to the Barangay system of the Philippines with no national or regional governments necessarily. For these chiefs or really Barangay Captains as we would term them today, were "innumerable." They could not be numbered as they were so many. Just how wealthy were they?

In addition to their lands, slaves, mines, etc., these chiefs wore 10-12,000 ducats of gold on their person in public not to mention what they stored at home. This is staggering. A ducat by today's standards is $150 in gold. 10,000-12,000 ducats which they wore candidly is valued at $1.5-1.8 million today. That is just the gold they wore. Absorb that. This was not just a few people. This was an innumerable group of likely many thousands and their wealth exceeds any legend in all of history.

Tagalog royalty in red (the distinctive color of his class) with his wife.
Boxer Codex, 1590. Public Domain. [299]

The Middle Class:

Tagalog royal couple in red, the distinctive color of their class.
Boxer Codex, 1590. Public Domain. [299]

> *"Likewise the **individual subjects** of these chiefs have a **great quantity of the said jewels of gold**, which they wear **on their persons** -- bracelets, chains, and **earrings** of solid **gold, daggers of gold**, and other very **rich trinkets**."*
> – *Guido de Lavezaris, 1574 [135]*

The Middle Class of those employed by these Barangay Captains of sort, still had an abundance of gold that they wore on their persons openly similar to that pictured on the previous page. We are aware the Boxer Codex labels them "royals" but Lavezaris delineates this in enhanced resolution. This is not the image we are taught in any sense regardless. This is a description of an affluent kingdom not just it's king or leaders but the entire populace and all of it's citizenry. Before you attempt to dismiss this, remember, we are about to show you archaeology which proves this along with other historic sources.

Take a good look at the jewelry pieces in these illustrations from 1590. Lavezaris and De Morga were not inventing a story that would not actually benefit their case anyway as they were the conquerors trying to justify the rape and plunder of a land. They would be better served by the Jesuit narratives 50 and 100 years later, or even Rada's, forging an image of a savage people who were in need of rescue by civilization just as the colonists claimed everywhere.

They do not record this abundance in South America, Mexico, the Caribbean nor even Africa however. Nothing like this and in this very Boxer Codex, you will find chapters illustrating and describing the Japanese, Chinese and other Asian peoples but not illustrated like this. The disparity even between the nations in the Far East in comparison to the Philippines is substantially less significant in gold and luxury in presence. It is no surprise the Boxer Codex labels these as royals which they certainly would have appeared to a Spaniard. However, Lavezaris defines these three classes and the gold worn in this illustration better matches his Middle Class description than it does the Upper Class.

The Lower Class:

> *"These are generally seen among them, and **not only the chiefs and freemen** have plenty of these jewels, but **even slaves possess and wear golden trinkets upon their persons**, openly and freely."* –Guido de Lavezaris, 1574 [135]

Once again, he reiterates eloquently that there are three distinct groups in social structure in the Philippines in those days. Some political

Highland Igorot Warrior from Cagayan Valley or Cordillera Highlands (Possibly Ibanag).
Boxer Codex, 1590. Public Domain. [299]

correctness radars flash when they see this word slaves. However, the Biblical slave and those of antiquity were not treated as African slavery in chains but it simply meant one had to work in the employ of another. In ancient times, this was usually to repay a debt more than anything. There is no indication these so-called "slaves" were anything near what is described in the evil Trans-Atlantic Slave Trade.

This class of people were merely employees yet even this Lower Class possessed and wore gold upon their persons, openly and freely. This is also very telling as to the low crime rate of this arcane people. The fact that even the Upper Class would feel safe enough to wear so much gold in public and all classes did so on different levels, indicates no one was stealing really. Again, we use these illustrations from the Boxer Codex as we believe Lavezaris described. Feel free to review the entire Boxer Codex and insert whichever illustrations you feel best fit.

In affirmation of this history, Antonio de Morga records:

> *"**All these islands are, in many districts, rich in placers and mines of gold**, a metal which the natives dig and work. However, since the advent of the Spaniards in the land, the natives proceed more slowly in this, and content themselves with what they already possess in jewels and gold ingots, **handed down from antiquity and inherited from their ancestors**. This is considerable, for **he must be poor and wretched who has no gold chains, calombigas [bracelets], and earrings.**"*
> —Antonio de Morga, 1609 [134]

We learn from this quote the very same understanding that one must be "poor and wretched" if they did not own plenty of gold just as Lavezaris structured and the Boxer Codex demonstrates. Also, there was such abundance of gold, the native Filipinos were content with what they had which was "handed down from antiquity" "from their ancestors." They inherited this gold and likely over thousands of years as this is the land of Ophir whose gold rush began likely before 1000 B.C. This is overlooked in academia as are these letters in this sense.

Observe how Hernando Riquel who travelled with Juan Salcedo on the first landing in Mindoro in 1570 describes the Filipino skill in mixing gold compared to Jeremiah's description of the very same people of Uphaz or Ophir and Tarshish.

> At Mindoro, the people had:
> *"…given two hundred taels of impure gold, for they possess great skill in mixing it with other metals. They give it an outside appearance **so***

natural and *perfect*, and so fine a ring, that unless it is melted they *can deceive* all men, even the *best of silversmiths*. While in this port of Mindoro..." –Hernando Riquel, 1570 [341]

Jeremiah 10:9 KJV
Silver spread into plates is brought from *Tarshish*, and *gold* from *Uphaz*, the *work* of the *workman*, and of the *hands* of the *founder*: blue and purple is their clothing: they are all the work of *cunning men*.

These are both describing the same people of Ophir (Uphaz) and Tarshish as cunning and possessing great skill as the workmen and founder in working with gold. Also, Daniel mentions blue and purple is their clothing and even in the 1500s we see the same theme in the Boxer Codex as well of blue and purple clothing illustrated much of the time. [299] However, to see this written history multiple times is already proof enough. To then, see it illustrated in the same era as well is double proof. However, some would still view this as a conspiracy to mischaracterize the Philippines even though that would be antithetical to the Jesuit purpose but no matter. This has now been fully confirmed in archaeology in the Surigao Treasure which up until recently has been on display at the Ayala Museum in Makati City Philippines and pieces even toured New York. This is documented in numerous places as well.

"When Filipino worker Berto Morales was digging on a government irrigation project in 1981, he literally struck gold. But what he found that day was worth more than its weight—he had uncovered *evidence of a lost civilization*...

On Friday, Asia Society New York unveiled its exhibition Philippine Gold: Treasures of Forgotten Kingdoms, displaying more than 100 gold artifacts on loan from the Ayala Museum and the Central Bank of the Philippines in Manila. Most objects trace back to the *Kingdom of Butuan* — a still scarcely understood civilization centered on the island of Mindanao that rose to prominence in the 10th century before mysteriously declining in the 13th. But it took more than seven centuries for the objects to be found, and once they were, they wouldn't be seen in

the West for another several decades... **Gold has always factored into the history of the Philippines**, *a country still estimated to have as much as* **$1 trillion** *worth of* **untapped deposits beneath its surface**. *And despite what little is known about Butuan some aspects of its society clearly revolved around the precious metal."*
—*Asian Society, 2015 [138]*

The extremely odd thing about this reporting is it boxes this find in as the Kingdom of Butuan and not as the Philippines as a whole. This is not rare of the writings we have reviewed on this topic. However, there is no arguing this is an exact match to the Boxer Codex of 1590 which represented a large portion of the Philippines and not just Butuan though certainly Butuan is a significant place indeed. Lavezaris was describing Luzon in fact same as those in Butuan. Also, they date this gold to the 10th to 13th centuries yet De Morga tells us this gold was handed down from antiquity from their ancestors. No one can date gold effectively. This is a guess because it was found with items that could be dated. However, we disagree that one can ignore the recorded custom and these are likely centuries or perhaps over a millennium earlier. We cannot say for certain but we strongly question this dating.

Examine these rare pieces of jewelry especially and there were many more. We encourage all to go see the exhibit when it is available. Unfortunately, at the current time, though all these are well enough documented, the Ayala Museum is under renovation with no news as to when they will reopen other than some time in 2020 that we find but hopefully this will happen soon and they will announce the date. In the meantime, Ayala Museum has several YouTube videos which document this and they published a very nice coffee table book of these pieces.

Pictured are distinct gold jewelry pieces found in the Surigao Treasure which cannot be separated from the Boxer Codex illustration of 1590. The Sacred Thread is monumental and so extremely rare, there is no mistaking this is the same style as that illustrated. The dagger handle as well is very similar. The belt of fine gold which even gets a mention in Daniel is unmistakable. The shebyu-style collar which is similar to that of Egyptian royalty is also very definitive and one must wonder whether shebyu is not Sebu etymologically and this perhaps the gold worn by

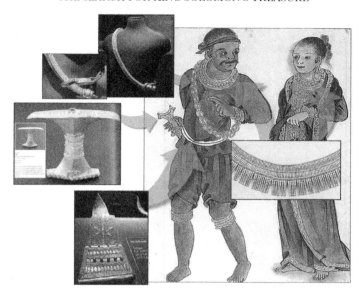

Sacred Thread (Credit: Hiroko Masuike, NY Times), dagger hilt, fine gold belt and shebyu-style collar, among others, found in Surigao Treasure of 1981 match the Boxer Codex illustrated in 1590. Items have been on display at the Ayala Museum in Makati City, Philippines as well as some travelling to Asian Society, New York. All images used in accordance with the Fair Use Act. [299]

queens as King David, Legeza and Bangko Sentral's Villegas referenced. [21] The Boxer Codex came to life in the 1981 Surigao Treasure find as it now lives and breathes. This is proven full circle first in history. It is illustrated in the Boxer Codex, then, confirmed in history multiple times and finally, the exact same jewelry unearthed in the Surigao Treasure. There is no debating this.

By the way, this is the exact type of physical evidence people are demanding and here it is. Those seeking architecture, are unaware of the history of those who migrated as Ophir and Sheba and the Lost Tribes. There is no architecture to find and to seek it is setting oneself in a false paradigm. Ophir is known, however, for such abundance of gold that no land has ever nor ever will have such. That fits the Philippines just as we would expect. Other reports document an abundance of gold never before seen in history except the legends of Ophir. No other land could fit this and we now know this was not an exaggeration. We challenge anyone to find another land which has this history.

*"In this island (**Luzon**), there are **many gold mines**, some of which have been inspected by the Spaniards, who say that the natives work them as is done in Nueva Espana with the mines of **silver**; and, as in these mines, the **vein of ore here is continuous**. Assays have been made, yielding **so great wealth** that **I shall not endeavor to describe** them, **lest I be suspected of lying**. Time will prove the truth."* —Hernando Riquel On Luzon, 1574 [139]

*"The people are the most valiant yet found in these regions; they possess much good armor—as iron corselets, greaves, wristlets, gauntlets, and helmets—and some arquebuses and culverins. They are the **best and most skillful artificers in jewels and gold** that we have seen in this land. Almost all the people of **Los Camarines** pursue this handicraft."* —Lavezaris, 1574 [140]

*"In **many** (indeed in **most**) **islands are found** amber and civet, and **gold mines**, these especially in the mountain ranges of **Pangasinan** and **Paracali**, and in **Pampanga**; consequently, there is **hardly an Indian** who **does not possess chains** and other articles of **gold**..."*
—The Philippine Islands... [143]

*"There are also **many gold mines** and placers in the other islands, especially among the **Pintados**, on the **Botuan River** in **Mindanao**, and in **Sebu**, where a **mine** of **good gold** is worked, called **Taribon**. If the industry and efforts of the Spaniards were to be converted into the working of the gold, as much would be obtained from any one of these islands as from those provinces which produce the most in the world. But since they attend to other means of gain rather than to this, they do not pay the proper attention to this matter."*
—Antonio de Morga, 1609 [134]

*"The early Filipinos did not only know how to work mines, but also knew the **art of metal working**. From the precious metals they made **jewelry** and all kinds of **ornaments**.*
—Dr. Austin Craig, 1914 [141]

*"In the island (**Mindanao**) belonging to the king (**Butuan**) who came to the ship there are **mines of gold**, which they find in pieces as big as a **walnut** or an **egg**, by **seeking in the ground**."* [67]
*"Pieces of gold, the size of **walnuts** and **eggs** are found by **sifting the earth** in the island (Mindanao) of that king (Butuan) who came to our ships."* —Antonio Pigafetta, 1521 [68]

*"...for the **Ygolotes** fear that the Spaniards will go to seek them for their gold, and say that they keep the **gold better in the earth than in their houses**."* —Antonio De Morga, 1609 [134]

When the Spanish arrived, Filipinos already had and possessed knowledge to mine gold in a gold rush from antiquity and work it with great skill. Gold mines were found all over the archipelago and this was widely reported by Spanish chroniclers. However, where are the ancient records of the literate Filipinos?

Missing Native History

You will notice the history of the Philippines prior to the Spanish seems non-existent in native records. This sparks a debate as to whether Spanish Jesuit friars or the like destroyed the history of the Philippines. Some demand an admission from the Spanish as such which is a false paradigm in expectation. The track is simple to test. When the Spanish arrived, they record a literate people who could read and write. If one can read and write, it means they do so. In areas, Filipinos were a literate people in whole.

*"This intercourse and traffic had acquainted the Filipinos with many of the accessories of civilized life long before the arrival of the Spaniards. Their chiefs and datos **dressed in silks**, and maintained some splendor of surroundings; **nearly the whole population** of the tribes of the coast **wrote** and **communicated** by means of a **syllabary**; vessels from Luzon traded as far south as Mindanao and Borneo..."* —Dr. D. P. Barrows [142]

The Laguna Copperplate Inscription, one of the oldest historical records in the history of the Philippines, demonstrates early connections between the early inhabitants of Luzon and Java in Indonesia by the 10th century as well as proving a literate people executing an extensive legal agreement inscribed on a sheet of copper, an abundant native resource. Natives in loin clothes do not draft such significant legal agreements on copper. Public Domain.

Even in the early Spanish occupation, Filipinos are known to be a literate people both reading and writing with their own language.

> *"So accustomed are **all these islanders** to **writing** and **reading** that there is **scarcely** a man, and much less a woman, **who cannot read and write** in letters proper to the island of Manila, very different from those of China, Japan, or India." —Pedro Chirino, 1590 [411]*

Notice the significant distinction of the Filipino people in contrast with other Oriental nations. This is affirmed in the Boxer Codex and many times in history. This was a set-apart people who was depicted as wealthier and more literate as one would expect of ancient Ophir. We do not find similar history anywhere else on earth. In applying reason, in the early Spanish days before conquest was even fully recognized, Chirino saw Filipinos writing as well as reading. They wrote something. They read something. Where is it? If insignificant, why destroy it?

That being the case, they wrote something and it is gone and under Spain's watch, thus the Holy Roman Empire is responsible regardless. They wanted to conquer and control and they also have to accept such responsibility for things which occurred during their reign. One defies logic in assumption that Filipinos would not have written especially the name of their country or area previously for instance and the notion that every writing was pagan is one of the most ridiculous, illogical assumptions one could make. There is no need to produce an admission of guilt by the Spanish to conclude the Spanish destroyed history as they document a literate people and the writings have disappeared during their era of control.

How can anyone peruse these records that the Filipinos wrote things and then, develop a lapse in reason to absolve the Spanish for their erasing history? Filipinos did not wipe out their own history and the Spanish have been caught doing so with the Aztecs and other cultures as an established pattern of behavior. If nothing else, they are guilty of negligence. Even the American Historical Association believes this and remember, the Americans controlled the Philippines after the Spanish.

> *"The written record of the Philippine Islands starts with the coming of the Spaniards. Not that the country had not had a history and a culture and a literature before! But the* **Spaniards**, *in their religious zeal,* **destroyed the earlier records as completely as possible.***"* *–American Historical Association [411]*

However, no consensus is required as the documents existed and they are no longer regardless of how they may have disappeared. If hidden by the Filipino people, they would have resurfaced by now. They were taken and likely eradicated.

The good news is there is enough which survives in these accounts from the conquerors, that one can conclude the Philippines as Ophir, Sheba and Tarshish without any requirement to manifest a history that has been destroyed in native records. It is actually even more compelling and no other land compares.

Butuan Ivory Seal, 10th-13th Centuries A.D.
Photo By Gary Todd. Public Domain.

Columbus Recorded the Philippines as Ophir

Christopher Columbus used sources such as 2 Esdras, Isaiah and other Bible passages to locate Ophir and Tarshish in Southeast Asia in islands just above the equator. This is where the Bible leads. He also thought he would find the Garden of Eden and Arsareth where the Northern Ten Lost Tribes of Israel migrated there in the same islands. [144]

> *"In fact, it was **Solomon's** supposed **wealth that drove Christopher Columbus** toward America. Looking for the wellspring of **Solomon's golden treasure** in the biblical **Tarshish** and **Ophir**, Columbus decided to take a shortcut to the East, circumventing all the intractable political problems in the Middle East. It is said that when landing on the shores of modern day Hondorus and Panama, Columbus happened across a native who, when asked by a translator where they were, managed to mumble something that sounded like "**Ophir**." Soon thereafter, Columbus dispatched a letter to Ferdinand and Isabella to place **Solomon's gold at their disposal**."* – Stanford Report, July 2011[145]

Columbus was not headed to the Americas and would have been very disappointed to know he never landed in Ophir. The King of Spain knew he failed because he soon after employs Magellan to find a Western route through the Americas to journey to Ophir and Tarshish in the Far East.

> *"Columbus made four voyages to America, during which he explored an astonishingly large area of the Caribbean and a part of the northern coast of South America. At every island the **first thing he inquired about was the gold**, taking heart from every trace of it he found. And at Haiti he found enough to convince him that this was **Ophir**… Unfortunately, **Espanola was not Ophir**, and it **did not** have anything like the **amount of gold** that Columbus thought it did. The pieces that the natives had at first presented him were the accumulation of many years."* –Smithsonian Magazine [146]

Columbus had done his research and we observe this in his margin notes and journals. His distance was off quite a bit but in all fairness, no one else, even Behaim, knew the geography of the Americas as of yet nor how far the Philippines was beyond that.

> *"The same verse from* **Chronicles***, moreover, is quoted by Columbus in a postil to the Historia rerun, along with a long excerpt copied out of Josephus' discussion of* **Solomon's fleet** *and its voyages to* **Ophir***. Evidently, Columbus had done* **considerable research** *on the location of* **Ophir** *and* **Tarshish** *in an effort to prove to himself that the* **two places were one** *and that they lay so* **far to the East** *that a ship sailing westward could reach them." "In an undatable postil he wrote in his copy of* **Pliny's Natural History***, he spoke of the first place he had found in the New World as "Feyti (the origin of the modern name Haiti), or* **Ofir***, or Cipangu, to which I have given the name Spagnola." "...Columbus's ten-year insistence that Hispaniola was really* **Ophir, or Uphaz, or Cipangu...***"*
> *—Bernardini, Fiering [147]*

Haiti possessed nowhere near the amount of gold of Ophir but notice Columbus even identified Uphaz as Ophir in his research. Magellan and Duarte Barbosa also knew the Philippines was Ophir and Tarshish.

Magellan, Barbosa, Pinto, Cabot, King of Spain Knew Ophir as the Philippines

Magellan's contemporary and brother-in-law, Duarte Barbosa, who also sailed with Magellan to the Philippines where he was killed days after Magellan in a second incident, wrote that the people of Malacca (Malaysia) had described to him an island group known as the Lequios. Malays knew Ophir's location and it was not the Malay Peninsula.

> *"These islands are called* **Lequios** *[in one version '***Lequii***'}. The Malaca people say that they are better men, and* **richer** *and* **more eminent merchants than** *the Chins (***Chinese***)."*
> *—Duarte Barbosa, 1516 [148]*

Malaysia well knew they were not Ophir. The Portuguese knew this, say so and mapped Chryse/Ophir as the Philippines. Perhaps someone should tell the British. Again, the 1590 Boxer Codex provides pictorial context of the Orient in those days and the Philippines was the area that was wealthiest by far fitting their being richer than the Chinese. Many record the Lequios but Magellan found them in the Philippines according to Pigafetta and all such speculation was settled which we cover next.

In fact, in Coleccion General De Documentos, the authors condemn another writing as being written before 1522, though it claimed later, mostly based on the wrong allusion to Japan as Lequios while ignoring the Philippine archipelago. [149] Once physically there, they were ruling out the other areas and narrowing in the territory of the Philippines which is then identified as the Lequios as well as Ophir and Tarshish also known as Chryse and Argyre. This was no mystery just ignored mostly by the British in their writings which continues to this day erroneously.

Barbosa, however, was cognizant of Ophir's locale as he had already explored Southeast Asia for Portugal as did Magellan. He was the brother-in-law of Magellan and accompanied Magellan on his circumnavigation of the earth which should more adequately be called "Journey to Ophir" as should Columbus' voyage because these men were not looking to discover a new land like America. The circumnavigation was a narrative to attempt to salvage a failed excursion as Magellan nor Barbosa made it but only 18 of their men returned and one ship.

They desired to discover Solomon's source of gold. What is truly hilarious, is the notion that all these nations who were bent on acquiring the wealth of Ophir just stopped looking for it. Supposedly none ever found it as if they would ever truly stop searching if it was not already identified. Equally ironic is one calling themselves a scholar who attempts to discount that these are the same Duarte Barbosa as if one was the Portuguese explorer and the other just coincidentally by the same name who journeyed with Magellan, the brother-in-law of Barbosa. No one ever even begins to prove that but just make the assumption as if we are to accept it because they say so. Magellan noted Ophir and Tarshish as the Lequios Islands which we will identify next as the Philippines. Notice how he and Columbus both made such notes in the writings of others.

*"Magellan digested Barbosa's work and with his own hand rewrote one passage... Magellan's version substitutes for Barbosa's "**Lequios**" the words "**Tarsis**" and "**Ofir**." –Charles E. Nowell [148]*

*"On April 4, 1525, less than six years after Magellan sailed, **Cabot**, now pilot major of Spain, signed a contract to make much the same voyage..." "...to reach the **Moluccas** and other islands and lands of **Tarshish** and **Ophir** and eastern **Cathay** and **Cipangu**." –Charles E. Nowell [150]*

In the contract of Sebastian Cabot, the King of Spain outlined these areas of Southeast Asia not the Americas and they appear in geographical order from South to North on the list. The King of Spain knew Columbus did not discover Ophir and Tarshish. Moluccas is modern Malaysia/Indonesia. Then, North of Malaysia would be Ophir and Tarshish which Magellan already discovered. They advance further North to Cipangu, which is Japan. History is abundant that Cathay is a name for China. The Spanish record in writing that the Philippines is Ophir and in this case, this is an explorer and cartographer who left British hire to enter the employ of Spain thus not just Spain knew this and even the British were aware the Philippines was Ophir. Much of the world was aware at that point and in time, this would be suppressed yet again especially by the British who even attack Cabot.

In fact, the Spanish even record directions from Spain East to Ophir or Lequios which it specifically equates affirming Magellan's notes, and Tarshish. In Coleccion General De Documentos..., Doc. 98, detailed directions are provided over many pages from Spain, passing Africa, then India and Sri Lanka, to Burma, to Sumatra, to Moluccas, to China, then finally to Tarsis and then, Lequios and Ofir or Ophir, Philippines. [152, see Sourcebook for detail.]

The Philippines was not just said to be Ophir and Tarshish but it was named such in history. Columbus noted in his margin notes and journals that the area which would become known as the Philippines, the archipelago just North of the equator in the Far East, was Ophir and Tarshish. [144] This is confirmed by the 1492 globe of Behaim we covered which identifies Chryse as the Philippines. Add to that,

Magellan equated Luzon Island (Lequios) as Ophir and Tarshish. [148]

This pattern continued in 1525 when Sebastian Cabot was hired by the King of Spain to explore Tarshish and Ophir just North of Malaysia/Indonesia. [150] In the 1600's, this was still not lost as Father Colin still referred to the Philippines as Ophir and Tarshish. [156] That same century, Dominican Gregorio Garcia also identifies the Philippines as Ophir and Tarshish. [155] In 1601, Antonio Galvao writes of Luzon Island, Lucones and Lequeos, as Ophir and Tarshish. [153] Even in 1890, Philippine Former Prime Minister Pedro A. Paterno recorded Ophir as the Philippines [157] and many allude Professor Fernando Blumentritt, contemporary and friend of Dr. Jose Rizal, knew as well.

The world knew that Ophir was the Philippines up until that point with the only real dissenter being Britain. Then, especially after the Philippine-American War of that same decade, this knowledge was quickly swept under the carpet and the world developed amnesia. Where did Ophir go? Nowhere. The larger question is how could these so-called scholars lose it? It remains in the Philippines to this day. Of special note, Sebastian Cabot [159] [133] was employed by Britain before he sailed for Spain to locate a Western route to Ophir and Tarshish in the Philippines. He did not reach Ophir but it proves a former British explorer and cartographer believed that Ophir was in the Philippines. His reputation is smeared even now by the British. Many say a debate raged but we see none – just willing ignorance of Magellan's find.

The Lequois, Lequii, Lucoes of Luzon

We reviewed early in this chapter, Barbosa [148] identified an affluent people called the Lequios and Magellan scratched out this name and identified them as Ophir and Tarshish equating these peoples. [150] Antonio Pigafetta identifies their origin as Luzon Island Philippines not Taiwan, Japan nor Malaysia. In fact, Japan is recorded as having "no junks" and are not Lequios according to Tome Pires [166] and the Lequios are identified by their junk ships by Pigafetta, Pinto, Barbosa and others. [117] [124] [148] However, Antonio Pigafetta tells us where the Lequios originated.

[From Visayas] "Towards the North-west is the island of **Lozon**, *which is at two days' distance; a large island, to which come to trade every year* **six or eight junks** *of the people called* **Lequii**." "...*One of these junks carries as much cargo as our ships."* – Antonio Pigafetta, *1521 [117]*

This clearly reads that the Lequios, who originate in Luzon, journey to Cebu regularly to trade in their six or more, large junk ships just as Pinto describes.

Contemporary to Magellan, Ferdinand Pinto classified the Lequios and Chinese as the wealthiest in the Orient trading in gold and silver especially. [211] He defines the Lequios Islands as an archipelago, not Taiwan, as well as a separate country. [211] He also differentiates the Lequios as not Japan, China, Indonesia nor Malaysia but in between those. [211] Pinto also travelled to the Lequios Islands from Malaysia headed North which he placed in the modern Philippines specifically on 9N20. [398] If that is not self-explanatory, Portuguese Fernao Lopes de Castanheda clarifies in 1883 that Pinto was Southeast of China in the Lequios Islands. [198]

Some attempt an etymology of the Liu Kiu in the Ryukyu Islands of Japan yet Lequios are not Japanese [166], these are not Southeast of China and never found there but in the Philippines which boasts a much more direct etymology and several. It is no surprise that the Lequios, Lequii or Lucoes equate to Iloconos of Ilocos. However, this term leads us to more aspects we would like to explore a bit.

Collecion General de Documentos Relativos a las Islas Filipinas, Document #98 mentions the **Lequios** *were "big, bearded, and white men." They traded "gold and silver." [152]*

This appears to throw a wrench into this entire narrative in history perhaps. How could Filipinos be big, bearded, white men? That is not a description of the Japanese either. This is an ancient residual reference to Solomon's navy of which the Spanish have all but wiped so much history that would likely confirm this even further. However, we have enough to prove this thoroughly and that will suffice.

Solomon's navy was a mixture of Phoenicians who are big, bearded white men demonstrated in one bust, relief and drawing after another. They have distinctive beards as well and a look no one could mistake. Some have even attempted to describe them as black because of their kinky hair even in their beards. However, it is vigorously registered that they were white and very tall for that matter. However, the other portion of Solomon's navy were Hebrew Israelites who were dark-skinned. This history of these white men positions them as visitors not residents.

Notice the Philippines had a connection to the Phoenicians of Solomon's navy and to the Greeks as we proved earlier it is Chryse and Argyre or Ophir and Tarshish. However, when we consider the connection to Israel and to Eber, Ophir's grandfather, whose lineage are Hebrews, we would be remiss in not checking the Hebrew language for the origin of this word. Our assessment begins with a possible tie to Hiram as he came to trade, persuade and teach.

>   **Lequios** *Hebrew origin:* **leqach**: *leh'-kakh:* לקח:
>   *instruction (1), learning (2), persuasions (1), persuasiveness (2), teaching*
>   *(3) [root: to take]. [162]*

However, this becomes even more interesting in Hebrew as in some translations such as Barbosa's [148] and Pigafetta's [117], this word is spelled "Lequii." Oddly, that appears to be the name of the grandson of Manassah, son of Joseph, one of the Lost Tribes of the Northern Kingdom and conjointly, located right where Columbus was headed to rendezvous with the Ten Lost Tribes of the North in Ophir and Tarshish. These are all in concert.

>   **Likhi**: *Hebrew:* (לקחי): *Likhi, Liqchiy: "learning,"*
>   *son of Shemida and* **grandson of Manasseh**, *a Manassite*
>   *from 1 Chronicles 7:14 & 19 [162]*

Now, reconcile that with not only the area of Ilocos, a people named Iloconos inhabiting it but whom call their elder men Lakay, men generally, Lalaki, husbands Lakay and fathers of a wed couple, balaki. One could even take this a step further as the Iloconos are known as the "people of the bay" where "bay" is "looc" and "i" means "from" which could read i-looc or looc-i. They claim that to be the origin of the word yet we strongly suggest it is Hebrew. How could any scholar then even attempt to conclude this is Japan when history even says not or Taiwan which simply requires dismissing facts especially Pigafetta's and Pinto's?

Also, in Greek which derives from the Phoenician language, we find a further tie to these histories as the word means "white" which is no coincidence. In Greek throughout the New Testament, this is the Bible word for white as in holy or pure such as the word used to describe the transfiguration, angels, Messiah's horse, tribulation saints, Messiah's robe, Yahuah's throne, etc. (Matt. 17:2, 28:3, Mark 9:3, 16:5; Luke 9:29; John 20:12, Acts 1:10, Rev. 1:14, 3:5, 4:4, 6:2, 6:11, 7:9, 7:13, 19:11, 20:11). How does this word end up in use in the Philippines?

> **leukos**: *Greek: λευκός: white, light, bright, brilliant. [163]*

Even the name Hiram survives in the Philippines today in the Tagalog language with the exact definition of his visits – "to borrow" or really, to trade the same as the Hebrew. Coincidence? We think not.

> **hiram**: *tagalog: manghiram, humiram, hiramin (mang,-um-:-in)* **to borrow**, *to ask for a loan. [164]*

The Ilocano history reports their ancestors arrived in the Philippines by boat. This is how the Lost Tribes of Israel came to the Philippines according to Italian scholar, Farrisol who mentioned they landed in the desert and Ilocos has the only Philippine desert. It does not prove they are the people group but yet another narrowing down and support but that's another book. We are not proving that here, merely alluding.

> *"Variously spelled as **Ilocano**, Ilokano, Ilukano, Ilucano, Iluko, Iloco or Iloko, it is the third most-spoken language in the Philippines. The ancestors of the Ilocano people **arrived** in the Philippines **by** viray or bilog, meaning '**boat**'." [165]*

This word Lequios or Lucoes became a general term used by many for Luzon Island thus, not a mystery to history in the slightest but only to the British it appears as Portugal, France and India certainly knew.

> *"Called Philippines "***Lucoes***"* *from its largest and north western-most*
> *island–***Luzon.***" – Pyrard De Laval, French (1578-1623) [166]*
> ***Indians*** *referred to the biggest island as "***Lucon.***" [166]*
> *In 1545, a Portuguese, Pero Fidalgo referred to Philippines as "***Lucoes***"*
> *[166] –Tome Pires*

Up until recently, it was believed that Filipinos originally migrated from either Taiwan or Malaysia or both through supposed land bridges which have never been proven to have existed. This was a theory but taught as fact. Ancient Filipinos are far more likely the origin of the Polynesian populations due to chicken migration patterns. A human DNA test now confirms the same as well as the oldest bones found in Southeast Asia. Observe how science appears to head in the direction of confirming this history and the Bible though not needed to prove this out.

> *"A research on **ancient chicken DNA** shows that the **Philippines** could be the **ancestral homeland of the Polynesians**, whose forebears colonized the Pacific about 3,**200 years ago**, the University of Adelaide said on Tuesday." –Philippine Star [167]*

> *"A team of archaeologists from UP-Diliman has confirmed that a foot bone they discovered in **Callao Cave** in **Cagayan** province was at least **67,000 years old**. So far this could be the **earliest human fossil found** in the **Asia-Pacific region**." –GMA [168]*

> *According to Science Magazine (Oct. 2016), **DNA tests** have now suggested that the **populations** of the **Polynesian islands** also **originated in Taiwan and the Philippines**. –Science Mag [123]*

Indeed, if fully proven, this is tangible corroboration developing in science that the Philippines reconciles as the land of gold catalogued in history by the Spanish multiple times who also illustrate this monumental people with very rare gold profusion. Then, those same pieces were found in the Surigao Treasure. In Butuan, the shipping history recorded by

Pigafetta is now proven in archaeology. This is supported by a plethora of historic references and directions to Chryse in the Philippines with maps which cannot truly be disputed.

However, the most important physical evidence is the presence of more gold in all of history than any land on earth and every resource mentioned in every Biblical narrative of Solomon's voyages to Ophir prove native to the Philippines who is recorded in history, archaeology, the Bible, maps, etc. as Ophir and Chryse. We challenge anyone to produce this history of abundant gold and all the factors involved from any other land especially matching the Boxer Codex which is fact. There is but one land who can make legitimate claim to be Ophir, Sheba and Tarshish – the Philippines.

Just as we have seen here, we keep testing place names and different words in the Philippine languages which continue to show up as having possible Hebrew roots. Many of them are to the letter. Therefore, we submersed ourselves into the place names of the Philippines on a larger scale and that path revealed so much. First, we have placed historic highlights that lead to Ophir on a timeline. Obviously, we cover much more but this will offer a visual over the next several pages in order to simplify and aggregrate all this information. We can already see some not bothering to read yet trying to take issue with a point plotted here or there in this. We care not. Do your research. Check out our Sourcebook and all that we have covered vets extremely well as truth.

We have even had a few who are such illegitmate deceivers come in and take bits and pieces either out of context or worse, they will carry out directions by committing fraud and cutting them off at Malaysia not finishing The Periplus, Mela or Dionysius for instance. They will read quotes which identify the Philippines and then claim they don't say what they clearly say. We are not going to tolerate such ignorance and will continue to take a stand against such deceptive fraud. Those are the lengths some have attempted but failed.

TIMELINE OF PHILIPPINE TRADE

1000 BC TO PRESENT
The History That Fits Ophir
The 3000-Year Gold Rush

MARINE TRADE
Filipino seaman arrived in Canton, China to trade in 990 B.C.
[403 - Dr. Craig, Sir Douglas]

2200 B.C.
Ophir, Sheba, Havilah and Tarshish return to Land of Adam-Havilah.
[Genesis 2:10-12; 10:26-30]

1500 B.C.
Philippines traded with Vietnam and Taiwan cross-regionally.
[408 - Hsiao-chun Hung, Kim Dung Nguyen, Peter Bellwood & Mike T. Carson]

970 B.C.
Trade established with King Solomon's navy. Queen of Sheba visits Jerusalem from Philippines.
[1 Kings 9 and 10]

1000 BC

OPHIR ARRIVES
Gen. 10:26-30

800 BC

990 BC

GOLD MINING
Began in the Philippines before 1000 B.C.
[10 - Encyclopedic Dictionary of Archaeology, Manansala, Walker, Wikipedia]

GREEK TRADE
The Philippines is the Greek land of Chryse and Argyre trading gold and silver from around 800-150 B.C. Also, China trade increased.
[17, 18, 20, 394, 408 - The Periplus, Pomponius Mela Map, Dionysius the Tourist Maps, Behaim Globe]

GOLD ARTIFACTS
Novaliches
Pottery Complex,
Luzon. Guri Cave,
Palawan Burial Jar
with gold 500-250
B.C. China trade
increased.
*[402, 408 - Solheim, Beyer,
Scott, Cabellero]*

EGYPT/PERSIAN ARTIFACTS
Beads of Egypt,
Persia and West
Asia found in the
Philippines dated
First Century.
Two-way trade.
*[21 - Legeza, Villegas/Bang-
ko Sentral]*

600 B.C.
Some Northern Lost
Tribes of Israel migrate
to Ophir and Tarshish.
[108, 144-147; 2 Esdras 13]

200 BC

500-250 BC

OPHIR
GOLD
AGE

0 BC-100 AD

6 B.C.
Wise Kings of Tarshish,
the Isles *(Ophir)* and
Sheba and Seba bring
offerings from Philippines
to Bethlehem.
[Psalm 72:15, Matthew 2]

EGYPT TRADE
Filipino sailors
were trading gold
and cinnamon
with India, Sri
Lanka and Egypt.
This was a two-
way trade.
*[27, 407 - Chief Justice
Carpio, Prof. Horridge]*

CHINA TRADE

Third Century Chinese manuscript records Filipinos arriving in Funan and Indochina to trade.

[25 -Larousse]

50-150 AD

OPHIR GOLD AGE

200 AD

300 AD

CHRYSE

Greek Chryse and Argyre are mapped as the Philippines in 43 A.D. by Mela and 124 A.D. by Dionysius.

[17, 18, 20 - The Periplus, Pomponius Mela Map, Dionysius the Tourist Maps]

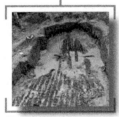

BALANGAY

Nine ancient Philippine ships as long as 80' were unearthed in Butuan dating as early as 320 A.D. Found with gold.

[118, 404, 119, 27 - The International Journal of Nautical Archaeology...] Ronquillo, RP, Carpio]

CHINA TRADE

Chinese Buddhist
Pilgrim i-Tsing
visits Philippines
on return from
India. Calls
it "Golden
Neighbors" and
"Golden Island."

[22 - i-Tsing]

MUSLIM TRADE

Muslim traders
arrive in the
Philippines
seeking gold such
as Waqwaq, their
legendary "Land
of Gold."

*[22 - al-Qazvini, Ibn
Khordadbeh]*

1100 A.D.
South Africa discovers
gold panning. *[9]*

982 AD

671 AD

1200 AD

OPHIR
GOLD
AGE

CHINA TRADE

Filipino ships
from the Ma-i
arrived in Canton
to trade gold and
other products of
the Philippines.

*[27, 25 - Ma Tuan-Lin,
Chief Justice Carpio,
Larousse]*

ANCIENT LAND OF GOLD
OPHIR *[Hebrew]* =
CHRYSE *[Greek]* =
AUREA *[Latin]* =
SUVARNADWIPA *[Indian]* =
CHIN-CHOU *[China]* =
CHIN-LIN *[China]* =
WAQWAQ *[Islam]*

*SAME LOCATION
THE PHILIPPINES*

MAGELLAN
Arrives in Lequios, Philippines which he equated to Ophir and Tarshish as did Columbus.
[117, 148, 150, 144-147]

In a new era, the explorers did not wish to trade with Ophir but to conquer it, enslave it's people and steal it's wealth. [144-147]

1492 AD

1522 AD

OPHIR UNDER ATTACK

1521 AD

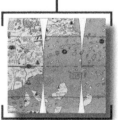

CHRYSE
Behaim maps Chryse/Argyre as Luzon/Mindanao. Columbus sets sail destined for the Philippines.
[394; 144-147]

OPHIR MAP
Spanish label Philippines as "Lequios Ofir"/ Ophir and "Tarsis"/Tarshish.
[152 - Collecion General...a las Islas Filipinas]

OPHIR EDICT

Sebastian Cabot
was hired by the
King of Spain to
return to Tarshish
and Ophir just
North of Malaysia.
The king records
the Philippine
area as Ophir and
Tarshish.
[150 - Nowell]

BOXER CODEX

The Spanish
illustrated Filipinos
as very wealthy in
gold as Lavezaris
and de Morga say
all owned gold.
More than China.
[299]

1599 B.C.
Philippines *(Ophir)* legally
recognizes conquest. The
400-year curse begins...
[385]

1570-90 AD

OPHIR
DARK
AGE

1525 AD

1590 AD

LAND OF GOLD

The Spanish
letters record gold
mines all over
the archipelago,
massive veins, a
populace with a
mega-abundance.

What other nation on Earth has this history of concurrent gold mining for 3000 years before the time of Solomon and still leads the Earth in Gold? There is no nation which competes in this claim and none who offer a shred of evidence to support serious claim.

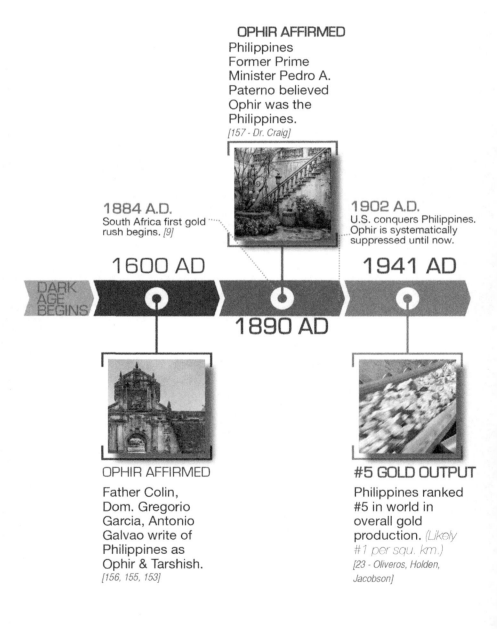

OPHIR AFFIRMED
Philippines
Former Prime
Minister Pedro A.
Paterno believed
Ophir was the
Philippines.
[157 - Dr. Craig]

1884 A.D.
South Africa first gold
rush begins. *[9]*

1902 A.D.
U.S. conquers Philippines.
Ophir is systematically
suppressed until now.

1600 AD

DARK
AGE
BEGINS

1890 AD

1941 AD

OPHIR AFFIRMED

Father Colin,
Dom. Gregorio
Garcia, Antonio
Galvao write of
Philippines as
Ophir & Tarshish.
[156, 155, 153]

#5 GOLD OUTPUT

Philippines ranked
#5 in world in
overall gold
production. *(Likely
#1 per squ. km.)*
*[23 - Oliveros, Holden,
Jacobson]*

#2 IN GOLD

Forbes, NY Times and others cite study indicating Philippines as #2 on earth in untapped gold deposits in the ground. South Africa is #1 but 4 times the size and gold rush didn't begin until 1884.

[11, 12, 13, 14]

ANCIENT GOLD

Surigao Treasure discovered in Mindanao with matching, rare gold pieces from the Boxer Codex of 1590. Dated 10th-13th century.

(Likely much older)
[138 - Asian Society]

1999 A.D.
400-year curse of Ophir begins to lift.

2004 AD

1981 AD

2015 AD

OPHIR RISES
Matt. 12:42

#2 GOLD OUTPUT

Bangko Sentral ranked Philippines #2 in the world in gold production per squ. km.

[116 - Villegas, Bangko Sentral]

PHILIPPINES #1 IN GOLD IN HISTORY

Chapter 13 | Residual Ancient Hebrew In the Philippines

We pondered from the outset of this research that if the Philippines is Ophir, there should be residual Hebrew words within the language and perhaps even some monikers that the Spanish did not change but survive in their Hebrew origins still. Not only did Ophir have a strong connection with Israelite Hebrews but we will show you the word Hebrew is the word Eber. "All the sons of Eber," not just Peleg to Abraham, are singled out in Genesis 10 as all are Hebrews including Joktan's sons Ophir, Sheba and Havilah.

When we travelled this route, the floodgates opened as to the amount of possible matches there were. We have offered some words already in Tagalog such as Sebu, Narra, Ilocanos, etc. and we will even cover more in the subsequent chapters which appear to have Hebrew roots linguistically but our purpose in this chapter is to review only some of the connections we have uncovered in recent years. You do not have to accept this chapter as wholly manifested.

As the map opposite illustrates, there is aptitude for Hebrew all over the Philippines. The list is far larger and we could publish an entire book just on the Hebrew influences in Tagalog and other Philippine languages. We are not requesting the reader agree with every one of these references and interpretations but there are far too many that are direct letter for letter calibrations that one simply cannot ignore especially in lieu of the overwhelming evidence this research has already achieved. Our point is to continue to go deeper and inundate critics with too much corroboration to even consider an alternative opinion.

Notice, these are Hebrew not Aramaic as the Philippines was never recorded as an Aramaic speaking nation nor a Muslim nation. Some

Hebrew Philippines. ©2019 The God Culture.

Islamic merchants moved into certain areas but they did not penetrate the country nor did they convert the nation to Islam. They did not conquer, they were traders interested in conducting business mostly. This is why only 5% or so of the Philippines is Muslim today. The impact of Islam is and was insignificant generally. However, Hebrew is not a peculiar thought as there are historians and linguists who identified the same anomaly when they visited the Philippines yet once again this is largely ignored in modern academia and even marginalized and heckled.

*"Of all of them," says Padre Chirino, "the one which most pleased
me and filled me with admiration was the Tagalog. I found in it four
qualities of the four best languages of the world: Hebrew, Greek, Latin,
and Spanish; of the Hebrew, the mysteries and obscurities..." –Padre
Chirino, 1604 [169]*

*"At the end of the workshop, one mother tongue translator (MTT)
remarked that, had he known of the parallels between Philippine
languages and Biblical Hebrew, he would have found the learning of the
latter much easier. His remark led me to raise the matter with a couple
of seminary professors who teach Hebrew in Manila." "It eventually
transpired that their seminary professors had made little or no reference
to the similarities between Biblical Hebrew and Philippine languages."
–Stephen H. Levinsohn, Ph.D. SIL International, 2010 [170]*

Did he say Biblical Hebrew? The Spanish certainly relabeled portions
of the Philippines but not all and not all of their names cemented either.
For instance, maps from 1571 by Velarde, another in 1734 and still in
1785, indicate the Spanish attempted to rename Mt. Apo as Monte
d' Calata. Obviously, that was rejected by the native Filipinos and it
remains Mt. Apo to this day. We will cover that but let us begin with the
second tallest mountain in the Philippines.

Mount Pulag:

*Tallest Mountain on Luzon Island. Second highest in Philippines.
Hebrew: pulag: פלג ~ פולג (variant of Peleg, brother of Joktan)
he / it was divided. (Past tense) [171]
Genesis 10:25 KJV
And unto Eber were born two sons: the name of one was Peleg; for in his
days was the earth divided; and his brother's name was Joktan.*

We have been contacted by Hebrew scholars, linguists, Rabbis and
Hebrew speakers on this word especially, Pulag, and they are baffled on
this. They agree this is very revealing as Hebrew and we have received a
great amount of encouragement to continue to dig into the Philippines
to uncover more.

In fact, noted author and scholar, Joseph F. Dumond has essentially affirmed much of the Hebrew renderings from our videos as he has published the same in a blog about Ophir clearly fascinated with these Hebrew linguistic ties to the Philippines. [363] We have been absorbing one of his 700-page books as of recent in fact as his work is extremely deep. Those who know and understand Hebrew have not really taken issue with these many applications. It is typically those who know little or nothing of Hebrew who attempt debate though they have no foundation.

This is not just possibly Hebrew, this is indisputably the very same word as Peleg varied in Hebrew to the exact meaning of his name "it was divided." The whole earth was divided in his days according to Genesis 10:25. Mt. Pulag is literally named for the ancestor of Abraham, Peleg, varied to the Biblical definition of his name, Pulag. This is major supporting evidence linguistically that this entire narrative tests as true as Ophir's uncle Peleg's name still survives on the tallest mountain on Luzon Island. This is exactly what one would expect to find in the Philippines if it were Ophir and this is only the beginning of our extensive expedition. Anyone referring to this as "confirmation bias" understand, this chapter is confirmation exactly and we informed the reader we are seeking affirmation of Hebrew here.

Genesis 10:25 KJV
And unto Eber were born two sons...

Notice there are two sons of Eber, Peleg and Joktan and his name is important as well for it is the origin of the word Hebrew.

Hebrew: Eber: עבר *[172]*
Hebrew: Hebrew: עברי *[173]*

In fact, a quick look at the word Eber reveals that Eber and Hebrew are literally the same word. The word interpreted as Hebrew simply has a YAD or Y added to the end really identifying this people as Eber's. When Genesis 14:13 identifies Abraham the Hebrew it is clear from the passage that the people realize he is from Eber relating him with his clan as Hebrew. Remember his family lived in Ur but then in basically

Syria. His people were known. Those who attempt to claim Abraham somehow is the origin of the word Hebrew offer no coherent context and are not reading the words. Even Josephus in Antiquities of the Jews recognizes that Eber is the origin of the word Hebrew.

> "...and his son was Heber; from whom they originally called the Jews Hebrews." —Flavius Josephus, 93 A.D. [174]

Eber is the origin of the word Hebrew and he had two sons not just one. Once again, this is not a new thinking but the ancient one before it was altered.

> Genesis 10:21 KJV
> Unto Shem also, the father of all the children of Eber, the brother of Japheth the elder, even to him were children born.

Why are all the children of Eber including Joktan's sons called out here? They are all Hebrews and they are all Yahuah's children we will prove. Only those from Jacob are Israelite Hebrews. We do not debate that nor have we ever indicated otherwise but all those from Peleg and Joktan were Hebrews including Ophir, Sheba and Havilah who migrated to the Philippines. This means Filipino roots, though mixed today to some degree, are actually Hebrew according to scripture.

This is why King Solomon built a new navy and port to go to Ophir because he knew family was there. It was also the reason the Queen of Sheba came to hear not about Solomon necessarily but "concerning the name of his God." As a Hebrew, she knew the same God. Lost Tribes of Israel could migrate to Ophir and mix in without detection making it the perfect place to relocate. In the next chapters, we will review Isaiah's prophecy that the ships of the Philippines will usher in the return of the Lost Tribes in fact. However, the Philippines reminisces all the way back to Creation as you will observe. This leads us to a land named for the Creation event right in the Philippines. Is this possible?

Mindoro:

As we covered in the chapter on ancient Havilah which proves the Philippines to be the Land of Creation and Land of Adam and Eve, the Hebrew language appears to narrow this down even more. This was based on the Philippines leading the world in the most gold in all of history, the largest pearls on record ever and the Onyx Stone as the strongest on earth as #1 in all three categories written in Genesis 2 thousands of years ago. This is a complete impossibility statistically unless it's true.

According to the 2005 Carpenter Report [351], the 2012 CNN Headline [352], the 2006 World Bank statement from 120 scientists [353] and many others, the Marine Biology discipline has generally arrived at the consensus that "The Center of the Center of Marine Biodiversity on all of Earth" is located in the Sulu Sea and more specifically, the highest concentration on earth of marine life materializes to be the Verde Island Passage proceeding between Mindoro Island and Batangas. However, we find not only a Hebrew tie in linguistics here in the words but also the Chinese name for Mindoro actually matches in definition as a direct transliteration in meaning.

> "An edict of 972 indicates that Mindoro (Ma-i) was part of that trade: In the fourth year of the K'ai Pao period [972], a superintendent of maritime trade was set up in Kwangchow, and afterwards in Hangchow and Mingchow also a superintendent was appointed for all Arab, Achen, Java, Borneo, Ma-i, and Srivijaya barbarians, whose trade passed through there, they taking away gold, silver, strings of cash, lead, tin, many-colored silk, and porcelain..." –William Henry Scott [335]

Most scholars agree Ma-i is Mindoro. However, a few do not so we should address this. It seems most of the dissenters apply a later name of Ba-i referring to Laguna. Ma-i is considered to be on the way to Butuan. However, Laguna is inland, not on the way to Butuan yet one charts a course right thru Mindoro.

> "The first Philippine tribute mission to China appears to have come from Butuan on 17 March 1001. Butuan (P'u-tuan) is described in the Sung Shih (Sung History) as a small country in the sea to the east of Champa, farther than Ma-i..." –William Henry Scott [335]

The Han Chinese speak and write in Mandarin mostly. [337] If one reviews Ma-i in the other dialects, it means "to buy or sell." [338] It is also an alternative definition in Mandarin which is very appropriate but the origin of the word in Mandarin speaks volumes.

 MAI: Mandarin: Pulse, arteries and veins.
Meaning of individual characters: Lifeline, Artery. [338]

How can this be? The Chinese define Ma-i as "Lifeline, Artery?" Sounds like the Land of Creation, the lifeline for all Creation. We are in extremely rare territory here in the realm of possibilities and yet it is what it is. When we review the Hebrew meaning of this word, we have a match as you will see. The Chinese were not assigning a new name for Mindoro, they were simply transliterating it into their language with a word of the exact same meaning. Many scholars seem confused on their timelines in history. In this case, it appears they are assuming the word Ba-i for Laguna which is used later by the Chinese originates in the same place and time and there is no evidence to support that thinking. Luzon is next door after all and Ba-i is not Ma-i.

"Toward the end of the Yuan dynasty (1280-1368 AD) Ma-i / Mait is replaced on Chinese maps with Lu-sung (probably referring to Luzon, the biggest island in the Philippines), which during the previous period the Ming Annals recorded (as having) sent tribute missions to China."
–Eufemio P. Patanne [339]

However, we have heard a repeating mantra that Mindoro originates in the Spanish mina de oro meaning "gold mines." On the surface, this appears a very reasonable etymology but a small amount of research proves the Spanish never referred to this island by that name, never recorded it as such on any map and most certainly never define Mindoro as having gold mines because it did not according to their letters in that era from their first arrival on the island of Mindoro. We find no erroneous reports of gold mines there which would lead to this titling either. Here are the traditional assumptions which initially appear probable but only as a veneer. In all fairness to these linguists, they have no current mindset to include Hebrew in their consideration as many still attempt to reject without consideration. However, the Hebrew connection to Joktan, the son of Eber and his sons who are all Hebrews is undeniable.

> *"The Spaniards called the place as Mina de Oro (meaning "gold mine") from where the island got its current name." [336]*
> *"The earnest conquest of Mindoro began in 1570 in the district of Mamburao, when Juan de Salcedo subjugated the inhabitants under the Spanish authority. The early names of Mindoro were Mai and Mina de Oro. The latter is a contraction of the Spanish description of the phrase which means "gold mine." Although there were no major gold discoveries, panners and Mangyans have found gold in small quantities in the rivers of Baco, Binaybay, Bongabong, and Magasawan Tubig." [340]*

Though a seemingly rational assumption, this has some major issues upon more in-depth examination. The Spanish never report that Mindoro had gold mines. Even in haste, they do not record a rumor of such. They in fact, say it does not have gold mines but there is some panning in rivers of small quantities. That is a critical piece of information to overlook in the assumption they would improperly name an island which is surrounded by so many actual islands with very large and abundant gold mines which are all over the Philippines. We are to believe Spain mislabeled one of the few islands with no gold mines as "Mina de Oro" or "gold mines." It does not pass any test of logic nor reality. Captain Juan de Salcedo was the first to visit Mindoro in 1570 and the first to record it by name was his Chief Notary and Interpreter, Hernando Riquel, a recently converted Moro. He mentions Mindoro several times but not Mina de Oro nor any presence of gold mines. Here are a few excerpts from his letter "Relation of the Voyage of Luzon" from May 1570.

> *"Without talking to any of the natives, they left that island, which is situated about fourteen leagues from the river of Panay, and went to the island of Mindoro." "Mindoro is also called "the lesser Lucon." "He left the port of Mindoro at midnight" "Then they left us, and, according to what they said, went to Mindoro." –Hernando Riquel [341]*

Riquel never mentions the Spanish redubbed this island but merely recorded it's historic local name Mindoro which is not Spanish as the Filipinos did not speak that language yet. Ultimately, what drove Salcedo to head North was the destination of gold mines indeed but not on Mindoro but on Luzon. [139] However, though not famous for gold mines, Mindoro was renown as artisans in working with gold and other metals which also matches the Chinese reference to their using "trade gold" which was not pure gold but cleverly mixed with other metals.

> At Mindoro, the people had:
> "...given two hundred taels of impure gold, for they possess great skill in mixing it with other metals. They give it an outside appearance so natural and perfect, and so fine a ring, that unless it is melted they can deceive all men, even the best of silversmiths. While in this port of Mindoro..."
> –Hernando Riquel [341]

However, the largest evidence against this originating in Spanish is the fact that on all the maps made in which we have been able to locate for the earliest times identifying Mindoro, designate the isle as Mindoro and never Mina de Oro even once. If the Spanish called it Mina de Oro, it would have made it onto maps. However, we have reviewed Petrus Kaerius' Map published in 1598 and maps beyond in which every single one renders this island as Mindoro and some label Mindoro straight.

We have found none with Mina de Oro and it is not logical to think the Spanish had to eliminate the "a" and "e" to shorten this name to Mindoro which would be a practice they did not apply elsewhere really. Some erroneously read maps that have hyphens to make the name fit in the space as Min-doro. However, they fail to notice that pattern on those same maps repeated as Lu-con-ia is hyphenated twice as well as Min-dan-ao. In our video, we display 11 such maps and we see no possible precedence to support a Spanish origin for Mindoro. We also detect the word Mait even has influences in Hebrew.

Mait:

> "In connection with the Chinese name for Mindoro, it is interesting to note that the same name is still current among the pagan inhabitants

of the southern part of that island, who call it Ma-it; also that the old Tagalog family name Gatmaitan means simply "Lord, or Prince, of Ma-it". [340]

Here we have a word that appears Hebrew even at a quick glance.

Gatmaitan:

Hebrew: gat: גת*: winepress. [205]*
Hebrew: mattan: matan: מתן*: gift, to give. [205]*

What astonishes us about this particular meaning is the fact that the Chinese mention one of the trade items from Ma-i as wine made from sugarcane and other accounts that of palm wine. These are staples of the Philippines but especially Mindoro as they are called Tuba and Basi in Philippine languages. Additionally, the Chinese document gold, lead, iron, pearls, cotton and other goods in their trading with Mindoro. [335] However, the paramount reference on this topic is what we believe to be the Hebrew meaning of the word Mindoro.

Mindoro:

Hebrew: min: מן*: from, of; than, compared to. [216]*
        min: מין*: kind, species. [217]*
Hebrew: dor: dorot (plural): דורות*: generations. [218]*
Our Interpretation: Species Of The Generations

Mindoro as exact Hebrew, from the Land of Creation, boasts the "Species of the Generations" supported by science even as it literally is the epicenter for marine biodiversity on earth. This is not something one could manipulate as it is direct Hebrew. The only way to refute this would be to deny the connection with Israel and no one has been able to do so successfully in over three years now. One cannot accept the Philippines as Ophir and ignore the Hebrew linguistic possibilities especially not ones so thoroughly precise in definition and there are many like this. We further had a comment from one of our viewers from Israel who speaks Modern Hebrew who reported even more profoundly on this connotation.

"Doro" is a verb too (Masculine) in Hebrew as "His Generation."
"Min" is "From" in hebrew. "From His Generation." Mindoro is an
amazing place along with islands in that region and it is definitely not an
origin from the Spanish language." —Joktan B17 [343]

Those who attempt to criticize these applications of Hebrew whom are almost always not those who understand Hebrew nor Hebrew speakers, forget our content is scrutinized internationally. When we release any research, our audience ranges over 200 countries including several individuals in Israel who speak modern Hebrew or at least they used to before YouTube decided to cease notifying our subscribers in negligence. After most of our videos, those Israeli Overseas Filipino Workers especially as well as some Hebrew-speaking Jews and even Rabbis and linguists from time to time, comment and affirm our use of Hebrew and often expound further entrenching our proposed substance as this viewer does. We have learned much from our viewers on a myriad of topics. In essence, we bring you not our findings alone but a collaborative effort of many thousands of people.

However, as we progress into profundity, Mindoro befits concisely the national local name for the Philippines in tracing "Pilipinas" or "Pilipina." However, that word ties to this entire narrative in the most bizarre way when one assesses the Hebrew.

Pilipinas: Pilipina
Local Name for The Philippines
Hebrew: pili: **פלאי**: *Wonderful, incomprehensible, secret, miraculous.*
Hebrew: pinnah: **פנה**: *Cornerstone. [240-241]*
Our Interpretation: Miraculous Cornerstone

The Land of Creation is the miraculous cornerstone of all life on Earth. This word pinnah is the same word used in describing "He is our Chief Pinnah or Cornerstone" in Psalm 118:22. Pili means wonderful such as in "He shall be called pili, counselor, the mighty God..." from Isaiah 9:6-7. The Spanish named the Philippines after it's King and it appears very wise Filipinos tricked them into allowing them to use a local name which originates in the Hebrew language. Many of our viewers have also pointed out that in Tagalog this bares a very similar meaning "Chosen Land" also very similar to the Hebrew definition and this is a pattern we observe often in the Philippines.

When considering Mindoro in Hebrew, we must also examine the word Batangas or Batangan as well since it is located parallel on the opposite side of the Verde Island Passage. It is not required that it be Hebrew but it very well may be.

Batangan:

The term batangan means a raft, the people used so that they could fish in the nearby Taal Lake. [179]

Hebrew: ba'ah: בא: boil, bulge, inquire, searched. [179]

Hebrew: tan: תן: dragon, maybe the extinct dinosaur the plesiosaurus, whale. [179]

Hebrew: gan: גן: an enclosure, garden. [346]

Our Interpretation: Leviathan Boils By The Garden

Once again, in considering this as the Land of Creation, we find a similar tone in this reference. The dragon of the sea is called Leviathan in scripture and he is described in detail in Job as breathing fire thus causing the water to boil. He is mentioned in 2 Esdras as a coiling serpent in the sea and giant in scope. Gan Eden is the Garden of Eden in fact and interesting that we have that mixed into this word combination.

The Philippines has a character in their history called Bukanawa who is a coiled, giant sea serpent who is so tall, he blocks the moon. Of course, when the Jesuits hijacked that legend they added that he is a god as part of moon worship. We do not believe such feeble attempts to conceal what to us, is obvious. There is even a legend of disappearing ships in the areas of Romblon and Mindoro called the Romblon Triangle. [347] Is it merely happenstance that the area which is named perhaps for Leviathan or at least his Creation on the third day as 2 Esdras mentions, is known to have missing ships? Or is it the streams which flow from the bottom of the ocean floor into the Garden of Eden described in the Book of Enoch perhaps? We will examine that. Additionally, Taal Volcano in Batangas peaks our curiosity as well in Hebrew.

Taal Volcano and Lake: [212]

Hebrew: tahal: תהיל: *Called out or summoned for a specific purpose.*
"Where the Hebrew term "tahal" occurs in the Jewish Scriptures, the
Greek Septuagint uses the word "ekklesian" as the equivalent term, and
it is so translated over ninety times."

Did Taal call out again in 2020? Is it a coincidence this eruption occurred
the week between the Black Nazarene and Sto. Nino celebrations? Or
that Mt. Mayon also erupted in the same period a year or so prior? The
ekklesia in Greek is translated in modern Bibles as church. A prophetic
name for a prophetic people and one must wonder how such a stroke
of luck can occur. Pastor Paul Medrano, a Filipino OFW Pastor and
Seminarian from Saudi Arabia whom we had the pleasure of touring
the Philippines in conferences for a month, also confirmed that tahal in
Arabic carries this same meaning.

Visayas

There are many names in the Philippines especially Visayas that appear
to have Hebrew origins. Certainly, one could take issue with a definition
here or there but overall, there is no debating the Hebrew synergy
which should be present in Ophir and is. For instance, in considering
the Northern Kingdom Lost Tribes migration into the Philippines as
proposed by Columbus and Farrisol especially, it is difficult to ignore
Samar Island.

Samar Island:

Hebrew: samar: סמר: *he / it bristled. Past Tense. [175]*
Bristled in English:
1 (of hair or fur) stand upright away from the skin, as a sign of anger
or fear. 2 react angrily or defensively. 3 (bristle with) be covered with or
abundant in.
Our Interpretation: Standing Upright in Righteous Anger In Abundance

When the Lost Tribes entered the Philippines, it is highly probable they
would have used names to which they were familiar especially the Lost

Tribes of the Northern Kingdom of Israel. These originated in Samaria and descended from Pulag or Peleg. They were taken captive into Assyria and some left Assyria for the Isles of the East or Tarshish which is the Philippines. This word is not only likely of Hebrew origin but specific to the Northern Lost Tribes as it was their capitol in Northern Israel. On it's own, it may appear vague but in lieu of all this evidence, it appears to connect firmly especially when we get to prophecy next as the Queen of the South (Philippines) shall rise up in judgment and condemn this final generation. These etymologies continue to lead to possible Lost Tribes connections. Again, this book is not proving out the Lost Tribes migrations. However, there are several such possibilities in etymologies we will cover because they are there.

Masbate:

Hebrew: mas: מס: *forced laborers, taskworkers, serfdom. [362]*
Hebrew: batem: באתם: *you m. pl. came. [362]*
Our Interpretation: Captives Came

If one considers the Lost Tribes of Israel were serfs or slaves in captivity in Assyria which they left to migrate to the Philippines, then, the logical conclusion is that those captives came to the Philippines. Perhaps some settled in Masbate and named it such in Hebrew especially since it is right next to Samar likely named for Samaria. Just South of Masbate, we find Bohol which also appears in root as Hebrew.

Bohol:

Hebrew: bo': בוא: *to come and go. (motion) [206]*
Hebrew: hol: חול: *sand (as round or whirling particles)... usually sand of seashore, simile of numberlessness, vastness, so of Abraham's seed. [206]*
Our Interpretation: Travelling Industrious Merchants

Bohol appears to have been a bustling harbor perhaps in the territory of Sheba. Where this really gets interesting is the consideration that perchance the people of Bohol may have been sand as of Abraham's seed and even travelled further than imagined. There is even a centuries old claim from the Eskaya Tribe of Bohol that "they are descended from the builders of King Solomon's temple." –Jes B. Tirol [245] What possible context may have brought such a claim? Tirol concluded the Eskaya language was similar to Hebrew as well. We have reviewed modern scholars who wish to avoid such conclusions yet continue to notice the similarities with Hebrew. However, some marginalize Tirol because it doesn't fit their paradigm.

Returning to Creation, imagine if there were an island named after Adam and Eve's first-born daughter. According to the Book of Jubilees which testifies to the daughters and wives as well in the ancient lineages, her name was Awan. She must have been the most beautiful woman ever as she shared the most perfect of genes from the first created couple. Also, Cain married Awan and there is no alternative creation event. The Book of Jubilees annuls such. Cain was Adam's son and not satan's and Genesis says the same. Prove all things.

Palawan:

Hebrew: pala: פאלא: to be surpassing or extraordinary. [176]

Hebrew: awan: און: to eye, look at. [176]

Jubilees 4:1 (R.H. Charles) ...she (Eve) gave birth to her daughter Âwân...

Our Interpretation: Extraordinary First Daughter or Extraordinarily Beautiful

Palawan is certainly Extraordinary to observe in every sense but imagine it being named after Adam's first daughter. This would be unthinkable in any other land but that of Adam and Eve. Otherwise, Awan in Hebrew is beautiful to look at and that is certainly applicable to Palawan which is extraordinarily beautiful indeed.

Realize, we have already reviewed more Hebrew than should be possible even if we were somehow exaggerating. Calculate the odds and just the very nature of all of these very direct and mostly letter for letter references, and that alone makes a case even without all the staggering confirmations but with it, this becomes definitive.

Calamian:

Hebrew: cala: לא: to weigh, compare. [361]
Hebrew: maya'an: מעין: spring(s), fountain(s). [361]
Our Interpretation: Comparable Springs

In the next chapters, we will locate the Garden of Eden in this area with four streams descending down into it. This certainly is a large fluke if so. How about another island named in Hebrew for it's location overlooking the Garden of Eden?

Panay:

Hebrew: al panay: פני: over me: panay is over. [178]
Hebrew: panayim: פנימ: In front of, overlooking. [178]
Hebrew: pana: פנא: before the face of God. [178]

What is Panay Island overlooking or in front of? We will cover in a coming chapter, the Garden of Eden. This is a very appropriate Hebrew name for it's region and we are still only in Northern Visayas in references. The isle adjacent is equally confounding.

Bacolod:

Derived from Old Ilonggo bakolod. [187]
Hebrew: baka!: בכא: (pronounced baw-kaw'): (to a man) split! (imperative). [188]
Hebrew: lod: לד: head of a family of returning exiles, nativity. [189]
Our Interpretation: Head of Scattered, Returning Exiles

One must wonder what the history may be behind such words in Hebrew context. The assumption that all names derive from the Spanish era is ludicrous and even the Muslim era is likely not the case much of the time. The Philippines is far more ancient and the ancients named their land first and to assume otherwise, will lead to false paradigms in which modern academia is loaded as they are unaware of the Hebrew association.

Is this an indication of the split of the Northern Lost Tribes of Israel in Assyria, the returning exiles as they are predicted to return? We have no track to be sure but we continue to find these kinds of markers all over the Philippines. Also, we will cover in the next chapters, Isaiah prophesies that the Philippines will usher in the return of the Lost Tribes of Israel which also identifies that at least some must be there. Between Panay and Bacolod (Negros) lies a tiny island with a very interesting name when understanding the Hebrew.

Guimaras:

Hebrew: goyim: גוים*: nation, people. [236]*
Hebrew: aras: ארש*: betrothed, to engage for matrimony. [237]*
Our Interpretation: Betrothed Nation

One of the odd things with this word is "aras" is also the Filipino designation of the coins which are gifted as a part of the traditional Filipino wedding ceremony. A direct Hebrew tie to the Filipino languages. Who is the betrothed nation? The Bride of Messiah perhaps? This is amazing especially since such thinking is confirmed in one of the reported former names of this country as Maharlika.

Maharlika:

Former Name Associated with the Philippines
Hebrew: mahar: מהר*: to acquire by paying a purchase price, endow, surely, to bargain (for a wife), i.e. To wed. [238]*
Hebrew: lecha: l'cha: lekha: לך*: to/for/of you (indicating possession).*
[239]
Our Interpretation: His Bride Purchased With A Price

We all know this as a reference to His ekklesia in the last days. Very interesting. There are linguists who represent the general academic position on this word originating in the Sanskrit as Mahardhika. No doubt it seems sort of close, but here is the challenge to that thinking. They have not followed the word's migrations and evolution which requires one skipping and going back a generation and then changing the word and somehow we are supposed to believe that is logical etymologically.

This word migrated in use to Indonesia and Malaysia as Merdeka not Mahardhika. That word then travelled into Mindanao and was in use as Merdeka but not Mahardhika. However, we are then told we must believe that it is logical to say that the Filipinos took this word back to it's origin in Sanskrit and made it longer back to Mahardhika and then, transformed it into Maharlika with no historical basis in the slightest yet it is a direct Hebrew word when one audits it. We find it far more logical to acknowledge the connection to Israel and the Hebrew origin of Ophir than to execute such gymnastics which never relate.

How is it that Maharlika and Guimaras both lead in Hebrew to the Bride of Messiah? We will cover this in the prophecy chapter and then, all will come into focus. Yah's people are indeed in the Philippines. Some of these words have the same meaning in Philippine languages and Hebrew.

Mount Cabalian:

"The Hidden Mountain" [To Climbers and locals: 219]

Hebrew: chaba: חבא: Withdraw, hide. [220]

Hebrew: lian: ליאן: greatly, exceedingly, exceedingly beyond measure. [221]

Our Interpretation: Greatly Hidden

The locals and hikers in Leyte refer to this mountain as "The Hidden Mountain." However, in Hebrew, this means "Greatly Hidden." The probable origin is obvious. On Negros Island, there is a mountain with a very odd interpretation for consideration.

Mount Kanlaon

Hebrew: kana: קנה: he / it bought. (past tense) [222]

Greek: kan: καν: though, if so much as, at the least, even. [223]

Greek: laon: λαός: people of God. (Heb. 11:25) [224]

Our Interpretation: Bought People Of God

Now, we have another reference to a people purchased with a price in Hebrew. These are not just any words but the meanings are powerful in scope. Again, at this point in our journey, we have already proven the Philippines is Ophir. Therefore, this is to be expected and it is right there.

Binalbagan:

Hebrew: bin: בִין: *understand, discern, separated, the wise. [177]*
Hebrew: alba: עֲלוֹה: *alvah: rising [177]*
Hebrew: gan: גַן: *an enclosure, garden. [346]*
Our Interpretation: The Wise Rising By The Garden

   This may be another prophetic relation. There are so many to consider. The Surfing Capitol of Mindanao also poses an intriguing probability.

Mindanao

Surigao:

Hebrew: suri: sarai: שׂרִי: *My princess, my senate, noblewoman.[196]*
Hebrew: gaw-al': ga'al: גאל: *to redeem, act as kinsman-redeemer, avenge, revenge, ransom. [197]*
Our Interpretation: My Princess of Redemption

   When naming their child, Tom Cruise and Katie Holmes chose "Suri" which they say is Hebrew for "princess." This has been debated but in the context of Modern Hebrew which is Yiddish-infused. In ancient Hebrew, this is the same word as Sarai or Sarah in the Bible. The YAD on the end or "I" gives the noun a possessive form, and would mean My Princess. The supposed guessed Spanish origin from linguists is "surgir" meaning swift water. That is more sensible than most but still one does not know the origin of that word and that is incomplete but again at least logical in this case. However, the next one makes no sense. They then, suppose it may be derived from "suligao" which certainly appears close but they seem to ignore that it's meaning is "spring water" which is not what Surigao is known for but large surf in salt water and that is not spring water.
   In fact, looking deeper at the more ancient uses, we find it rendered as "zurigan." Now that is interesting because gan is the Hebrew word for garden. My Princess of the Garden? When we cover the prophecy of Messiah later, you will find he says the Queen of the South shall rise up in judgment and that fits this connotation indeed. It also could suggest Eve (Havah).

In considering the feminine characteristics of these words in Havilah, Davao really nails this. Even the government tourism signage in the area explains the origin of Davao is "davah," the aboriginal Obos name for the river. [366] That is Hebrew of peculiar note.

Davao:

Hebrew: davah: daw-vaw': דוה: to be sick (as if in menstruation):— infirmity. [180] (Note: Eve's curse similar to Havilah, childbirth).

We realize at first, this may wax crude but contemplate this perspective. There is a modern prophecy which we would not normally pay attention. It is from Cindy Jacobs whom we do not support nor know much about but this prophecy as we have vetted it, rings true. She identifies that the Philippines will be cleansed through the "bloodiest part." Little does she likely know Davao is literally the bloodiest part in Hebrew not just because of the turmoil there in the past. This prophecy is available on our YouTube Channel. [181] The menstruation female cycle is one of cleansing and this becomes very appropriate as it may be Eve as it ties to her curse from the Garden once again just like Havilah. We would expect this if the Philippines is Ophir. Next to Davao, is a mysterious island.

Samal Island:

Hebrew: samal: סמל: sergeant, image, likeness, symbol. [182]

Samal Island also has areas like Biblical Sion and Kanaan, the correct spellings of both. Is there something about this island which makes it a symbol or emblem for the nation? Just as Davao, we see it likely Samal will be greatly involved in the rising of the Philippines and it is right there in it's Hebrew name prophetically. Here is a very strong name in Hebrew.

Panabo:

Hebrew: pana: פנא: before the face of God. [178]
Hebrew: bo: בא: come and go. (motion) [206]
Our Interpretation: Come and Go Before the Face of God

There is no better definition of a people than those who come and go before the face of God. Around Mindanao, this pattern continues.

Mount Baya:

Hebrew: ba: בא: he / it come(s) or he / it came. [355]

Hebrew: yah: יה: the name of the God of Israel. [356]

Our Interpretation: Yah Comes

Pagadian:

Hebrew: paga: פגע: to meet, make intercession. [364]

Hebrew: daan: דן: leader, judge. [365]

Our Interpretation: Intercessors and Judges

Mount Matutum:

Hebrew: mot, matu: מוט: to totter, shake, slip. [213]

Hebrew: thummim, thum: תום: perfections in breastplate of the High Priest (Ex. 28:30), complete or perfect. [213]

Our Interpretation: Shaking of the High Priest

Unceasingly, we continue to unearth these kinds of references to the High Priest in the Temple, the rising, interceding, judging role of the Philippines in prophecy and the presence of Yahuah. How is this?

Balut Volcano and Island:

Hebrew: balut: בלוט: acorn. [214]

You may be aware of the delicacy (though not our favorite) of the premature duck egg, balut. However, an aerial view of this island reveals an island with trees in the pattern of the geometric shape of the top of an acorn. Perhaps coincidence but interesting. Even the entire island name Mindanao appears Hebrew.

Mindanao:

Hebrew: min: מן: from, of; than, compared to. [216]   min: מן: kind, species. [217] Hebrew: danot: דנות: they discuss. [231]

Our Interpretation: The Species Speaks

We can only speculate on the exact application of such a definition. However, in reference to the aforementioned prophecy from Cindy Jacobs where Davao will lead the cleansing of the nation, is it possible that Mindanao is denoting a similar meaning in Hebrew? Even Mt. Apo opens a different conversation. Not only did the Hebrews of Ophir and brothers migrate to the Philippines but also the Greek Tarshish supplied the ships for their journey. We find references to him on Mindanao especially but none more fascinating than the Greek loan word Apo.

Mount Apo:

Tallest Mountain in the Philippines
Greek: apo: **απο***: from, away (from something near), ago, at, because of, before, of separation of a part from the whole, of origin, of origin of a cause. [228 (selected definitions as there are many)]*
Tagalog: Ancestor, High Leader, Elders, Grandchild.

Most point to Apo as a Greek loan word not originating in the Philippine languages. How does Greek enter the Philippines in use especially in naming it's highest mountain and used in language as Grandparent/ elder or grandchild? Tarshish left his family migrating far away from his elders and likely some of his grandchildren. It makes sense. Leaving Mindanao and Visayas, a brief excursion around Luzon yields more of the same. However, the best transition is Cagayan which is positioned in different forms in all three regions.

Cagayan:

Hebrew: chaggayah: חגיה*: Feast of Yah, a Levite. Origin of name Chaggay or Haggai the prophet. [191]*

One sees this name utilized all over the Philippines in Cagayan Province in North Luzon, Cagayan de Oro and Cagayan Sulu in the Mindanao region, and Cagayancillo in Visayas. Examine the traditional etymologies on the origin of this word and there is no track whatsoever on it's actual root. Assumptions are made without an accurate historical paradigm. The assumption that the Spanish renamed everything is already disproven and to ignore the Philippines existence of a far more sophisticated society who named their own land prior to the Spanish is to ignore even Spanish chroniclers.

> *"Spanish documents in 1500s already referred to the area around Himologan as Cagayan. On January 25, 1571, the Spanish government granted this area, including what is now Northern Mindanao, as an encomienda to Juan Griego."* [192]

What is the origin of this name there and also in the other regions? There is a strong possibility, the Spanish did not name either of these areas Cagayan.

> *"According to Father Miguel Bernad, S.J. of Xavier University, "cagayan" comes from the Malayo-Polynesian word ag, which means "water". Ag is present in words like agus, agusan, and kagay. Agus means "flowing water", and agusan "place of flowing water". Kagay means "river" and kagayan is "place with a river."* [192]

> *"But according to Dr. Lawrence A Reid, Professor Emeritus, Department of Linguistics, University of Hawai`i, "cagayan" comes from an ancient Philippine word *kaRayan, which means "river". In an email sent to the Ancient Baybayin Scripts Network of Yahoogroups, Reid explained, "The evidence for the Proto-Philippine word reconstructable for river, kaRayan, comes from the Ilokano karayan, Central Agta kahayan, Itawis kayan, etc... Note that in all the languages that have a reflex of this form, it simply means 'river'. It is not a morphologically complex form. There is no language that reflects a form kagay. Nor is there any evidence that either the final -an was a suffix, or for that matter that the initial ka- was a prefix ...."* [192]

Even archaeology shows a thriving community in Cagayan de Oro in at least 350 A.D. Cagayan Province has a prehistoric history with the oldest bones of humans and animals found there. [192] Cagayan Sulu is mentioned by Pigafetta and also had a community prior to the Spanish. One scholar claims all it takes is the Malay word "ag" to determine an etymology of the word Cagayan. That's not logic and only a tiny piece of the word. It is not that he may not have a point, it is that he would go public with an opinion of unfinished research which we review consistently from many scholars. What if the Malay word "ag' actually originates in Cagayan instead as modern science proves that the Philippines populated the other Polynesian Islands and not the other way around. The land bridge theory has also crumbled and with it, many of their antiquated etymologies which need to be updated.

What about the other Cagayans? Another scholar attempts to connect "karayan," an Ilocano word, and "Cagayan." Are they now saying Ilocanos migrated to Visayas and Mindinao prior to the Spanish? There is no history to support that and before positing such a theory would it not be wise to consider such? In other words, it only takes "ayan" to connect the words yet would not "Cag" be a different word from "kar" in any language essentially. Is this really logic? They are guessing and these are not hypotheses as that requires educated reason. Instead, we find that the Hebrew word Chaga or Chag means "feast."

If only they were aware of the Hebrew associated through the sons of Eber and the alliance with Israel, many would see this as we. Yah is the name of God and even "yan" is Yah's Grace (יו). [199]. Some say the connection between these four areas is they each have a river. What rivers are even on Cagayan Sulu? They only have lakes. What about Cagayancillo and the Cagayan Islands? Still no significant rivers. Thus, half of the references already fail to support a meaning for rivers which is a stretched etymology that does not connect from a language not even prevalent in three of the four areas until centuries later.

In fact, in Cagayan Province, the people were already referred to as Cagayanos or Cagayanes when the Spanish arrived. Cagayan appears to us based on this evidence, to be of Hebrew ancestry. This is why the word is all over the archipelago because the Feast of Yah mattered all over. How can one think that the Queen of Sheba brought back nothing from Israel in way of answers of God if nothing else? Did the Wise Men just take some gifts there and visit the Son of God and just take selfies and leave as if they were on a pleasure cruise? It is far more likely they brought texts of scripture and great knowledge upon their return that they would have disseminated to the people all over the land of Ophir, Sheba and Tarshish.

Actually, the three Cagayan's in Visayas and Mindanao appear to serve a greater purpose as Cagayan de Oro is on the East border of the Garden of Eden. De Oro is said to refer in Spanish to "of gold" and thus Cagayan assumed river. However, Oros is the Greek word for "mountain" and the gold is in the mountains. [193] Cagayan Sulu is on the Southern border of the Garden. The word Sulu in Akkadian (Phoenician, spoken by Hiram, Solomon's Admiral) is "highway" and the sea was certainly the highway for Solomon's navy. [194] Cagayancillo is on the Northern border of the Garden. "Cilla" is Spanish for "tithe barn, granary, tithe." [195] This is a rather odd circumstance rendering the meaning Tithe of the Feast of Yah. We believe Cagayan is Hebrew in origin as it makes far greater sense than the attempt to connect rivers which are not there in half the areas and we see no support to assume an Ilocono origin of the names of three places in Visayas and Mindanao. Cagayan is far better rendered in Hebrew as "Feast of YAH" than contrived etymologies which have no real basis. As the Philippines is the Land of Creation thus the very region of the first Feasts, of all places on earth, Biblical feasts should be observed there and this will be restored.

Luzon

Abra:

Hebrew: abra: אבר*: Mother of a multitude. Short feminine form of Hebrew Abraham. [185]*

Likely the original gold region in Luzon, Abra is named in the feminine form after Abraham, the forefather of the Israelites as his ancestor's name Pulag, a direct variant of Peleg, brands the tallest mountain on Luzon not far from there. Gold mining and population in these regions far precede the Spanish. Linguists will claim this was named as "The Gap of Vigan" yet Abra is in the mountains and not a gap. Sure, there may be a narrow gap which the river bends along the route but why would one name the gold region after a gap. It appears to us the Spanish were more so attempting to hijack the word. Also, King Solomon's favorite concubine is recorded to have borne the name Abra. [186] Further South in Benguet, there is another mountain of Hebrew potential.

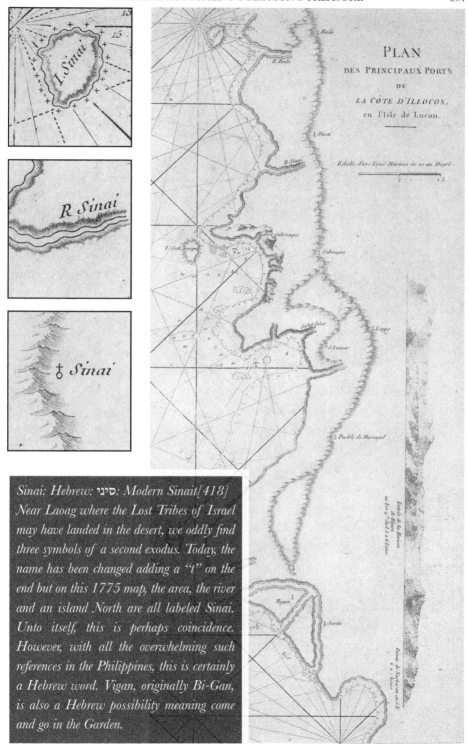

PLAN
DES PRINCIPAUX PORTS
DE
LA CÔTE D'ILLOCOS,
en l'Isle de Lucon.

Echelle d'une Lieue Marines de 20 au Degré.

Sinai: Hebrew: סיני: Modern Sinait[418] Near Laoag where the Lost Tribes of Israel may have landed in the desert, we oddly find three symbols of a second exodus. Today, the name has been changed adding a "t" on the end but on this 1775 map, the area, the river and an island North are all labeled Sinai. Unto itself, this is perhaps coincidence. However, with all the overwhelming such references in the Philippines, this is certainly a Hebrew word. Vigan, originally Bi-Gan, is also a Hebrew possibility meaning come and go in the Garden.

Kabayan:
Region at the foot of Mt. Pulag in Benguet.
Hebrew: chaba: חבא*: Withdraw, hide. [220]*
Hebrew: chabayah: חביה*: Yah has hidden. [354]*
Hebrew: yan: ין*: God's grace. [199]*
Our Interpretation: Hidden by God's Grace

This word is special as it also is used by Filipinos to identify their fellow brothers and sisters locally and abroad as Kabayan or Kababayan. Are the Overseas Filipino Workers also "hidden by God's grace?" Also, has Yahuah hidden a secret in an area known for the mysterious fire mummies of Kabayan which are human remains in caves there preserved through a lengthy dehydration and smoking process which sounds like something from Egypt. Do not forgot the ancestors of the Lost Tribes who came to the Philippines once lived in Egypt and this is located right next to Mt. Pulag or Peleg and we link trade there since ancient times. We could spend much time on mountain names especially but one that bares "to know praise" really captivated our interest.

Sagada: *Mountain Province of Luzon*
Hebrew: saga': שגא*: Laud, praise, exalt. [200]*
Hebrew: yada: ידע*: to know, knowledge. [201]*
         da'at: דעת*: opinion, knowledge. [202]*
Our Interpretation: To Know Praise

In this region, the Igorots have a very arcane custom reported as old as over 2000 years. They hang their dead in coffins from the top of tall mountains. It is almost as if this is a tradition that originates from the time before the Flood as if one knew the Flood was coming, they may attempt to give those ancestor's bones a chance at survival by transferring them to the highest ground possible hanging from a mountaintop. This is an area defined in Hebrew as knowing praise and the Igorots, too, offer a direct etymology in pronunciation.

Igorot:
Hebrew: iggereth: אגרת*: (eeg-ge-roht, iggerOt): A letter, an epistle. [226]*

What kind of writing may this refer? According to R.F. Barton writing in "American Archaeology and Ethnology" in 1919, "It (Igorot law) ranks fairly with Hebrew law." You will also find a similar calendar in the Igorot communities to that of the Bible. [227] Additionally, we have been exploring volcano names as well and many remember this tragic eruption from the 1980s.

Mount Pinatubo:

Hebrew: pinnah: פנה*: Cornerstone.* *[241]*
Hebrew: tub: טוב*: good things, goods, goodness.* *[204]*
Hebrew: bo': בוא*: to come and go. (motion)* *[206]*
Our Interpretation: Cornerstone of Goodness To Come

In Tagolog this means to raise. Is He raising His cornerstone of goodness to come? When we get to prophecy you may respond affirmative. However, how about a mountain that likely bares record to one of the most significant events of all time.

Mount Arayat:

Hebrew: ara: ארע*: Earth.* *[207]*
Hebrew: yaat: יעט*: Covered.* *[208]*
Ilocano: Rescue.
Our Interpretation: Earth Covered

As we find Adam's generations to Noah lived in Havilah, Philippines, we believe Noah would have built the ark on top of a Philippine mountain especially using Narra wood which is why King Solomon pursued it for the Temple. Noah was smart enough to know that mega-tsunamis would decimate anything in the impact zone thus he would have gone to higher ground so he merely had to deal with the rising waters instead. Also, he would have known that the best timber grows near the mountaintops. It is worth mentioning that Narra trees are native and common on top of Mt. Arayat. [209] These are Yahuah's ancient mountains and there is no better marker than one built by the Creator of all things.

Mount Banahaw:

Hebrew: banah: בנה: Build, built. [210]

Hebrew: Yah: יה: Creator God, short for Yahuah. [356]

Our Interpretation: Built by Creator God

The Hebrew word banah is the same used in the Creation account in Genesis 2:22 when Yahuah made (banah: built) a woman from Adam's rib. Many of these words are not just arbitrary but ones of the most significant meanings such as this. Another mountain of note is yet another very direct Hebrew reference.

Mount Mayon:

Hebrew: maya'an: מעין: spring of water. [361]

Until we visited there, we had no idea that the amount of water which originates from this volcano provides for families for many kilometers especially due to it's grade and it is known as the cleanest on Earth according to locals there. In addition, as Enoch nears the Garden of Eden, just to the North of it, he observes a mountain erupting with water. We see no evidence of Mayon erupting water but perplexing connection. Just to the South, Naga offers the same.

Naga:

Hebrew: naga: נגע: he / it touched. [215]

What did He touch in Naga? With all the other citations, it seems that a holy definition would make sense though this is very general and broad. However, Naga is a Hebrew word indeed. We even analyzed some of the popular fruits in the Philippines which appear appropriate in letters and definition.

Saba: Banana

Hebrew: saba: שבע: Satisfied, fulfilled, have one's fill of. [232]

In modern Hebrew this could also mean "grandfather." We can imagine when Solomon's navy first arrived or even Joktan's sons perhaps, they took one look at the abundant saba and ate and were satisfied and had their fill. The definition fits the fruit. Even the so-called Tree of Life, though not the actual tree that we can assess, seems to attach to Hebrew roots.

Buko: Coconut

Hebrew: buk'u: בוקעו*: they were split. [233]*

What does one do with the buko, they split it open. Intriguing prospect. With reservation, we even tackled what is referred to as the "Creator God of the Tagalogs" whom the Jesuits represent as a pagan god yet we question this because this emerges Hebrew. We explore this fully in an entire video thus this will be a brief.

Bathala: Ancient Creator God of the Tagalogs

Hebrew: bath: בת*: Hebrew measure (as a means of division) of liquids. [234]*
Genesis 1:6 KJV And God said, Let there be a firmament in the midst of the waters, and let it divide the waters from the waters.
Hebrew: ala: עלם*: a rib, to go up or ascend. [235]*
Genesis 2:22 KJV And the rib, which the Lord God had taken from man, made he a woman, and brought her unto the man.

These two words in Hebrew both point to the Creator God from scripture. Ask yourself how this is possible. We are aware of the narrative of Bathala being a pagan god which includes worship of Anitos or demons of sort. However, we cover this in our Bathala video, when the Jesuits ask the Filipinos about Bathala, they tell them they only worship Bathala and not the Anitos and not the bird. Of course, immediately after receiving their answer which one time even includes a warning by the Filipino not to worship anyone else, the Jesuits still continue to write about Anito idols, etc. We believe the ancient Filipino word on this as they are the ones who lived there and we observe this often in the historic record. Even the Presidential Palace provides astounding thought.

Malacañang Palace:

Name of the Presidential Palace in the Philippines

Hebrew: mal'ak: מלאך: from an unused root meaning to dispatch as a deputy; a messenger; specifically, of God, i.e. an angel (also a prophet, priest or teacher):--ambassador, angel, king, messenger. [242]

Hebrew: achyan: אחין: Hebrew name meaning "brotherly" or "fraternal." In the bible, this is the name of a member of the tribe of Manasseh. [243]

Hebrew: anan: ענן: Bring [244]
Our Interpretation: Righteous Priests to Bring My Brothers

This coincidentally fits the prophecy we will cover from Isaiah 60:9 and others where the Lost Tribes of Israel are literally ushered in by the ships of Tarshish which is the Philippines who are also the isles waiting for His law to be restored. Manasseh is not just any tribe but the tribe of Joseph's oldest son. His other son Ephraim was given the birthright but in Revelation, the two tribes of Joseph's sons are together as one. Without Manasseh and Ephraim, there can be no re-gathering of the Tribes of Israel as the birthright lies with them. Judah never received this birthright thus has no right to re-establish the land of Israel but they inherited the scepter and Messiah, who is from Judah, has possession of that scepter today and forever and it shall never depart from the throne of David as prophesied. Add to this we already covered the word Lequii referring to inhabitants of Luzon which is the name of the Grandson of Manasseh.

In fact, the Lost Tribes of Israel were also identified by region at least for one migration into an area beyond a river which the Pharisees have lost from their own Bible – the Targum Psuedo-Jonathan in Aramaic. Please note, we do not use this as scripture nor any writing of any Rabbi ever but simply the geographic name of this river where some of the Lost Tribes will be exiled and they offer extremely poor explanations because they are exploring the wrong lands. This is one of the warning verses to Israel if it breaks covenant with Yahuah.

Sambatyon River:

Exodus 34:10 Targum Psuedo-Jonathan: Warning To Israel
I will take them from there and place them on the other side of the
Sambatyon River.

The Rabbis even today have no concept of where this Sambatyon River is located nor the origin of the name. This is because they are unaware of the land this references as this is the language of that land not Hebrew, Aramaic, Latin nor Greek. None of the Bible languages apply as the root of this word. Notice the clues they offer which has been handed down yet they have no idea where this is still.

Jerusalem Talmud (Sanh. 10:6, 29c)
"According to the Jerusalem Talmud, however (Sanh. 10:6, 29c), the
exiles were divided into three. Only one-third went beyond the Sambatyon,
a second to "Daphne of Antioch," and over the third "there descended a
cloud which covered them"; but all three would eventually return." [348]
This legend is also mentioned in Josephus Flavius (Wars: 7:96-97) and
Greek author Pliny the Elder (Historia Naturalis 31:24)." [348]

"The first ascription of miraculous qualities to this river is found in the
*Talmud. When *Tinneius Rufus asked R. Akiva how he could prove*
that the Sabbath was divinely ordained as the day of rest, he replied,
"Let the River Sambatyon prove it" (Sanh. 65b). It was unnavigable
on weekdays because it flowed with strong currents carrying along stones
with tremendous force, but it rested on the Sabbath (Gen. R. 11:5).
These passages give no indication as to the supposed location of the river
or of the origin of its name. The only inference that can be drawn from
them is that it was located in Media. The most extensive description
of both its name and locality is given by Namanides (to Deut. 32:26).
He identified the river with the River Gozan of the Bible (e.g, II
Kings 17:6), explaining the name (on the basis of Num. 11:31) as
meaning "removed," i.e., the ten tribes were "removed" from their people.
Namanides also held that its name derived from its Sabbath rest, since
Sabbat was the local word for the Sabbath."[203]

Eldad ha-Dani claimed that the Sambatyon did not surround the land of the ten tribes but rather that of the children of Moses (Levites):

"The children of Moses are surrounded by a river resembling a fortress, which contains no water but rather rolls sand and stones with great force. If it encountered a mountain of iron it could undoubtedly grind it into powder." *[203]*

Before we continue in this channel of thought, please understand this is lined with leaven and there is much added as you can see. In fact, observe how they operate because this has been happening for over 2000 years and it is time we discern beyond such expansions. We could show you even more examples which just plain become ludicrous stopping just short of alien craft sightings in scope yet some esteem to modern Pharisees as scholars. When even a little leaven is added, it creates false paradigms (Gal. 5:9).

Matthew 16:6-12 KJV
Then Jesus said unto them, Take heed and beware of the leaven of the Pharisees and of the Sadducees.

As we catalogue these descriptions, the Sambatyon is known as Sabbath River. Where was the first Sabbath? In the Land of Creation which is the Philippines which is surrounded by the ancient Pison River from Eden. The Pison River is the Sabbath River by definition and no other river could fit. Even it's root definition, prophetically as it is a very ancient word, means "be scattered." It is almost as if Yahuah knew the Lost Tribes would migrate there. He did.

Pison:
piyshown: פישון*: increase, overflowing. [349]*
From Root Word: puwsh: a primitive root; to spread; figuratively, act proudly:—grow up, be grown fat, spread selves, be scattered. [349]

This river operates with such strength that it has strong currents carrying along stones with tremendous force, rolls sand and stones with great force and grinds mountains into powder. Again, this is leaven as you can see as they expand their story like the one-armed fisherman who "caught a fish this big." The Pison River was at the end of the Eden River System with the very deepest trenches on Earth as you will find in the River From Eden chapter later. It would have operated before the Flood with such force and still flows today with sand and rocks. It seems these Rabbis are a bit confused on their timeline and descriptions but enough has survived that their descriptions lead to the Philippines though none of them may ever admit it which is unnecessary to restore truth. Even more conspicuous, in the Tagalog language of the Philippines, the word Pison means "to crush or steam-roll."

Tagalog: pison: Steam-roller, to crush. [350]

Finally, they discuss this river forms a fortress around the Lost Tribes. Indeed, the Pison River surrounds the whole land of Havilah, Philippines. Even their reference that the Lost Tribes migrated into three regions fails to match their own reporting of their Mass Aliyah from 1948-1952 but does actually fit Isaiah 11 which identifies exactly three areas and only three for these mass migrations and they will return from those same three lands. The Ethiopic of St. Matthew takes this even deeper as it identifies the Lost Tribes hidden beyond the Sambatyon River in the Garden of Eden in a tropical area. This is the Philippines. We especially realized this when our viewers began to weigh in on this en masse as Filipinos recognized these words immediately.

"Sambatyon sounds like a Filipino word." – DeLaCruzer11
"Sabat in our native dialect means meet or to meet." – Aie Dns
"Sambat: Sabbath/Worship/Samba. Yon: Their." – Maniah Man
"Sabat in bisaya means to join." – Bangtan Sonyeondan
"We have this in iloilo as an ilonggo saying "indi na mag SABAT."
that means you are telling somebody to 'STOP OR REST' from giving
opinions, clarifications, etc.." – Geruin Fetalino
"sambat (Tagalog) n. point at which a road or river forks into two." –
Mon G
"Sambatyon is like 2 ilokano words combined. "Samba" is worship or

give praise, "tyon" is like the pronoun tayon in Ilokano which means "us." Just like saying in Ilokano "mangan tayon" - LET US EAT. So it might mean LET US WORSHIP." – froicabuling

Meet, Their Sabbath, Their Worship, Rest, Join and Let Us Worship all tie very nicely to the purpose of this River and to the Lost Tribes of Israel. Even the river that forks into two is exactly what the Pison River does when it surrounds the whole land of Havilah, Philippines. The Rabbis can stop (or Sabat) guessing on this from now on. They can know the truth. The Sambatyon surrounds the Philippines.

We could publish an entire book just on the many Hebrew possibilities in the Philippine languages as we hear from Filipinos on the topic almost daily and we continue to uncover so many more in our research. It is truly amazing. Regarding the Lost Tribes of Israel, this research continues to touch that topic but let us be clear, we have not made a case for such in this book and that is another whole book. We have a full series of over 25 videos on the Lost Tribes of Israel even testing modern Israel and the Bible does not lead there. Whether you accept every word as having such origin is immaterial but one cannot deny that the link is established and our criteria set forth has met the burden of proof for tertiary support.

....

Bulawan:

"birth of the first daughter"
Hebrew: bul: בול: produce, to bring forth, outgrowth [416]
Hebrew: awan: און: to eye, look at. [176]
Jubilees 4:1 ...she (Eve) gave birth to her daughter Âwân... Similar to Havilah in Hebrew!

Photo: Philippines. Piloncito (ca. 10th-11th Century) or "bulawan." Very Fine. 0.17 gms. Barnaby's Auctions. Piloncitos, a type of gold nugget with Baybayin Ma characters which could be a symbol for the nation of Ma-i. Used as one of the early currencies along with gold rings according to Bangko Sentral. [129]

Chapter 14 | Not Ophir
Other Claims Dismantled

Let's resolve right to the heart of the matter. The principal assertions for other regions who wish to be Ophir all either originate or are supported by the British. In essence, it is the British who are suppressing this history and geography of the Philippines initially with the assistance of America. Spain rebranded things and certainly operated with loathing distaste but still identified the Philippines as Ophir and Tarshish and the record reflects this in their writings. When Britain could not win a direct debate, they moved to offering confusion in making assertions of Ophir in multiple locations in which they cannot even agree with themselves nor do they ever substantiate anything which is clearly not their intention but to offer chaos and distraction which is a tactic we have seen often. This comes from so-called scholars yet their ignorance on the topic is the most profound we have seen.

All of this however, was performed under the rule of the Holy Roman Empire from the conquest to the hand-over from Spain to the U.S. who supposedly purchased the entire Philippines for the lump sum of $20 million. This confuses us greatly as why did the U.S. not then grant the Philippines their independence immediately if they were not yet another conquering power? Why would the Philippines have to fight for their freedom against America who clamped down on the Philippines around 1900 like any other colonial power killing as many as 2 million Filipinos in some estimates. They were finally granted their freedom in a sense after becoming America's battleground in World War 2 while the whole mainland America remained unscathed. Their stranglehold on the economy has continued until this day in many arenas.

Also, for a mere $20 million knowing the resources of the Philippines, why was the Philippines not offered the right to purchase it's own freedom at that time rather than selling it to the U.S.? If America was not a conquering power, it would have offered the Philippines that option. However, even in the Treaty of Paris of 1783, the United States is defined as part of the Holy Roman Empire to which the King of England remained Prince Elector and the Americans signed it too confirming such but under their British titles still servants of the crown. One cannot separate the two powers regardless of what narratives we have accepted. Unfortunately, as we reviewed in the chapter on history, that is when the world developed amnesia and misplaced Ophir in the 1890s or so.

However, even before then, Ethiopia began to assert claims not just of Ophir but the Queen of Sheba with her goat legs and hoof which is preposterous. That is their claim as well not ours. In all fairness, Ethiopia is a precious and special land but it cannot be Ophir in Ham's territory nor Ophir's brother Sheba. We have already covered that Ethiopia is missing resources on Solomon's list thus invalidated. They are West of the Red Sea not East thus disqualified. They are West of Iran thus ruled out. They are not islands thus any claim is just postulation. We have even seen one channel out there completely destroy it's credibility by attempting to move Shem's land into Africa including Israel, Babylon, Assyria and even Rome. In Africa? There is no logic which can do this and the rejection of European history does not justify such behavior as African maps say otherwise and so does the Book of Jubilees which was preserved in the Ethiopian canon.

The Bible is very deliberate Abraham lived in Canaan/Israel and went South into Egypt (Gen. 12:10) and then, upon leaving headed North back to Canaan/Israel (Gen. 13:1). However, they seem to be willing to go to any length as then, they claim the maps are all upside down. The problem is for those of us who have owned a compass and used it, Israel is still North of Egypt and one cannot change that. Pigafetta records in his journal in fact that he was in South America and the compass still pointed North. [79] If Ethiopia had any resemblance of a coherent declaration, we would be happy to consider it. They do not.

Some attempt a massive stretch that Abraham's grandson named Epher(עפר) is Ophir(אופיר) as the origin of the word Africa but even if that did match the name, which it does not, that's not Ophir from Joktan and actually would serve as evidence to the contrary. Having said that, that view lacks Biblical geography as Jubilees calls Africa, 'Afrâ(המזרח) not Ophir(אופיר) nor Epher(עפר). These are not the same words.

There is no history in Ethiopia to support such an allegation. There are no true archaeological finds, though claimed. The supposed Queen of Sheba gold discovery where they found no gold nor anything related to the Sheba who descended from the brother of Ophir fails. British Archaeologist Louise Schofield identified a temple which dated to 200 A.D. with artifacts of the same era not in 1000 B.C. when Sheba came to visit Solomon. There was a cave next to this temple which she believes would have gold inside, if the entrance were not blocked and she actually entered it that is. She did not but that did not stop the Guardian and others from picking up a dubious story with no factual evidence of the Queen of Sheba.

However, we keep bumping into Ethiopia who seems to make a claim for many things without ever producing evidence. We prove the Southern Kingdom of Israel migrated there among other regions in Africa on our channel so they have a good claim but not with Ophir and Sheba. However, they also declare they house the Ark of the Covenant in a small church yet many have been inside the entire church and no one has died approaching it nor has anyone ever found it there. Perhaps Indiana Jones could have saved a lot of time as well as Hitler in real life. Also, they claim to have the Gihon River from Eden running through a small portion of Ethiopia but this ignores the Genesis 2 passage entirely which says the Gihon surrounds the whole land of Ethiopia which in Bible times was all of Central Africa not Abysinia exclusively which was only a tiny sliver. This Blue Nile river surrounds nothing whether alone the whole land.

Further, Genesis 2:5 is clear it did not rain before the Flood as their was a mist which came up to water the face of the entire earth. The Blue Nile would not exist prior to the Flood as it's source is rainfall collected in the Lake Tana basin. Every Ethiopian chronicle is so royally divergent from the Bible origin as the Goat Lady Queen is not the right Sheba, the ark is not there or it would be found already if so and the Blue Nile would be "nil" (zero) prior to the Flood. Ethiopia should focus on the Lost Tribes narrative instead because there, they have foundation to reinforce a strong case.

The British are supporting this myth and propagating it with others at the same time which is their obvious tactic to suppress the real Ophir, Sheba and Tarshish. They can attempt but they have no collateral history, no where near the gold of the Philippines except South Africa who is not linked to Cush's grandson Sheba which is the wrong family anyway for this account. The Philippines possesses the actual gold today and in history, every resource, and no one can disprove this and then locate Ophir in Africa in any Biblical theory because the Bible says otherwise.

Yemen has the same challenges which we have covered especially obliterating the inaccurate etymologies from over a thousand years later which are not the progenitors of Mesha, Sephar and certainly not the Mount of the East which must also be in the Garden of Eden. We will expound in the next chapters. They do not natively maintain all the resources on Solomon's list. With these two areas being all of 3-4 months round trip journey from Israel down the Red Sea, not only can they not fit any description of the excursion, but the notion that King Solomon would wait once every three years to go there would be to accuse him of being complacent.

The best response they have for that is that Solomon waited every three years due to the tithe tradition of that time recorded in the Book of Tobit 1:7-8. However, they are not even reading such passages which clarify Tobit paid the tithe to the Temple the second year not the third when he gave undeviatingly to the widows and orphans not the Temple. Tobit was giving annually not every 3 years just to different causes each year. Ophir is not a land of widows and orphans nor was King Solomon's navy jaunting there to give a tithe but to trade for goods. One does not have those resources three months away and decide to wait three years to acquire them especially from Yemen nor Ethiopia who were already trading partners and Yemen giving tribute even. The challenge is there is no litigating that Ophir ever lived in Saudi Arabia nor Yemen nor Ethiopia thus there is no reconciling anything intelligible in researching these pontifications based in ignorance.

The debate Britain put forth, though never disproving Spain had found Ophir nor did they try head-on to address such, was quite the rage in the 1600's for over 200 years. Then, when Spain lost the war, the debate disappeared. It was never won by the British. They lost and still do.

Much of this case originates with Samuel Purchas from "Purchas His Pilgrims" in 1625. Purchas assumes Ophir in India and the British East Indies, only British territories of course. He cites historians who are basing their assumptions on etymology and uses antiquated geography ignoring Magellan completely. [246] He intimates Tarshish as Peru perhaps. This was a British find in which Sir Francis Bacon, the Freemason, was obsessed. Right or wrong, it proves though, the British did not believe Tarshish was Britain.

> *"Although he collected accounts of travels over the entirety of the known world, Purchas himself never set foot outside England. In Purchas his Pilgrimes, he tells us that he has never been "200 miles from Thaxted in Essex where I was borne." [247]*

> *"Purchas wrote Purchas his Pilgrimes under the patronage of the East India Company. The Company awarded Purchas 100 pounds to assemble the book and gave him access to many of the letters and manuscripts that Purchas would draw on in writing his magnum opus." [247]*

> *"The Rothschild family was one of the controller families of the East India Company." [248]*

Purchas was a Rothschild puppet paid to propagate the opposition to the Philippines as Ophir. That's called propaganda. Imagine even today, the founder of Facebook who has even at one time shut down our page and continues to attempt censorship at times, also happens to be a Rothschild family descendant. His is no rags to riches story nor one where he actually invented anything but stole someone else's great idea and he had access to the funding to make it viral as few would ever have.

Also, Purchas did not travel to the Philippines, India, Malaysia nor Peru. His position is solely based on antiquated scholarship who had lost Ophir when Spain surely found it. It was right in front of his nose but he was paid to explain it away. This is another example of willing ignorance as defined by 2 Peter 3. Permit us to test the more credible claim of India first as it has the resources and is in the right direction though it still cannot fit the narrative.

Britain's Assertion: India

India's challenge as Ophir per The Periplus is it's own history which details it's source of gold in ancient times was located in the isles East of India. This legend persisted in Sri Lanka as well thus, it would not qualify either as it is only an isle and not isles nor is it East of India. This is the only claim out there other than the Philippines that meets the burden in resources but history and the fact it is not an island crush it. We dealt with Malaysia already in Chapter 3.

> *A Dictionary of the Bible by Sir William Smith, published in 1863, notes "the Hebrew word for parrot Thukki, derived from the Classical Tamil for peacock Thogkai and Cingalese "tokei."*
> *—Sir William Smith, Smith's Bible Dictionary, 1863 [249]*

Smith focuses heavily in this writing on the Hebrew word Thukki which he never proves is Tamil. Yes, Thogkai and Tokei are sort of similar but a different language and one would need more to connect. Additionally, the word parrot which he seems to be focused never appears in any Bible translation even once. It is not in the *KJV, NKJV, NLT, NIV, ESV, CSB, NASB, NET, RSV, ASV, YLT, DBY, WEB, HNV, RVR60, VUL, WLC, LXX, mGNT, or TR* translations. Additionally, ancient words from scripture do not originate from other languages that are newer. The Book of Jubilees is clear, Hebrew was the "language of Creation" (Jub. 12:26-27).

Even Chabad, likely the largest Jewish group of synagogues worldwide, expresses this. *"We know from the Scriptures, that King Solomon imported tukkiyyim (parrots, in Modern Hebrew) from Tarshish. But according to the commentators and ancient translations, tukkiyyim is a reference to peacocks." [250]* Modern Hebrew is of no consequence in this as it is infused with other languages.

Thus no one has ever produced evidence that these were ever parrots but they are well recorded as peacocks. Even some modern translations will render this as baboons but the Philippines has those too. However, this is just a continued effort to confuse and a poor one.

Peacocks: Hebrew: tukkiy: תכיים: *TUKIYIM. [251]*

India has native peacocks as well as every resource as the Philippines except never as rich in gold and never known as the land of gold but their source of gold is Chryse/Ophir, Philippines. We covered in a Chapter 3 the history from The Periplus of the Erythaean Sea including it's directions East of India, Southeast of China and supported by Pomponius Mela's World Map of 43 A.D., Dionysius The Tourist's Map of 124 A.D. and the 1492 Globe of Behaim. These directions come from the Indians. Ophir is not India.

The Periplus records Indians all over the coasts of mainland India and in Ceylon (Sri Lanka) as acquiring their gold from an island to the East of India called Suvarnadhipa or Suvarnadwipa which means, "Islands of Gold." Mainland India is not considered islands. Some claim this may be Sumatra but there is no history to support that conjecture either. Certainly, there is gold in Sumatra but it does not compare to the Philippines which has always been the land of gold. In fact, on Mela's, Dionysius's and Behaim's maps, one passes Sumatra thus it is not Ophir. Even the British did not claim Sumatra as Ophir but the Malay Peninsula which we will cover. Regardless, this is more testimony India is not Ophir.

According to the Ilocos Sur Archaeology Project from the Philippines, in their published findings in 2015, Luzon Island with gold from the Abra area is Suvarnadhipa, "islands of gold." This is well supported with the right kind of archaeology, gold itself in massive abundance over thousands of years. [252] The case for the Philippines is too well-proven.

According to Nathaniel Ben Isaiah, a Bible commentator in the 14th century, in Jewish tradition (the Talmud), Ophir is in India based on word association yet again.

> *"Ophir is often associated with a place in India, named for one of the sons of Joktan." [253]*

There is no place in modern India named for a son of Joktan but we will address whom this likely refers. Perhaps he assigns the former capital of Tajikistan named Joktan but that would not be a son nor would it be

Ophir. Tajikistan is not that far from Meshad, Iran where Joktan once lived before their migration to Sephar, the Mount of the East which would become known as Ophir. This name would represent a residual reference to Joktan who once lived in that region very appropriately but not his migration. He is more likely referencing what he believes to be the name of Ophir in India which others have claimed erroneously.

"Alternative spellings of both variants... Opheir, Sophír, Sopheír and Souphír occur in the Septuagint..." (Σωφηρα) [254]

This leads to a poor assumption even Wikipedia hardly makes anymore. The assumption is this sounds like Ophir and it does indeed. The thinking is that Sophir is possibly an Egyptian name for ancient India. The problem is we cannot find any evidence.

In fact, a statue with Egyptian carvings in Iran circa. 500 B.C. has been unearthed demonstrating the Egyptian name of India as H-n-d-w-y-a. [255] This also matches the Hebrew name for India that appears twice in the Book of Esther (1:1, 8:9: הדו) and confirmed in the Book of Jubilees (9:4: הודו) in Hebrew as:

Photo: The Statue of Darius exhibited at the National Museum of Iran Archives de la Maison Archéologie & Ethnologie, René-Ginouvès, JP_V03. Mission de Suse. c. 500 B.C. On the left side of the base is a list of conquered territories rendered in Egyptian hieroglyphs. India is rendered in Egyptian as "H-n-d-w-y-a" which is very close to the word India. [255]

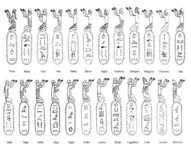

India: Hebrew: Hoduw: הדו: H-d-w or H-u-d-w [253]

Does Hoduw lead to Sophir? No. Nor does the Egyptian "H-n-d-w-y-a" but it is similar to the Hebrew word which makes sense but Sophir does not. That is because there is no such thing as the word Ophir being rendered as Sophir. They are confusing what the writers of the Septuagint were doing and you will find this to be very obvious.

> *1 Kings 9:28 Greek Septuagint*
> *And they came to Sopheira (Σωφηρα), and fetched from thence gold, four*
> *hundred and twenty talents, and brought it to king Solomon.*
> *Chrysion: gold (9x) [256]   Sopheira: ophir?*

Ooops! Did we get this wrong? Is Sopheira the same as the word Ophir? No, it is a substitute word that is very appropriate but it is not the word Ophir. Remember, Ophir is first recorded in Genesis 10. When you examine that in the Greek Septuagint, this becomes evident.

> *Genesis 10:29-30 KJV*
> *And Ophir, and Havilah, and Jobab: all these were the sons of Joktan.*
> *And their dwelling was from Mesha, as thou goest unto Sephar a mount*
> *of the east.*

> *Genesis 10:29-30 Greek Septuagint In Greek*
> *καὶ Ουφιρ(OPHIR) καὶ Ευιλα(Havilah) καὶ Ιωβαβ (Jobab) πάντες*
> *οὗτοι υἱοὶ Ιεκταν. καὶ ἐγένετο ἡ κατοίκησις αὐτῶν ἀπὸ Μασση ἕως ἐλθεῖν*
> *εἰς Σωφηρα(SEPHAR) ὄρος ἀνατολῶν. [257]*

Here we see a portion of the register of Joktan's lineage including Ophir which in the Septuagint is rendered as: Oupir (Greek: Ουφιρ). Thus, Ophir in Greek is still Ophir pretty much. However, Sopheira is the Greek rendering of the word Sephar. Ophir migrated to Sephar and from that point the name was changed to Ophir thus, we should be looking for Ophir not Sephar or Sophir in Greek. This is a dead end reference which leads nowhere though scholars have taken off on just this alone principally for centuries. Somehow, they never bothered to read the verse of origin for Ophir in Genesis 10 in Greek to realize the word Sophira is Sephar not Ophir. Of course, that may become inconvenient for their theories.

Therefore, every leg the British have attempted to set in place for a case for India as Ophir is now removed and their theory comes crashing to the ground. Indian history is apparent as they had a source of gold not in Mainland India nor Sri Lanka but isles to the East. The etymology of Sophir is not Ophir but Sephar and that land was renamed Ophir since about 2200 B.C. with no connection to India whatsoever. Egyptian history has no record of a Sophir referring to India but in antiquity, the Egyptians called India by a name very close to the Bible name of Hoduw. As we have witnessed in their translation of these two words of this narrative Ophir as Oupir and Sephar as Sophira, the Greek Septuagint would also translate the name of India more closely and accurately if they were referring to that same region. There are no legs left. Sorry Britain and India but we desire to know the true Ophir not fanciful legends in which usurp the true land of gold's history with no justification. It is time to refrain from positing bad theories.

Britain's Petition: Malay Peninsula

In the 1800's, Britain must have been becoming extremely desperate in this debate which they had already lost no doubt because they were lacking the one thing they needed most – the truth. In all their narratives we have reviewed, we do not see them attempt to tackle the position of Ophir in the Philippines directly but they ignore it and plant yet another Ophir flag in another area in confusion and chaos. In 1801, they tipped their hand too much and entered into an arena of what many would consider fraud as they continue to propagate an already old, disproven paradigm of Malaysia being Ophir. The Portuguese first conquered Malaysia and we have produced numerous quotes they believed Malaysia was not Ophir and Tarshish. Pinto recorded Malaysians providing directions to Ophir, Philippines. We showed you the progression and maps.

MT. OPHIR (Malay: Gunung Ledang)
"a mountain in the Gunung Ledang National Park located in Tangkak
District (formerly part of Muar), Johor, Malaysia." "It has been called
"Ophir" by British cartographers since at least 1801, based on a map
from that year." –Malaysia Tourism [258]

1862 British Map of
Malaysian Peninsula.
T. Moniot. Showing
Mt. Ophir. National
Archive of Singapore.
Public Domain. [259]

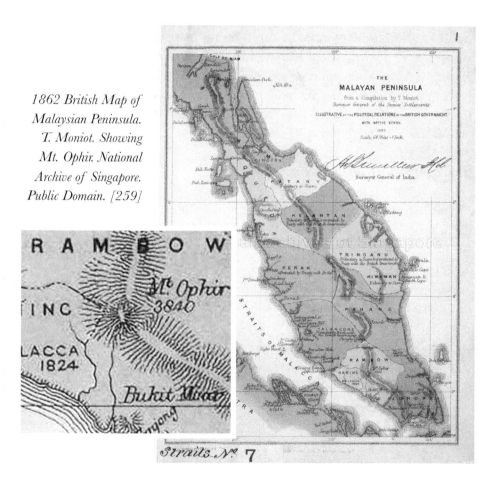

Who called it Ophir? The British cartographers according to the Johor Malaysian Tourism office. When reading this article from the Tourism office, they are careful to clarify Mt. Ophir is a British name and creation because they still call it Gunung Ledang even in their tourism article from 2014. The local Malays rejected this new British name. In the same era, it turns out there was a second mountain in which they also attempted to rebrand as Mt. Ophir – Mount Talakmau in Pasaman County, West Sumatra, Indonesia [254] which is actually in Ham's territory even not Shem's. Note the Portuguese who possessed these lands previously did not refer to Malaysia nor Indonesia as Ophir in the end as both Magellan and Barbosa, though sailing for the Spanish at the time but Portuguese prior, discovered Ophir in the Philippines. That second one did not stick at all. Frankly, in all of our research, though Britain attempts this stunt, we do not really find local Malays nor Indonesians making such claims as Ophir. They knew better.

One other very major challenge with this allegation is that Ophir (Chryse) and Tarshish (Argyre) are isles not a Peninsula. This fails any test of history and geography.

Britain's Claim: Peru

Even before Purchas published his books, the British Freemasons were already making the claim that Peru was Ophir.

> "The Alchemist" by Ben Jonson, 1610
> (Sir Francis Bacon's Freemason Friend) [261]
> MAMMON. Come on, sir. Now, you set your foot on shore
> In novo orbe; Here's the rich Peru:
> And there within, sir, are the golden mines,
> Great SALOMON'S Ophir! He was sayling to't
> Three yeeres, but we have reach'd it in ten months.
> (2.1.1–5) [399]

Believe it or not, since no one is out there disproving this disinformation, the myth continues to be kept alive because they will say no one knows where Ophir could be. When you offer up such nonsense, no wonder.

However, Ophir is well-attested as the Philippines and really nowhere else. We agree looking at the other claims, one would certainly arrive at the conclusion no one knows because they are meant to accomplish exactly that. They lead one in multiple directions in circles only to conclude, this just cannot be known. The Bible is not so vague nor is history and these positions are not even supported beyond very shallow guesses. Even Wikipedia on Ophir, has an article that makes the case for India and that takes up most of the article. The last paragraph is on the Philippines in a total misrepresentation of it's case with a few sentences about Documentos Relativos... but that document merely gives Spain's directions to Ophir. It is secondary support, not an actual view.

In 1966, this position resurfaced in modern archaeology thus it must be proven now right? Wrong. This claim comes directly from the Blogsite of Archaeologist Gene Savoy.

> *"Northern Peru at the headwaters of the Amazon River where he found a cave that housed three stone tablets or tables, one of which was roughly six feet long with carvings hewn into the stone in very ancient Hebrew and Phoenician that seems to say:*
> *(translation of these very ancient Hebrew and Phoenician glyphs is somewhat problematic. It is estimated that they are from around 900 BC at the time of Solomon's Temple construction, so the availability of scholars that are familiar with that old of writing is a problem so we need more research to absolutely verify the literal meaning of the inscriptions)."*
> *—Gene Savoy [261]*

Photo: Gene Savoy's Trip to Peru. Map By The God Culture. ©The God Culture. [261]

Even if these tablets were proven to have Phoenician writing distinctly from Solomon's era, it does not prove Peru to be Ophir. However, here is the bulkiest objection. The tablets map out a trip which we took the liberty of providing (previous page). They crossed the Atlantic Ocean not the Pacific as there is no point of entry by river on the West Coast of Peru. They travelled up the Amazon River (huge river), from the Atlantic Ocean. The people they encountered had gold. Explorers and merchants have been trading gold for thousands of years. Does that make every place that had gold no matter how much Ophir? Not remotely. This says nothing. So they had gold. A lot of lands did. Did they have $12 Billion of gold like Ophir supplied in 970-930 B.C.? Are they the number two nation on earth in untapped gold deposits? Do they have a concurrent history since before 1000 B.C. of having a gold rush? They would have to. Ultimately, this entire claim is based on the most simple-minded of approaches. Peru must be Ophir because it has…. P-R.

Even Samuel Purchas had to come clean on this one and conclude that Peru could not be Ophir. He recognized the absence of native resources in Peru for peacocks and ivory. He identifies the length of the journey cannot fit the three-year round trip of scripture. Indeed, Purchas too realized it was a 3-year journey. They also do not have red sandalwood. This is written in Old English from the original format of the writing of Purchas on this topic.

> *"Lastly, Peru could not be Ophir, if wee conceiue that SALOMON brought thence Iuorie; and Peacockes. For Peacockes they read Parrots, and for Iuorie they are forced to take it vp by the way in some place of Africa or India, which distraction must needs prolong the Voyage, which without such lets could not (as before is obserued) in three yeares bee performed." [262]*

In the end, Purchas dismissed Peru as Ophir but alludes Peru could still be Tarshish instead and this assuming India and the Indies (the British portion only of course) were Ophir. However, the trip to Tarshish in 2 Chronicles produced the same peacocks and ivory and must be three years as he just overcame Peru. In fact, the trip to Peru from the Red Sea to the East through the Indian Ocean and then the Pacific, would add about 2 or more years to the journey round trip thus every 3 years does not work in any sense. Peru cannot be Ophir nor Tarshish.

Britain's Demand: Britain is Tarshish

There is no separating Tarshish from Ophir. The ships of Tarshish go to Ophir and Tarshish and they return with the same resources from both lands because they are the same route in the same region as evidenced especially by the Greek gold maps of 43 A.D., 124 A.D. and the 1492 Portuguese Globe. When we covered all the scriptures involved, we realized that these isles are to the East of the Red Sea and not West. The Phoenicians already had routes established on the Mediterranean. It makes no sense for King Solomon, the wise, to build a new port and new navy on the Red Sea and hire Hiram from Tyre/Phoenicia who already had the largest fleet on earth and ports throughout the Mediterranean. Then, he would take a trip around Africa as much as four times the journey to re-establish trade they already had. The Phoenicians are documented to have traded with Spain and Britain in those days already for themselves.

> *2 Chronicles 9:21 KJV*
> *For the king's ships (Solomon's) went to Tarshish with the servants of Huram (Hiram): EVERY THREE YEARS once came the ships of Tarshish bringing gold, and silver, ivory, and apes and peacocks.*

> *1 Kings 22:48 KJV*
> *Jehoshaphat made ships of Tharshish to go to Ophir for gold: but they went not; for the ships were broken at Eziongeber.*

> *2 Chronicles 20:36 KJV*
> *And he joined himself with him to make ships to go to Tarshish: and they made the ships in Eziongeber.*

> *Psalm 72:10 KJV*
> *The kings of Tarshish and of the isles shall bring presents: the kings of Sheba and Seba shall offer gifts.*

Jeremiah 10:9 KJV
Silver spread into plates is brought from Tarshish… (Tarshish is a place)

Britain cannot be Tarshish as it does not have the resources on Solomon's list. It is missing native peacocks as the ones you see there today originate in India and has no Almug wood at least and the largest issue, it is not East and requires King Solomon to be, not so wise. Also, Britain is in Japheth's territory not Shem's and though Tarshish may be from Japheth, his father was Javan, founder of Greece not Britain which was never his territory. Because he had ships due to his inheritance of the Greek isles in Genesis 10 and clarified by the Book of Jubilees, Ophir and Sheba who were land-locked largely in Northeastern Iran, brought in Tarshish as their transport. Therefore, Tarshish obviously received part of the territory of Adam and Eve as payment as he should have. That is the Tarshish we must find and it is in Ophir not Britain nor even Greece but in Shem's territory where Havilah is located.

As there is no separating Ophir from Tarshish as they are in the same region, this is a major hurdle for Britain's claim as Tarshish as they place Ophir in India. So, essentially they somehow believe one can travel to India and around the world to Britain and return in three years back in 1000 B.C. That does not work. Some make this assumption because Britain has been a superpower in recent centuries but they fail to research British history from that era in which they have no documentation of a navy or ships essentially, no structure as a nation and there is no way for them to fit this narrative. So, why are they attempting to force this supported by the Rabbis today?

Unfortunately, that answer is very obvious. Since the ships of Tarshish usher in the return of the Lost Tribes (Is. 60:9), they require identifying as Tarshish in order to justify Britain's conquest of peaceful Palestine in 1917. They then, handed that land to Lord Rothschild in ownership through the Balfour Declaration. There's that name again. Many may not be ready to hear this but we test this narrative in our Lost Tribes Series and Modern Israel does fit prophecy indeed. However, not that of the returning Lost Tribes but instead those of Gog of Magog as the 1948 Mass Aliyah lists the territories from which mostly Ashkenazi (Japheth's son not Shem's) Jews (not even a Hebrew word) arrived in Palestine from the territories of Ezekiel 38 describing Gog, the prince demon's forces. However, they do not and must fit the territories of Isaiah 11. Use the Bible as your standard and prove all things.

Britain's Plea: Spain is Tarshish

Let us not forget that British Explorer Sebastian Cabot was hired away from the British by Spain to find a Western route through the Americas to Ophir and Tarshish. Not only did Spain know it was not Tarshish nor Ophir but Britain did as well and this was written into Cabot's contract even as we covered earlier. The King of Spain structured that agreement thus the King of Spain spent all this money contracting all these explorers to find Tarshish and Ophir in the Far East but never knew he was actually sitting in Tarshish the whole time? Ludicrous. We demonstrated that Columbus, Magellan, Pinto, Pigafetta, Barbosa all distinguished Tarshish was not Spain and so did the Spanish Jesuits in the 1600s all the way up until 1890. However, let's take this declaration straight on in Tartessus, Spain. Could that be the legendary Tarshish?

> *TARTESSUS, SPAIN*
> *"Tartessus, ancient region and town of the Guadalquivir River valley in southwestern Spain, probably identical with the Tarshish mentioned in the Bible. It prospered from trade with the Phoenicians and Carthaginians but was probably destroyed by the latter about 500 BC. The exact site of the town is not known, but archaeological evidence suggests it may have been near present-day Sevilla (Seville)."*
> – Encyclopaedia Britannica [263]

> *"Tartessus, a cultural grouping in south Spain between the lower Guadalquivir valley and the Guadiana which is often identified with biblical Tarshish. Tartessus developed from strong native roots from c. 750 bce by exploiting the rich metal resources in the hinterland of Onoba (mod. Huelva)."* −Oxford Clasical Dictionary [264]

No doubt the Phoenicians traded in Spain and got resources from there but that was not for Solomon as his navy was built on the Red Sea and headed East to Tarshish not West. Though this may almost sound similar to Tarshish, Tartessus is not Tarshish. Just the TAR. Do you notice the date upon which this city was founded? 750 B.C. That is over 200 years after Solomon's trip to Tarshish already flourished.

Once again, Spain is in Japheth's territory going to his son Meshech not Javan and Tarshish. That becomes the seat of power for Gog of Magog along with Tubal which is Central Europe. Essentially the Colonial powers, the Vatican, Rome, Germany are all under the prince demon's territory. Like Yahuah would place His Tarshish nor Ophir there.

In all fairness, Spain and Britain are resource rich. However, they must have those on Solomon's list to fit this narrative and they do not. Spain falls even shorter than Britain though as they have no native source of ivory, apes, peacocks, almug wood and it is West of the Red Sea not East. Lastly, at least Britain is known as Isles. However, Tartessus is on mainland Spain and thus not isles and that does not match either.

These claims are not only shallow and hollow, they fail the simplest of tests. There is no replacing the history, geography, science, language and especially Biblical markers which all point to the Philippines with these unsubstantiated and desperate assumptions on the part of the British. At the end of Chapter 9, we already offered a chart with this resource test. Only the Philippines fits. Attempting to even make a comparison using any of these is like saying a light bulb has the power of the sun. One could make the claim but never prove it and these claims do not.

Chapter 15 | We Three Kings
Of Philippines Are

We three kings of orient are
Bearing gifts we traverse afar,
Field and fountain,
Moor and mountain,
Following yonder star.
–John Henry Hopkins, Jr., 1857. General Convention
for the US Protestant Episcopal Church [265]

When he wrote "We Three Kings of Orient Are" in 1857, is it possible John Henry Hopkins, Jr. knew where they originated? Not only is it possible, but definitive as this was not the only song he composed on the topic. These next lyrics from another song written by Hopkins will enlighten.

WHEN FROM THE EAST THE WISE MEN CAME
1 Led by the Star of Bethlehem,
The gifts they bro't to Jesus were
Of gold, and frankincense, and myrrh.
*2 **Bright gold of Ophir**, passing fine,*
Proclaims a King of royal line; [265]

Essentially, Hopkins knew that the Orient he was talking about was the Orient of the Far East, the true orient and not the modern creation which includes Babylon. Even the song above, "Epiphany," identifies these as "eastern sages." Hopkins knew that these Kings came from Ophir and we know that to be the Philippines.

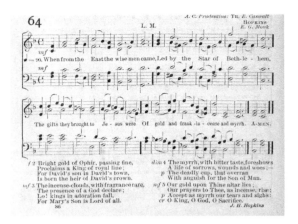

However, he may not have been so wise necessarily as all he had to do was read Psalm where King David tells us exactly where these kings would originate.

Psalm 72:10-15 KJV

The kings of Tarshish and of the isles shall bring presents: the kings of Sheba and Seba shall offer gifts. Yea, all kings shall fall down before him: all nations shall serve him. For he shall deliver the needy when he crieth; the poor also, and him that hath no helper. He shall spare the poor and needy, and shall save the souls of the needy. He shall redeem their soul from deceit and violence: and precious shall their blood be in his sight. And he shall live, and to him shall be given of the gold of Sheba: prayer also shall be made for him continually; and daily shall he be praised.

This is King David's prophetic prayer of his coming lineage but he is far more detailed than given credit if one simply reads the passage. When you read this chapter in the Catholic Bible, it begins with brackets boxing in a false paradigm from the start reading "[Of Solomon]." We take major issue with such thinking as it is proven wrong multiple times in context easily. King Solomon never had all kings nor all nations serve him. Only the Kings of Arabia paid him tribute (1 Kings 10:15) not the whole world in any sense even the known world of his day. Solomon could not "save the souls" of the needy nor could he "redeem their soul," those are Messianic qualities reserved exclusively for the Son of Yahuah

God. Prayer is not being made for Solomon continually as he's dead but Messiah and only Messiah is praised daily not Solomon. In other words, there is absolutely nothing about the passage which identifies Solomon. This is Jesus(Yahusha).

Where do these kings originate who will bring Messiah gifts after His birth? Tarshish, the isles (Ophir, isles of the East), Sheba and Seba. Seba has a derivative in Hebrew in Saba or Sabah now in Malaysia but formerly part of the Philippines or really, Sheba. [61] By definition, Seba is assimilated as a territory, in this context, by Sheba. We now know where these lands are as all of them identify the modern Philippines. Ophir is Luzon, Sheba is Visayas with Seba as it's territory or Sabah, and Tarshish is Mindanao. It was the Land of Creation named Elda, rebranded Havilah after Havah's curse of childbirth and after the Flood, the land of gold. They brought gold, frankincense and myrrh just as the Queen of Sheba brought the same when she gave to the Temple project and these are the ancient elements used in Adam's very first sacrifice which is why they matter specifically.

Certainly, the Philippines qualifies as the land of gold which we have already supported. However, some would challenge that frankincense and myrrh only originate from Ethiopia and Yemen. That is a false paradigm. We already showed you the Philippines as a tropical rainforest has literally every Biblical spice in scripture including extra-biblical books. We have tested them all and only one is unknown as a lost reference in connecting it to modern spices thus no ones knows, but otherwise, it is one hundred percent. The Philippines has multiple cousins to frankincense and myrrh and in Bible times never once is the word frankincense ever used as it is Old French.

Greek: λίβανος: Libanos: frankincense (2X). [266]
Hebrew: lĕbownah: לבונה: frankincense(15X), incense(6X). [267]

Notice, six times, this word translates more generally as spices or incense not as specifically the modern frankincense which is assumed. There is no debating this Hebrew word originates in the word laban which is Hebrew for white. However, to claim frankincense as the only white incense is simply untrue. The very word frankincense is of Old

French origin so let us not pretend that a language that did not exist until long after the Bible was written indicates the origin of this Bible word in use for thousands of years. The assumption of the Rabbis is this only refers to a tree that originates in Ethiopia but Adam did not fly to Ethiopia after exile from the Garden and return to the Far East. In fact, he acquired frankincense from the skirts of the Mount of the East. Thus it was native to the Far East and it is to the Philippines. Once we locate that land, and we have, then, we identify the spice. Otherwise, that would be backwards reasoning.

We wonder if ancient Filipinos were not aware of this false claim of the Rabbis in declaring frankincense only derives from one tree from Ethiopia and no where else. The reason is the Filipino word for frankincense is kamanyang and very strangely the word chaman in Hebrew has a possible appropriate application.

> *Hebrew: Chaman:* חמנ: *From Habakkuk 1:2: Chaim Ben Torah*
> *"...the idea of wealth or pleasure that is obtained through violence, oppression, theft, etc. Includes predatory lending, ponzie schemes, corrupt businessmen who put others out of business to enhance their own. Ultimately, it carries out the idea of enhancing your own power, wealth and/or pleasure at the expense of another person." [268]*

> *Hebrew:* חמס: *châmâç:*
> *violence; by implication, wrong; by metonymy unjust gain. [269]*

Did ancient Filipinos know when using this name for this spice, that there was a back story that this representation was taken from their land and given to another? We cannot prove this but it is probable.

The Philippines has species in the same Burseraceae family as frankincense and myrrh even labeled as frankincense in fact.

> *"Manila elemi, from Canarium luzonicum, one of the best known and single largest source of the world's supply of elemi." [271]*
> *Philippine frankincense and myrrh:*
> *Burseraceae family (same as frankincense and myrrh)*
> *Gum Elemi (Manila Elemi) (soft): Canarium commune*

"From the Philippines. Elemi produces a bright lemony, woody fragrance with a hint of fennel, frankincense and grass. Elemi is a cousin to myrrh and frankincense (Boswellia carterii) and is often referred to as "the poor man's frankincense," as it is a bit easier on the pocket." [270]

Pili (Manila Elemi) (soft): Canarium genera,
Canarium ovatum, Canarium luzonicum
From the Philippines. Cousin to Myrrh and Frankincense. [271]
"The elemi tree is related to frankincense, myrrh and opoponax, all belonging to the Burseraceae family. When lacerated, the bark yields a sharp, green, and pungent, white or yellow oleoresin. Elemi has properties and uses similar to Frankincense; ergo, also referred to as "Poor Man's Frankincense." France has been the largest single market, followed by Germany, and increasingly by Japan." –Godofredo U. Stuart Jr., M.D.

Notice the differentiation in scientific names yet these are both the Pili tree which is likened to frankincense in properties and uses but because it is cheaper (not blessed by the Rabbis), it is known as "Poor Man's Frankincense." In other words, it is frankincense. Let us not be fooled by semantics. Chemically this is just as much a candidate for the Biblical frankincense as Ethiopian frankincense especially since the word frankincense is Old French not a Bible word. This is another case of Western infusions leading to misunderstanding. Dr. Stuart delineates this perfectly though not attempting to connect to the Bible.

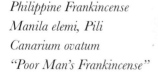

Philippine Frankincense
Manila elemi, Pili
Canarium ovatum
"Poor Man's Frankincense"

"Both Canarium luzonicum and C. ovatum are locally known as pili.
The Manila elemi of commerce is derived from both species. There is
a confusing sharing of common names and scientific names between
Canarium ovatum (pili) and Canarium luzonicum (sahing)." –
Godofredo U. Stuart Jr., M.D. [271]

The scientific varieties of Pili tree represent that at some point in history, these were considered separate as both frankincense and myrrh. Nine of seventy-five known canarium species are found in the Philippines. [271] These originate in the Land of Creation where Adam lived not Ethiopia where he did not. It's Hebrew name likely unveils this in a miraculous way literally.

פלאי: *pili: wonderful, incomprehensible, remarkable, secret, miraculous.*
[240]

We continue to encounter Hebrew throughout the Philippines encompassing the archipelago and this time this ties perfectly to the gift given to Messiah, the wonderful, incomprehensible, remarkable, miraculous one and the gift matches the land even from which it came – the Land of Creation. Both frankincense and myrrh must originate in the Land of Creation as Adam used them both in the first sacrifice, the Queen of Sheba brought them to Jerusalem for the Temple and these "Three Kings" (six) brought them all from the same area of ancestry.

It is the reason they have significance to Yahuah and there is no inserting Ethiopia into any of these narratives in backwards reasoning because Rabbis named a tree there frankincense and in Yemen myrrh as if they have a clue as to the actual ancient Biblical spices. You do not begin this kind of research with the false narrative that boxes in reason. You locate the Land of Creation and then, determine the true origin of the elements in the story which does not include Ethiopia. Therefore, to claim these essential oils must only emanate from trees there is the exact type of rationalization that has lead to losing Ophir. It came from Havilah not from Ethiopia nor Saudi Arabia/Yemen and nothing in the Bible ever says otherwise but fully identifies Havilah, Ophir, Sheba, Tarshish and the Land of Creation in the East as the Philippines. That is likely why in Bukidnon, Mindanao there is a rich agricultural area called Libona with the same sound as the Hebrew Lebownah.

We would be remiss, however, in not acknowledging the Philippines has a second name for c. luzonicum as "sahing." Could this also be Hebrew?

shachah: שׁחה: to bow down [372]

The Ancient Hebrew form of this name is "sahah" really not "shachach" which employs Yiddish rules and is not actually Hebrew. Adam, Sheba and the Wise Kings all bowed down in reverence as they offered these divine gifts. One gift bore the meaning of "wonderful, miraculous" and the second "to bow down." We cannot dream of a more appropriate Hebrew connotation in this instance. Analogous to the Hebrew is the Tagalog meaning where "pili" means "chosen" and "sahing" is defined as "tree sap," which is spice, thus "chosen spice."

It is assumed that Ethiopian frankincense has a concurrent history as the Biblical frankincense. We do not find that to be established especially since this Old French word did not exist until 300 A.D. or later meaning it is not a Bible word. Add to that, Jeremiah combines frankincense with sweet cane or sweet calamus from Sheba which both originate in the Philippines but neither in Ethiopia as we already proved (Ch. 7). The Biblical frankincense was not settled to originate in Ethiopia but was known as elemi as historical fact and one cannot overlook this.

> *"After the Middle Ages the resin from the Boswellia frereana tree, a Somalian variant (Maydi) of the genus that gives as frankincense, was referred to as "elemi." Its inclusion in Coptic incense (i.e. the incense used by the Coptic Christian church of Egypt), helped the confusion, as elemi is frequently a participant in incense blends." [373]*

The Middle Ages ended in the 1500s and Ethiopia's white incense was still confused as "elemi" just as the Manila Elemi. That would be because elemi is frankincense. The Biblical frankincense is not the Ethiopian variety though it is a fine substitute in use. It is not from Havilah and the Land of Creation so though it may have perceived value, Pili or Manila Elemi instead has far greater value to Yahuah and He says so. We'll take

His Word. Elemi is also myrrh in application and archaeology.

> *"Elemi's use in embalming, found in sarcophagi buried in ancient tombs has been celebrated through the ages. The ancient Egyptians championed elemi in the intricate embalming process..."* [373]

The famous Biblical funeral ritual oil was myrrh used in Egypt as well. Archaeology confirms the Egyptians were using "elemi" because it is the Biblical myrrh as well and it originated in the East. In fact, the Wise Men came from the East. Yemen is hardly East.

However, even today, the Manila Elemi has been rediscovered though you do not hear much on international news. Did you know major luxury brand perfume manufacturers from Europe and the U.S. are utilizing Manila Elemi in their perfumes, colognes, skin creams and other products?

> *"No less than international luxury brand Chanel now carries pili, internationally known as the Manila elemi tree (Canarium ovatum) in its newest product, the Ultra Correction Lift for facial skin rejuvenation.*
>
> *The product advertisement reads: "At the heart of the Pacific Ocean, the island of Luzon holds the secrets of a tree with moisturizing properties: the Manila elemi." –Philippine Daily Inquirer, 2011* [374]

It is rather ironic that pili in Hebrew means secret. It is quite the suppressed spice and the perfume companies know this and benefit as Manila Elemi is much cheaper than the Rabbi-blessed Ethiopian frankincense. They can mix it in as frankincense.

> *"In 2003, 361,386 kg of the resin valued at $528,336 was exported to France, Germany, Japan, Spain, Switzerland and the United States, the Philippine Forestry Statistics showed."*
>
> *"Manila elemi is evident as fragrance component in other luxury perfumes, such as Gucci by Gucci Pour Homme, Dior Homme Sport for Men, Marc Jacobs Bang for Men, Donna Karan DKNY Women,*

Revlon Pink Happiness for Women, Ralph Lauren Extreme Polo for Men and dozens more."
—Philippine Daily Inquirer, 2011 [374]

This Who's Who List of luxury brands is elite company for the Philippines. Most Filipinos and much of the world probably have no knowledge of this. If this were a spice of far lesser quality, would posh lines carry it and mix it with the highest quality of spices? Of course not. It is an endorsement that pili ranks fairly with these other optimal products.

> *"In the world's perfume industry, the pale yellow Manila elemi oil is often used as middle note because of its medium aroma strength that blends well with lavender, rosemary, frankincense, sage, myrrh, patchouli, vetiver and other international fragrances." [374]*

This would not be in such company if it was not of like properties and quality. The only reason the Philippine frankincense is called "Poor Man's Frankincense" is because it is lesser expensive. When they mix it with frankincense one must wonder how much they might use as they may well replace almost all of the frankincense with Manila elemi.

Therefore, short of being chemists and declaring the Ethiopian frankincense and the Philippines the same exact, which is not necessary, we vehemently suggest that the Canarium ovatum (pili) and Canarium luzonicum (sahing) are the only appropriate candidates as the Biblical frankincense and myrrh which must originate from the land of Adam and Havah – Havilah. Adam offered these two elements in the first atonement offering and they are the original. The Queen of Sheba journeyed from this same land to offer these same spices to the Temple project. Now, the Three (really 6 or more) Kings emulate these tantamount oblations of paramount implication.

We know they brought frankincense, myrrh and gold not from Ethiopia but from the East in what the passage describes as a two-year excursion. This time, the Red Sea port was still broken up as it was in the days of Jonah and they would have travelled all the way around Africa to the Mediterranean Sea to get to Judaea. They did not need to divert a layover in Ethiopia to trade for frankincense as they already had the true, authentic spices of scripture as their gold of the correct Queen of Sheba from the Brother of Ophir. The real question is how did we all miss this for so long? We even know the Philippines had the ships.

With this in mind, we can now read Matthew's account of the Wise Men and understand whom they were. They were not Magi from Babylon who are those who would likely wish to murder the Son of Yahuah God as they attempted with Daniel whom those same theologians claim Daniel redeemed them. They ignore that Daniel moved to Persia even before Babylon was conquered and the Magi did not like him and he did not retire a Babylonian but a Persian. He was in Susa in the Palace of Darius and he died there in Susa not Babylon. So the claim that Daniel trained Babylonian Magi to look for Messiah is occult thinking.

In fact, consider when the wise men came to Herod on their way to Bethlehem, Herod inquired as to the time in which the star appeared in the East sky. Yes, the East sky meaning the sky in the East in Ophir, Philippines. They told him but Matthew does not report the time until Herod is outraged when they did not return and he sent his men to kill all two years of age and below. In other words, he had been told that the star appeared about two years previously. Messiah was a toddler when they arrived. Consider however, that you are a Babylonian Magi who just saw the star of the Son of Yahuah appear in the sky and so excited that you wait two years to take what would be less than a one month journey to Bethlehem. You would not be very motivated to see the Messiah would you? Instead, imagine this two-year journey at sea from Ophir, Philippines around Africa and through the Mediterranean Sea to get to Judaea.

This is the reason it took two years for the Wise Kings, yes they were Kings according to David, to travel to Bethlehem. That makes far more sense than unmotivated pagan priests who would have no right to be notified in the first place.

We observe the illustrations of the Wise Men arriving on camels which are not Biblical as they usually depict them arriving at Messiah's birth erroneously and no camels mentioned. Even if it was in scripture, there is no reason to believe they would take any other land transportation from the port in which they landed but a camel in those days. Just as with the Queen of Sheba, some jump to assumptions that just are not in the text.

Finally, this journey would also require the star just as in Revelation in the narrative of the seven churches to be an angel not a star. We are fully aware of the theories out there arising out of a software program predicting star patterns. The problem is the supposed alignment they discuss did not occur for 20 minutes whether alone two years as the angel led them all the way to Bethlehem where it changes directions multiple times and then stopped over the head of toddler Jesus(Yahusha). There is no star which can do that and no star pattern that could possibly fit.

Ultimately, there are those who use this software program to attempt to identify the birthdate of Messiah. However, we have proven from scripture especially Luke's very brilliant writings that Messiah was born on the Biblical Feast Day of Covenant Renewal called Shavuot in Hebrew and Pentecost in Greek. Watch our "When Was Jesus Born" videos for the full evidence and you will find we narrow it down to the year, the month and then, the exact day. However, that Feast Day occurs in early June or so each year no where near December 25 which is the infamous birth and rebirth season of the sun god in history. We encourage all to research that.

This passage also addresses the number of Wise Kings, yes kings, who came after Messiah's birth. With the list provided in David's prophecy in Psalm 72, we know that there were more than three kings however. There were at least six kings total. So, why would Hopkins narrow that down to three in his song? Actually, this fits the precedent established in scripture as ancient Ophir was divided into three territories just as it is today – Ophir as Luzon, Sheba as Visayas with Seba/Sabah and thirdly, Tarshish as Mindanao. Thus, the commentaries claiming this theologian was unaware there were more than three kings are likely lacking context as well as those claiming the Bible never defines these as kings when David most certainly did. This in no way conflicts with Matthew's use of the Greek word Magos translated as the "wise men" in Matthew 2:1, 2:7, and 2:16.

> *Greek:* **μάγος***: Magos:*
> *a Magian, i.e. Oriental scientist; by implication, a magician -- sorcerer,*
> *wise man. [273]*

Daniel's "Wise Men" were not Magi and that is false. In Daniel 5:8, they were identified as:

> *Hebrew:* חכים*: chakkîym: Wise Men (Aramaic origin). [274]*

However, the problem with this in scholarship is even the Greek Septuagint renders Daniel 5:8 in Greek and this was well circulated in the day of Matthew even in the Dead Sea Scroll community. Here is the rendering in Greek:

> **σοφός***: sophós: Wise Men. [275]*

Many already know Sophia is wisdom in Greek and it is obviously not the same word as Magos. The word is just not there. Thus the use in Matthew does not reconcile this but is clearly not Babylonian magicians. This originates in a false paradigm of scholarship where one will only look at the English word from the Hebrew Old Testament and they compare that only in English to the same translation from Greek in the New Testament. Then, they go backwards and apply that assuming the "wise men" in Hebrew in Daniel must be the "wise men" from the Greek in Matthew as if Matthew was referring to Babylonian Zoroastrian Priests. The problem is it is backwards reasoning. Upon further testing, if it were the same Babylonians, it would have the same Greek word as is used in the Greek Septuagint for Daniel 5:8, yet it does not. This term for Babylonian wise men is used 12 times in Daniel and never is it indicated the same in the Greek as Matthew. Thus, they cannot be the same application. We can vet this further as Matthew uses the word Magos other times.

> *Matthew 23:34 KJV*
> *Wherefore, behold, I send unto you prophets, and wise men (Magos: μάγος), [273] and scribes: and some of them ye shall kill and crucify; and some of them shall ye scourge in your synagogues, and persecute them from city to city:*

Are we really expected to believe Jesus(Yahusha) said he sent Babylonian magicians and sorcerers equated to the prophets and scribes to minister as messengers to His people? Do you know any sorcerers and magicians called by Him nor being persecuted and killed for His sake? Ridiculous and unscholarly by any measure, this is a slap in the face to Matthew who wrote this as well as the prophets whom these "wise men" are likened. This is a definition that has been very confused by the doctrines of men over the years and it is time we fix it because the "wise men" of Matthew do not originate from Babylon as David told us they would be kings who originate from the Philippines. Those men who came from there were righteous as they are equated to prophets and scribes not only in Matthew but in prophecy coming also demonstrating Ophir's righteousness. Wow!

Having said that, we keep finding traditions in the Philippines which predate Catholicism and do not originate there. For instance, there is the blessing of the elders where you place the back of your hand against their forehead in blessing. That does not appear Catholic in origin and it looks to us more the tradition in which Jacob and his sons blessed. Has anyone else noticed the high rate of circumcision in the Philippines? Also, this is not a Catholic tradition and let's not pretend the nation was ever truly penetrated by Islam because that fits no history we have reviewed and still only about 5% are Muslim today so how do you get 93% of males who are circumcised? You would not. This seems Biblical.

This is a residual part of the ancient Ophirians who learned the practice from Israel likely at the time of the Queen of Sheba and continued since. When the Lost Tribes of the Northern Kingdom left Assyria for the Philippines, they took an oath of rechabite, righteous priests, to live in temporary housing such as tents or in the Philippines, nipa huts would become a much more practical way of housing that would adhere to the oath. Then, we find a tradition like Bayanihan where some Filipinos relocate their houses with the help of their neighbors as they are temporary in a sense. Is this a residual custom of the ancient Ophirian? It certainly is not of Catholic origin.

In fact, the King of Zubu (Cebu) who was first to convert to Catholicism is recorded by Pigafetta as turning against his successor after Magellan was killed by Lapu Lapu. Knowing he turned against and even killed Duarte Barbosa at that time, this was a scathing rebuke of the Spanish and all of their trappings including Catholicism especially. Thus, ancient Filipinos rejected Catholicism. Certainly, the lines sounded good as Magellan explained Jesus because the ancient Ophirian well-knew it was their ancestors who brought Messiah gifts after His birth. However, follow this through logically a little further and you will realize the Philippines already knew Jesus(Yahusha) long before the Roman Catholics or really, Holy Roman Empire came.

No wonder Jesuits changed the Bible to attempt to obscure this meaning which is very obvious when we just read it. Just look at their deceptive rendering of the Three Kings, Caspar, Melchior and Balthazar (all names made up in 500 A.D.) originating in Persia and Arabia leading to the wrong places away from the Philippines. Yet somehow, we are supposed to continue to follow this false tradition and others from those who conquered and stole from the Philippines over what the Bible actually says. We hope you will decide to follow the Bible instead.

In fact, has anyone ever wondered why the Philippines has the longest Christmas celebration on earth at over three months? That, too, predates Catholicism as we already established Ophirians knew Jesus(Yahusha) personally and directly from the time He was two years of age as the

Kings brought Him offerings. When one looks at the actual birthdate of Messiah which we prove to be the Feast of Shavuot/Pentecost known as the Day of Covenant Renewal in basically early June, you will notice a pattern here. That is the culmination of the Spring Feasts of the Bible which begin in the first Hebrew month with the Passover season and end in the Feast of Shavuot, the birth of Messiah. Though they are celebrating the wrong time of year thanks to Catholicism, Filipinos appear to continue this tradition of a three-month celebration ending with the Birth of Messiah when their ancestors observed the sign in the sky of the Star of Bethlehem.

This is also why we believe this practice is likely rooted in the Spring Feast celebration of three months. Further support for this comes from the parol, a giant five-pointed star, which is the center of the Filipino celebration and not the Christmas Tree which Jeremiah 10 rebukes as pagan along with it's six or eight-pointed star of Remphan. It would be no surprise the land of the Wise Kings would have the longest celebration of Messiah's birth even commemorating the three kings in the very end.

This celebration may have been Catholicized over the years but it is not Catholic in origin and actually appears to have truly Biblical ancient roots. Process my friends as we transition to the next chapter which will make your brain explode as all this research merges to interpret prophecy not from us but Messiah, Isaiah and Ezekiel. All these years, we did not understand whom they were foretelling and now we can reveal this people because they specify these same three lands.

Three Kings from Ophir, Sheba and Tarshish. Filipino men from Boxer Codex 1590. [299]

Chapter 16 | Prophecy of Ophir, Philippines

Restored Prophesies of Ophir, Sheba and Tarshish

Prophecy is so abundant once you identify Ophir, Sheba, Tarshish and the Isles of the East at the ends of the earth. We will locate the Rivers from Eden in the next chapter, then the Garden of Eden and the Mount of the East. However, we have a well-fortified position now and we do not require them for this restoration of prophecy. You will find the Philippines is in the Bible many times. The future of the Philippines is one of the most documented nations in prophecy and this is significant.

Isaiah's isles of the East are the perfect starting point and these will build to the end with three prophesies that will blow your mind like never before. Please note we are not nor do we wish to be prophets. We have little use for most modern prophecy as it is usually vague enough that anyone could glean some kind of meaning from it. Having restored this history and geography, we simply now know whom Isaiah, Ezekiel and Messiah especially were referencing – the Philippines.

> *Isaiah 40:31-41:2 KJV*
> *But they that wait upon the Lord shall renew their strength; they shall mount up with wings as eagles; they shall run, and not be weary; and they shall walk, and not faint. Keep silence before me, O islands; and let the people renew their strength: let them come near; then let them speak: let us come near together to judgment. Who raised up the righteous man from the east, called him to his foot, gave the nations before him, and made him rule over kings? he gave them as the dust to his sword, and as driven stubble to his bow.*

Hebrew: צדק מזרח: *Mizrach Tsedeq: Righteous Priests From the East. [276]*

We will observe this pattern continuously in these scriptures. These isles in the East will judge the New World Order and the final generation not on Judgment Day but now. In order to become a judge one must have an adherence to the law or they have no measure by which to judge. Wait til you find out Yahuah will restore His law in this archipelago. There is an organization which attempts to usurp this prophecy for one man who sits at the top collecting the money of course. This Hebrew word is not simply the word for "man" but "men." It is the word for "priests." Do not allow any one man to snatch the prophecy of an entire nation. No one man can fulfill this. This is explained in the other prophesies.

> *Isaiah 46:11 KJV*
> *Calling a ravenous bird from the east, the man that executeth my counsel from a far country: yea, I have spoken it, I will also bring it to pass; I have purposed it, I will also do it.*
> *Hebrew:* `ayit:* עיט*: Bird of Prey [65]*
> *Hebrew:* 'iysh:* איש*: Man, Men, Great men [65]*

This is fascinating because this ravenous bird from the East from a far country tells us much. First, this word is the word for man but could also be men or great men. How do you exercise His counsel? One must judge righteously which requires one also living righteous. This word ravenous bird or `ayit refers to a bird of prey – an eagle. Some do not realize that the afar isles in the East at the ends of the Earth actually have the largest eagle on Earth. When we mention this, there are those that look up one quick reference or another which make claims but we are not making a claim here. The Philippine Eagle is the very largest eagle. There are essentially seven categories by which to determine the largest. Some seize on one whose talons are bigger which we find impertinent in this pursuit and others focus only on wing portion or wing chord.

This is not arbitrary. Here is data determining the largest eagle from The Haribon Foundation supported by Dr. Robert Kennedy of the Harvard Museum of Natural History.

"Based on a very limited available number of specimens and selected external measurements, we have the following: [66]

Haring Ibon: Philippine Eagle

Total Length (from tip of bill to tip of longest tail feather):
1. Haring Ibon *(average) = 1021 mm or 1.021 meter*
2. *Harpy Eagle (average) = 900.75 mm or 0.90075 meter*
3. *Golden Eagle (single) = 884 mm*
4. *Kenyan Eagle (single) = 855 mm*
5. *American Bald Eagle (single) = 829 mm*

Bill Gape
1. Haring Ibon *= 73.66 mm*
2. *American Bald Eagle = 71 mm 3. Harpy Eagle = 64.75 mm*
4. *Golden Eagle = 60 mm*
5. *Kenyan Eagle = 55 mm*

Bill Culmen
1. Haring Ibon *= 72.33 mm*
2. *Harpy Eagle = 51 mm*
3. *American Bald Eagle = 50 mm 4. Golden Eagle = 45 mm*
5. *Kenyan Eagle = 45 mm*

Bill Height
1. Haring Ibon *= 50.66 mm*
2. *Harpy Eagle = 36 mm*
3. *American Bald Eagle = 33 mm 4. Kenyan Eagle = 33 mm*
5. *Golden Eagle = 27 mm*

Tarsus (Foot length)
1. Haring Ibon *= 145 mm*
2. *Harpy Eagle = 121.25 mm1.*
3. *Kenyan Eagle = 115 mm*
4. *Golden Eagle = 110 mm*
5. *American Bald Eagle = 95 mm*

Talon (Hind toe claw)
1. *Harpy Eagle = 64.75 mm*
2. *Kenyan Eagle = 62 mm*
3. **Haring Ibon** = *55.66 mm*
4. *Golden Eagle = 55 mm*
5. *American Bald Eagle = 39 mm*

Wing Chord
(from bend or shoulder to tip of longest primary feather)
1. *Golden Eagle = 654 mm*
2. **Haring Ibon** = *608.66 mm*
3. *American Bald Eagle = 570 mm*
4. *Kenyan Eagle = 545 mm*
5. *Harpy Eagle = 544.75 mm [367]*

The Haring Ibon (Philippine Eagle) tops in five of the seven external measurements, namely, total length, bill gape, culmen, bill height and tarsus. The Harpy tops in one out of seven measurements, namely the talon which is really impertinent. In the wing measurement or wing chord, Haring Ibon is only second but the Harpy Eagle is fifth. Frankly of all of these, talon length should not even be considered and this is really five of six in which the Philippine Eagle leads but regardless even in the two categories in which it does not lead, it is number two and number three. In the Olympics or Sea Games, that would be called a Gold Medal. The Philippine Eagle is the largest eagle on earth and since it originates in the isles of the East, it is the prophetic analogy being employed by Isaiah especially when he consistently specifies the isles in the East at the ends of the Earth (Ch. 8). That is not Africa, Yemen, Peru, Britain nor Spain and even India begins the Far East but is not at the ends of the Earth.

The Philippines fits every descriptor being engaged in this verse. No single prophet nor apostle can as they cannot be the Philippine Eagle which is a national symbol of all the people not one man. No one man gets to own that and anyone that attempts such claim is no prophet but is behaving as the Holy Roman Empire when it arrived demanding tribute because they say they are superior not because they actually are. Indeed, they conquered for a while but those days are over and what is Spain now? Insignificant on the world scene. What is the U.S.? There are many who believe it too has run it's course as the world leader and on it's way to decline. Regardless, they are not this eagle from prophecy nor is the Holy Roman Empire as both are eagles of lesser significance in this regard.

> *Isaiah 41:3-5 KJV*
> *He pursued them, and passed safely; even by the way that he had not gone with his feet. Who hath wrought and done it, calling the generations from the beginning? I the Lord, the first, and with the last; I am he. The isles saw it, and feared; the ends of the earth were afraid, drew near, and came.*

What isles? The ones who are at the ends of the Earth. The same in the land of the beginning who will fear Yahuah once again and revive His ways. We just read the isles will come near to judgment and this is saying the same. Notice these prophesies are not that far apart in Isaiah even. That is due to the fact that they are connected. This is Ophir, Philippines.

> *Isaiah 41:9 KJV*
> *Thou whom I have taken from the ends of the earth, and called thee from the chief men thereof, and said unto thee, Thou art my servant; I have chosen thee, and not cast thee away.*

More confirmation from the ends of the Earth and chief priests again. The Philippines is not cast away.

> *Isaiah 42:4 KJV*
> *He shall not fail nor be discouraged, till he have set judgment in the earth: and the isles shall wait for his law.*

The Philippines is awaiting the renewal of His law. This will happen as you will find, it is confirmed multiple times. He sets judgment, restores

His law and where? In these isles first. This next prophecy is a Filipino prophecy to the core. Singing is not just something many enjoy, it is in their prophetic DNA. How did Isaiah know this?

Isaiah 42:10 KJV
Sing unto the Lord a new song, and his praise from the end of the earth, ye that go down to the sea, and all that is therein; the isles, and the inhabitants thereof.

Isaiah is speaking to the Philippines who love to sing and most do not know why. It is because singing is in their very prophetic DNA as a commonality. This is not to one group but "the inhabitants thereof..." "all that is therein the isles." The Philippines will sing a new song from the throne room of Yahuah and it will not be karaoke. This is their calling. They are the isles who sing His praise at the ends of the Earth. There is no fitting Indonesia and Malaysia into that category especially. Indonesia is even in Ham's territory not Shem's and has no history of serving Yahuah. Otherwise, there are no other isles which qualify.

Once again, this is not new but an ancient talent of Filipinos as they have always loved to sing. Isaiah says so and history agrees as evidenced in De Morga's 1609 description of singing Filipinos.

"...and they time their rowing to the accompaniment of some who sing in their language refrains by which they understand whether to hasten or retard their rowing." —Antonio de Morga [279]

Filipinos have been singers all along singing their way from one location to the next at sea even. They would speed up or slow down their pace based on the cadence of the leader in song. Isaiah affirms this.

Isaiah 42:11-13 KJV
Let the wilderness and the cities thereof lift up their voice the villages that Kedar doth inhabit: Let the inhabitants of the rock sing, let them shout from the top of the mountains. Let them give glory unto the Lord, and declare his praise in the islands. The Lord shall go forth as a mighty man, he shall stir up jealousy like a man of war: he shall cry, yea, roar; he shall

prevail against his enemies.
Hebrew: kedar: קדר: *dark, turbid: dark-skinned. From the verb (qadar),*
to be or become dark. [280]

Most scholars would again immediately speculate that Kedar must refer to the son of Ishmael but we just saw the isles that sing are in the East not Saudi Arabia. Filipinos are dark-skinned. What isles does Saudi Arabia even have? They essentially have rocks not isles. This is the Philippines and it will prevail against it's enemies.

Now that is prophecy. Not ours, Isaiah's restored and Ezekiel also affirms. Certainly, Isaiah is not "new doctrine." These next three are monumental in scope because they characterize a Philippines who embodies a position of authority on the world stage. For those who do not believe this can happen, remember this is Isaiah, Ezekiel and Messiah and none of us can ever legitimately conclude they are wrong. They cannot be. These will come to pass because they must. This is Isaiah's promise to the Lost Tribes of Israel upon their return.

Isaiah 60:9 KJV
Surely the isles shall wait for me, and the ships of Tarshish first, to bring thy sons from far, their silver and their gold with them, unto the name of the Lord thy God (Yahuah), and to the Holy One of Israel, because he hath glorified thee.

What isles? Not Britain. This is why they wish to plunder the title of Tarshish though they are in the wrong direction without the resources nor any history whatsoever to bolster a position. What isles does Isaiah prophesy? The ones in the East he said are waiting for His law. He begins with exactly that here. Then, he invokes Tarshish, Philippines so there is no doubting. Finally, he prescribes that this is the isles of Tarshish which is the land of silver and gold or Ophir. Could he not disencumber this with ample detail any further? There is certainly no need. This is the Philippines and they will usher in the return of the Lost Tribes of Israel which has not happened yet according to scripture especially Ezekiel 39. In fact, in the account of Gog of Magog (note it's "of" not "and" in these two chapters), Magog is Russia but though Gog originates there, that is not his seat of power. His seat of power is Tubal or Central Europe including the Vatican and Germany and Meshech, the colonial powers of Britain, France, Spain, Portugal, Netherlands, etc. This prince demon with his forces attacks Israel and only three areas are listed as protesting and standing against him. He is the same demon who colonized the Philippines in the 1500s and the Philippines will rise and condemn him and his allies.

> *Ezekiel 38:13 KJV*
>
> *Sheba, and Dedan, and the merchants of Tarshish, with all the young lions thereof, shall say unto thee, Art thou come to take a spoil? hast thou gathered thy company to take a prey? to carry away silver and gold, to take away cattle and goods, to take a great spoil?*

> *Hebrew:* כפיר: *kephîyr, kef-eer'; a village (as covered in by walls); also a young lion FROM:* כפר: *kephar, kaw-far' to cover, purge, make an atonement, make reconciliation, cover over with pitch. [281]*

Again, this is where some attempt to force Britain into this when it is interpreted "young lions." However, the word in Hebrew is also defined as "a village as covered by walls." Anyone visiting the Philippines quickly notices that the entire nation is a walled village. Most properties are fenced in with large concrete walls or the like. In fact, notice the priestly language in the original root of this word to make atonement and reconciliation, not Gog's seat, Britain.

This is a further fit to the rest of Isaiah's prophesies about the Philippines in context as Ezekiel knew as well the significance of this land. This is not Britain. Sheba, Philippines and Tarshish, Philippines will be joined here by DDN which is Dodan not Dedan, both DDN as there are no vowel points, representing the brother of Tarshish who we also can trace to the East. [156] Note, Dodanim is plural with "im" and his name is DDN/Dodan. The Philippines will condemn Gog and his allies for his stealing and killing and they will be the only nation on earth who does so. Finally, this is the most important of prophesies and it merely affirms the rest. This one comes from Jesus(Yahusha).

Matthew 12:42 KJV (Parallel in Luke 11:30)
The queen of the south shall rise up in the judgment with this generation,
and shall condemn it: for she came from the uttermost parts of the earth to
hear the wisdom of Solomon; and, behold, a greater than Solomon is here.

The Queen of the South still remains a designation of Cebu and Iloilo to this day and she will rise up. This means Messiah knew she would be put down for a season. She will judge this generation which is the final generation as in the passage, He defines this era where people will be seven times more demon possessed. Who came to hear the wisdom of Solomon? The Queen of Sheba. This is the Philippines which ascends to a position on the world amphitheater. It will have a say in judgment of the world and it's hierarchy. This is significant. We believe we are already beginning to witness the grass roots move which will lead to this fulfillment. Ezekiel even confirms the timing as Sheba, Tarshish and DDN, Philippines rise up early in the narrative not at the end.

When Magellan arrived in the Philippines, Antonio Pigafetta recorded various journal entries about their religion. There were some Muslims but very few isolated to a small island likely Cagayan Sulu or in pockets. He mentions some who include idol worship as he has to justify the entire expedition and what would follow which everyone well knows was normal for Colonialists.

Some of this author's ancestors were Native American Indians who were all but wiped from the face of the earth when they rebranded them "savages." We also see the term in history "barbarians" which by definition should really mean anyone whose land and resources they wish to steal and justify through "Survival of the Fittest" Doctrine. That theory has been used to indemnify the colonial governments from legal liability for their actions. If they be a lesser evolved species, then, by all means, they are entitled to their stuff and their land, right? Wrong. That's evil and China is still attempting such in the South China Sea.

These are nations using the Bible and the spread of Christianity as their exoneration for evolutionary principles of sheer evil. We saw this before the Flood which the Book of Jubilees explains in detail, the Nephilim offspring of the Watcher Fallen Angels behaved this way and they are described as "every imagination of their heart was evil continually."

They branded created humans who were Yahuah's Creation as a lesser species and this is the same thinking. There is no scripture which tells us to "go into all the world" and conquer. Any country or religion using the Bible to dismiss that kind of evil behavior is a filthy rag to the Creator who demands we respect life.

However, Pigafetta, in his desire to catalog everything, also records a different people who have all but been erased from taught history. For these people, had but one God, the Creator of all things and their worship was authentic like that of Adam. The fact that this would make it into his logs without alterations is amazing yet this journal sits in museums today even in Gog's Britain, Gog's Italy and Gog's Yale University. This is monumental. There is a reason as well why we do not refer to ancient Ophir as idol worshipers or ones serving multiple gods. They certainly were not Muslims according to Pigafetta but when he asks, they indicate an authentic worship that demands history change.

> *"Then he asked whether they were Moors or Gentiles, and in what they believed. They answered that they did not perform any other adoration, but only joined their hands, looking up to heaven, and that they called their God, Aba. Hearing this, the captain was very joyful, on seeing that, the first king raised his hands to the sky and said that he wished it were possible for him to be able to show the affection which he felt towards him."* –Antonio Pigafetta [282]

This group of Filipinos are not idols worshippers but perform **NO OTHER ADORATION** or worship. Just one God. They purely joined their hands, looked to Heaven and cried out to their Abba. Talk about odd. Where did they get the title Abba? That is not any of the 99 names of Allah even in Islam. [413] It is the very title used by Messiah Himself whom ancient Filipinos knew long before Catholicism was even founded. Remember they already met Messiah when they brought Him gifts after His birth long before Catholicism was even a religion. They did not need to wait for Catholicism to bring it to them nor did it. Instead, it drove Him away but this will change.

Abba: Αββα: "The Father, My Father"[406]

Mark 14:36 KJV
And he said, Abba, Father, all things are possible unto thee; take away
this cup from me: nevertheless not what I will, but what thou wilt.

Romans 8:15 KJV
For ye have not received the spirit of bondage again to fear; but ye have
received the Spirit of adoption, whereby we cry, Abba, Father.

Galatians 4:6 KJV
And because ye are sons, God hath sent forth the Spirit of his Son into
your hearts, crying, Abba, Father.

Paul uses this as well emulating Messiah with this endearing title, My Father, but how did it come to be used in the Philippines? The thinking has been ancient Filipinos were natives wearing loin clothes of no sophistication just waiting for Magellan to come and save them from their savage ways. Funny, why did they kill him then? And then, his brother-in-law, Barbosa and other captains in the King of Zubu's final rejection of all things Spanish? And then in a naval battle where they chased the Spanish into the South out of Visayas with over 200 ships? That is not an acceptance of Catholicism nor the Spanish. The reason is there were a number of people throughout the Philippines that maintained this authentic worship and were not going to allow their nation to begin to worship idols. Again, remember Pigafetta was paid to write a history of people that he must classify as a lesser species and yet, things like this slip in often as he reports that which he observes throughout his journal. This makes them the most believable portions.

Ancient Ophir worshipped Yahuah not false gods generally and that is according to Pigafetta not us and confirmed by Psalm. There may have been pockets of other types of worship but this is representative of Ophir and the others are not. This was a land of Hebrews that descended from Eber. They knew who Yahuah was and this was reconstituted in the time of the Queen of Sheba at least and reinvigorated in the days of the Three Kings not to mention the influx of Lost Tribes.

The Queen of Sheba did not donate to the Temple a pagan. She did so as a devout Hebrew which she was – not an Israelite Hebrew but from Eber. They were not conquered for over 3500 years in history after arriving in Ophir. Certainly, they may have strayed but especially when the Lost Tribes of the Northern Kingdom immigrated there, there was a new infusion of the lifestyle of a rechabite, a holy priest of Yahuah. No they are not the Serpent's Seed.

The Philippines was never overcome by the Muslims nor Chinese. Even the Portuguese stopped short in Malaysia and Indonesia as they likely knew Ophir was a power and protected. Spain failed on it's first attempt returning with a crew of only 18 survivors really with their tails between their legs. It would take overwhelming force later to subdue the Philippines led by new religious practices which would cause them to profane their authentic worship which was it's intent.

However, though the King of Zubu was deceived for a few weeks, there is no evidence he continued in Catholicism. In fact, there is evidence to the contrary. First, once Lapu Lapu rose killing Magellan, days later this same King of Zubu followed his lead. This account appears in Pigafetta's Journal in the British Museum. The island that supposedly was first to embrace Catholicism is also the first to veto it and they did so with the strongest possible acts.

> *"We then elected in the place of the captain, Duarte Barbosa, a Portuguese, and a relation of the captain's, and Juan Serrano a Spaniard. Our interpreter, who was a slave of the captain-general, and was named Henry, having been slightly wounded in the battle, would not go ashore any more for the things which we required, but remained all day idle, and wrapped up in his mat (Schiavina). Duarte Barbosa, the commander of the flag ship, found fault with him, and told him that though his master was dead, he had not become free on that account, but that when we returned to Spain he would return him to Dona Beatrice, the widow of the captain-general; at the same time he threatened to have him flogged, if he did not go on shore quickly, and do what was wanted for the service of the ships." – Antonio Pigafetta, 1521 [282]*

Understand that Magellan's will, which Barbosa as his brother-in-law would have been likely aware, actually declared Henry (Enrique) a free man upon Magellan's death. Henry may have been abreast. [383]

"The slave rose up, and did as though he did not care much for these affronts and threats; and having gone on shore, he informed the Christian king that we were thinking of going away soon, but that if he would follow his advice, he might become master of all our goods and of the ships themselves. The King of Zubu listened favourably to him, and they arranged to betray us. After that the slave returned on board, and showed more intelligence and attention than he had done before. Wednesday morning, the 1st of May, the Christian king sent to tell the two commanders that the jewels prepared as presents for the King of Spain were ready, and he invited them to come that same day to dine with him, with some of his most honoured companions, and he would give them over to them. The commanders went with twenty-four others, and amongst them was our astrologer named San Martin of Seville. I could not go because I was swelled with a wound from a poisoned arrow in the forehead. Juan Carvalho, with the chief of police, who also were invited, turned back, and said that they had suspected some bad business, because they had seen the man who had recovered from illness by a miracle, leading away the priest to his own house." –Antonio Pigafetta, 1521 [282]

Inspired by Lapu Lapu's victory, this is a story of intrigue in which the King of Zubu changed sides. He no longer supported the Spanish nor remained Catholic. You cannot make a stronger statement of rejection than killing those who brought Catholicism.

"They had hardly spoken these words when we heard great lamentations and cries. We quickly got up the anchors and, coming closer to the beach, we fired several shots with the cannon at the houses. There then appeared on the beach Juan Serrano, in his shirt, wounded and bound, who entreated us, as loudly as he could, not to fire any more, or else he would be massacred. We asked him what had become of his companions and the interpreter, and he said that all had been slain except the interpreter." –Antonio Pigafetta, 1521 [282]

Duarte Barbosa and the other leaders were killed by the King of Zubu and his men. The Catholic Church and Holy Roman Empire no longer retained his support and allegiance. This will happen again as the Philippines awakens. However, there are numerous sources out there who wrongly confuse Barbosa's death into the day Magellan was killed which is not true as he was voted his replacement.

> *"Barbosa's uncle Diego, warden of the castle of Seville, was Magellan's father-in-law, and Barbosa himself accompanied the explorer in his famous voyage around the world. Both met their deaths in a battle with Filipino tribesmen on the island of Cebu."* — Encyclopedia.com [384]

Not only was this a wholesale repudiation of Magellan, Barbosa and everything European including their religion and their King, but when the Spanish returned to Mactan forty years later in 1565, Filipinos there were not worshipping the Santo Niño idol left behind.

> *"We stopped at an island where Magallanes's men were killed..."*
> *As we have just said, they declared that not only they would not give us anything, but that they were willing to fight us. Thus we were forced to accept the challenge. We landed our men and disposed the artillery of the ships, which were close to the houses of the town, so that the firing of the artillery from the said ships and the arquebuses on land drove the enemy away; but we were unable to capture any of them, because they had their fleet ready for the sea. They abandoned their houses, and we found in them nothing except an image of the child Jesus, and two culverins, one of iron and one of bronze, which can be of no service to us; it is believed that they were brought here at the time of Magallanes."*
> *—Letter from Royal Officials of Filipinas from Cubu, 1665 [381]*

The inhabitants of Mactan took everything from their houses of value and fled except very minor items. All that remained from their houses was two culverins and the Santo Nino idol left by Magellan in Cebu. He did not leave this idol in Mactan. Perhaps Lapu Lapu secured it from the King of Zubu as a trophy of sort. However, there is zero evidence this statue was worshipped that entire time between 1521 and 1565 in Mactan. In fact, the people of Mactan were sending a message in leaving behind practically only this one thing. They did not worship it and stating "we think you left something when you were here last."

There is no coherent narrative of Cebu nor especially Mactan accepting Catholicism in the end in Magellan's days. They rejected his religion and one cannot rebuke any more strongly than killing the messenger and his replacement in separate events.

What the Holy Roman Empire was attempting to achieve was to deceive Ophir into incorporating an idol into their worship in any sense. They knew the context would not matter as Yahuah always rejects any infusion with other gods even if their name happens to be Jesus, Mary nor any saint. The Jesuits perceived they could especially focus on the child Jesus because they knew they were in the land of the Three Kings who visited Jesus(Yahusha) as a small child. Why would this be necessary?

In order to rape and pillage the land of Adam and Eve, they would require permission. As witnessed by Magellan, Barbosa and others, Ophir was not an easy target as they failed in their first attempt even unto death. Yahuah protected the land. They needed to have this hedge removed. Here is how they tricked the Filipinos upon their return and this remains in practice today.

We constantly receive the attempts to parse words where the Catholic Church will literally deny with the waive of a hand what is obviously a practice. Notice, those pictured [next page] are incorporating idols into their worship. Much worse, that is not an image of Jesus but documented as that of the false god Ploutus as a child, even the curls. He is the god of wealth known in the Bible as Mammon and it's his image as pictured to the right from 400 B.C. long before Messiah or Mary was born. Archaeology proves this and you can view this statue Munich.

Also, history tells us this is the same image on display in Cebu today. This is the Child Jesus statue mentioned in Spanish letters according to "The Philippines Islands, 1493-1802 – Vol. 02 of 55" as introduced by the Spanish Catholics and used in worship as Jesus, the Son of God on pages 7, 17, 150, 152, 163, 202, 241, 291 and 304 just in 1 volume. That is a false god idol period as the image of Ploutus before Jesus. They do not have to worship him directly which is where they attempt to deceive, they only have to incorporate him and they become an abomination to Yahuah. Our response is if they are not worshipping him, then they will have no issue smashing those idols right now and eliminating them in any sense since they are extraneous anyway. If not, they are worship.

Sto. Nino is the image of the Greek god Ploutus!

Cephisodotus the Elder, Eirene, daughter of Fallen Angel Poseidon, bearing the false god child Ploutos, 380-370 BC. Gallery of Classical Art in Hostinne. Glyptothek in Munich. Public Domain. This is the image brought by the Spanish as Sto. Nino. This is not Jesus. Background image is from the Sto. Nino Basilica Minore del Santo Nino. [272]

We have actually had some even prominent Catholics come into our channel and comment or send replies elsewhere. One such defender actually claimed the Catholic Church and Jesuits never propagated this Sto. Nino as Jesus yet even a quick Wikipedia search documents Pope Paul VI did in writing to coronate this child Jesus in a Papal bull in 1965 and Jesuit articles play along and praise this day as well as the statue even telling stories supporting it's worship and supposed miracles. They brought it. Now, we will deal with the heart of this matter.

Without going into major detail, this would include worshipping idols among those who did not previously. Why? The Second Commandment which the Jesuits erased from the Ten Commandments and replaced with Thou Shalt Not Covet a second time in 9 and 10 which is one commandment not 2. In any other profession, that is called fraud. Here's the trick. When one breaks the Second Commandment and includes idols in their worship regardless of how they attempt to justify it, they suffer a curse to the Third and Fourth Generations. The Philippines has been under that curse. However, the reason this is coming to light now, is that timeframe is up and it is time for this curse to end.

This is worship! *Cebu City, Philippines - January 15, 2016: People attending the opening Sinulog Mass in front of the Basilica of Santo Nino holding up Santo Nino, a religious vested statue of the infant Child Jesus.*

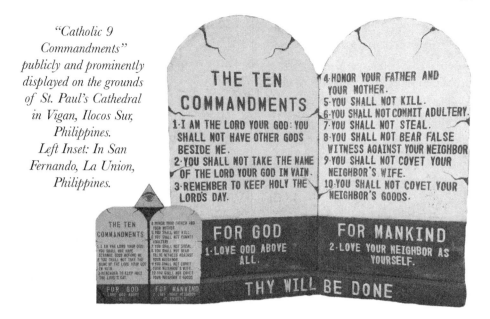

"Catholic 9 Commandments" publicly and prominently displayed on the grounds of St. Paul's Cathedral in Vigan, Ilocos Sur, Philippines. Left Inset: In San Fernando, La Union, Philippines.

Do you notice anything missing from these tablets? How about duplicated? Any ancient occult symbology even? These are the Catholic Ten Commandments on display pretty much all over the Philippines. We do not care who paid for this as some attempt to deflect, as these are the Catholic Commandments according to their own Catechism. Some are in Tagalog but the commandments remain consistent as these are actually the NINE Commandments not ten. The Tenth Commandment is duplicated as nine and ten, "thou shalt not covet" which are the same sentence. What is omitted is the Second Commandment. The one the Jesuits tricked Ophir into disobeying. The one that comes with a curse of about 300-400 years.

> *Exodus 20:4-6 KJV*
>
> *Thou shalt not make unto thee any graven image, or any likeness of any thing that is in heaven above, or that is in the earth beneath, or that is in the water under the earth. Thou shalt not bow down thyself to them, nor serve them: for I the Lord thy God am a jealous God, visiting the iniquity of the fathers upon the children unto the third and fourth generation of them that hate me; And shewing mercy unto thousands of them that love me, and keep my commandments.*

At the risk of offending some, we would be remiss in not mentioning the times within all these wonderful prophesies from Isaiah, of his warning to these isles. We would not show love by suppressing this. Why does Isaiah rebuke these same isles four times in this midst? He says they have an issue with idols (Is. 41:29, 42:8,17, 43:10-11).

How long has it been since the Philippines was conquered by Spain? Magellan did not conquer the Philippines, he lost, failed and died. It was February 13, 1565 that the Philippines was conquered according to Spanish records but that was principally Cebu not the whole Philippines. In fact, it was not until 1599, until the Philippines legally recognized the Spanish sovereignty over the Philippines. [385] Even at that point, the entire Philippines was not subdued. However, our countdown begins as of that date since it was legally recognized by the Philippines. 400 years would then bring us into the future into 1999. The shift from Spain to the U.S. is inconsequential as the curse was still active no matter whose rule and let us not pretend the U.S. was not representative of the same Holy Roman Empire as the Treaty of Paris of 1783 says they were. Some say the Philippines gained it's independence after World War II but if that were the case, they would have taken over their own economy at that point and much of it remained in foreign control up until recently. As the clock turned into the 21st century, the strangle-hold of this curse the Jesuits brought begins to loosen. Today, we believe even more but this still requires the repentance of a nation which must happen.

Today, the trick continues as many do not realize this image has origins long before Mary was ever born. It is not her face, nor her Biblical titles nor any attribute for which Mary should be nor would want to be associated as they are all the worship of the ancient goddess. She has different names but her image has been consistent for thousands of years and Mary looked nothing like her. Here is the ancient goddess beginning 500 years before Mary was even born and she does not look Hebrew like Mary either. Notice her face remains the same through history no matter the name she has been rebranded.

Jeremiah also rebukes this ancient goddess 500 years before Mary by her Biblical name numerous times as Ashteroth or Asherah or Astar. In history, she is the Harlot of Babylon, a consort to the gods who birthed a child as a supposed virgin yet she was an harlot. She is not Mary as Mary

STATUE OF LIBERTY FACE
UNCRATED IN N.Y. 1885

THE PIETA BY MICHAELANGELO
OUR LADY OF SORROWS CATHOLIC CHURCH, ST. LOUIS, MO

Mary's statue is the image of the ancient goddess!
This is the image of the ancient goddess known by many names from as early as 500 years before Mary was born. The statue called Mary is that same image thus a false goddess.

was righteous and precious. She is called the "Queen of Heaven" even in Jeremiah and he rebukes her and Yahuah hates her. It is bad enough that this image is included in worship and Mary elevated to goddess status which she would hate. However, what is worse is that this image of Isis appears all over the Philippines.

Many say, they do not require this statue in their worship and that is great to hear. Isaiah says get rid of it. It brings a curse and continues to do so. Any image of this ancient goddess, which is never Mary, included in any worship of any sort, breaks the Second Commandment. We do not care if you wish to remain Catholic but if you wish to participate in the rising of the Philippines without suffering judgment, it is better to remove this idol. Let go of it then. This must go and we care not what your religion, there is no bringing the image of this Harlot of Babylon into your worship. Do not demean Mary in calling her this Harlot and associating her with that title. May we all deal with this in our homes and on our properties. No one needs this idol no matter what your religion and it is time for it to be removed. Do not endanger your household in continuing a curse which should end. We have shown you Messiah says this will end. (Matt. 12:42).

These so-called "missionaries" did not arrive to better a society of barbarians. They came to plunder the Estate of Adam. Just research

Dole, a Jesuit missionary who stole land, overthrew the king and queen in Hawaii and now has one of the largest canning empires in history because that is what a missionary stands for. Enriching themselves? They took the wealthiest nation on earth, the Biblical land of gold and resources and transformed it into what is defined in modern times as a third world country. There is no other appropriate definition but evil.

> *"The friar missionaries did not bring about the first settlement and conquests under Legaspi; they did not blaze the way in wildernesses and plant the flag of Spain in outlying posts long in advance of the soldiers, the latter profiting by their moral-suasion conquests to annex great territories for their own plunder; they did not find bloodthirsty savages, wholly sunk in degradation, and in the twinkling of an eye convert them to Christianity, sobriety, and decency; they did not teach wandering bands of huntsmen or fishermen how to live peacefully in orderly settlements, how to cultivate the soil, erect buildings (except the stone churches), and did not bind these villages together by the sort of roads and bridges which we have today, though they had considerable share in this work, especially in later time; they did not find a squalid population of 400,000 to 750,000 in the archipelago, and wholly by the revolution wrought by them in ways of life make it possible for that population to increase by ten or twenty times in three centuries." –Ibid. [136]*

Revelation 12 Explained

Revelation 12:1-17 KJV
And there appeared a great wonder in heaven; a woman clothed with the sun, and the moon under her feet, and upon her head a crown of twelve stars: And she being with child cried, travailing in birth, and pained to be delivered. And there appeared another wonder in heaven; and behold a great red dragon, having seven heads and ten horns, and seven crowns upon his heads. And his tail drew the third part of the stars of heaven, and did cast them to the earth: and the dragon stood before the woman which was ready to be delivered, for to devour her child as soon as it was born.

And she brought forth a man child, who was to rule all nations with a rod of iron: and her child was caught up unto God, and to his throne.

And the woman fled into the wilderness, where she hath a place prepared of God, that they should feed her there a thousand two hundred and threescore days.

And there was war in heaven: Michael and his angels fought against the dragon; and the dragon fought and his angels, And prevailed not; neither was their place found any more in heaven. And the great dragon was cast out, that old serpent, called the Devil, and Satan, which deceiveth the whole world: he was cast out into the earth, and his angels were cast out with him. And I heard a loud voice saying in heaven, Now is come salvation, and strength, and the kingdom of our God, and the power of his Christ: for the accuser of our brethren is cast down, which accused them before our God day and night. And they overcame him by the blood of the Lamb, and by the word of their testimony; and they loved not their lives unto the death. Therefore rejoice, ye heavens, and ye that dwell in them. Woe to the inhabiters of the earth and of the sea! for the devil is come down unto you, having great wrath, because he knoweth that he hath but a short time.

And when the dragon saw that he was cast unto the earth, he persecuted the woman which brought forth the man child. And to the woman were given two wings of a great eagle, that she might fly into the wilderness, into her place, where she is nourished for a time, and times, and half a time, from the face of the serpent. And the serpent cast out of his mouth water as a flood after the woman, that he might cause her to be carried away of the flood. And the earth helped the woman, and the earth opened her mouth, and swallowed up the flood which the dragon cast out of his mouth.

And the dragon was wroth with the woman, and went to make war with the remnant of her seed, which keep the commandments of God, and have the testimony of Jesus Christ.

One of the greatest mysteries in prophecy which has eluded scholars is Revelation 12. Most immediately migrate to astrology and there is no biblical precedence to interpret His prophecy through the paradigm of star patterns named for His adversaries. In fact, we examine every scripture that appears to classify constellations in the English and studying out the Hebrew and Greek, there is not one which even refers to a star cluster which commemorates the Watcher Fallen Angels and their Nephilim offspring. Talk about "doctrines of demons."

Instead, with this restored geography in mind, we now understand the Philippines to be far more important than once perceived. To ignore this, would be a huge oversight. Understandably, scholars are unaware largely of this thinking thus they will never interpret this prophecy with accuracy in our opinion.

Remember, this is prophecy and we are simply attempting to examine one which no scholar has ever explained with precision. This is a future event as all of Revelation is according to John in his opening. We see dual symbology here in which the woman appears physically in Heaven but these symbols which surround her distinguish a land as well which will protect her and she will flee into it's wilderness. This land is described as clothing the woman in the sun, the moon at it's feet, twelve stars in it's crown, having a wilderness or desert, likely an island or on the coastline in the ocean where a great tsunami could form and it has the great eagle. Do any of these seem familiar? We believe so.

The Philippines is known in it's National Anthem, "Lupang Hinirang," as the "Land of the morning" or sun. [382] Some English translations then render "child of the sun returning." It is well known geographically as the area in which the sun rises in the Far East just as Japan is the "Land of the Rising Sun" in almost parallel longitude to the Philippines. The Philippines would envelope this woman in the warmth of the sun.

The moon is also at the feet of the Philippines. Many may not realize that Islam in origin, is the worship of the moon god, Hubal, who was the Allah (chief god) of Mecca whom Mohammed then decreed as the only god. He even adopted his crescent moon and star symbology which hales from Babylon originally. The largest population of Islam on Earth, resides in Indonesia at the feet of the Philippines. In fact, Islam's stronghold in the Philippines today is in Southern Mindanao and other islands at it's feet. [386]

When one examines the map of the Philippines, just North of Luzon (the head) are exactly twelve islands which form a circle. They are called the Babuyan Islands which to the locals are known as the "burning islands." [387] Thus, crown of twelve stars.

Many assume because this is a woman, it is the bride or the church (ekklesia). However, she is a virgin, spotless bride on the Day of Judgment who does not birth a child previously (Eph. 5:27, 2 Cor. 11:2). This woman is Israel who in scripture is known as the travailing woman (Is. 66:7-9, Mic. 4:10, 5:2-3, Gen. 37:9-11). The man child, Israel, is taken before the throne of Yahuah redeemed from the earth and raised in Heaven. However, not just anyone but 12,000 from each of the twelve tribes totaling 144,000 as a First Fruits offering. Many confuse the innumerable multitude of martyrs in Heaven (Rev. 7:9) but 144,000 is numbered and these are even separated in the King James Version. John says this is a future event and written after Messiah's ascension thus not Him. Mary birthed Jesus(Yahusha) on Earth not in Heaven.

We prove this out thoroughly over six videos on our channel on YouTube, however, this is a brief explanation. The Great Red Dragon is satan very clearly identified in the passage. However, as we have dual symbology on Earth for the narrative of the woman, we believe we see the same here. The country it identifies however, does not qualify a people as satanic in any sense nor are they even involved. However, it is an indication of the position in which satan will be cast down to the Earth geographically.

On Earth, adjacent to the Philippines is a nation which has identified as the dragon for thousands of years. This country is the "greatest" or largest in population on all of Earth thus fits. Finally, red is it's color of identity in many applications. These are not foreign designations but those accepted by this land of itself. This is China. Again, the Chinese people have no association with this prophecy other than they happened to pinpoint an area on Earth in which this event will occur. Satan is cast down in the South China Sea next to the only desert of the Philippines in Laoag. He will attack with a tsunami which the Earth will swallow protecting the woman and the land.

We also have the two wings of the great eagle transporting the woman deeper into the wilderness. That represents the Philippine Eagle yet again.

The Philippines is the woman originally known as Havilah, the land of childbirth or the travailing woman. Even it's geographic shape on a map looks like a woman. Remember, this is prophecy and we cannot prove it like geography. You do not have to agree with this interpretation but test it for yourself.

Chapter 17 | Rivers From Eden: Revealing Havilah

"If you drained all the water away, it would look exactly like a river system with bends and meanders, except there are no trees along the banks..."

− Dan Parsons, PhD, sedimentologist, University of hull, uk to bbc news (who travels the world to study undersea rivers) [160]

It shall cover the whole [earth] with its shadow
[and its crown] (shall reach) to the [clouds];
its roots (shall go down) **to the Abyss**
[and all the rivers of Eden shall water its branches].

− Hymn 14, (formerly 10), The Thanksgiving Hymns
Qumran Scrolls (iQH, 1Q36,4Q427-32) [414]

Along the way in this search for truth, we uncovered clues which kept leading to the Rivers From Eden of Genesis 2. We already covered the Pison River which surrounds the whole land of Havilah also known as the land of Adam and Eve (Havah) which is defined by gold, pearl and the onyx stone in which the Philippines leads the earth in all three categories. We, then, unraveled the Hebrew meaning of Uphaz which is the gold of the Pison River in ancient Havilah, Philippines tying Ophir and Havilah. The Bible is truly the most brilliant document ever written as thousands of years ago it pinned this down though we lost it in translation.

Then, we settled Parvaim gold ties Ophir to the Garden of Eden which makes sense as the Garden would be right next to Havilah where Adam and Eve were exiled just to the East. We will cover the Garden of Eden and locate that next. However, aren't we told the Rivers From Eden are somewhere in the Middle East? Indeed, we are and now we will dismantle that completely while we also locate all five Rivers From Eden. We agree with those of you who are skeptics as we, too, never thought this would lead this far and yet it does. Examine the evidence and test it for yourself. Can you prove this to be wrong? If you cannot, then you must at least consider this as truth.

We call this chapter of this book a theory still yet it vets far better than any other as it is the only theory on the location of the Rivers From Eden which actually engages the account in Genesis 2 and all others fail miserably. We have dedicated eight videos of maybe 6 total hours to this and it deserves a book of it's own but for the purposes of locating King Solomon's legendary land of gold, we will break this down as best we can in brief.

Why head in this direction? We test everything. Once concluding the Philippines was Ophir and the Land of Adam and Eve, Havilah, we must answer the immediate question that arises. If Havilah is surrounded by the Pison River From Eden which branches from the source River From Eden, then we should detect this acclaimed tributary. In doing so, this should lead us to the River From Eden and the entire system. Most scholars have scarcely reflected on the cosmology of the antediluvian world.

The Bible tells us far more than we realize about the layout and ecosystem of the pre-flood existence. Prior to the Flood, the water system of the earth was described as five mega-rivers with fountains of the great deep within. There is no mention of a world ocean but we did not see a firm balance for exactly how much of the earth was water and how much land prior to the Flood until we studied 2 Esdras. We are aware some hear of an Apocryphal book and immediately dismiss it. However, before you dismiss this one, understand it is published in the Authorized 1611 King James. In fact, Matthew 24:37-38 expresses a margin note anchoring that Jesus(Yahusha) is quoting from 2 Esdras.

Therefore, before dismissing this inspired writing, consider Messiah did not and He used it thus we have every right to as well especially for pre-flood geography which is all we are looking for here not doctrine. Just as the Dead Sea Scroll Thanksgiving Hymn (Left) which places these rivers in the abyss or bottom of the ocean deep, this will enlighten all of us to the primeval Earth with a more exact image on this topic which Genesis requires further clarity.

> *2 Esdras 6:42 KJVA*
> *Upon the third day thou didst command that the waters should be gathered in the seventh part of the earth: six parts hast thou dried up, and kept them, to the intent that of these some being planted of God and tilled might serve thee.*

> *2 Esdras 6:47 KJVA*
> *Upon the fifth day thou saidst unto the seventh part, where the waters were gathered that it should bring forth living creatures, fowls and fishes: and so it came to pass.*

> *2 Esdras 6:49-52 KJVA*
> *Then didst thou ordain two living creatures, the one thou calledst Enoch(In Job 40: Behemoth), and the other Leviathan(In Job 3, 40, 41; Ps. 74, 104; Is. 27); And didst separate the one from the other: for the seventh part, namely, where the water was gathered together, might not hold them both. Unto Enoch thou gavest one part, which was dried up the third day, that he should dwell in the same part, wherein are a thousand hills: But unto Leviathan thou gavest the seventh part, namely, the moist; and hast kept him to be devoured of whom thou wilt, and when.*

BEFORE THE FLOOD, ONLY 15% OF THE EARTH WAS WATER.

2 Esdras narrows this down to a percentage we can understand. Only one-seventh of the Earth before the Flood was water which is approximately 15%. This is extremely significant as there are many who lose sight that the ocean did not exist at that time but was formed by the Flood. Even before finding this, we felt Genesis says pretty much

that but now we have affirmation. Today, 70% of the Earth is water which is almost all (97%) the newly formed World Ocean after the Flood which is 4.5 times more water than before the deluge occurred. This is a completely different paradigm which is why it eludes most scholars and even science must reconsider all pre-flood data. *[378]*

The reason this matters is Genesis 2 is depicting the only major aqua nerve system on the Earth at that time. It is important to understand this especially in locating the Rivers From Eden which once again the Bible waxes vivid when you adhere to and believe it. Modern science even agrees though they hardly know it. This is a lot less water, no ocean and a lot more land. A different ecosystem and no one can interpret anything found prior to the Flood without understanding this including it's affect on dating carbon-14 among other methods. The whole world changed and we do not feel most scholars truly understand the implications and magnitude of this event. Before challenging this, review it thoroughly because we will overcome many objections throughout this chapter and you will find our position Biblical and actually scientifically sound when you test it. Some push back immediately that the Creation account uses the word "seas" in English and that is a fair point except the English translation is not actually representing oceans in context.

> *Genesis 1:10 KJV*
> *And God called the dry land Earth; and the gathering together of the waters called he Seas: and God saw that it was good.*
> *Hebrew: yam:* **יָם***: sea, mighty river (Nile), salt sea. [283]*

The Hebrew yam can mean sea but it also is used for mighty river and even the Salt Sea or Dead Sea which is not a sea but a lake. Yam is obviously a generic word referring to a large body of water not narrowing down the specifics of their details nor does such requirement exist. This word is not a definitive word for ocean nor does Genesis 1-6 ever describe an ocean but just five mega-rivers which we will locate with perhaps lakes we call basins today. Notice, the Bible cites five not four and any so-called theory which only attempts to locate four has already failed. Therefore, since there was no World Ocean prior to the Flood but only 5 Rivers From Eden encompassing only 15% of the earth, we should be able to locate these on the bottom of the ocean floor. In all fairness, no scholar could have possibly seen this prior to the 1970's until the ocean floor was then mapped. However, we have never seen anyone understand this. We will test it thoroughly and you will see for yourself how this matches scripture. Job mentions a word defined as underground streams in application that fascinates this line of thinking.

> *Job 28:10-11 KJV*
> *He cutteth out rivers among the rocks; and his eye seeth every precious*
> *thing. He bindeth the floods (nahar: נהר) from overflowing; and the thing*
> *that is hid bringeth he forth to light.*
> *Hebrew: nahar: נהר: stream, river, (underground) streams.*
> *Job 28:11 usually understood of (underground) streams. [284]*

This word Nahar is the same word used to describe all five Rivers From Eden and they are the source of the Flood which Job is expressing here. However, they are all rivers. Nahar only means rivers or streams or (underground) streams but never means rain, snow, ice caps, springs, a lake or even a geyser. We mention this because there are actual disinformation channels out there who have gone that route and they are not reading the passage nor do they seem to care. However, Job, who deals with Genesis several times, mentions in the context of Creation, Yahuah cut out rivers or underground streams which caused the Flood. Let us review a graphic reproduction of National Geographic's mapping of the bottom of the ocean floor from NASA(right) and see if you observe anything which might begin to come into focus.

This mapping of the ocean floor is monumental as it actually reveals the source River From Eden as previously described by Dr. Parsons which also must be a river and a very large one. Science characterizes this as the Mid-Ocean Ridge and they break it up into several names but then define it as one continuous, undersea mountain range. Mountain range? Ask yourself this question, would you define a river which sinks to the depth of over 6 miles and several miles wide by the mountains on it's banks which convey far less significance? Would you especially do so if this continuous river was 65,000 kilometers (40,000 miles) long? [400] We term this misrepresentation of the facts before us.

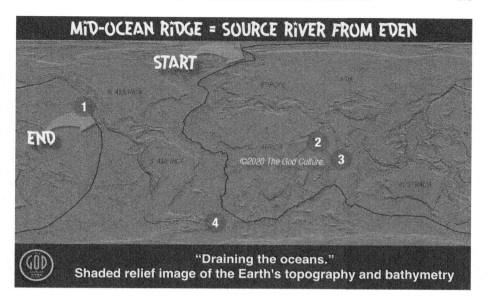

NASA/Goddard Space Flight Center Map of the oceans drained with Mid-Ocean Ridge filled in with blue representing water if the oceans were drained down to the bottom of the ocean with only the deep ridge still filled. There are four places in which this River From Eden branches into heads meeting the Oceanic Trench System. Emphasis added along with continents titled and numbering by The God Culture. [285]

What defines this is not the lesser mountains on it's shores but the actual 65,000 kilometer-long, overlooked river in the center. [400] Test it's depths and you will find it to be downhill all the way around the world which it must. This source of the world water system flows from the shallowest Arctic Ocean deeper into the Atlantic Ocean, below into the Indian Ocean and further sunken across the Pacific Ocean where it terminates. You are looking at the mammoth River From Eden itself.

Without it's four tributaries, the Mid-Ocean Ridge envelopes maybe 2% of the entire earth's water volume. Jubilees identifies lakes as well.

Jubilees 2:7 R.H. Charles (1903)
And on that day He created for them all the seas according to their separate gathering-places, and all the rivers, and the gatherings of the waters in the mountains and on all the earth, and all the lakes, and all the dew of the earth...

This is consistent with Genesis as Jubilees remains. Again, yam interpreted seas means large bodies of water generally not necessarily oceans. These have separate gathering places yet today, regardless of how many names they label them, there is only one World Ocean. Waters in the mountains would be essentially lakes but there was no precipitation yet. Essentially, we have mega-rivers described as five in Genesis 2 and lakes. The dew came from the mist that comes up from the earth as Genesis 2:5 explains.

The River From Eden initiates in the North Pole which we identify as Eden not to be confused with the Garden of Eden planted in the East which we will cover in detail later. The river, then, operates continually across the Earth down between the Americas and Europe, then under Africa into the Indian Ocean and all the way under Australia into the Pacific Ocean until it reaches the coast of Mexico. Therefore, these must be downhill in slope which is a challenge for other theories. As the source river for the other four mega-rivers, scientifically, it must essentially be larger in volume than the other four branches which flow from it and that concurs. It has an average depth of 2.5 km (1.55 mi.) and an average width of 100 km (62.5 mi.). This is massive.

However, in order for it to manifest the River From Eden, it must have four heads which branch accordingly and we will show you it has exactly four. This river has the purpose to water the Garden of Eden which we will find at the end of it's entire system. Also, note, it leaves Eden as it "went out of Eden." Eden and the Garden of Eden are two different places in scripture as the Garden is planted "eastward" or "to or toward the East." Many miss a worldwide perspective and get stuck in the Middle East trying to force rivers that did not even exist prior to the Flood nor could they have as there was no rain.

Genesis 2:10 KJV
And a river went out of Eden to water the garden; and from thence it was parted, and became into four heads.

We will take a closer look at the ocean floor and demonstrate that these four heads are the beginning of the Oceanic Trench system which each synchronizes in impact with the Mid-Ocean Ridge. We will identify each river from here. Understand, however, some of the areas of these trench systems have been filled in places due to sediment from modern rivers dumping into them over the continental shelves and some from the Flood. Therefore, they may not all still appear contiguous but once were and still there.

> "A few trenches are partially filled with sediments derived from the bordering continents." [286]

> "Trenches that are partially infilled are known as "troughs" and sometimes they are completely buried and lack bathymetric expression." [286]

1. Pison River

Genesis 2:11-12 KJV
*The name of the first is **Pison**: that is it which compasseth the whole land of Havilah, where there is gold; And the gold of that land is good: there is bdellium and the onyx stone.*

In Chapter 5 on Havilah, Land of Eve, we found that the Philippines leads the world in these three resources which define it as Ancient Havilah – gold, pearl and the onyx stone. To date, it maintains a leadership position in all three as it is the historic forerunner in gold abundance, has no rival in largest pearls on Earth and possesses the strongest onyx and marble from Romblon. Therefore, the Pison River must surround this whole land of the Philippines.

You can observe the culmination of the 65,000 kilometer Mid-Ocean Ridge off the coast of Mexico essentially. At that point begins a series of Oceanic Trenches which travel all the way up the coast of America to Alaska, then, over to Russia, down to Japan and splits and surrounds the whole land of the Philippines especially. This is the ancient Pison River, the first River From Eden that branches from the main source river. It is positioned at the end of the entire Eden River System yet it is ranked first. This is because Hebrew writing initiates from right to left or East to West in direction. Therefore, the Eastern-most river would be first.

World map, shaded relief with shaded ocean floor. With Oceanic Trenches labeled. Map from Alamy based on National Geographic. [401]

As we continue to the next chapter, you will find this is where the Garden of Eden is watered as well. Again, in understanding water gravity, it has to flow downhill unless there is some sort of jet or like force applied. Notice, the very deepest trenches on all of earth are right here near the Philippines. Mariana's Trench is deepest, the Tonga Trench second and third, the Philippine Trench. This is not coincidence. It fits exactly the Biblical narrative and confirms the Philippines is Ancient Havilah and Ophir surrounded by the legendary Pison River.

As we zoom in, one can see just how pronounced this trench system is. Observe, the Manila Trench, Negros Trench and Sulu Sea Basin on the West side of the Philippines causes this network to encompass the whole land of the Philippines as it must. Prior to the deluge, the Philippine archipelago was one island essentially. That which we call islands today, were the Mountains of Eden. It was the land of Adam and Eve where the first child was born and man was created. What we find amazing as we review geographic characteristics especially of the Philippines land mass, it almost appears like the trenches in the ocean to the East form what appears in the shape of a womb. Does it not appear on the map, the Philippines seems a child who is being birthed exiting that womb as the Land of Creation where life began? We see that as likely though not something we can prove.

The map to the adjacent top left identifies numerous trenches by name which were linked prior to the Flood as one river. Science, unaware, labels these by many names but they constituted one continuous river in antiquity. Aforetime, the surface of the Pacific Ocean outside of these trenches and the Mid-Ocean Ridge was dry land. Many recall the fabled Lemuria. It is no sunken continent that disappeared into the sea. It was inundated and overcome by the new World Ocean as was Atlantis. If one desired to discover a treasure trove of prehistoric archaeology, they would need to penetrate into the Flood sediment there on the bottom and entire large societies would emerge. However, man has no such capabilities in this age. Is it not odd that the Flood buried this and Atlantis to such degrees that we cannot even locate them today?

On the bottom, we have rendered a cleaner view expressing dry land with only the Mid-Ocean Ridge and Oceanic Trenches pronounced for clarity. We will publish all the trench maps as well. For these five rivers to fill 10-13% or so of the Earth with water adding lakes for the remaining 2% perhaps, they must be global and larger than any rivers in our age. None of our modern rivers could possibly qualify.

So far, we have the River From Eden and the Pison River identified and fully matching the descriptions in Genesis 2. You will find that continues. For the sake of this book, we could stop here but it would leave everyone with questions. What about the other rivers? They have to match in order to make this work and they do. This next tributary in description assists in really nailing down this thinking as in order for a river to surround the Philippine Islands, it must be on the ocean floor and the same rule will apply with the Gihon River around Africa.

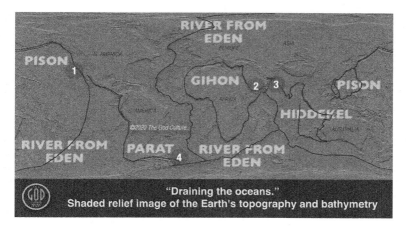

"Draining the oceans."
Shaded relief image of the Earth's topography and bathymetry

2. Gihon River

Genesis 2:13 KJV
And the name of the second river is Gihon: the same is it that compasseth
(cabab: סבב) the whole land of Ethiopia (Kuwsh: כוש).
Compasseth: Hebrew: cabab: סבב: to turn, turn about or around or
aside or back or towards, go about or around, surround, encircle, change
direction. [287]

We are seeking a river that surrounds all of Ethiopia as "compasseth"
means surrounds or encircles essentially. Genesis then says the whole land
which affirms the meaning. The challenge with this is most in modern
times do not know where Ethiopia was considered when the Bible was
written? They are confused by modern Ethiopia being named such
because in history until the 1800's, it was always identified as Abysinia.
Their name is appropriate as they were part of ancient Ethiopia but a
very small sliver. In order to understand where this river is located, we
must understand this because there is no modern river surrounding the
whole land of modern Ethiopia (Abysinia).

Ethiopia: Hebrew: Kuwsh: כוש: Cush
Ethiopia (19x), Cush (8x), Ethiopians (3x)
Cush: "black." Cush (or Ethiopia), the name of a son of Ham, and of
his territory; also of an Israelite:—Chush, Cush, Ethiopia.
Translated 8 times as Cush: 6X - Name of Ham's Son (who lived
in Ethiopia), 1X - Cush the Benjamite (Psalm 7:1), 1X - Ethiopia
(Isaiah 11:11 w Egypt and Pathros) [288]

One of the theories out there is there is a Kush in Iran and Afghanistan.
However, that is not referenced ever in the definition of this son of Ham
who would not live in Shem's territory. Many of these theories can be
obliterated just by understanding Biblical geography. Cush as Ham
means "black" or "burnt" which is fitting to the lands Ham inherited.
Do we ever see Iraquis, Assyrians, Persians or Afghanis referred to as
black in the Bible? No. The Hindu Kush is a new name with no basis
in this narrative and cannot be used to locate the ancient Rivers From

Eden. Hindu Kush was not used for Indian mountains until 1000 A.D. and Kush or Koh is the Aveston word for "mountain" not the son of Ham who had no association with that area as he lived in Africa.

> *"The name Hindu Kush is, from a historical point of view, quite young. It is missing from the accounts of the early Arab geographers and occurs for the first time in Ebn Battuta (ca. 1330; tr., p. 53; Le Strange, Lands, p. 350)."* – Encyclopaedia Iranica [379]

> *"The name Hindu Kush derives from the Arabic for "Mountains of India."* Its earliest known usage occurs on a map published about AD 1000."* - Encyclopaedia Britannica [380]

This Bible word Cush is virtually always associated with Ham's son Cush who inherited part of Africa. His land became known as Ethiopia as even the Bible confirms numerous times and he acquired the West coast of Africa as well which Canaan abandoned according to history and Jubilees. Indeed there was a Kushite Kingdom in Abysinia 2000 years later but maps show the entire area of Ethiopia as far larger as early as 450 B.C. There certainly was but it only represented a small portion of the land of Cush. Ancient maps demonstrate this fact from 450 B.C. all the way to the 1800's so there is no real debate. Some just do not know history much of the time and draw assumptions inaccurately.

In the days the Bible was written especially, ancient Ethiopia was far larger than modern Ethiopia. In 450 B.C., Herodotus identifies Ethiopia as all of Central Africa. [p.281] Remarkably, the South Atlantic Ocean is titled the Ethiopian Ocean. Why would it carry that connotation if Ethiopia was a small country on the other coast with no affiliation? It would not. This practice continued all the way through until the 1800's. In 43 A.D., Pomponius Mela's Map of the World also indicates Ethiopia as sprawling all the way across Africa from East to West Coast displaying twice even and again, the Ethiopian Sea which would be out of place in name if Ethiopia was just Abysinia. [p.281]

In 1467, The 4th African Map identifies Media Ethiopia just South of Egypt, Ethiopia Sub Egypt for much of the East coast and Ethiopia Interior from West to East coast all the way across Africa. [p.281] On our channel we show probably 20 or so maps that further confirm this but you get the picture. In fact, many of these demonstrate modern Ethiopia labeled as Abysinia. Ethiopia was never only Abysinia but much larger until the last two centuries. Genesis was written by Moses in some time around 1700 B.C. therefore, his mindset and understanding of geography was not our modern one. Even as late as 1611 when the King James was first published, those translators did not see Ethiopia as any less than all of Central Africa from East to West coast.

Therefore if this third Gihon River from Eden must surround the whole land of ancient Ethiopia, then it must surround the entire continent of Africa. It is not a tributary running through it and even the Nile does not fit especially since it's source is rainfall which did not exist in Genesis 2 in verse 5. It must surround the whole land which places it on the bottom of the ocean floor. We have never seen a coherent theory on this one in the slightest. However, connecting to the Mid-Ocean Ridge leads to a Trench system which just so happens to surround the whole land of Africa or ancient Ethiopia. Later in this chapter, we provide a map of this as well as the trenches and basins that surround Africa so you can visualize.

On a final note, there are theories which claim the Gihon Springs in Israel must be the Gihon River. However, it is a very small spring 325-meters long, a straight line thus surrounds nothing, and 6 cm in width. Certainly, they must be jesting to suggest that was an ancient River from Eden. It is a spring which is not Nahar (river) neither time it is used in scripture. Also, where is the source River from Eden which must feed it which also must connect to 3 other rivers which also do not exist? In order to make such connection, they express an underground river which is fiction and try to connect it to rivers such as the Tigris and Euphrates which it would have to flow uphill more than once in order to be that source. Science fails this quickly. It is one of the most ludicrous theories we have ever reviewed and truly unscientific and unbiblical in every sense. The Book of Jasher even mentions the Gihon overflowing a first time before the Flood in response to the Nephilim. Supposedly it flooded one-third of the earth. We cannot confirm that but we know it most certainly was not the Gihon Spring. Those posing such theory are promoting Zionism not Bible.

Herodotus' map of the world. Public Domain. [289]

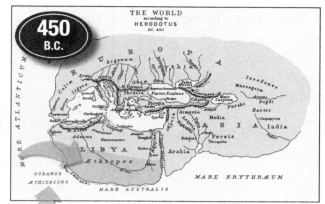

World Map of Pomponius Mela. Public Domain. [18]

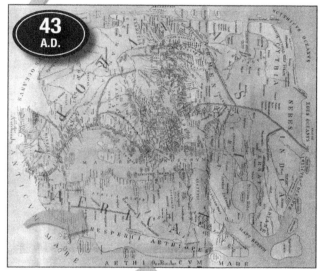

Ptolemy Cosmographia. Public Domain. [290]

3. Hiddekel River (Never Tigris)

The third river once again is accompanied by a description that one cannot ignore yet they do. In fact, they even replace the Hebrew word on this one with a modern river – the Tigris. That is erroneous.

> *Genesis 2:14a KJV*
> *And the name of the third river is Hiddekel: that is it which goeth toward the east of Assyria.*

East of Assyria means East of Assyria. That seems simplistic yet the traditional theory on this is far from reading the Bible. For one, there are some translations which insert the Tigris River spuriously and it misleads many. The logic almost seems reasonable. However, it is a complete misrepresentation of occult origin.

Even if the Bible said this was the Tigris River, it would have to match scripture and the entire Eden River System in order to be the modern Tigris. After all, these are the Rivers From Eden from Creation. It would be no surprise to have countries copying these names but that would not make them the River From Eden. For instance, there are seventy places on Earth named "Eden." [291] Does this make them all the Garden of Eden? Of course not. There are twelve places on earth named "Ararat" but does that really mean there were twelve arks? [291] There are four places even named "Hell" on earth. [291] However, we are pretty sure we have not been warning people that they may someday go to Michigan if they are not in relationship with the Messiah. This is a logical fallacy and no way to treat scholarship yet this thinking penetrates as the basis for many theories we encounter on many ancient topics regarding geography. The modern Tigris and Euphrates both have to concur with the actual descriptions from Genesis 2 or they are not theories. Here's the challenge with most modern rivers in this entire paradigm. None of them existed prior to the Flood. How can we assert that?

> *Genesis 2:5-6 KJV*
> *And every plant of the field before it was in the earth, and every herb of the field before it grew: for the LORD God had not caused it to rain upon*

the earth, and there was not a man to till the ground. But there went up a mist from the earth, and watered the whole face of the ground.

It seems many scholars have missed a few verses before the Rivers From Eden. These rivers cannot be created by rain and snowmelt. If they are, then they did not exist prior to the Flood as there was no precipitation but a mist which went up from the earth to water the whole face of the ground. This is how we perceive the modern Tigris and Euphrates and even the Nile and Amazon Rivers are already disqualified. They are not antediluvian entities because their sources are all rain and snow. Neither is fueled by a larger River From Eden which cannot be rain and snow as there was none in Genesis 2 if that even could make sense. This also means no snow caps on mountaintops as their source is rain and snow as well. Not only is this a problem but in order for these to harmonize with the River From Eden system, they also must have the identical source – the River From Eden which fuels all four of it's branches. There is no injecting multiple roots.

> *"The Tigris begins in Lake Hazar, which is located in the Taurus Mountains. The lake measures 14 miles at its maximum length and has a maximum width of 3.7 miles. The source is located in eastern Turkey, about 16 miles southeast of the city of Elazig and about 50 miles from the origin of the Euphrates." [292]*

A lake which derives it's water from rainfall, is not the River from Eden nor was their rain before the Flood. It is assumed the modern Tigris and Euphrates can somehow be inserted into this narrative and that is fairly accepted in consensus which is why we seek no such because in this instance scholars are simply acquiescing to be unsound. First, both must have the same source river and this indicates their sources are 50 miles apart. That is not the River From Eden and this never works. The Euphrates has two sources that both stem from rain and snowmelt.

> *"The headwaters of the Euphrates are the Murat and the Karasu rivers in the Armenian Highland of northeastern Turkey." [293]*

Both the Murat and Karasu rivers originate in the mountains from rain and snow. The modern Euphrates cannot be a River From Eden. Sure it at least conveys the name of a River From Eden but the real reason is the occult Creation account of Sumer begins right there between the Tigris and Euphrates. That's the occult not the Bible which places Creation in the East. This is why we keep seeing things lead to Babylon not because the Bible supports occult narratives. That is very backwards and a thinking that should never enter the scholarly community.

Even other modern rivers that some attempt to insert just cannot fit this description. The Nile originates from Lake Victoria mostly and that is filled with precipitation. It is not the River From Eden and it's source did not exist in Genesis 2. [294]

The more major challenge we have to the traditional view on this is the assumption, and it's an extremely poor one, that the Hiddekel River must be the Tigris River because the one other time it is used in scripture is in Daniel as he had a vision on the Tigris River when he writes Hiddekel. This is biblically illiterate yet permeates mainstream scholarship and most pastors. Did Daniel ever live on the Tigris River? No. When he had that vision in fact, he was not even in Babylon but in Susa, Iran at the Palace of Darius nowhere near the Tigris River which he never lived on or near. Is the Tigris River really never referenced in scripture by another name in Hebrew that it would be associated with the Hiddekel River from Eden? Of course it has a Hebrew name.

First, before consulting Daniel who never lived on the Tigris River and never mentions the Tigris by it's Hebrew name for obvious reason, we should consult a Lost Tribe of the Northern Kingdom as they were taken to Nineveh and surrounding areas right by the Tigris River which Daniel never lived. In the Book of Tobit, he literally comes out in Tobit 6:1 and identifies the Tigris River as TYGRYS(תיגריון) in Hebrew. [295] That is not Hiddekel. However, there is a Hebrew name for the Tigris.

1 Kings 14:15 KJV
*For the LORD shall smite Israel, as a reed is shaken in the water, and he shall root up Israel out of this good land, which he gave to their fathers, and shall scatter them **beyond the river**, because they have made their groves, provoking the LORD to anger.*

Isaiah 7:20 KJV
In the same day shall the Lord shave with a razor that is hired, namely,
*by them beyond **the river, by the king of Assyria**, the head, and*
the hair of the feet: and it shall also consume the beard.

The Lost Tribes of the Northern Kingdom were taken captive into Assyria beyond the Tigris River. The Southern Kingdom was later taken to Babylon which is on the Euphrates River mostly especially the palace where Daniel lived on or near. "The River" in Hebrew is the Tigris River. Why? It is to the Hebrews, the river of abomination where the occult was birthed as their legends begin there at Babel. There is a Hebrew word Euphrates used several times but the Tigris is only referred to as "The River" in Hebrew mentioned 26 times or so in scripture, usually referring to Northern Lost Tribes. Judaea from which Daniel originates never lived in Assyria. Here is a list of the mentions of the Hebrew Name for Tigris as The River in the King James Version twenty-six times for your consumption:

> *Ha Nahar. "The River" (*הנהר*): 2 Chronicles 9:26; 1 Kings 14:15;*
> *Ezra 4:10, 4:11, 4:16, 4:17, 4:20, 4:23, 5:3, 5:6, 6:6, 6:8, 6:13,*
> *7:21, 7:25, 8:36; Nehemiah: 2:7, 2:9, 3:7; Isaiah 7:20, 8:7, 11:15,*
> *19:5, 23:3, 27:12; and Jeremiah 2:18.*

However, let us deal directly with the story of Daniel. Daniel was taken from Judaea into Babylon as a child as essentially a slave where he lived in or by Nebuchadnezzar's palace on the Euphrates River not the Tigris. In fact, the Euphrates ran right through the middle of this palace complex.

Daniel 1:4 KJV
Children in whom was no blemish, but well favoured, and skilful in all
wisdom, and cunning in knowledge, and understanding science, and such
as had ability in them to stand in the king's palace, and whom they might
teach the learning and the tongue of the Chaldeans.

By the 8th chapter of Daniel, Daniel is still at the King of Babylon's service as he was brought to the palace to interpret the handwriting on the wall just before this. However, King Belshazzar would be the last king of Babylon and he would soon be killed. Daniel in chapter 8 though is in Susa or Shushan, Iran in Persia. He was by the River Ulai for that vision which is no where near the Tigris River nor did he live near the Tigris when in Babylon. He never lived there.

> *Daniel 8:1-2 KJV*
> *In the third year of the reign of king Belshazzar a vision appeared unto me, even unto me Daniel, after that which appeared unto me at the first. And I saw in a vision; and it came to pass, when I saw, that **I was at Shushan in the palace**, which is in the province of Elam; and I saw in a vision, and I was **by the river of Ulai**.*

In chapter 9, Babylon had been defeated and Daniel was still in Susa, Iran in the Palace of Darius the Persian King. There was a complete power shift prior to that as Babylon is conquered.

> *Daniel 9:1 KJV*
> *In the first year of **Darius** the son of Ahasuerus, of the seed of the Medes, which was made king over the realm of the Chaldeans;*

Now, you can see the progression of where Daniel lived leading up to his dream in which he invokes the Hiddekel River the only other time it is used in scripture. Years have passed and Cyrus the Great is now King of Persia. Daniel's vision occurs in Iran.

> *Daniel 10:1-5 KJV*
> *In the third year of Cyrus king of Persia a thing was revealed unto Daniel, whose name was called Belteshazzar; and the thing was true, but the time appointed was long: and he understood the thing, and had understanding of the vision. In those days I Daniel was mourning three full weeks. I ate no pleasant bread, neither came flesh nor wine in my mouth, neither did I anoint myself at all, till three whole weeks were fulfilled. And in the four and twentieth day of the first month, as I was by*

the side of the **great river, which is Hiddekel;** *Then I lifted up mine eyes, and looked, and behold a certain man clothed in linen, whose loins were girded with fine* **gold of Uphaz:**

Daniel was in Susa, Iran where he is even recorded as expiring near the Persian Gulf on the Iranian side near the River Ulai which is mentioned by name before yet he invokes the Great River Hiddekel. Great River? He is referring to the River From Eden indeed but that is not located in Assyria but East of it and he is East of Assyria at this point. Daniel is right next to the Persian Gulf in Iran not Babylon nor Assyria. The Trench system on the bottom of the Indian Ocean East of Assyria runs right up to the Persian Gulf. The Tigris nor Euphrates would be involved as they both originate in the mountains of Turkey and flow downhill from the mountains into the Persia Gulf not the other way around which some even attempt such theory. Thus they would have to flow backwards to be injected into this narrative. First let's review the detail of the ocean floor on this one. [below]

World map, shaded relief with shaded ocean floor. With Oceanic Trenches labeled. Map from Alamy based on National Geographic. [401]

Iran even has nice beach resorts in these areas today and Daniel would have had more freedom in Persia than in the Babylonian Palace as a slave. You can see the massive Mid-Ocean Ridge here which connects with the Trenches around the Indian Ocean leading to the Persian Gulf especially. Daniel literally meant he was next to the original Hiddekel River which was on the bottom of the ocean floor right in front of him.

There is one channel who created multiple videos with the childish line how did Daniel breath on the bottom of the ocean floor. Very simple. He never had to go to the bottom of the ocean floor. In fact, when one reviews the Book of Jubilees 8 mapping of Noah's division of the earth between his three sons, you will find Shem's territory extends from Saudi Arabia over to the coast of Africa. Jubilees 8:15 equates the continental shelf of Africa "to the banks of the Gihon River." Daniel

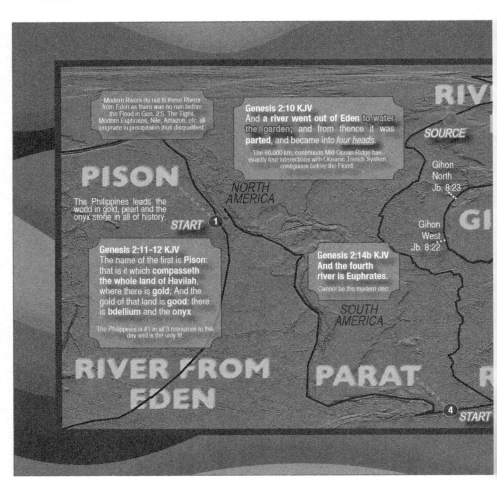

was standing on the Persian Gulf on the banks of the Hiddekel River on the continental shelf. Therefore, no qualification is met by the Tigris River whatsoever and time to remove it from consideration. Below is a full mapping of all 4 rivers with the scripture for your review and clarity.

4. Parat River (Not Modern Euphrates)

Finally, the last river is the Euphrates or Parat in Hebrew but it cannot be the modern Euphrates which originates in rain and snow melt. It would have to flow backwards to work and there is no River From Eden feeding it nor connecting it to the three other branches at the same time. None of the narrative makes sense. However, we find the fourth and final branch of the Mid-Ocean Ridge (River From Eden) next to South

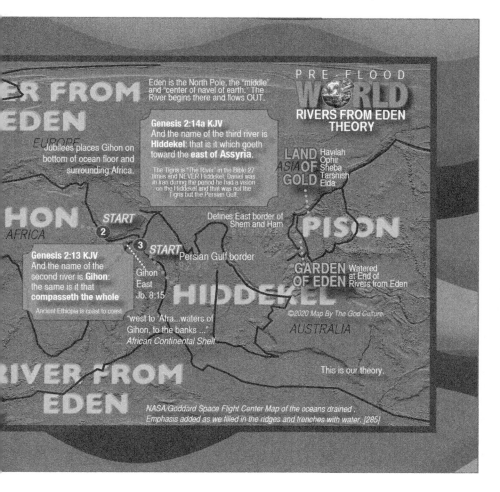

America running up it's coast (Map on bottom right). Oddly, Parat is rendered in Tagalog as well meaning "salty" and with the fountains of the great deep within, this whole system is salty. This is the fourth position where the Mid-Ocean Ridge veers into another leg. Exactly four and a perfect balance conforming to every detail of Genesis 2. You will find no other theory which does.

The Rivers From Eden are not that difficult to identify when we apply the accurate mindset. The one where the Bible is viewed as truth and the standard of measurement. With this foundation, we have adequately located the Rivers From Eden and in terms of Solomon's land of gold, they lead right there to the Philippines at the very end of the Eden River System where it waters the Garden of Eden. All of this can be seen in clear view and we will locate the Garden of Eden in the next chapter.

Featured to the right are the other three detailed maps of the ocean floor surrounding Africa where the Gihon flows. In the midst of the Indian Ocean, the Hiddekel runs and climbing up the coast of South America where the Parat or original Euphrates, the one named before the Flood, exists. They are still there and continue to serve a purpose.

One thing we find extremely interesting is that the Filipino word "Tagalog" breaks down as "taga" and "ilog" meaning "People of the River." Yet, we do not find a significant modern river in the whole Philippines that would define the inhabitants of the thousands of islands. No common denominator found in modern times. Should they not be referenced as the "People of the Ocean" instead. Here we have yet another clue that reveals this theory as they are the "People of The River" – the Pison River from Eden. Now it makes sense and no surprise in the land of Havilah.

Why are we dealing with so much confusion on this issue today? Remember, over 2000 years ago Jude warned the enemy, the Pharisees and Gnostics, had already penetrated the ranks of the early ekklesia (church) even then. That is a long time of mixing and confusing which is their greatest talent described multiple times as leaven or an additive rising agent. Their applications do not interpret but expand. This is why we all must prove all things. Peter warned us that in the last days would come scoffers who would operate in "willing ignorance" justifying their own lusts for power and material luxuries who would attack the

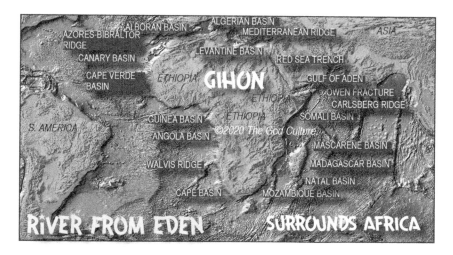

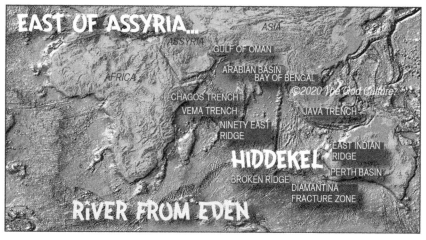

foundations of the Bible. They would deny the Biblical narratives of Creation, the Flood and the Deity of Messiah and we are right there today in the heart of this. We do not have to be deceived however. We can discern for ourselves when we know His Word.

2 Peter 3:3-7 KJV
Knowing this first, that there shall come in the last days scoffers, walking after their own lusts, and saying, Where is the promise of his coming? for since the fathers fell asleep, all things continue as they were from the beginning of the creation. For this they willingly are ignorant of, that by the word of God the heavens were of old, and the earth standing out of the water and in the water: Whereby the world that then was, being overflowed with water, perished: But the heavens and the earth, which are now, by the same word are kept in store, reserved unto fire against the day
of judgment and perdition of ungodly men.

The Flood in today's seminaries continues to be misunderstood drastically as even Creation Science employs occult lines within unknowingly. In Sunday School, most of us have heard that it rained forty days and nights and somehow that flooded the whole earth up to the tallest mountains. Realize even a child recognizes that sounds like a fairy tale. In response, a scientist took the challenge and calculated that rain would have had to have fallen at such a rate that the friction would have caused the waters to boil at such high temperatures, the ark

Hydrothermal Vents. Fountains of the Great Deep.

and all that was therein would have disintegrated. Perhaps his math was accurate. The problem is that is not a Biblical narrative and he could have saved a lot of time by simply reading. However, we observe that much more than we should. What does the Bible say?

The cause of the Flood was "all the fountains of the great deep" bursting forth first and then, the windows of Heaven were opened though not for 40 days and nights but for 150 days. The ark landed on that 150th day when the fountains were stopped and the windows shut as the Flood was at it's peak 15 cubits above the tallest mountain. Job describes and locates these fountains of the Great Deep and this is amazing revelation.

> *Genesis 7:11 KJV*
> *In the six hundredth year of Noah's life, in the second month, the seventeenth day of the month, on that day all the fountains of the great deep were broken up, and the windows of heaven were opened.*

> *Job 28:4 KJV*
> ***The flood breaketh out from the inhabitant;***
> *even the waters **forgotten of the foot**:*
> *they are dried up (**Brought Low**),*
> *they are gone away (**shake**) from men.*

The Flood broke out of the Fountains of the Great Deep which is the inhabitant of the Rivers from Eden who are found at the foot or bottom of the ocean floor. They are forgotten. The translators were fine on this but no where near exact to the Hebrew. However, without understanding the paradigm, this would be difficult for any man. They are dried up is not true to the Hebrew use.

> *dried up?:* דלל*: dâlal: H1809: [392]*
> ***brought low** (3x), dried up (1x), not equal (1x), emptied (1x), fail (1x), impoverished (1x), made thin (1x).*
> *Gesenius Hebrew-Chaldee Lexicon: To **hang down**, be **pendulous**, to **swing**, to **wave**. As a **bucket hanging in a well**...*

This is not "dried up" but better rendered "brought low" exactly where the Rivers from Eden are at the foot of the ocean. They are gone away is also an odd rendering.

> *gone away?:* נוע: *nuwa`: H5128: [392]*
> *to **quiver, totter, shake, reel, stagger, wander, move, sift, make move, wave, waver, tremble***

This is the location where 80 percent of the volcanic eruptions on Earth take place and men are shaken. [393] The largest zone for earthquakes and volcanoes on all of earth is not on land but in the bottom of the ocean deep in the Mid-Ocean Ridge and Oceanic Trenches or the Rivers from Eden just as Job said they would be.

These fountains of the great deep have been found today right in the middle of this River from Eden System we have identified. Science terms them Hydrothermal Vents and they introduce warmth into the depths of the ocean which is integral in protecting our ecosystem to this day. They introduce salt and minerals into the sea in essence serving to chemically balance the harmony of the entire ocean with other factors. Yahuah has not forgotten His rivers. These fountains are still there and only found in the midst of the River from Eden system known to science as the Mid-Ocean Ridge(Eden River) and the Oceanic Trenches(Four Heads). We will likely see them fully functioning in the end when the ocean once again disappears when there is "no more sea." (Rev. 21:1).

All of this is connected to this day, to the entire circulation system of the ocean. Without the Rivers from Eden, life on earth would likely fail. The Great Ocean Conveyor Belt or Thermohaline (Temperature and Salt) Circulation literally begins at the same point where the Mid-Ocean Ridge or River From Eden begins and follows the same path largely until it gets off track in the Pacific Ocean for obvious reason but then returns right back to the same Northern point just South of the North Pole with surface currents. This is where circulation falls back to the ocean floor in the world's largest waterfall. This is no coincidence.

The Fountains of the Great Deep operated at Creation, still today and continue to the end times when they will stand still for three hours meaning they will continue to operate until that point and after.

AT CREATION: 2 Esdras 4:7 KJVA

And he said unto me, If I should ask thee how great dwellings are in the midst of the sea, or how many springs are in the beginning of the deep, or how many springs are above the firmament, or which are the outgoings of paradise:

IN THE END TIMES: 2 Esdras 6:24 KJVA

At that time shall friends fight one against another like enemies, and the earth shall stand in fear with those that dwell therein, the springs of the fountains shall stand still, and in three hours they shall not run.

Science has introduced theories of Pangea, one supercontinent that existed before the Flood. Of course, their theory requires millions of years they do not have. Some attempt to inject that this supercontinent divided in the days of the Flood. If this had happened, you are not reading this book as we would all be extinct. No life would likely survive such a massive shift in tectonics causing the largest earthquake the world would have ever seen. That is not scientific.

Some discuss the mountains rose out of the seas yet from what sea did Mt. Everest rise? It is in the middle of a continent. Would not the impact of tectonic plates colliding with such monumental force also cause the extinction of life as we know it especially to move the Himalayas to ascend to more than five miles into the sky and abruptly? If we are on continents floating on magma yet spinning and colliding at 1,000 miles per hour at the equator, does this not defy science?

No one is thinking this through. We continue to hear so many theories and no one proves anything anymore. These fountains of the Great Deep have been found and are said in 2 Esdras to not only operate from Creation but continue through to the end times. Again, we label this a theory and we are not scientists. However, examine it with scripture and you will find this is the only theory on this topic which actually matches the Bible and science for that matter. This system leads us to the Garden of Eden.

Chapter 18 | Locating the Garden of Eden In the Philippines

"My Last Farwell" ("Mi Ultimo Adios")
"Farewell, my adored Land, **region of the sun** *caressed,*
Pearl of the Orient Sea, *our* **Eden lost,**
With gladness I give you my Life, sad and repressed;
And were it more brilliant, more fresh and at its best,
I would still give it to you for your welfare at most."
– Dr. Jose Rizal, December 30, 1896 (Eve of his execution). Original
in Spanish. English translation by Encarnacion Alzona & Isidro Escare
Abeto. [296]

Did Dr. Jose Rizal know more about the Philippines than we are told? On the eve of his execution, he wrote this poem in which he referred to the Philippines as the "region of the sun" which is important in identifying the land of Chryse/Ophir, "Pearl of the Orient Sea" which is crucial in revealing the land of Ancient Havilah next to the Garden of Eden and "our Eden lost" as if he knew this was in fact the long lost location of the Garden of Eden perhaps.

One must wonder if Rizal had other writings which may have been smuggled out of his prison of exile but no such speculation is needed to locate the Garden of Eden which has actually been recorded since very ancient times and exact directions even. We will delve into this realm though we were hesitant at first. Can we really find the Garden of Eden in the Philippines?

When we first started researching Ophir, we received correspondence from many Filipinos who told us that not only was the Philippines Ophir but it was the location of the Garden of Eden. Knowing the ramifications and monumental effort it might take to authenticate that, we carefully answered that was not something we could prove at that time. In other words, we did not believe we would ever find the Garden of Eden in the Philippines. We, as many of you reading this book, were steeped in the mindset that the Garden of Eden may have been destroyed by the Flood and regardless, we knew there were two or more terrible angels guarding the entrance with a flaming sword that turns in every direction. We certainly were not planning to go there even if we were fortunate enough to locate it.

We found Ophir and after the Three Kings revelation, we migrated over to another topic in our Flood Series where we were not even seeking the Garden of Eden but wished to restore belief that the Biblical Flood account was accurate. As we sought secondary support for Noah's division of the earth we decided not to just read Jubilees 8 again but to map it out so all could understand what Noah did and did not mean. These can be very confusing if one does not have a map in front of them researching each place name to make sure they are in the right spot and following the directions turn by turn. In addition, we have read so many commentaries on Jubilees which never used a map and they are all over the place even stumbling over the same tract of land more than once as if Noah was sloppy. He was not as the mapping would reveal.

We already covered the Rivers From Eden which lead us to Ancient Havilah, land of Adam and Eve in the Philippines which we also tested the Genesis 2 passage and each resource defining that island is not only found native and in abundance but the Philippines leads the world as number one in all three categories. It is not as if there is even a second land who could lay claim. However, that alone does not mean the Garden must be in the Philippines except the purpose of the River From Eden system is to water the Garden and that is the very end of the entire system. Thus, we should find it there but how?

Some read the Genesis 2 Rivers From Eden and poorly assume the Garden of Eden must be between the modern Tigris and Euphrates Rivers yet we already proved that requires ignoring Genesis 2 which is clear there was no precipitation on the Earth at that point. There is also nothing which leads there and that is the occult creation myth not Bible.

Here are a couple of odd things to consider, and this is the Bible waxing brilliant yet again. If the whole face of the Earth is watered by this mist and the Garden is watered by the Eden River system, then the Garden of Eden is not located on the whole face of the Earth. How could this be? Where would it be then? This is actually already defined in the Hebrew word which is translated as Garden. It is hard to believe we have yet to read a commentary which actually explores this Hebrew word but virtually all accept the word Garden yet they should not leave it at that as the first definition is not garden.

Hebrew: gan: גן *:* **enclosure**, *garden. [346]*

The first definition of the Hebrew words Gan Eden are "Enclosure of Eden." It was also a garden, an enclosed garden. Certainly, in many passages especially it's creation was a planting of a Garden. Some question how the Garden would have sunlight and yet this is the Holy of Holies of Yahuah on Earth. His light is sufficient just as the sun and moon will disappear in Revelation and we will no longer need it because we have His light after the Day of Judgment. In many cases, these very ancient Hebrew words, do not carry just one meaning but they convey all the definitions as they have come to mean different things in different applications over the millennia. This is why when Adam and Eve were exiled from the Garden, the angels were not placed on the North, South nor West but only on the East. The exit from the Garden is on it's East side where Adam was exiled.

> *Genesis 3:23-24 KJV*
> *Therefore the Lord God sent him forth from the garden of Eden, to till the ground from whence he was taken. So he drove out the man; and he placed* **at the east of the garden** *of Eden Cherubims, and a flaming sword which turned every way, to keep the way of the tree of life.*

Adam was exiled to the East of the Garden and the angels placed on that side as well to guard it from his attempting to re-enter. Notice their true purpose, to "keep the way of the Tree of Life." Yahuah told us it would be a disaster if Adam and Eve in their fallen state now ate from the Tree of Life. This would mean the Garden is located West of where Adam and Eve were exiled as they were ejected to the East of the Garden. We already know they lived in Ancient Havilah, land of Havah(Eve) where the first childbirth occurred which is it's Hebrew meaning and this land tests as the Philippines and no other land. Therefore, somehow the Garden of Eden is enclosed down within the Earth just West of Havilah, Philippines. We are aware there is a doctor out there claiming to understand scripture saying we made an "alleged mistake" on this. Though we will leave this anonymous, he claims the Garden must be to the East of Havilah based on what he represented in his emails to a viewer in which they forwarded to us with questions at his request evidently. We have no issue with his asking questions or even challenging and are glad he is following the research. This is why we are not calling him out. However, this position must be clarified so people are not confused by this.

> *"So TGC (The God Culture) setting the Garden of Eden or the Temple in Sulu which is WEST is Questionable."*
>
> *"...In EZEKIEL 8.16 prayer must be Directed to East. the True location of Garden of Eden is Pacific, but TGC points a wrong Direction in Sulu which is West. It's ABOMINATION"*

Obviously, this doctor is reading in fragments, one of the greatest fallacies of modern scholarship and did not seem to notice the context of those whom are praying not just to the East but to the SUN. That is sun worship called by many names such as Mithraism, Zoroastrianism, Mazdaism, etc.

This passage never commands us to pray to the East in this fashion but the opposite, it calls this and the two other scenarios of those weeping for Tammuz (false sun god of ancient Sumer/Assyria/Babylon/Persia) an abomination. Thus, he has it backwards. If only he had read even a paragraph before, he is the one propagating abomination as acceptable worship.

Ezekiel 8:13-18 KJV
He said also unto me, Turn thee yet again, and thou shalt see greater abominations that they do. Then he brought me to the door of the gate

of the LORD's house which was toward the north; and, behold, there sat women weeping for Tammuz. Then said he unto me, Hast thou seen this, O son of man? turn thee yet again, and thou shalt see greater abominations than these. And he brought me into the inner court of the LORD's house, and, behold, at the door of the temple of the LORD, between the porch and the altar, were about five and twenty men, with their backs toward the temple of the LORD, and their faces toward the east; and they worshipped the sun toward the east. Then he said unto me, Hast thou seen this, O son of man? Is it a light thing to the house of Judah that they commit the abominations which they commit here? for they have filled the land with violence, and have returned to provoke me to anger: and, lo, they put the branch to their nose. Therefore will I also deal in fury: mine eye shall not spare, neither will I have pity: and though they cry in mine ears with a loud voice, yet will I not hear them.

No, these were not holy elders but the ones who dragged the nation of Israel into idol worship and Yahuah hates this practice this doctor claims is supposed to be ours. No thank you. We get such objections from time to time but have yet to receive a coherent debate even from such scholars especially. This one certainly is not a challenge.

Also, even if they were to pray to the East from Jerusalem, and this passage does not say so, that is merely an indication that the Garden is East of Jerusalem at best. The Sulu Sea is East of Jerusalem thus qualifies fine. There is no passage that ever states Adam prayed to the East nor East specifically from the Philippines. This is not Islam and this shows a very mixed up doctor in the basics of theology. Unfortunately, we are finding several such not because they desire to be so but because our seminaries are shallow and peddling the doctrines of men requiring memorization or let us call that what it is, programming rather than teaching them to discern and test all things for themselves. If you have made it this far in this book, you are already aware of several such doctrines of men regarding Biblical geography, history, science, prophecy, etc. such as the Queen of Sheba with the leg and hoof of a goat. That is a colossal misrepresentation and occult infiltration and this doctor represents the same unknowingly.

We will expound on this even more in the next chapter as we locate the Mount of the East which is inside the Garden of Eden as Enoch sacrificed there inside yet at the same time protrudes out of the Garden of Eden as Adam sacrificed on the same mountain after his exile. He was no longer in the Garden yet accessed the Mount of the East. In the Biblical narrative, Enoch, the great prophet who was seventh from Adam is not identified as residing in Heaven.

> *Genesis 5:23-24 KJV*
> *And all the days of Enoch were three hundred sixty and five years: And Enoch walked with God: and* **he was not***; for God took him.*

One day, Enoch disappeared from among men yet did not die as confirmed in Hebrews.

> *Hebrews 11:5 KJV*
> *By faith* **Enoch was translated** *that he* **should not see death***; and was not found, because God had translated him: for before his translation he had this testimony, that he pleased God.*

Again, these verses only mention that Enoch was taken but this does not specifically say that Enoch resides in Heaven. Jubilees clarifies this and much of Genesis.

> *Jubilees 4:23-24 (R.H. Charles, 1903)*
> *And he was taken from amongst the children of men, and we (the angels)* **conducted him into the Garden of Eden** *in majesty and honour, and behold there he writes down the condemnation and judgment of the world, and all the wickedness of the children of men. And on account of it (God) brought the waters of the flood upon all the land of Eden; for there he was set as a sign and that he should testify against all the children of men, that he should recount all the deeds of the* **generations until the day of condemnation***.*

Sometimes scripture is so masterful it confirms itself over and over. Jesus(Yahusha) tells us no man has ascended up into Heaven. Only He will and He did. Enoch did visit Heaven but he did not ascend there to reside as he was conducted into the Garden of Eden where he would replace Adam as High Priest. In fact, he will remain there until the Day of Judgment.

> *John 3:13 KJV*
> And **no man hath ascended up to heaven**, *but he that came down from heaven, even the Son of man which is in heaven.*

The Flood waters were brought on all the region of Eden and note, we will demonstrate the Garden of Eden is not Eden but was planted to the East of it. Enoch is the Great Scribe who writes in the Garden to this day and will be there until the Day of Judgment thus it survived the Flood in tact. The Tree of Life in the midst of the Garden survives in Revelation 2:7, 22:2 and 22:14. Jubilees provides further clarity.

> *Jubilees 4:25-26 (R.H. Charles, 1903)*
> And **he** *(Enoch)* **burnt the incense** *of the sanctuary, (even) sweet spices acceptable before the Lord on* **the Mount**. *For* **the Lord has four places on the earth**, *the* **Garden of Eden**, *and the* **Mount of the East**, *and this mountain on which thou art this day,* **Mount Sinai**, *and* **Mount Zion** *(which) will be sanctified in the new creation for a sanctification of the earth; through it will the earth be sanctified from all (its) guilt and its uncleanness through-out the generations of the world.*

Some may question the Book of Jubilees as scripture, inspired and canon. Chapter 21 of this book will test this book, 2 Esdras and Enoch since we use them principally to locate only the Rivers and Garden of Eden. If you are feeling skeptical on Jubilees, skip ahead and read that chapter first and your questions will be answered in full as we find Jubilees quoted by the Qumran community, Jesus(Yahusha), John, Paul, Luke and Peter and even the early church fathers, 2 Esdras was recited even by Jesus(Yahusha) Himself and the Book of Enoch has a whole paragraph essentially quoted in Jude.

According to Jubilees, Yahuah has four Holy Places on Earth. The Mount of the East is located in the Garden of Eden, Mt. Sinai and Mt.

Zion. When Enoch entered the Garden, he sacrificed on the Mount of the East there from inside the Garden. Adam also sacrificed on the Mount of the East, the Holy Mountain in the Garden of Eden when exiled from outside of the Garden. Thus, we can also identify the Mount of the East above the surface. Otherwise, Adam would not have been able to access it from atop.

> *Jubilees 3:27 (R.H. Charles, 1903)*
> *And on that day on which* **Adam** *went forth from the Garden, he offered as a sweet savour an* **offering, frankincense, galbanum,** *and* **stacte,** *and* **spices** *in the morning with the rising of the sun from the day when he* **covered his shame.**

We will use an historic reference outside of the Bible to further support this not for scripture but geography to better understand. This is not scripture.

> *Cave Of Treasures*
> *And Adam and Eve went down in . . . . of spirit over the mountains of Paradise, and they found a cave in the top of the mountain, and they entered and hid themselves therein.*
> *And Adam took from the skirts of the* **mountain of Paradise,** **gold,** *and* **myrrh,** *and* **frankincense,** *and he placed them in the cave, and he blessed the cave, and consecrated it that it might be the house of prayer for himself and his sons. And he called the cave "ME`ARATH GAZZE" (i.e. "CAVE OF TREASURES"). [71]*

What mountain of Paradise is this? The Mount of the East that protrudes out of the Garden of Eden. Adam offered the first atonement and there is no passage to indicate he ever sinned again in his entire 930 years. He retrieved gold, frankincense and myrrh from the sides of that mountain meaning they grow there natively and all three are native to the Philippines. These are the same gifts brought by the Queen of Sheba and the Three Wise Kings (6 or more) from Ophir, Philippines. Some attempt to insert Africa into this but Africa is not East of the Garden, it is far West as you will see and in Ham's territory and we will show you it must be in Shem's on his Eastern border which is no where near Africa nor Iraq nor Israel which is all the way on his Western border not East.

Remember, the sons of Joktan migrated East of Meshad, Iran to Sephar, the Tree of Life in the Garden of Eden and the Mount of the East, the Holy Mountain in the Garden of Eden. This is Sephar or Parvaim or Sephar-vaim another name for the gold in the Temple. That is the same as Ophir which is the same as Uphaz, the Gold of the Pison River or Ancient Havilah. These all tie together firmly in the Hebrew and there is no separating them. Our Rivers From Eden theory locates this land as Philippines firmly. However, there is concrete evidence and exact directions that were written thousands of years ago which does not even require such associations though they do affirm it.

The Book of Jubilees outlines in Noah's division of territories exact directions to the Garden of Eden. For a full mapping of these directions in all of Chapter 8, view our Flood Series Parts 3 and 4 and you will find when following this on a map, this makes perfect sense. Get ready to have your mind blown because this is monumental. No wonder the Book of Jubilees was censored by the Pharisees.

In the division of Shem's territory, Noah is very deliberate in his language. He begins to describe the location of the Garden of Eden and identifies that it is the permanent Holy of Holies of Yahuah on Earth. This is not Israel's temporary Temple which is gone and only lasted a few centuries. Many overlook that.

> *Jubilees 8:18-19 (R.H. Charles, 1903)*
> *And Noah rejoiced that this portion came forth for Shem and for his sons, and he remembered all that he had spoken with his mouth in prophecy; for he had said: 'Blessed be the Lord God of Shem And may the Lord dwell in the dwelling of Shem.'And he knew that the* **Garden of Eden is the holy of holies, and the dwelling of the Lord,** *and Mount Sinai the centre of the desert, and Mount Zion - the centre of the navel of the earth: these three were created as holy places facing each other.*

As you follow this full mapping, it begins in the North Pole, then a river in Russia that cannot be any other river. Though the name is lost to history, it's description is perfection. The territory advances South

Shem's Southeastern border.

to India to Saudi Arabia and to the coast of Africa on the banks of the Gihon River. It then turns to the Far East crossing the Indian Ocean all the way to Shem's Eastern border beyond India.

> *Jubilees 8:16 (R.H. Charles, 1903): SHEM'S TERRITORY*
> *…And it extendeth towards the* **east, till it reacheth the Garden of Eden,** *to the south thereof, [to the south] and from the east of the whole land of Eden.*

The Garden of Eden is on Shem's Eastern border. That cannot be Africa nor anywhere in the Middle East. It is a small stretch North of the Southeastern border of Shem. Noah repeats that Shem's territory travels to the East of India or the Far East as verse 21 specifies:

> *Jubilees 8:21 (R.H. Charles, 1903): SHEM'S TERRITORY*
> *"And he (Noah) knew that a blessed portion and a blessing had come to Shem and his sons unto the generations forever… and the* **whole land of the East and India…***"*

Shem's Division from Noah.

Asia.

From Jubilees 8

(See our publishing of the Book of Jubilees for full-sized, detailed color maps)

Ham's Division from Noah.

Southern Hemisphere except Asia..

From Jubilees 8

(See our publishing of the Book of Jubilees for full-sized, detailed color maps)

Japheth's Division from Noah.

Northern Hemisphere except Asia.

From Jubilees 8

(See our publishing of the Book of Jubilees for full-sized, detailed color maps)

Then, the next verse identifies Ham's territory which begins in Africa of which all is Ham's and none Shem's. However, Shem's territory already reaches the shores of the East coast of Africa blocking Ham from entering the Indian Ocean to the East on that portion as Ham's territory which cannot stumble over Shem's. Therefore, the directions progress from Africa to the West across the entire Southern Hemisphere beyond South America and to the Far East where the Garden of Eden is positioned. Some attempt to claim because Ham's territory is to the right of the Garden, that somehow places it in Africa but that thinking would mean Shem would have to have a portion of Africa which he does not and all the directions become royally discombobulated as a result. Crossing the Gihon could be any direction as it surrounds Africa.

Even the Hereford Mappa Mundi c. 1300 (below) and the Turin Map c. twelfth century (Ch. 3) place the Garden of Eden or Paradise in the Far East in the same position as Dionysus the Tourist from 124 A.D. (Ch. 3) and Mela of 43 A.D. (Ch. 3) locate Chryse, the Greek isle of gold known as Ophir in Hebrew. The Turin Map ties the Garden to Chryse and all lead to the Philippines.

"Hereford Mappa Mundi." circa 1300. Inset left. Public Domain. [302]

1 - **The Paradise**, *surrounded by a wall and a ring of fire and a great river (Pison River).*

2 - The Ganges and its delta.

3 - The fabulous Island of Taphana, Sri Lanka.

4 - Rivers Indus and Tigris. (Turn to corner to the East and you are in Paradise, Philippines)

Again, follow the map and it is clear. Remember, we are in Ham's territory in the directions and we cross the Gihon River from Eden (not a modern river) from Africa into the sea of Mauk documented as the South Atlantic named after Ham's wife and around the Southern Hemisphere in these directions. Most neglect that the Gihon surrounds all of Africa thus when Ham crosses it, it could be in either direction. That is not a clue but what he cannot do is cross into what is already mapped as Shem's territory. There is no overlapping nor can there be as there is a curse pronounced on anyone who lives in their brother's land thus Noah would be precise and he was.

> *Jubilees 8:22-23 (R.H. Charles, 1903): HAM'S TERRITORY*
> *And for Ham came forth the second portion, beyond the Gihon towards*
> *the south* **to the right of the Garden**, *and it extends towards the*
> *south and it extends to* **all the mountains of fire**...
> ...**till it reaches the right of the Garden of Eden**.

Ham received the Southern Hemisphere or the "hot" lands especially. Africa, South America, Australia and even Indonesia which these directions now become very specific. We are in the Far East as we must be in the directions as we are near Shem's Eastern border, East of India and Noah then, defines Shem's Southeastern border while also clarifying his East border. He identifies Ham's in both directions as well.

This is why the Aborigines of Australia, Indonesia, South America, etc. have similarities to Africa. The assumption is they came from Africa and perhaps they did but they are in their territory of Ham all the same. Ham's name means "hot" or "burnt" or black and so does his son Cush for which Ethiopia (all of Central Africa) is named. Noah had the genes to carry all of the races across the Flood as all men are precious to Yahuah. This is why Noah had a different appearance which worried Lamech, his father, yet he was fully human but described much like an albino.

Hebrew: Cham: **חם***:* **hot**. *[301]*
Hebrew: Cush: Kuwsh: **כוש***:* **black**, *Ethiopia. [288]*

Ham's border with Shem in Southeast Asia.

This border to Shem's South in the Far East and Ham's North also defines Shem's East as it lines up with the Philippine Trench, is defined as "all the mountains of fire." Obviously, this cannot be a reference to all volcanoes on Earth as you have all three territories and confusion nor can it even be the Ring of Fire which also falls in all three regions. This is more pronounced. When one is in that part of the world, they quickly realize that Indonesia has a name for it's 147 volcanoes which derives from Noah's directions here in Jubilees.

They call them Gunung Gunung Api in Javanese which just so happens to translate into English as Gunung meaning mountain, Gunung twice meaning plural or mountains and Api is fire – Mountains of Fire. [300] Here we are with a reference which survives to this day preserving the location of the Garden of Eden which is just to the North of this border. The northernmost volcano happens to be on the border of Sabah, Malaysia (Philippine owned in history) and Indonesia. That is how this island was split between two countries, Noah did it just as he split what is now Moscow as it's river is the border set by Noah between Europe and Asia. Modern Russia is in violation. This identifies the Southeastern border of Shem's allotment as the border of Malaysia and Indonesia today to the South and to the East lining up with the Easternmost volcano, essentially the Philippine Trench, or the ancient Pison River.

Therefore, Indonesia is in Ham's territory and so is everything in that area to the East of the Philippine Trench which Noah is using the ancient Pison River as the border just as he uses the Gihon in Africa and the Hiddekel later. Noah knew where the Rivers from Eden were and his mapping matches our theory.

This is why Indonesia cannot be Ophir as it is in Ham's territory nor can Solomon Islands which are inappropriately named as they have never been known for gold. Nor is Ophir, New Zealand, a modern concoction which is Ham's territory as well. The Garden of Eden can be located just to the North of Sabah, Malaysia in the Sulu Sea even scientifically.

Now that you can see the Chapter 8 full mapping (full details are available in our publishing of the Book of Jubilees), in Chapter 9 of Jubilees, Shem, Ham and Japheth divide their first portions of their territories to their sons all around the area of Babel in perspective, in which they all migrated from the East. We used this passage in Chapter 4 but the mapping would be out of context there. To the right, we have produced a mapping of Jubilees 9 for your perusal. Take special note that Arphacsad, ancestor of Ophir lived in Iran as that was his territory and Canaan stole Israel. Also, this now identifies the seat of power for Gog of Magog, the nemesis prince demon of the end times who tries to conquer the world. He is originally from Magog which is Russia but his throne is established in West and Central Europe.

Hebrew Markers in the Land of Creation

As we covered before, the Carpenter Report [351], CNN [352], World Bank [353] and many others now record the Sulu Sea specifically the Verde Island passage from Mindoro to Batangas as "The Center of the Center of Marine Biodiversity on Earth" and as we established, that indicates the origin of life on Earth not old bones of humans nor animals. Therefore, this even proves out scientifically as that is just above the Garden of Eden which is enclosed within the Earth. Somewhere to the East there is an entrance and we do not claim to have found the entrance nor do we wish to attempt to enter. We believe we even find support in the Hebrew name of a large underwater reef famous for

Shem, Ham and Japheth initially divide their vast worldwide territories in the region near Shinar to which they all migrated from the East (see Noah's Ark Landing Map at the end of this chapter). This is only their division prior to the destruction of the Tower of Babel. They spread out beyond into their full territories after and this is when Ophir, Sheba and Havilah relocated far away from Babel and into the Far East with Tarshish.

diving in the center of the Sulu Sea in fact just above the Garden.

Tubbataha Reef
Hebrew: Tub: טוב: *good things [204]*
Hebrew: ba: בא: *in the [355]*
Hebrew: Ta: תא: *chamber [305]*
Hebrew: Ha: הא: *The [306]*
Our Interpretation: The Good Things in the Chamber

To what chamber might this be referring? Perhaps the enclosed Garden of Eden just below. If this is coincidence, calculate the odds of such impossibility.

For further support, we consult the Book of Enoch as Enoch was taken around the world by the angels and he describes the world especially as he is approaching the Garden of Eden.

2 Enoch 8:4-7 (The Book of Secrets translated by Platt)
*And **two springs** come out which send forth honey and milk, and their springs send forth oil and wine, and they **separate into four parts**, and go round with quiet course, and **go down into the PARADISE OF EDEN**, between corruptibility and incorruptibility. And thence they go forth along the earth, and have a **revolution** to their **circle** even as other elements.*

It just so happens that when travelling along the Pison River or Philippine Trench, there are two entry points through the rear spine of the Philippines or in ancient times perhaps two streams. These would split into four streams and go round about the interior of Visayas around the ancient mountains of Eden until they go down into the Garden of Eden just below the Sulu Sea in the Earth. As the ocean floor was dry land prior to the Flood, this would seem to indicate they enter the interior of the Earth where the Garden of Eden is enclosed. Even today, you will hear many stories of very mysterious currents throughout these areas of Visayas especially around Romblon and Surigao (Northern tip of Mindanao) right around these two entrances. In fact, the word Romblon may actually be even more telling as it appears to be Hebrew

Romblon:

Hebrew: rom: רום: *on high, of direction, elevation. [307]*
Hebrew: bl: yabal: ybl: יבל: *watercourse, stream. [308]*
Hebrew: N: נ: *letter NUN: continue, offspring, heir [310]*
Our Interpretation: Upper Streams of the Heir (in the Garden?)

We already covered Panay which in Hebrew is overlooking likely the Garden, Mindoro meaning "species of the generations" and so many more in this vicinity which lead in this same direction.

One must wonder if even the fabled Biringan City may actually have ancient roots in the narrative of Enoch who was taken from mankind into the Garden of Eden just below the Philippines where he still resides. Remember, that is the Holy of Holies just below the Philippines. It is no wonder this people is such a happy people despite all the hardship they have faced. Of course, over time all kinds of things have been added into the story as it becomes a sort of ghost tale. However, the legend says righteous people disappear and are taken into Biringan City never to return. There are descriptions which no one has ever entered nor left other than Enoch, Adam and Eve perhaps thus no one could possibly describe it. However, what is extremely odd is we have yet another word here that may be of Hebrew origin and appropriately so.

Biringan City, Samar:
Legend of the Mysterious, Hidden City

Hebrew: BIRI: בראי: *creative one [309]*
Hebrew: N: נ: *letter NUN: continue, offspring, heir [310]*
Hebrew: GAN: גן: *Hebrew: an enclosure, garden. [298]*
Our Interpretation: Enclosed Garden of Heir of Creative One

We actually take a tour around Visayas finding all kinds of place names of potential Hebrew origin such as Binalbagan, Samar, Calamian, Palawan, Cebu, Bohol, etc. A further look into many of the mountains reveals even more. However, whether one agrees with every definition or not, it is very hard to dismiss in lieu of the exact directions from the Book of Jubilees and all the other factors aligning in the Philippines. The Book of Enoch sheds a little more light on this as well as he describes his approaching the region of the Garden of Eden. Enoch even describes trees which sound like those of the Philippines.

Enoch Affirms Jubilees' Location of Garden of Eden

> *1 Enoch 31:1-3*
> *And I saw another mountain on which there were trees, and there flowed out water, and there flowed out from it, as it were, a nectar whose name is* **styrax** *and* **galbanum***. And beyond this mountain I saw another mountain, and on it there were* **aloe trees***, and those trees were full of a* **fruit***,* **which** *is* **like an almond***, and* **is hard***. And when they take this fruit it is* **better than any fragrance***.*

Styrax and Galbanum are found in the Philippines natively as is aloe despite a limited history which assumes that Egypt is the origin of aloe because they drew it in ancient times. It is rather ludicrous to think the plant only grew there on all of earth just because they illustrated it. However, this nut like an almond and hard sounds to us like the Pili Tree of the Philippines and it is the source of frankincense of the very best fragrance which is impossible odds.

> *1 Enoch 32:1-2*
> *And after these fragrances, to the north, as I looked over the mountains, I saw seven mountains full of fine* **nard***, and fragrant trees of* **cinnamon** *and* **pepper***. And from there, I went over the summits of those mountains, far away to the* **east***, and I went over the Red Sea, and I was far from it, and I went over the* **Angel Zotiel***.*

The Philippines has nard, cinnamon and pepper natively as well. This Red Sea reference as Enoch is in the Far East is to the Indian Ocean. He is beyond the Indian Ocean in a group of mountains which after the Flood we call islands. He is in the Philippines. His mention of the Angel Zotiel is a reference to one of the angels who guards the entrance to the Garden of Eden as there are at least two as cherubim is plural. These trees sound Filipino in nature and as a side note, we explored the original fig whose leaves were used to cover Adam and Eve.

Philippine Fig Leaf Best Fits the Story of Adam and Eve

Adam and Eve covered their shame with fig leaves when they realized they were naked in the Garden following their trespass (Gen. 3:7). As critics have noted, the average fig is ill-shaped and extremely inelegant for this application. After all, how did Adam get this to stay in position as normally pictured? However, the Philippines has a native fig which is only known to be indigenous there which satisfies this narrative. It's long leaves grow up to 30 inches of appropriate disposition well-suited for Adam and Eve to fashion a sort of grass skirt. Ficus pseudopalma is a species of fig known by the common names Philippine fig, dracaena fig, and palm-leaf fig. In nature it is endemic to the Philippines, especially the island of Luzon.

Philippine Fig Leaf.
The perfect orientation for Adam and Eve.
Endemic and rare to the Philippines.

Common Fig Leaf.
This design would require
intricate weaving not present
in the narrative.

1 Enoch 32:3-4

And I **came to the Garden of Righteousness**, *and I saw beyond those trees many large trees growing there, sweet smelling, large, very beautiful and glorious, the* **Trees of Wisdom**, *from which they eat and know great wisdom. And it is* **like the carob tree**, *and* **its fruit is like bunches of grapes** *on a vine, very beautiful, and the smell of this tree spreads and penetrates afar.*

What tree is Enoch referring to here which looks like a carob tree and it's fruit is like bunches of grapes on a vine but this is a tree, beautiful with penetrating smell. We believe this is Lanzones.

1 Enoch 32:5-6

And I said: "This tree is beautiful! How beautiful and pleasing is its appearance!" And the Holy Angel Raphael, who was with me, answered me and said to me: "This is the **Tree of Wisdom**, *from which* **your ancient father** *and ancient mother, who were before you*, **ate and learnt wisdom***; and their eyes were opened, and* **they knew** *that* **they were naked**. *And they were* **driven from** *the* **garden**.*"*

Lanzones appears to be the Tree of the Knowledge of Good and Evil in Enoch's description as it is a perfect fit in every way. Could there be such a history that Lanzones could be poison?

Lanzones originates in the Tagalog word Lason for "poison to morals or mind." [410] This is perfectly fitting and very similar to the Hebrew "Lashon" which denotes essentially a poison tongue in some applications and even a golden wedge or bar in others tying to Ophir and Havilah. [410] To the right, you will notice insets of the Carob and Lanzones Trees. Notice the leaves and branches are very similar as Enoch recorded. The Lanzones fruit certainly appears as grapes growing on a tree as described.

Can we really say this? Well, we were not there but in reading Enoch's very obvious reference this does match. However, we are not the first to say so as Philippine legend concurs. It was purged of such poison but one must ask how this can possibly end up matching the Book of Enoch.

The Legend of Lanzones (Ang Alamat ng Lansones)

"Lansones is actually derived from the word lason, which is Tagalog for "poison." There was once a time when the pale yellow globes lived up to their sinister name.

The cream-colored clusters were said to have originated from Paete, Laguna. They were so poisonous that even the ants on it's branches died on the spot. But all that changed when a kindly old man named Mang Selo paused to rest under a shady tree while passing through the thick Paete forest, only the notorious Lansonses trees were nearby.

Faint from hunger, Mang Selo fell asleep and dreamt of a beautiful angel who plucked a fruit from the lansones tree for him to eat. Sensing his reluctance, the heavenly being pinched the tiny fruit to draw out the poison. Mang Selo awakened to find fruit peelings on the ground next to him. His curiosity and hunger soon overcame his fear of the lansones, and he cautiously peeled one and bit into it.

His gamble paid off, and he ended up relishing the fruit's sweet, refreshing taste. In gratitude to the angel who had saved him from hunger, he spread the word that lansones were no longer poisonous, and that the brown spots on it's skin were the fingerprints of the benevolent spirit who pinched the poison away." [312]

lason:
Tagalog: n. 1. poison;
2. poison to morals or mind
(origin of word lanzones) [410]

Lanzones fruit grows like bunches of grapes on a tree. Notice how the leaves and branches of the Lanzones tree resemble that of the Carob tree just as Enoch describes.

lashon:
Hebrew: לשׁון:
babbler, evil speaker, language,
talker, tongue, wedge (of gold)
(one with a poison tongue) [410]

CAROB TREE

LANZONES TREE

According to this oral legend passed through the generations in Laguna, Lanzones was once known to be poison. Where might a legend like that derive? The Book of Enoch yet again? An angel removed the poison and the tree was good to eat after that. Of course, this is a legend and there is no need to verify the story as much as we realize, legends like this usually have some sort of basis in ancient events many times. In this case, this happens to match what Enoch was describing in the Book of Enoch. Thus, we believe there is a connection. We do not need this association to prove our position but it's existence is additional support we thought worth mentioning and there are other accounts as well.

SunStar Philippines [311] and ABS-CBN [304] report on a Camiguin Island legend in which lanzones is also recorded as poison. Both add occult factors of witchcraft but in all three of these accounts, the lanzones tree is ultimately purified of poison and good to eat. So enjoy. We will.

Add to that the strong possibility the other tree in the neighborhood fits the Pili Tree which is like an almond but more so, that is the tree for Manila elemi which has two incense resins likened to frankincense and myrrh. Coincidence? We think not.

One last query posited often is the distance for the ark to travel to Turkey from the Philippines may be too far. This is another false paradigm as Noah's ark could not possibly have landed Northwest of Shinar (Babel, Iraq). Genesis 11:2 and Jubilees 10:19 firmly place the descendants of Noah East of Shinar. That cannot be Turkey nor Armenia.

There is no overcoming that period. Then, there is the challenge of the ark landing at Flood peak meaning it could only have rested on one mountain on all of earth – the tallest. The ark landed on day 150 which is the same day the fountains of the great deep and windows of heaven were stopped. It rained for 150 days not 40 according to the narrative as that is just a time stamp for when the ark was lifted. The Flood crested to 15 cubits above the tallest mountain and the ark being about 18 cubits below the water level could only have hit that one mountain.

One could attempt to make all the mountains move to satisfy this but then they have a massive problem with the Bible which not only locates the ark landing but firmly states mountains do not move from their places until Revelation of course. Yes, they blow their tops but they do not move positions. Some even are shaken but generally, they are anchored to a foundation which is immovable according to scripture.

The ark landed in the mountainS of Ararat, the highest land. Mt. Ararat in Turkey is in the wrong direction, 12,000 feet too short, not even the highest land in it's own region, not mountains as the closest are over 250 km away, etc. From Mt. Ararat in Turkey, Noah would not have seen other mountaintops as Genesis says he did. The dove would have found land in two directions. However, in the Book of Enki, the Nephilim also built an ark which landed in Turkey on their Mount of Salvation now called Ararat or near there. That's not Noah.

We believe remants of Japheth's first cities have been discovered in the Indus Valley Civilization dated to about 4000 B.C. These are among the oldest such finds in history. There is a Ma'uk region named after Ham's wife, Ne'elata Ma'uk, in India. This follows Ham's naming the South Atlantic the Ma'uk Sea also named after her. An empire rose from that area around 600 B.C. or so bearing the regional name of the Ma'ukhari Empire. Oddly, there is an area on Everest called Arkhale as if the ark is here. In fact, even the Nepalese name for Mt. Everest, Sagarmatha, reveals much as it means "Forehead of the Ocean and Sky." When was Everest considered such forehead especially of the ocean and sky? During the Flood it was the forehead of both at the same time.

The Garden of Eden is in the Philippines just under the Sulu Sea. However, we also locate this Holy Mountain, The Mount of the East which is mentioned in Jubilees in the midst of the Garden. This brings us back to the beginning narrative of Ophir and Sheba who migrated to Sephar, the Mount of the East.

Noah's Ark landed at Flood peak which must be the tallest mountain and Noah's descendants came to Shinar (Iraq) from the East not Turkey but the Himalayas. No one has found the ark nor would Noah, the carpenter, leave the only good wood left.

ARK LANDED AT FLOOD PEAK:
150 days = 5 months (Same day Waters Stopped)

GENESIS 7:24 KJV (Cf. 5:27)
And the waters prevailed upon the earth an hundred and fifty days

GENESIS 8:4 KJV (Cf. 5:28)
And the ark rested in the seventh month, on the seventeenth day of the month, upon the **mountains of Ararat**. (150 days, SAME)

15 CUBITS ABOVE TALLEST MOUNTAIN

GENESIS 7:19-20 KJV
And the waters prevailed exceedingly upon the earth; and **all the high hills**, that were under the whole heaven, **were covered. Fifteen cubits** upward did the waters prevail; and the mountains were covered.

JUBILEES 5:26 KJV
Fifteen cubits did the waters rise above all the high mountains

NOAH'S
ARK LANDING
HIMALAYAS
TALLEST MOUNTAIN
EAST OF SHINAR
AFTER THE FLOOD

GENESIS 11:2 KJV
And it came to pass, as they **journeyed from the east,** that they found a plain in the land of **Shinar; and they dwelt there.** Cf. 10:19 "For they **departed** from the land of **Ararat eastward to Shinar**" Cf. 8:21 **Ararat East of Media.**

EUROPE

Mt. Ararat in Turkey has the wrong name, in the wrong direction, 12,000' too short, is not mountains but is the site where the Nephilim claim to have landed when they survived.

SHEM
ASIA

2/3s of World Population Lives within this Area

JAPHETH
NORTHERN HEMISPHERE

SHINAR
ASSYRIA
BABEL

MT. EVEREST
Mt. Lubar in Ararat Mts (5:28)
Sagarmatha "Head of Ocean"
Arkhale, Nepal

Note Olive Trees are native to the Himalayas.

NOT TURKEY NW!
MUST BE EAST
OF SHINAR!

Mediterranean Sea

WHOLE
WRONG
DIRECTION

ISRAEL

EAST OF SHINAR

JAPHETH WEST
FIRST CITY
Adalaneses
Indus Valley
7:13-17

HAM SOUTH
FIRST CITY
Ne'elata Ma'uk
Ma'ukhan Empire, India
7:13-17

SHEM EAST
FIRST CITY
"Sedeq Eta Lebab"
East Side of Everest
7:13-17

CHINA

Notice the same directional pattern of Shem to the East, Ham South and Japheth North West continues in Noah's division as the son's first cities just after the Flood.

4000 BCE
Farming Settlements
Emerged Just After Flood

INDIA

Philippines

START
HAVILAH

GARDEN OF EDEN
Sabah, Malaysia

Indian Ocean

AFRICA

HAM

SOUTHERN
HEMISPHERE

ONLY THE TALLEST MOUNTAIN COULD FIT!

GENESIS 8:9 KJV (ALL MOUNTAINS STILL UNDER WATER)
But the dove found no rest for the sole of her foot, and she returned unto him into the ark, for **the waters were on the face of the whole earth.**

GENESIS 8:5 KJV (Cf. 5:30)
in the tenth month, on the first day of the month, were the tops of the mountains seen
(IF they were not seen before, they were ALL covered. Closest mountains to Mt. Ararat, Turkey = 250+ km)

AUSTRALIA

MOUNTAINS DON'T MOVE!
From their places. Not until the end times.

GENESIS 49:26
"everlasting hills"

DEUTERONOMY 33:15 KJV
"ancient mountains... lasting hills"

©2020 Map By The God Culture.

THE ARK:
30 Cubits Tall (50')
18 Cubits Below
Water Level (9m/30')
IT COULD HAVE ONLY HIT
1 MOUNTAIN – THE TALLEST.
1 Cubit = 20"

PSALM 104:5-8 KJV
Who laid the **foundations of the earth**, that it should **not be removed for ever.** Thou coveredst it with the deep as with a garment: the **waters stood above the mountains.**

Chapter 19 | Pioneer the Mount of the East In the Philippines

The next logical progression after locating the Garden of Eden in the Sulu Sea would be to find the Mount of the East. We believe we can do this as well though this will not be quite as scientific as the previous. However, the information is compelling and worthy of review. Once you test it, you may well come to the same conclusion. Let's review a different rendering of Enoch's sacrifice in the Garden of Eden.

> *Jubilees 4:25*
> *(Rabi-Kohan Shalomim Y. Halahawi, Ph.D, N.H.T. Min.)*
> *And he (Enoch) burnt the incense of the sanctuary, (even) sweet spices acceptable before the Lord on the **Mount Qater**. [40]*

Rabi-Kohan Halahawi, identifies the Mount of the East in Jubilees by name as Mount Qater or Qatar. Why would this be named such? Enoch made smoke sacrifices on this mountain as did Adam upon his exile. Also, in Kabbalah which he may be involved, the highest rung of the Tree of Life is named Keter which is the same word. We do not follow Kabbalah and reject it in every sense but the Hebrew is still Hebrew and useful in this case.

> *Hebrew:* **Qatar***:* קטר*: to make sacrifices of smoke, incense. [314]*

We begin with narrowing down the shape of the Garden of Eden. Logically, we believe the presence of oil pockets in the Sulu Sea will assist in identifying the shape as if there is a deep oil pocket miles deep, then likely the Garden is not found there. We took a map of the oil deposits around that area and begin to see a clearer picture. In fact, we notice an opening to the East becomes more pronounced which we will explore. The reason is the Mount of the East in order to be both inside the Garden and outside must be on the very Eastern tip of the Garden protruding out even beyond what is the World Ocean today. In ancient times this was a mountain but today we call it an island.

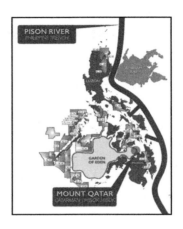

Mapping the Garden of Eden shape by the presence of oil pockets.

This appears to open up and lead right to Camiguin Island where the tallest summit would be Mt. Hibok Hibok. Could this be Mt. Qatar? Oddly, this is Hebrew yet again and not just any Hebrew but that which bears a very appropriate meaning and not in just one name but both names of this mountain as it has an international name, Mt. CATARman.

Mt. Hibok Hibok (Hiboc-hiboc volcano):

Hebrew: **hiboch***!: !היבוך ~ !היבוך: an imperative meaning (to a man) be embarrassed! [315]*

How can this possibly be the case? How can Hibok(Hiboch) be a direct and matching Hebrew word which essentially means "sorry" specifically to a man like Adam for instance. In translation, this is Mount Sorry! Sorry! with exclamation marks even and in the Hebrew definition rendered Hiboch!-Hiboch! Was Adam not embarrassed when he made an atonement sacrifice on this very mountain named for this purpose. Of course, this is impossible enough until you consider there is a second international name for this same mountain – Mt. Catarman. Catar or Qatar? As in smoke sacrifices? As in the Mount of the East where Ophir migrated and where Adam and Enoch sacrificed?

Mt. Catarman (Mt. Hibok Hibok International Name)

Hebrew: **Qatar***:* קטר*: to make sacrifices of smoke, incense*
Hebrew: **Maan***:* מען*: purpose, intent. [314 & 316]*
Our Interpretation: Intended to Make Smoke Sacrifices

Mt. Hibok Hibok, Camiguin Island, Philippines.

We are wading in absolutely impossible territory here. A mountain with two names that appear of Hebrew origin both in definition bridging Adam's first sacrifice of atonement. That is compelling.

Also, we mention the antediluvian Mount of the East is not just the tallest summit but the entire island of Camiguin. If you visit this area, you will find it is a true paradise even for the ancients. On Camiguin you find numerous freshwater springs, hot springs and even soda springs (maybe Adam made his own Soda – kidding). It is rich in agriculture and very abundant in what may well be the Tree of the Knowledge of Good and Evil – Lanzones. A sweeter variety of Lanzones for which Camiguin is famous and bears such legend.

In examining the word Camiguin, it originates in etymology in the Philippines as kamagong which is a hard, black wood related to the ebony tree. Somehow the Philippines seems to be omitted from some of the lists of habitats for ebony yet they have an island named for it. We do not find a direct Hebrew etymology for this entire word though Kam is entirely appropriate for the context and Agon is Greek.

Kamagong (Camiguin origin):

Hebrew: kam: קם*: he / it get(s) up [317]*

Greek: agon: ἀγών*: a gathering, contest, struggle (in the soul)*

(a masculine noun, and the root of the English words, "agony," "agonize") – properly, a contest (struggle), a grueling conflict (fight); (figuratively) positive struggle that goes with "fighting the good fight of faith" (1 Tim 6:12) [318]

Would Adam not get up or rise? He repented the next day. Was he not in agony, conflict, struggle? Did he not atone fighting the good fight of faith? These coalesce. However, when one looks at the fruit of the kamagong tree which is named Mabolo, perhaps this becomes a little clearer and in context.

Mabolo:

Hebrew: mabo: מבוא*: entrance, a coming in, entering. [319]*

Hebrew: lo: לא*: not, no. a. not (with verb - absolute prohibition). b. not (with modifier - negation) c. nothing (subst). d. without (with particle). e. before (of time). [320]*

In terms of the ancient mountain or modern island of Camiguin (kamagong), is this identifying that it is perhaps not an entrance to the Garden of Eden? Or that it is an entrance before time? Or that it is the act of entering before time? It is difficult to know but what is not difficult is to connect the etymology of this word Mabolo to Hebrew once one understands whom Joktan and his sons were as Hebrews and their connection to Israel on multiple levels. Just because the Mount of the East may protrude there from the Garden, does not mean the entrance is there. Perhaps it is elsewhere. We admit, we have not found the entrance to the Garden nor terrible angels.   We even had a viewer named Geni comment on our YouTube stream that "in Leyte, parents warn their disobedient children, "ipapatapon kita sa Mt. Hiboc Hiboc" which in English means to "put into exile on Mt. Hibok Hibok." Is it yet another coincidence that this tradition has been handed down through the generations that just as Adam was exiled from the Garden to Mt. Sorry Sorry whose purpose is to make smoke sacrifices, so might our misbehaving children be punished there? We have learned much from this exchange as Filipinos have added to our research constantly even steering us in directions at times.

Another viewer, Giovanni, commented "been to the top of hibok hibok many times small group of people dwell there amazing that on the top earth is mixed with many kinds of sea shells.. the place is called maitum...black in English." Does Maitum have possible Hebrew origins as well?

Maitum:

Hebrew: Mai: maon or main: מעון: abode, habitation. [321]

Hebrew: Tum: תמים: tummim: Plural of tom; perfections, i.e. (techn.) One of the epithets of the objects in the high-priest's breastplate as an emblem of complete Truth -- Thummim. [322]

Our Interpretation: THE DWELLING OF THE HIGH PRIEST

This certainly could have Hebrew roots and we cannot imagine a more appropriate definition as Adam was the first High Priest among men. To some, these Hebrew connections are considered a stretch and we understand their position but realize to entrench oneself there in light of all this overwhelming evidence is no longer supported by logic. If the Philippines is Ophir, there must be a connection to Hebrew and throughout this book, whether you accept every interpretation we offer in that vein or not, one cannot dismiss this link especially with the many direct Hebrew correlations that should cause academia to reconsider the Jesuit etymologies of an incomplete history.

Therefore, we believe a logical mapping of the Sulu Sea and Visayas considering oil deposits reasonably leads to the very East of the Garden of Eden as Camiguin Island. This mountain has incredible support in

Hebrew etymologies supporting it as the ancient Mount of the East upon which Adam sacrificed atop and Enoch sacrificed inside of the Garden of Eden. We cannot prove this out in the detail of the case for Ophir but when one piles all the evidence on top, this makes sense.

This is Yahuah's Holy Mountain – The Mount of the East from Genesis 10 and Jubilees. One of His four Holy places on Earth and it is connected to the Garden of Eden where His Holy of Holies resides. This is far more significant than Israel's temporary one. Instead of migrating to Israel where a Temple no longer stands and His presence no longer resides for certain Feasts, everyone should be visiting the Philippines where His permanent Holy of Holies still exists on Earth. Enoch remains inside at the base of this very mountain – Hiboch! Hiboch!

Photo: Idyllic White Island, an uninhabited white sandbar located off the northern shore of Mambajao in Camiguin island, Philippines.

Chapter 20 | Examining Extra-Biblical Texts Used in this Book

The entire modern Old Testament canon was found in Qumran with the exception of the Book of Esther. For many of these books, these are the oldest copies found and some were complete such as the 24-foot long Isaiah Scroll. After over 70 years, we still know little about this community yet the archaeology, writings of the community and the large compound found there confirm these were the Aaronic Levite Priests, the sons of Zadok, who had been exiled to the Wilderness of Judaea by the Hasmoneans and Pharisees. They were the Temple High Priests replaced by a new unbiblical order. However, today, the world allows the Pharisees to teach us about this community. No wonder we know so little. This was the base of operations for John the Baptist and his disciples where he baptized Jesus(Yahusha) and was visited by Him later privately. It is among the most well-documented New Testament communities on record and the church does not even know because it is too busy defending a control narrative that the other books found with the Old Testament are somehow cursed when Jesus(Yahusha) and John the Baptist set this library as a time capsule. In 1947, the voice in the wilderness cried out yet again. Did you hear it?

In this book, we have used three principal resources outside of the modern canon of the Bible – the Books of Jubilees, 2 Esdras and Enoch 1. Some may not be familiar and some may vehemently object not because they have read these books for themselves and tested them likely, but because they have heard they are scary. We understand as we used to proclaim the same things until we began following the edict to "prove all things." Remember, we are using these for geographic and historic purposes mainly. However, having tested them far beyond such, we wish to address things you should know and may not have learned in seminary nor from churches. We did not.

Book of Jubilees

It is our responsibility as individuals to prove things and know the Word for ourselves. For if we do not in this age, we will be deceived. How can we say the Book of Jubilees is appropriate to cite in this book? First, as an historic context, copies of the Book of Jubilees have been found dated as far back as 150 B.C. Thus, it is extremely appropriate to use at least as a secondary historic and geographic support which is how we mostly use this.

We are not quoting Jubilees for doctrine in this book but it has geographic data not found in Genesis and it is very useful. However, even so, on our channel, we get comments often that we dare not ever read or even touch this book because it is not in the modern canon. However, it most certainly was in the Bible, many just do not realize.

We prove in our Original Canon Series that John the Baptist lived and operated in Bethabara(Greek) or Betharabah(Hebrew). This is a well-documented site in the Bible and also on ancient maps from the oldest map of Judaea. The Madaba Tile Map in Jordan c. 6th century demonstrates this all the way to the maps published up until 1901. For it was around that period (1917 especially) that the world forgot where Bethabara was. See, Bethabara somehow retains it's modern Muslim name as those controlling history in Israel refuse to restore it to the Qumran area where it belongs.

Left: Jordan. Madaba (biblical Medeba) - St. George's Church. Fragment of the oldest floor mosaic map of the Holy Land - the Jordan River and the Dead Sea. Right: 1770, Bonne Map of Israel. Rigobert Bonne 1727 – 1794.

The Qumran community was the sect of John the Baptist – a group of especially Aaronic Levite Priests who were ejected from the Temple by the Hasmoneans whom they call in the Dead Sea Scroll community documents, the "sons of darkness" while referring to themselves as the "sons of light." When the Hasmoneans conquered Judaea and especially the Temple literally fulfilling the Psalm 83 war in every sense, they installed themselves as High Priests replacing the Sons of Zadok. That was the lineage of Aaron, the Levite brother of Moses and first High Priest of the Tabernacle. Scripture is clear only an Aaronic Levite bloodline priest could serve as High Priest and no other and since the days of Solomon, that was to be a son of Zadok specifically. These were the teachers and keepers of scripture.

The Qumran community writings such as the War Scroll especially condemn this identifying the Hasmoneans, their priests and entire infrastructure as the "sons of darkness" whom the "sons of light" would battle to the very end in Revelation-style language. The Pharisee nor Sadducee parties did not exist until the Hasmoneans also installed them in 165 B.C. after this "Hasmonean Revolt." We cover this in detail on our channel. However, those calling themselves scholars that have not bothered to read the writings of the Dead Sea community and then, ignorantly claim a Pharisee wrote the Book of Jubilees are simply guessing and behaving badly.

In fact, Jubilees condemns the Pharisee lunar calendar as pagan as well as other practices. Pharisees are on record as forbidden to write such books in that era in their own doctrine. The D.S.S. lumps them in with the "sons of darkness." There is no placing any Pharisee, Sadducee nor even Essene in this Qumran community which were the ancient lineage of Aaron who were supposed to serve as the High Priest and other critical roles in the Temple but exiled which is the reason they were in the Wilderness of Judaea including John the Baptist.

It is very laughable to listen to a modern Pharisee attempt to justify that no one knows where this library originated yet it is right there in the caves next door to a compound. They claim there are over 1,000 graves there and that compound would not have supported 1,000 people yet they seem oblivious to the fact that John the Baptist lived there and baptized there, even Messiah was first baptized there, and drew crowds of many thousands upon which some perhaps expired or wished burial.

Also, no one knows how long that community was kept up but at least since the time the Levites were run out of the Temple in about 165 B.C. That is over 200 years or 4-5 generations in that age thus a group of about 200-250 consistent inhabitants would represent 1000 graves. Of course, there is no requirement that all of them must live there.

There is very strong evidence that these were not Essenes whose headquarters according to Pliny the Elder was in Ein Gedi, 25 miles South of Qumran. There is never one mention in the Dead Sea Scrolls of Essenes but many of the Levite priests of Aaron, sons of Zadok, etc. These were the keepers of scripture and they continued to do so in Qumran yet they have been marginalized falsely classified as Kabbalistic Essenes with zero evidence. This is a lie.

In fact, there was a great archaeological find in Ein Gedi, 25 miles South, which has been deemed "The Essene Find." That was their headquarters and they were not keepers of scripture nor righteous men according to the Bible. However, we have all heard about how they were somehow the librarians and therefore, we must not accept their library. The problem is it was John the Baptist's library we are rejecting with no investigation. It is time to breach this topic in far more depth which we cannot here.

Then, they find multiple copies that are clearly not originals but copies and attempt a dating. The dating is fine but to represent this as the date of original writing is ludicrous as Moses wrote this book over 1000 years before these copies were created. Some even reference scribal errors and this too is to claim a scribe whose ministry was to study his scrolls memorizing them in Hebrew ready to copy them in exactness would become a haphazard practice of clowns who did not care about the sacred nature of the text in which they were responsible. If a scribe made an error which would also be checked by many eyes and easily caught, it was no error but a purposeful changing of scripture.

The Dead Sea Scrolls were not found all over the Dead Sea, they were in Qumran or Bethabara thus representing the scroll library of John the Baptist's community. The Book of Jubilees was the number six most numerous scroll found and even in the same scroll jar as Genesis which is very appropriate. We have no issue using a book from John the

Baptist's library in which Messiah was baptized and even took other trips staying there according to scripture. He likely reviewed this library and endorsed it. However, we do not need to leave this to speculation. The Qumran community uses the Book of Jubilees as authoritative.

> *"With 14 or 15 attested copies, the book of Jubilees is undoubtedly one of the best-documented texts of the Qumran library. Moreover, it is cited as an authoritative source in a sectarian work, the Damascus Document (CD 16:2-4), and seems to have been equally important to the Qumran community."* – Gabriele Boccaccini, 2005 [323]

Not only was Jubilees equally important to the Qumran community, it is quoted for law as Torah which makes sense since Moses wrote it.

> *The Damascus Document, 4Q266, fr. 8 i, 6-9, 50 B.C.–100 A.D.:* *(For God made) a Covenant with you and all Israel; therefore a man shall bind himself by oath to return to the Law of Moses, for in it all things are strictly defined. As for the exact determination of their times to which Israel turns a blind eye, behold it is strictly defined in the Book of the Divisions of the Times into their Jubilees and Weeks. And on the day that a man swears to return to the Law of Moses, the Angel of Persecution shall cease to follow him provided he fulfills his word: for this reason Abraham circumcised himself on the day that he knew.* [324]

The Pharisees were not using Jubilees even then nor it's calendar. They continue as they quote right out of the Book of Jubilees chapter 23 verse 2. Where does the Qumran community derive the exact determination of the times and their definitions of how to keep Torah or the law? These are strictly defined in Jubilees which bares alternative titles in history such as the Book of Division as it records Noah's division of the earth in territories between his three sons (Ch. 19). They believed the Law of Moses included the Book of Jubilees thus, Torah and used it as the Torah Calendar rejected by the Pharisees. Also, the Book of Jubilees is the source of quotes in the New Testament by Jesus(Yahusha), John, Peter, Paul and Luke and not arbitrarily so but for doctrine not found anywhere else in the Old Testament. Everyone should know this.

John 1:1-3 KJV
In the beginning was the Word, and the Word was with God, and the
Word was God. The same was in the beginning with God. All things
were made by him; and without him was not any thing made that was
made.

The margin notes from the KJV anchor this passage in origin to Psalm 33:6 which is not it's source.

Psalm 33:6 KJV
By the word of the Lord were the heavens made; and all the host of them
by the breath of his mouth.

What is John doing here? Nowhere in the Old Testament does it ever define the Messiah to come as the Creator of all things along with Yahuah. Certainly this anchor in Psalm is not a direct link to that. This should be a challenge to many scholars as this has no root in the modern Old Testament. Is John manufacturing new doctrine however? No, he is quoting the prophecy of Messiah from the Book of Jubilees. Proverbs 8:22-23 and 30 are also cited in the margin note but they all pertain to wisdom not identifying Jesus(Yahusha) as creating all things alongside Yahuah.

Jubilees 16:26 (R.H. Charles, 1903)
And he (Abraham) blessed his Creator who had created him in his
generation, for He had created him according to His good pleasure; for He
knew and perceived that from him would arise the plant of righteousness
for the eternal generations, and from him a holy seed, so that it should
become like Him who had made all things.

Who is the plant of righteousness for eternal generations who descends from Abraham? Only Messiah. All things were made by Him and that originates not in any of the Old Testament but firmly from the Book of Jubilees. Psalm certainly does not directly say such and this should haunt scholars. There is so much in this one passage that we could spend a chapter on what are the first direct prophecies of Messiah as they really originate in the Book of Jubilees. Moses did not always repeat himself in Genesis and Jubilees fills in blanks. This is not the only time John quotes Jubilees.

> *John 14:26 KJV (Words of Messiah)*
> *But the Comforter, which is the Holy Ghost, whom the Father will send in my name, he shall teach you all things, and bring all things to your remembrance, whatsoever I have said unto you.*

> *Jubilees 32:25 (R.H. Charles, 1903)*
> *And Jacob said: 'Lord, how can I remember all that I have read and seen?' And he said unto him: 'I will bring all things to thy remembrance.'*

That's an exact quote word for word and though not as monumental in doctrine and ramifications as the first verse, significant none-the-less.

The writer of Acts whom many attribute as Luke quotes a timeline for the burning bush which appeared to Moses forty years after Moses entered Midian. Read the Exodus account and you will not find any indication of a dating on this but only the 40 years they wandered in the wilderness. Where did Luke get this?

> *Acts 7:30 KJV*
> *And when forty years were expired, there appeared to him in the wilderness of mount Sina(i) an angel of the Lord in a flame of fire in a bush.*

> *Jubilees 48:1-2a (R.H. Charles, 1903)*
> *And in the sixth year of the third week of the forty-ninth jubilee thou didst depart and dwell <in [2372 A.M.] the land of Midian>, five weeks and one year. And thou didst return into Egypt in the second week in the second year in the fiftieth jubilee. And thou thyself knowest what He spake unto thee on [2410 A.M.] Mount Sinai.*

The author is quoting the timeline from the Book of Jubilees which does not derive in the modern Old Testament. We deduce if the writer of Acts and John can quote the Book of Jubilees, we can certainly use it as geographic support for this book.

This next scripture is actually one of the things that Jubilees is criticized as this claim that Moses received assistance from angels on Mt. Sinai in writing is not found in Torah yet no one seems to realize, the writer of Acts says the same thing. Thus to reject Jubilees over this obscure point is to also condemn Acts and we are confident those critics would not apply this consistently on that topic.

We disagree with that and so does Luke who says the Torah was received by Moses by the "disposition of angels." This is a major issue for scholars as they would have to condemn Luke for this as he is quoting a doctrine not found in the entire Old Testament. How dare he say Moses received some of the law from angels which is not found in Torah. Some will argue Yahuah wrote the law with his finger but they fail to read that was specific to the 10 commandments and their 2 tablets not all of the law. Nothing in scripture disagrees with this and here we have the New Testament affirming Jubilees in a manner that is not against the Old Testament. How could Luke add to the Word, to the Torah even? He did not as he is quoting the sixth book of the Torah – the Book of Jubilees which was well-noted as such.

> *Acts 7:53 KJV*
> *Who have received the law by the disposition of angels, and have not kept it.*

> *Jubilees 1:26 (R.H. Charles, 1903)*
> *And He said to the angel of the presence: Write for Moses from the beginning of creation till My sanctuary has been built among them for all eternity.*

> *Jubilees 1:13 (R.H. Charles, 1903)*
> *And they will forget all My law and all My commandments and all My judgments, and will go astray as to new moons, and sabbaths, and festivals, and jubilees, and ordinances.*

In fact, Jubilees had already prophesied that Israel would break Yahuah's law just as Luke mentions. He was reading Jubilees and quoting it because it was scripture. No one can criticize Jubilees for it's position of the angel of the presence writing down the first portion of Genesis. Moses was not alive in that era and scholars even criticize him for that portion without cause.

> *2 Corinthians 5:17 KJV*
> *Therefore if any man be in Christ, he is a new creature: old things are passed away; behold, all things are become new.*

> *Jubilees 5:12 (R.H. Charles, 1903)*
> *And he made for all his works a new and righteous nature, so that they should not sin in their whole nature for ever, but should be all righteous each in his kind alway.*

In the margin in the KJV, it anchors Paul's New Creature to Isaiah 43:18-19. However, once again not only is that not a direct quote, it has nothing to do with the nature of man. It simply says Yahuah will "do a new thing." A new thing is not a new creature nor a new and righteous nature which are precise in context. Paul is quoting the Book of Jubilees on one of the most important doctrines of the entire New Testament and scholars are rejecting the origin of that doctrine because they fail to conduct a little research. Paul uses a second time a term he is quoting directly from Jubilees which also does not appear in the Old Testament.

> *Galatians 2:15 KJV*
> *We who are Jews by nature, and not sinners of the Gentiles...*

> *Jubilees 23:23a (R.H. Charles, 1903)*
> *And He will wake up against them the sinners of the Gentiles…*

Paul does it again and Jesus(Yahusha) joins him when both use a term "son of perdition." We cannot find this term in the entire Old Testament even once. However, it seems to be quoting the Book of Jubilees and though it may appear to be a simple term, this has powerful implications in determining whom the beast will be. Did Jesus(Yahusha) quote Jubilees?

2 Thessalonians 2:3 KJV
Let no man deceive you by any means: for that day shall not come, except
there come a falling away first, and that man of sin be revealed, the son
of perdition;

John 17:12 KJV (Words of Messiah)
While I was with them in the world, I kept them in thy name: those
that thou gavest me I have kept, and none of them is lost, but the son of
perdition; that the scripture might be fulfilled.

Jubilees 10:3a (R.H. Charles, 1903)
...And hast saved me and my sons from the waters of the flood, And hast
not caused me to perish as Thou didst the sons of perdition...

This becomes extremely important as the sons of perdition in Jubilees prior to the Flood are Nephilim – the offspring of the Watcher Fallen Angels not men. They are not redeemable according to Enoch and that is why Jesus(Yahusha) says they are the lost he could not save. Paul links that the Beast will be part Nephilim. Messiah quoted Jubilees.

The next one as a quote actually originates in the very heavenly tablets that are the source for the first chapters of Genesis written by an angel. We even sing about this one as it comes from James but where did James learn Abraham was called "the friend of God." Once again, we do not find an exact reference in the Old Testament. Genesis is not the same.

James 2:23 KJV (Brother of Messiah)
And the scripture was fulfilled which saith, Abraham believed God, and
it was imputed unto him for righteousness: and he was called the Friend
of God.

Jubilees 19:9 (R.H. Charles, 1903)
...for he was found faithful, and was recorded on the heavenly tablets as
the friend of God.

Finally, Peter quotes Jubilees as well in concept. The KJV anchors this to Psalm which could fit but not as directly as the Book of Jubilees does.

2 Peter 3:8 KJV
But, beloved, be not ignorant of this one thing, that one day is with the Lord as a thousand years, and a thousand years as one day.
Psalm 90:4 KJV MARGIN
For a thousand years in thy sight are but as yesterday when it is past, and as a watch in the night.

Jubilees 4:30 (R.H. Charles, 1903)
And he lacked seventy years of one thousand years; for one thousand years are as one day in the testimony of the heavens and therefore was it written concerning the tree of knowledge: 'On the day that ye eat thereof ye shall die.' For this reason he did not complete the years of this day; for he died during it.

Jubilees becomes a far better match than Psalm. These are direct references and not veiled ones nor stretches. The only origin of these scriptures in the New Testament from Jesus(Yahusha), John, Paul, Luke and Peter is the Book of Jubilees which was written long before but at least documented copies were found in Qumran dating to about 200 B.C. which is 200 years or more before these New Testament quotes. Therefore, we have no issue using the Book of Jubilees as we have and we encourage all to begin reading this book and testing it thoroughly as scripture, Torah, inspired and canon. The Apostles believed it was, deriving monumental and significant doctrine from the Book of Jubilees which does not derive from the modern Old Testament Canon. Jubilees has always been scripture, inspired and canon all along.

THE BOOK OF JUBILEES
"...an ancient Jewish religious work of 50 chapters, considered canonical by the Ethiopian Orthodox Church as well as Beta Israel (Ethiopian Jews), where it is known as the Book of Division." "It was well known to Early Christians, as evidenced by the writings of Epiphanius, Justin Martyr, Origen, Diodorus of Tarsus, Isidore of Alexandria, Isidore of Seville, Eutychius of Alexandria, John Malalas, George Syncellus, and George Kedrenos. The text was also utilized by the community that originally collected the Dead Sea Scrolls." [325]

Therefore, the Qumran Community documented and preserved the Book of Jubilees as scripture and Torah even. The Apostles continue to even derive significant doctrine from the Book of Jubilees including Messiah solidifying it as scripture and Torah. The early church fathers quoted and used the Book of Jubilees in their sermons as scripture and Torah. Then, though the Catholic Church usurped the throne of Jesus(Yahusha) censoring scripture and adding to it, the Ethiopian Church continued Jubilees as canon all the way until today. These copies were rediscovered by the Western world in Ethiopia but remained in consistent circulation as scripture which does not require the West nor do they have an opinion on the matter unless they can prove it not scripture which they never have.

In fact, this was taken back to Britain and translated from the Ethiopic Geez language into English in 1903, forty years before it was even found in the Dead Sea Scrolls. Then, we found it in Hebrew even and now that it has been translated into English. It proves this remained preserved in the Geez language of Ethiopia. Some scholars then handcuff Yahuah claiming He has to preserve it only in Hebrew in His promise but that is a false paradigm yet He did preserve it in Hebrew as well after all though never does the Bible say He has to.

Please identify one modern scholar in the past 2000 years who has more authority than the patriarchs of our faith who in some cases travelled with the Son of God Himself. There is no Pope nor Cardinal nor Bishop nor Rabbi nor modern Apostle nor any position which can overrule scripture and one has to accept their authority in order to reject the Book of Jubilees. Thus, we are not suggesting convening a council to induct this into the canon as men are unlikely to do so. However, we can all restore this even cautiously in our readings as we should. Never-the-less, our use of Jubilees as an historic book of geography is accurate and well-attested.

2 Esdras

The books of 1 and 2 Esdras are also considered part of a series written by Ezra and the Rabbis refer to it as 3 and 4 Ezra as 1 Ezra is what is called Ezra and 2 Ezra is Nehemiah. Thus, 3 Ezra is 1 Esdras and 4 Ezra, 2 Esdras. Regardless, we won't spend much time on this in this book as we have the best kind of direct evidence for this book and should require no further in order to quote it is as geography as we do regarding the pre-flood world. Esdras is not just used by the Apostles but even the 1611 King James Version anchors this quote from the lips of our Messiah as originating in 2 Esdras. Remember, the KJV translators translated 2 Esdras into English and included it in the Original 1611 KJV. They would not have bothered to translate this if not useful. Though we have heard the contrary from the pulpit so many times in error, the Original 1611 King James Version records Messiah quoted 2 Esdras.

Matthew 23:37-38 Authorized 1611 KJV. [326]
O Jerusalem, Jerusalem, thou that killest the prophets, and stonest them which are sent unto thee, how often would I have gathered thy children together, even as a hen gathereth her chickens under her wings, and ye would not! Behold, your house is left unto you desolate.

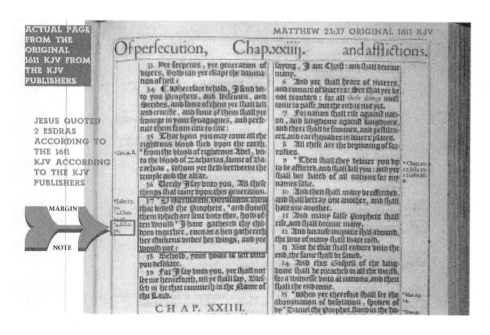

Original Authorized 1611 King James Bible. [326]

2 Esdras 1:30-33 KJVA

I gathered you together, as a hen gathereth her chickens under her wings: but now, what shall I do unto you? I will cast you out from my face. When ye offer unto me, I will turn my face from you: for your solemn feastdays, your new moons, and your circumcisions, have I forsaken. I sent unto you my servants the prophets, whom ye have taken and slain, and torn their bodies in pieces, whose blood I will require of your hands, saith the Lord. Thus saith the Almighty Lord, Your house is desolate, I will cast you out as the wind doth stubble.

The 1611 Authorized King James Version anchors this quote from Messiah in Matthew 23:37-38 as originating from 2 Esdras 1:30 from the Original 1611 Authorized King James Version in which it was included. It was also translated into English by these same scholars. Yes, Messiah quoted the Book of 2 Esdras. Why would we be told not to read something He quoted? The 1560 Geneva Bible renders the exact same anchor with 2 Esdras as Messiah's source for this passage. [313] Thus, which scholar, theologian, pastor today can overrule those translators of these credible first English editions claiming this book is to be censored when Jesus(Yahusha) used 2 Esdras? Who are they to overrule Messiah as well? Therefore, we are firmly comfortable quoting this book as Messiah did. His use is one of doctrine in fact. If one's doctrine is not following that of Messiah, who are they following?

Book of Enoch

Once again, we merely use portions of the Book of Enoch 1 for geography and resources that allow us to further test these findings. To ignore such, would not mean we could not prove our case but why leave something out that is a secondary source of confirmation and quoted at the very least, as useful and likely scripture by Jude.

Jude 1:12-15 KJV

These are spots in your feasts of charity, when they feast with you, feeding themselves without fear: clouds they are without water, carried about of winds; trees whose fruit withereth, without fruit, twice dead, plucked up by the roots; Raging waves of the sea, foaming out their own shame; wandering stars, to whom is reserved the blackness of darkness for ever. And Enoch also, the seventh from Adam, prophesied of these, saying, Behold, the Lord cometh with ten thousands of his saints, To execute judgment upon all, and to convince all that are ungodly among them of all their ungodly deeds which they have ungodly committed, and of all their hard speeches which ungodly sinners have spoken against him.

Let us remember Jude was written in the 1st Century A.D. yet Enoch 1 in the Dead Sea Scrolls was dated to about 200 B.C. In fact, according to John Strugnell, former chief editor of the official Dead Sea Scrolls editorial team, a complete copy of the Book of Enoch in Aramaic was found in 1956 and microfilmed which he witnessed. It is said to be in the hands of "private collectors." Therefore, Jude is not just noting the prophet Enoch said something here but clearly quoting his book which Jude would have had access to in Qumran which we now have and was considered scripture by the Qumran community as it was the third most found scroll there. That's more copies than most of the Torah and you will not find this prophecy quoted by Jude in any of the Old Testament.

1 Enoch 1:3-9 (R.H. Charles, 1917)
Concerning the elect I (Enoch) said, and took up my parable concerning them: The Holy Great One will come forth from His dwelling, And the eternal God will tread upon the earth, (even) on Mount Sinai, And appear from His camp And appear in the strength of His might from the heaven of heavens. And all shall be smitten with fear And the Watchers shall quake, And great fear and trembling shall seize them unto the ends of the earth. And the high mountains shall be shaken, And the high hills shall be made low, And shall melt like wax before the flame And the earth shall be wholly rent in sunder, And all that is upon the earth shall perish, And there shall be a judgement upon all (men). But with the righteous He will make peace. And will protect the elect, And mercy shall be upon them. And they shall all belong to God, And they shall be prospered, And they shall all be blessed. And He will help them all, And light shall appear unto them, And He will make peace with them. And behold! He

cometh with ten thousands of His holy ones To execute judgement upon all, And to destroy all the ungodly: And to convict all flesh Of all the works of their ungodliness which they have ungodly committed, And of all the hard things which ungodly sinners have spoken against Him.

Jude was debated at one time and overcome as it was included in the New Testament canon and continues to be. Therefore, if it is permissible for Jude to quote the Book of Enoch in large part, it is certainly acceptable for us to use it as geographic support in locating the Garden of Eden. The fact that scholars have ignored such for so long, explains why the Dark Ages have continued until today in understanding the Bible.

Finally, on a small scale, we use a fragment from the Cave of Treasures, 2 Enoch, and the Life of Adam and Eve. All of these books are not scripture in our opinion and do not survive in full even. Neither was found in the Dead Sea Scrolls. We use the one quote from each simply as a geographical marker and that is it just as one might use Greek mythology or other historic sources as peripheral support. We will not attempt to prove they are scripture as they are not nor do they need to be to glean geographic information that merely further affirms what we already proved.

We encourage all to discern and pastors should be teaching discernment not censorship. We have been drawn into a false paradigm as the Pharisees (modern Rabbis are Pharisees in origin according to the Jewish Encyclopedia) have lined this topic with their leaven in so many ways.

There is such control over this narrative and having tested it thoroughly, we find the church is buying a massive load of Pharisee leaven and needs to wake up. Although there were no New Testament books found there, this was the New Testament community of John the Baptist. Messiah placed His endorsement being baptized and travelling there more than once. Test this.

Chapter 21 | Conclusion
The Rise of Sheba

It was inaugurated "in the beginning." Yahuah God spoke "let there be light..." and the land of gold came into being as the mouth of light (ophir: אופיר). That light would be used to create all things. Yahuah executed bath (בת: separated the waters from the waters). He spoke everything into existence but when He approached the sixth day, Yahuah knelt down and scooped the soil of Elda called Adamah ('adamah: אדמה: soil from its general redness). Placing His fingerprint on mankind, Yahuah sculpted man from red soil. First man was "red-skinned" or a medium brown skin tone. If he were either extreme as white or black, scientific probabilities near impossible. In history, red skin is considered that of the Native American Indian or the Filipino.

After Havah's (Eve: הוה) creation from the "ala" (עלה: rib) of Adam, they were taken into Gan Eden (גן עדן: Garden of Eden) which Yahuah planted there in Qedem (to the east: קדם). This would define the East for all generations which appellation remains. Adam and Havah ate of the Lanzones Tree of the Knowledge of Good and Evil resulting in exile from the Garden and were returned to their land of Creation which would convey Havah's curse from the Garden – Havilah (childbirth: חוילה). Adam would sacrifice atonement on Mt. Catarman, or Hibok Hibok (Qatar: קטר: to make sacrifices of smoke; Maan: מען: purpose; hiboch!: היבוך!: sorry).

Encircled by the Pison River (פישון) and abounding in gold, pearl and the onyx stone, this land of Qedem would witness the first births of mankind where Adam's generations, except Cain, would inhabit chronologically until the days of Noah.

Upon completion of the ark of Opher wood (wood of Ophir: na'ara: נערה), the Great Flood enveloped the estate of Adam and the whole Earth. All the fountains of the great deep were broken up and the windows of heaven poured. However, His marine life endured and has continued to diversify as the "epicenter" site of creation preserved in Mindoro (min: מין: species; doro: dorot (plural): דורות: generations). Noah's progeny bearing seeds and the surviving spawn of land animals, were lifted from the mountain of Havilah (Arayat; ara: ארץ: earth; yaat: יעט: covered) and propelled by the waters for 110 days until the Flood was ceased. At Flood peak, the ark rested on the tallest mountain on Earth to the East of Shinar (modern Iraq) in the "highest land" (mountainS of ararat: אררט). Noah's sons – Shem, Ham and Japheth settled in villages to the East, South and West of the Himalayas for a time. Their descendants would then migrate to the plains of Shinar from the East to settle on The River of abomination – the Tigris which is not a River from Eden but the origin of the reconstitution of the occult which once almost destroyed the Earth and will again.

The grandson of Noah would unearth a stone containing the occult religion of the antediluvian cult of the Nephilim giants which once devastated Yahuah's Creation resulting in the Flood to save man, animals and plants. During this time, the sons of Hebrew (Eber: עבר; Hebrew: עברי) from Shem's posterity were named prophetically for their impending return to their ancestral homeland of Adam's estate. Ophir (Aupyr: אופיר: mouth of light), Sheba (shebu'a: שבועה: first Sabbath in Land of Creation) and Havilah (חוילה: Land of Havah) lived in Meshad, Iran near Shinar. They would testify to the destruction of the Tower of Babel.

Embarking aboard the ships of Tarshish, the mariner son of Javan (Greece from Japheth), these patriarchs pioneered to Havilah returning to Sephar (ספר: Tree of Life in Garden of Eden) and The Mount of the East (qedem: קדם:Yah's Holy Mountain in Garden of Eden). What were the Mountains of Eden and the Isle of Havah, had transformed into over 7,000 islands since the Flood.

Erudite acclaim would travel the world in time and everyone would know once again the origin of Adam and his land of gold, frankincense and myrrh. A millennia would pass until King Solomon constructed the first navy to reach this arcane homeland of his forefathers. The land of the Hebrews known for the gold and spices of Adam's first sacrifice in Havilah, would be rebranded as Ophir, Sheba and Tarshish.

it's time to
RISE
MATT 12:42

"The queen of the south shall rise up in the judgment with this generation, and shall condemn it: for she came from the uttermost parts of the earth to hear the wisdom of Solomon; and, behold, a greater than Solomon is here."

SHEBA/SEBU, PHILIPPINES   Matthew 12:42 KJV (Luke 11:30)

Upon the arrival of Solomon's fleet in Ophir, the Queen of Sheba, ancestor of the ancient Sheba, brother of Ophir, heard of the fame of Solomon concerning the name of Yahuah whom she was acquainted as her God. Intrigued by the prospect of her cousins reaching the Promised Land on the Western border of Shem realizing the dream of her founders Joktan and Peleg, this empress desired to return to Jerusalem with Hiram's ships to question and to give to the Temple of Yahuah under construction as Adam once did. She arrived at Eziongeber on the Red Sea with Hiram's flotilla and commandeered camels to sojourn through the desert to Solomon's capitol (344 km North).

Once her queries were satisfied, the Queen offered the first fruit offering to Yahuah as was custom from the Estate of Adam in gold, frankincense and myrrh with precious stones added. She would then exit never to be heard from again awaiting the promised Messiah of their people. But her tale would become legend and her gifts continue in use to this day.

A millennia later, on the Feast of Shavuot (shebu'a: שבועה: First Sabbath in Land of Creation), the priests of the isles of Qedem in Ophir witnessed an angel in the East sky. They perceived this was the sign of the promised Messiah of antiquity they anticipated. These Kings prepared for a two-year expedition that would result in their introduction to the Son of Yahuah. The ships of Tarshish would return to Jerusalem and there, they would first meet these Babylonian priests in Herod and

INDEPENDENCE DAY (PHILIPPINES):
June 12, 1898

ON MODERN HEBREW CALENDAR:
SIVAN 22 in 1898
7 (SHEBA) DAYS AFTER SHAVUOT
(Jubilees dates Shavuot as Sivan 15 not 6.
That is the Birth of Messiah.)

Sheba/Shebu'a (Shavuot plural)/Sebu

"...for the Ygolotes fear that the Spaniards will go
to seek them for their gold, and say that they keep
the gold better in the earth than in their houses."
—Antonio De Morga, 1609 [1324]

the Pharisees. As was their ancient custom from the Estate of Adam, these magi brought their gold, frankincense and myrrh from the Land of Havah and set it at the feet of Messiah in oblation of First Fruits.

Another millennia would pass and this antique protected region would see encroachment from the Muslims, the Chinese and others but no one conquered this society. They continued under Yah's shelter and the Babylonian priests who usurped from Solomon and conquered the Temple began to become aware of this zone. These sons of darkness would increase in power and reach as their Babylonian empire folded into the Medo-Persian kingdom which became the Greek empire which transformed into the Roman Empire just as Daniel predicted. In those days, these alchemists were merely advisors to these conquering monarchs prior. Now, in the final empire for the first time since they lost power in the Flood, they would become the dictators and their mixed bloodlines of angelic incursion would commence in dominating mankind once again just as the days of Noah. This miry clay mixed with iron of Rome (Dan. 2:43) began to set their sites to possess the full Estate of Adam. They were not interested in trading but they would follow the footsteps of their fathers.

In order to execute their fruits to steal, kill and destroy (John 10:10), they anticipated an obstacle to overcome. They had to convince the people of Ophir to turn against their nature of serving Yahuah and break the second commandment which would result in a curse to the third and fourth generation. This would give them license to rape and pillage this wealth of Adam. They began with the introduction of a small, unassuming idol of Yahuah's son as a child which bore the image of their ancient god Tammuz or Ploutus. This worked in the land of the Three Kings for a few weeks in Sebu until Ophirians realized the distortion and renounced the intruders and their religion killing their captain, then, his brother-in-law and replacement days later, and eventually, responding with an armada of significant ships of Ophirian design expelling the enemy from their land.

This attempt failed in 1521 as that expedition of five large ships returned to Spain with one remaining and aboard, a crew of only eighteen. However, these Babylonian sorcerers would return forty years later in force. They would subjugate Ophir in convincing the people to include an idol in their worship. They began with the child Jesus again and advanced to the veneration of His mother whose image was their ancient moon goddess known as Ishtar, Isis, Semiramis, Selene, Allat, etc. Those priests even added others from their repertoire of deities who were concealed as saints. They changed the ten commandments erasing the second commandment to never include these idols in one's worship duplicating the tenth. Breaking this commandment leads to a 400-year curse on their descendants and so it was. Ophir would succumb.

By 1599, Ophir, now called the Philippines christened after their Babylonian ruler, acquiesced and officially recognized the conquest of it's inhabitants and thus, the Estate of Adam was transplanted and usurped illegally. The citizenry who was once so prosperous and blessed would now watch the Estate of Adam being eroded and used to fund the rise of the beast from the headquarters of the prince demon named Gog in Western and Central Europe (Ez. 38-39). This was foretold by the prophets and Messiah. However, this is not the end of this story but the onset of what will become the new beginning of all things to which this populace will find themselves central. The empire struck back but the jedi shall return – not the occult mind-melting form of Hollywood but the righteous priests of the East who will execute His counsel (Is. 41:1-2 and 9, Is. 46:11).

In the transition into the twenty-first century, this 400-year curse is coming to an end. Sheba who had been subdued will now rise up and judge her conquerors (Matt. 12:42) as well as Gog (Ez. 38:13). Joined by Tarshish (Ez. 38:13, Is. 60:9) and the Isles of the East in Ophir, united in purpose, this nation will usher in the return of the Lost Tribes of Israel it protects (Is. 60:9). They will see the restoration of the Estate of Adam seven-fold as the thief has been found (Prov. 6:31). It will again become a protected land (Rev. 12:15-16) who will first repent of it's abandoning Yahuah and it's role (Is. 41:3-5). This people will then restore the ways of Yahuah in His Sabbath (Is. 41:3-5) and the Cagayan Feasts (Chaggayah: חגיה: Feast of Yah) which first began in this region of Sebu. They will reinstate His law and commands (Is. 42:4, Is. 60:9) and return to a place of judging righteously in Him (Is. 41:1-2, Is. 46:11) and then, the Philippines will see the reinstatement of Adam's priestly line of judges (Is. 42:4, Is. 41:1-2, Is. 46:11, Ez. 38:13, Matt. 12:42).

All of the inhabitants of these isles at the end of the earth shall sing a new song of worship (Is. 42:10). As a people, it will condemn this Babylonian sorcery publicly and openly with vigor (Matt. 12:42, Luke 11:30, Ez. 38:13). For this is the last stand where a standard will be raised which even the beast system can no longer penetrate (Rev. 12:15-16). Together, with Nineveh (modern Kurdistan), these isles will rise up in judgment as the two witnesses sending prophets from among them to Jerusalem in the last days (Matt. 12:41-42, Rev. 11). The question is, will you be among them? Or will you stand in their way?

For this land of gold is not such for man's purposes and these magicians will never acquire it in the end. All will be returned to Yahuah and they will disappear. This gold has heavenly value and purpose to the end. Tobit records the gold of Ophir will be used to pave the streets of New Jerusalem (Tobit 13:17). This is a coating of Adam's original atoning sacrifice covering the streets of over 2,000 km. in length by 2,000 km. in width in the Holy City to come (Rev. 21:16-18). Remnant believers will walk this path of righteousness and anointing. There shall be none working abominations and iniquities for the first time since the era of Adam. Just as the first days of Creation, there will be no sun nor moon but the light of Jesus(Yahusha) will illuminate Ophir once again (Rev. 21:23). The sea will vanish (Rev. 21:1) and Rivers From Eden revealed.

We will not repeat the error of King Solomon whose sin lead down

"Consider the lilies how they grow:
they toil not, they spin not;
and yet I say unto you,
that Solomon in all his glory was
not arrayed like one of these."
–Luke 12:27 KJV
JESUS (YAHUSHA)

it's time to
RISE
MATT. 12:42

a dark path ceding a portion of Adam's Estate from Ophir transferring into the hands of the Babylonian priests for the first time. That is the fuel they used for the entire World Empire of which Daniel warned. Solomon even realized in the end in writing Ecclesiastes, that all those trappings using Adam's Estate for one's own gain and pleasure is vanity and meaningless. It produces no good fruit.

Ecclesiastes 1:1-11 KJV

The words of the Preacher, the son of David, king in Jerusalem. Vanity of vanities, saith the Preacher, vanity of vanities; all is vanity. What profit hath a man of all his labour which he taketh under the sun? One generation passeth away, and another generation cometh: but the earth abideth for ever. The sun also ariseth, and the sun goeth down, and hasteth to his place where he arose. The wind goeth toward the south, and turneth about unto the north; it whirleth about continually, and the wind returneth again according to his circuits. All the rivers run into the sea; yet the sea is not full; unto the place from whence the rivers come, thither they return again. All things are full of labour; man cannot utter it: the eye is not satisfied with seeing, nor the ear filled with hearing. The thing that

hath been, it is that which shall be; and that which is done is that which
shall be done: and there is no new thing under the sun. Is there any thing
whereof it may be said, See, this is new? it hath been already of old time,
which was before us. There is no remembrance of former things; neither
shall there be any remembrance of things that are to come with those that
shall come after.

There is nothing new under the sun. The same contest since the early age of Jared, the sixth from Adam and father of Enoch (Gen. 5), was being waged in the time of King Solomon and is afoot today. The days of Noah have returned and the progeny of twisted fallen angels desires to entrap mankind (Matt. 24:37, Luke 17:26) as we do not wrestle with flesh and blood but the very principalities and powers of darkness (Eph. 6:12). This is what happened to the Philippines. The sons of darkness. In contrast, we are the sons of light just as John the Baptist and his Dead Sea Scroll community at Bethabara (Qumran) recorded. The final clash of the sons of light verses the sons of darkness is underway in our time. This is why we need the full armor of Yahuah daily (Eph. 6:11).

We have entered an era where many of our churches desire to bottle-feed with milk and shallow doctrine. They avoid the meat of the Word in order not to offend. They wish to be "seeker friendly" and "politically correct." Some have become a single message pulpit only for salvation which is the most elementary levels in theology. We even receive routine challenges especially on this topic where people have been programmed to tell us to only focus on salvation and nothing else. That is simply ignorance. To behave in such manner is to be absent the Holy Spirit who convicts and offends with the truth which we all need regularly. Without such diet, we will die spiritually and He will spew us out of His mouth.

Revelation 3:15-17 KJV
I know thy works, that thou art neither cold nor hot: I would thou wert
cold or hot. So then because thou art lukewarm, and neither cold nor hot,
I will spue thee out of my mouth. Because thou sayest, I am rich, and
increased with goods, and have need of nothing; and knowest not that
thou art wretched, and miserable, and poor, and blind, and naked

As former evangelists, we have witnessed the impact of the modern "altar call." In following through with these supposed converts, we have continually observed most never made a life-altering decision and little to nothing had been done to foster relationship with Yahuah through His Son, Yahusha. This is in part because few are practicing discipleship but mostly because salvation is not a prayer – it is a lifestyle. When one is truly saved, they cannot fall away. However, much of the church does not even understand the definition of salvation. It does not derive from the writings of Paul but from the words of Messiah who expresses this very clearly.

> *Matthew 7:15-23 KJV*
>
> *Beware of false prophets, which come to you in sheep's clothing, but inwardly they are ravening wolves. Ye shall know them by their fruits. Do men gather grapes of thorns, or figs of thistles? Even so every good tree bringeth forth good fruit; but a corrupt tree bringeth forth evil fruit. A good tree cannot bring forth evil fruit, neither can a corrupt tree bring forth good fruit. Every tree that bringeth not forth good fruit is hewn down, and cast into the fire. Wherefore by their fruits ye shall know them. Not every one that saith unto me, Lord, Lord, shall enter into the kingdom of heaven; but he that doeth the will of my Father which is in heaven. Many will say to me in that day, Lord, Lord, have we not prophesied in thy name? and in thy name have cast out devils? and in thy name done many wonderful works? And then will I profess unto them, I never knew you: depart from me, ye that work iniquity.*

All is vanity without relationship with Yahuah through His Son Yahusha who is the only way, the truth and the life (John 14:6). Only Jesus(Yahusha) is, not Mary nor any saint. This is a life decision not a prayer. It requires one to choose relationship with Him. There is no easy way and that requires time and obeying His commands. Who is He turning away in this passage? Pagans? No. Christians performing at fairly high levels casting out demons, prophesying and performing miracles in His name even. How can Christians possibly enter the category of not saved? Once we are saved are we not always saved?

That is not actually scripture but a doctrine of men. One clue is the fact

that in all the salvation scriptures typically used, absent are the words of Messiah who defines His relationship which should matter most. Think about the message we are sending to unbelievers when they hear all they have to do is say a prayer and they are saved forever. It sounds too good to be true because it is and they know better. This is why many seem cross-eyed when you repeat the programmed lines of following twelve salvation scriptures as if that remotely represents the Bible nor the Gospel. The Gospel begins in Genesis 1:1 and without such context, many are never going to listen because they have stumbling blocks as Paul said. Some need to be educated first in a far deeper way and the church is generally lacking such depth.

Some challenge saying this is work or works. Take that up with Messiah, He said it. However, since we are supposed to establish deeper relationship with Him on the Sabbath and yet, one cannot work on the Sabbath, it is clear that is a modern definition from oblivion and does not represent the Bible. Developing relationship with Him requires effort indeed but it is not work according to the Word nor is obeying Him. We would not encourage you to inform your spouse that loving them is work. In John 15, Jesus(Yahusha) further defines salvation just as the Lost Tribes must return in the vine. That's not modern Israel indeed.

John 15:1-10 KJV

I am the true vine, and my Father is the husbandman. Every branch in me that beareth not fruit he taketh away: and every branch that beareth fruit, he purgeth it, that it may bring forth more fruit. Now ye are clean through the word which I have spoken unto you. Abide in me, and I in you. As the branch cannot bear fruit of itself, except it abide in the vine; no more can ye, except ye abide in me. I am the vine, ye are the branches: He that abideth in me, and I in him, the same bringeth forth much fruit: for without me ye can do nothing. If a man abide not in me, he is cast forth as a branch, and is withered; and men gather them, and cast them into the fire, and they are burned. If ye abide in me, and my words abide in you, ye shall ask what ye will, and it shall be done unto you. Herein is my Father glorified, that ye bear much fruit; so shall ye be my disciples. As the Father hath loved me, so have I loved you: continue ye in my love. If ye keep my commandments, ye shall abide in my love; even as I have kept my Father's commandments, and abide in his love.

He abides in us but we are also to reside in His presence. To abide in Him requires effort but again, it is not work. To bear much fruit is also effort but again, not considered work in scripture. Salvation is certainly a free gift and there is nothing any of us can do to replicate what Messiah has done for us. However, it is free if you accept it and you have to do something. You have to develop relationship. You are to bear much fruit or regardless of whom any of us think we are, we will be cut off and burned in the fire. He is referring to Hell. This is serious. How do we abide in His love? If we keep His commandments. Do we know His commandments? They have never changed generally.

> *Matthew 5:17-20 KJV*
>
> *Think not that I am come to destroy the law, or the prophets: I am not come to destroy, but to fulfil. For verily I say unto you, Till heaven and earth pass, one jot or one tittle shall in no wise pass from the law, till all be fulfilled. Whosoever therefore shall break one of these least commandments, and shall teach men so, he shall be called the least in the kingdom of heaven: but whosoever shall do and teach them, the same shall be called great in the kingdom of heaven. For I say unto you, That except your righteousness shall exceed the righteousness of the scribes and Pharisees, ye shall in no case enter into the kingdom of heaven.*

When does heaven and earth pass away? Not until the Day of Final Judgment when they are made new (Rev. 21:1). Messiah did not abolish the law and He says not one letter of the law will pass until then. This means His law remains applicable today.

The writings of the prophets may be aged but they are never old. There is no such thing as an Old and New Testament – only the writings of the prophets and apostles. One church attempts to take credit for compiling the Bible but we now know John the Baptist already housed a library of scrolls which we would call the Bible today though they changed it. As the last great prophet, name one Pope, Archbishop, Cardinal nor Priest who outranks him. You will find none. The Word is precious even powerful and cuts like a two-edged sword. However, when one waters it down, it does not just lose it's power, it is no longer His Word. The Pharisees do this with their leaven rendering the Word of none effect (Mark. 7:13), against His commandments (Mark. 7:9). However, is there really a difference in this modern doctrine which steers to the same leading lambs to slaughter? We are to keep His commandments. His covenant remains His covenant and the New continues in basis in the Old. At least that is what Jesus(Yahusha) said. One can disagree but then they would be creating their own gospel never truly preached by any apostle.

We live in precarious times in which we must be prepared. Though the Philippines will experience a great revival, we are in the midst of the Great Falling Away predicted by Paul (2 Thess. 2:1-3).

No one wants a diluted gospel and Messiah rejects it. The Philippines will restore His ways first and as a nation. Some may question how this could happen but we assure you, the Holy Spirit is capable and the word of Messiah in Matthew 12:42 nor Ezekiel or Isaiah will return void and empty but will accomplish that which they were set out to accomplish. We are not prophets. However, now we know whom these prophesies address and they must come to pass. The Philippines will begin in repentance first and many around the world will follow.

> *2 Chronicles 7:14 KJV*
> *If my people, which are called by my name, shall humble themselves, and pray, and seek my face, and turn from their wicked ways; then will I hear from heaven, and will forgive their sin, and will heal their land.*

This land needs healing and His forgiveness before restoration can begin. This requires a people humbling themselves in prayer truly seeking Him in repentance turning from their wicked ways. We have all been tricked in ways by the wiles of the enemy. This is not about condemnation, it is about the responsible path to rising again. He will execute His promise to forgive and heal not just a few but this entire archipelago.

> *Joel 2:25 KJV*
> *And I will restore to you the years that the locust hath eaten, the cankerworm, and the caterpiller, and the palmerworm, my great army which I sent among you.*

The locust has eaten much but He will restore those years in this generation in the Philippines and beyond. Mankind may view these islands as outcasts, but He will bring health again.

Jeremiah 30:17 KJV
For I will restore health unto thee, and I will heal thee of thy wounds, saith the LORD; because they called thee an Outcast, saying, This is Zion, whom no man seeketh after.

Just as in the days of Job who lost everything but remained faithful to Yahuah, so will be the reward of those who return to Him. Not for monetary gain but for the sake of restoring a nation in Him.

Job 42:10 KJV
And the LORD turned the captivity of Job, when he prayed for his friends: also the LORD gave Job twice as much as he had before.

This people will then turn to Him and then, to their neighbors and they will gently restore them as well. When you procrastinate in this, you are hurting others by not restoring them and continuing in ways not His.

Galatians 6:1 KJV
Brethren, if a man be overtaken in a fault, ye which are spiritual, restore such an one in the spirit of meekness; considering thyself, lest thou also be tempted..

Then, we enter the realm of restoration and this will be the most exciting time to be alive. He will revive this people and restore them to their former covenant blessing as they restore His ways. This will not be accomplished in greed and Yahuah cannot be haggled or bargained. He will do so because He said He will. This reclamation and recovery will not tarry. This is a sincere society who is already sensitive to the desire to please Yahuah and many hearts are already being prepared. We witness this in recent festivals like the "Jesus Reigns" worship event which attracts over 150,000 Cebuanas annually. However, that is not even scratching the surface as you begin to see the return of the days of the Acts of the Apostles. The isles of the sea at the ends of the earth will sing for the majesty of Yahuah (Is. 24:14-16, Is. 42:10-14).

The first thing for all of us to reclaim is revitalizing the name of Yahuah God. He has a name and it is in scripture over 6,800 times. There is no authority who can suppress nor overrule this. It is about time we use it instead of generic replacement titles like Lord which is actually Ba'al in Hebrew. We provide charts and explanation of our rendering next but His name is YHWH, YAHUAH.

Then, we must restore his Sabbath, the seventh day of the week which is His since Creation. He made it for man to rest with Him. Some worry about church but you can go to church on Sunday without violating His Sabbath or Shabbat. However, Saturday is your day with Him regardless. This is about relationship not organization. You either desire to please Him and follow His ways or you do not. Remembering Sabbath is His fourth commandment but far predates Moses.

Finally, the isles of the East will see the restoration of His law (Is.42:4) including His Seven Feast Days not replacement holidays of pagan origin in worship of His enemies – the sun and moon gods and goddesses. It matters not how attractive those festivals may be. If you eat food sacrificed to idols, He will reject you. We offer comprehensive teachings on YouTube but you will find Messiah, His disciples and the early church kept these feasts and never celebrated Christmas, Easter, etc. He is not silent on this matter.

Isaiah 1:14-18 KJV
Your new moons and your appointed feasts my soul hateth: they are a trouble unto me; I am weary to bear them. And when ye spread forth your hands, I will hide mine eyes from you: yea, when ye make many prayers, I will not hear: your hands are full of blood. Wash you, make you clean; put away the evil of your doings from before mine eyes; cease to do evil; Learn to do well; seek judgment, relieve the oppressed, judge the fatherless, plead for the widow. Come now, and let us reason together, saith the LORD: though your sins be as scarlet, they shall be as white as snow; though they be red like crimson, they shall be as wool.

Amos 5:21-24 KJV

I hate, I despise your feast days, and I will not smell in your solemn assemblies. Though ye offer me burnt offerings and your meat offerings, I will not accept them: neither will I regard the peace offerings of your fat beasts. Take thou away from me the noise of thy songs; for I will not hear the melody of thy viols. But let judgment run down as waters, and righteousness as a mighty stream.

We will never find a scripture that justifies our behavior because He "knows our heart." In fact, you will find He truly knows our heart and one cannot seek first His kingdom while keeping that which He rebukes outright (Matt. 6:33). For instance, Yahuah hates Easter and the goddess it represents known as Astar (עשתרת) or Ishtar (Jer. 7:18, 44:17-25). She is the "Queen of Heaven" some attempt to attribute to Mary erroneously and Easter is her day of fertility rituals replacing Yahuah's feast. The Passover season holds the calendar to the events of Messiah's death and resurrection not Easter which is never a Biblical Feast. Even the one time it is used in English required outright fraud on the part of translators as the same Greek word, pascha, used 29 times is always interpreted Passover except this once. It also refers to Herod keeping pascha and his family converted to Israel's religion and kept the Feasts not Easter (Luke 22:27). However, eating food or participating in that which is sacrificed to idols is forbidden in His kingdom (1 Cor. 10:28, 8:1-13, Acts 15:29). No excuses.

He entered Jerusalem on the donkey on the same day the Passover lamb enters on Abib 10 and was crucified on Passover as our Passover Lamb. He is the Passover yet we celebrate Easter? (1 Cor. 5:6-8)

He despises Christmas as Jeremiah points out in specifically rebuking the Christmas Tree as pagan (Jer. 10:2-8). This Shavuot/Pentecost replacement is the birth and rebirth of the harlot's son – the sun god Mithra, Tammuz, Horus, etc. Yahuah hates All Saints/Souls Day as Abraham likens such celebration to the ways of Canaan the cursed whose descendants will be wiped off of the Earth (Jub. 22:16-24). This is a counterfeit for the Feast of Tabernacles where we recognize we live in temporary housing and bodies. Their intent is to profane and He warns His people perish for lack of knowledge (Hos. 4:6, Is. 5:13).

If you wish to celebrate Messiah's birth, follow the apostles' example. They were doing so in the upper room on Pentecost/Shavuot when the Holy Spirit came. We prove this in "When Was Jesus Born." For his death and resurrection, he died on Passover and rose on the Feast of First Fruits as He was our First Fruits offering from among the dead (1 Cor. 15:20-23, Rom. 8:23).

His Feasts begin in the Spring from March through June, as Passover (not Easter), Unleavened Bread, First Fruits and Shavuot/Pentecost (not Christmas) which began on the seventh day of Creation right here in this land of Havilah. The Feast of Sebu is Shavuot in which Philippine Independence follows 7 (Sheba) days after. The Fall Feasts all bear prophetic meaning including the Day of Atonement, Feast of Trumpets and Feast of Tabernacles (not All Saints Day). Seven (Sheba) Feasts in seven (Sheba) months. These are forever in your generations (Lev. 23:14, 21, 31, 41). These are not Jewish Feasts. They are for all believers and always have been as even the "stranger among you" is identified multiple times in these scriptures (Ex. 12:49, Num. 9:14, 15:26-29, Lev. 16:29, 18:26, 19:34, 17:12). These are gentile believers who are under the same law as Hebrews in blessings and curses. Salvation is not a New Testament concept in origin.

This is the strong deception unraveling before us. Even some pastors today will vehemently oppose keeping these Feasts while defending their pagan replacements not even realizing what they are doing. As we once were, they are programmed with canned responses in seminary. Many will tell you these have passed away yet Messiah says not (Matt. 5:17-20). However, it is the ultimate hypocrisy to then, keep the feast they say has passed by participating in idol replacements instead.

Will you restore the ways of Adam, Enoch, Noah, Abraham, Jesus(Yahusha) and the patriarchs of our faith? Or will you continue to follow the ways of Cain the evil from before the Flood and Canaan the cursed after? Will you return to the nature of your ancestors who knew Abba Yahuah or continue to justify worship of the wrong god by more recent deceived ancestors? We already know many will accept this challenge because Messiah, Isaiah and Ezekiel already said so. It is time to RISE UP and be Restored in Him! Selah.

FEASTS OF YHWH

PASSOVER

1st month day 14 (mar-apr)
2020:Apr. 8 2021:Mar. 27 2022:Apr. 15

UNLEAVENED BREAD

1st month days 15-21 (mar-apr)
2020:Apr.9-15 2021:Mar. 28-Apr. 3 2022:Apr.16-22

FIRST FRUITS

1st month day 16 (mar-apr)
2020:Apr. 11 2021:Apr. 3 2022:Apr. 16

SHAVUOT

3rd month day 15** (may-jun) [not 6th]
2020:Jun. 9 2021:May 25 2022:Jun. 14

TRUMPETS

7th month day 1 (sep-oct)
2020:Sep. 19 2021:Sep. 7 2022:Sep. 26

ATONEMENT

7th month day 10 (sep-oct)
2020:Sep. 28 2021:Sep. 16 2022:Oct. 5

TABERNACLES

7th month days 15-21 (sep-oct)
2020:Oct. 3-9 2021:Sept. 21-27 2022:Oct. 10-16

*Date Calculations for our personal worship from United Church of God, MyJewishLearning, Chabad and others and dates vary as all are approximations. **Jubilees 15:1-4 says Shavuot is the 15th not the 6th.

Restoring His Ways: His Sabbath

If the Sabbath were insignificant, why is it mentioned 137 times in the Bible? If Messiah had done away with it, why is it observed by the disciples after His ascension? (Acts 2:1-4, 13:14-16,13:42-44,18:4, 1 Cor. 7:19, 11:1) Why did the early church keep it as well? If it was temporary, why does scripture profess the Sabbath is forever in your generations for a perpetual and everlasting covenant by a statute forever? (Ex. 31:13, 16, Lev. 16:31, 24:8) Why did Jesus(Yahusha) say he did not come to abolish it? (Matt. 5:17-20) In fact, why does He declare Himself "Lord of the Sabbath" (Mark 2:28) only to abolish it which He says He would not? (Matt. 5:17-20) Why would He create a day for man and then eliminate that day altogether? (Mark 2:27)

For this is the Day of Rest created for man (Mark 2:27) to rejuvenate in the presence of our Creator. He knows we need that and without it, we will never have the needed fuel nor will we ever apply our full armor. (Mark 2:27) This is never a suggestion but in Israel, to defile this day in many references, would mean death (Ex. 31:14-15, 35:2). On this day, we are to conduct no work not even cooking, nor to indulge in our own pleasure but strictly to focus on Him in a state of rest (Ex. 35:3, Lev. 23:3, Deut. 5). Even when Yahuah rained manna from Heaven, He refrained on the seventh day (Ex. 16:26).

Did Messiah void the law? No (Matt. 5:17-20). Did Paul? No (Rom. 3:31, 2:13, 7:12, 7:22). Did Luke? No (Acts 24:14, 25:8). Paul's responses to gnostic teachings and Pharisees are never repudiating the law which he says is holy, just and good. His context is one of application of the law which is not the Pharisee nor gnostic way of additives and leaven.

It is time to restore His Sabbath in your life. Selah.

Photo: Incredible turquoise-colored Kawasan
waterfalls located on Cebu Island, Philippines.

REMEMBER THE SABBATH
TO KEEP IT HOLY...

שבת

Ex. 20:8

"I delight in the law of God..."
Paul in Romans 7:22 KJV

"Therefore the law is holy,
and the commandment
holy and just and good"
Paul in Romans 7:12 KJV

"...on the contrary,
we establish the law"
Paul in Romans 3:31 KJV

שבא
SHEBA
oath, seven [61]

שבו
SEBU
take captive [60]
properly, will; concretely, an affair (as a
matter of determination):—purpose.

שבועה
SHEBU'A
oath, week, seven
first Sabbath [59]

1646

[62]

Sebu = Sebat = Sabbath

Restoring His Ways: The Name of God

Many ask why we pronounce Yahuah for the name of God and Yahusha for the name of the Son. We offer a full teaching on YouTube in The Name Of God Series on this. The Father's name is actually recorded as four Hebrew letters (YAD-Y, HEY-H, WAW-W, HEY-H) over 6,800 times in the Hebrew scriptures and has been removed and replaced with generic titles such as Lord. This is the doctrine of the Samaritans not that of the Tribes of Israel nor anywhere in all of scripture. Some Rabbis will even claim Abraham did not know the name of God, yet using this same name of YHWH, the Creator told Abraham His name and says so three times in the Word. Abraham spoke His name and so did Isaac, Rebecca and Abraham's servant. Thus, this is the doctrine of men attempting to hide the name of God likely because He is not their God as they are the Samaritans who conquered Judaea and the Temple in the Hasmonean Heresy according to the Qumran community writings which calls them "sons of darkness." This is why they erase Yahuah's name, the Son's name and even the name of His people which is never Jew–not Hebrew.

This is well-proven out in the precedence of scripture as many of the prophets have the name of God rendered within their names and definitions. The standard is already set in Hebrew such as Elijah which is actually EliYAHU. There are many such examples that establish YAHU as the beginning of His name not JEHO in which "J" does not even exist in Ancient Hebrew, Greek, Aramaic, Latin, Old French, Old German nor Old English. Equally, there is no arriving at this as YAHW or YAHAW either as the names of the prophets preserve this as YAHU.

When the Son came in the flesh, He tells us He came in His Father's name. He meant this literally as the first 3 letters of His name in Hebrew are the exact same as YAHU. His name is pronounced phonetically as it must as Ancient Hebrew never had nor did it ever require vowel points which the Masoretes added around 1000 A.D. unnecessarily. These were pronounced for thousands of years without vowel points. Even His people were defined and branded with His name in theirs as they are the YAHUdim never Jews which is not Ancient Hebrew, Greek nor any language through which the Bible was translated. His name is YAHUSHA with YAHUSHUA also being appropriate as it also appears as a variant in scripture. May we restore these Bible names. Selah.

YAHUAH

יהוה

HEY WAW HEY YAD

Hebrew reads right to left.

Ancient Semitic/Hebrew					
Early	Middle	Late	Name	Picture	Meaning	Sound

AH
U

Y

H AU U H AY
YAHUAH

YAHUSHA

"YAHU IS SALVATION"

יהושע

AYIN SHIN WAW HEY YAD

NO "J"

NO "V"

NO VOWEL POINTS

AHS U HAY
YAHUSHA

YAHUdim יהודים
Yah's People (Never Jews, Yah's)

YAHUdah יהודה
"Yahu Be Praised" (Tribe of Judah)

Ha YAH היה
I AM or THE YAH

EliYAHU אליהו
"My God Is Yahu"

| Bibliography

1. "Two Hebrew Ostraca from Tell Qasile." Journal of Near Eastern Studies. Vol. 10, No. 4 (Oct. 1951). By B. Maisler. p. 265.

2. "The Prehistory of the Balkans: The Middle East and the Aegean World, Tenth to Eighth Centuries B.C., Part 1." By John Boardman. Cambridge University Press. 1982. p. 480.

3. "The Age of Solomon: Scholarship at the Turn of the Millennium." By Kenneth A. Kitchen. Edited by Lowell K. Handy. BRILL 1997. p. 144.

4. "Itineraria Phoenicia Studia Phoenicia 18." By Edward Lipinski. Peeters Publishers. 2004. p. 197.

5. "King Solomon's Wall Found—Proof of Bible Tale?" By Mati Milstein, National Geographic News. Published Feb. 27, 2010.

6. "Ophir." Strong's Concordance #H211. Blue Letter Bible.

7. "Light." Strong's Concordance #H216. Blue Letter Bible.

8. "Fires." Strong's Concordance #H217. Blue Letter Bible.

9. 1. Department of Archeology, University of Cape Town Rondebosch 7701. By Duncan Miller, Nirdev Desai & Julia Lee-Thorp. South Africa Archeology Society Doodwin Series 8, 91-99, 2000. University of the Witwatersrand, Johannesburg. p. 1-2. 2. "History Of Gold In South Africa - In The Witwatersrand". The South Africa Guide. Minerals Council South Africa. Mar. 7, 2010.

10. 1. "Ancient Mining: Classical Philippine Civilization." Wikipedia. Extracted August 9, 2019. and "Cultural Achievements of Pre-Colonial Philippines." Wikipedia. Extracted August 9, 2019. 2. "The Edge of Terror: The Heroic Story of American Families Trapped in the Japanese-occupied Philippines." By Scott Walker. Thomas Dunne Books. St. Martin's Press. New York. Chap. 3 - The Gold Miners, 1901-1937. p. 44. 3. "Philippine Civilization and Technology," By Paul Kekai Manansala. Asia Pacific University. 4. "Encyclopedic Dictionary of Archaeology – Philippines, the." Compiled by Barbara Ann Kipfer, Ph.D. Kluwer Academic/ Plenum Publishers. New York, London, Moscow. 2000. p. 436.

11. "Miners Shun Mineral Wealth of the Philippines." By Donald Greenlees. NY Times. May 14, 2008. Citing The Fraser Institute.

12. "Trillion – Dollar Philippine Economic Goldmine Emerging From Murky Pit." By Ralph Jennings. Forbes Magazine. Apr. 5, 2015.

13. "Mining for Gold in the Philippines." By Nicole Rashotte. Gold Investing News. Sept. 10th, 2019.

14. "China vs. Philippines." Index Mundi Factbook.

15. "Ophira." hebrewname.org.

16. 1. "Early Mapping of South East Asia." By Thomas Suarez. Periplus Editions (HK) Ltd. Fig. 30 and 31. Chryse and Argyre. Entire Chapter. 2. "Pomponius Mela, Chorographia Bk II, from Pomponius Mela's Description of the World." Translated by Frank E. Romer. University of Michigan Press. 1998. Sections 3.67-3.71.

17. "The Periplus of the Erythraean Sea, Travel And Trade In The Indian Ocean By A Merchant Of The First Century." Translated from the greek and annotated by Wilfred H. Schoff, Secretary of the Commercial Museum, Philadelphia. Longmans, Green, And Co. New York. 1912. Section 63-64. Original housed at The British Museum (Add. MS 19391).

18. "World Map of Pomponius Mela, 43 A.D." Rotated for north up and be comparable with modern maps. Reconstruction by Konrad Miller (reconstructed in 1898). Mappae Mundi Bd. Vi. "Rekonstruierte Karten", Tafel 7. Public Domain.

19. Antiquities of the Jews — Book VIII, Chapter 6:4 and 7:1. Flavius Josephus.

20. 1. "The World According to Dionysius Periegetes, from Bunbury's A History of Ancient Geography Among the Greeks and Romans, From the Earliest Ages Till the Fall of the Roman Empire." 1879. High Resolution image from Alamy. Public Domain. 2. "Weltkarte des Dionysios Periegetis." 1898 Reconstruction by Dr. Konrad Miller. Mappae Mundi Bd. Vi. "Rekonstruierte Karten." Public Domain. Wikimedia Commons. 3. "This Map Exists Only As A Reconstruction". E. A. Bunbury. History of Ancient Geography, Volume 2. p. 490. J. B. Harley. The History of Cartography, Volume One, p. 172. C. Dilke, O.A.W., Greek and Roman Maps. pp. 56, 71, 143-144. Cited by myoldmaps.com.

21. 1. "Tantric Elements in pre-Hispanic Philippines Gold Art," By Laszlo Legeza. Arts of Asia, July-Aug. 1988, pp.129, 131 and 137. 2. "Ginto: History Wrought in Gold." By Ramon N. Villegas. Manila: Bangko Central ng Pilipinas. 2004. p. 45.

22. 1. "Yijing (i-Tsing)." Wikipedia citing: "A Record of Buddhist Practices Sent Home from the Southern Sea, also known as the Nanhai Jigui Neifa Zhuan and by other translations." Buddhist travelogue by the Tang Chinese monk Yijing (i-Tsing) detailing his twenty five-year stay in India and Srivijaya between the years 671 and 695 ce. p.41 & p.17. 2. Further support from: Chau Ju-Kua: his work on the Chinese and Arab trade in the twelfth and thirteenth centuries, entitled Chu-fan-chi by Chau Ju-Kua, 13th cent; Hirth, Friedrich, 1845-1927; Rockhill, William Woodville, 1854-1914. p. 160. 3. "Wak Wak." Wikipedia citing "Wakwak history" from G. R. Tibbetts; Shawkat M. Toorawa; G. Ferrand; G.S.P. Freeman-Grenville (22 August 2013). "Waqwaq". In P. Bearman; Th. Bianquis; C.E. Bosworth; E. van Donzel; W.P. Heinrichs (eds.). Encyclopaedia of Islam (Second ed.). Brill Online.

23. 1. "Mining amid decentralization. Local governments and mining in the Philippines." By William N. Holden and R. Daniel Jacobson. The Authors Journal compilation. 2006. United Nations. Published by Blackwell Publishing Ltd., 9600 Garsington Road, Oxford, OX4 2DQ, UK and 350 Main Street, Malden MA 02148, USA. p. 189. 2. University of Santo Tomas. "Philippine History Hand Out #1 - Philippine History Early..." PHIL HIST 100. p.1.

24. "The 10 Richest Women of All Time" By Kerry Close. Feb. 1, 2016. Money Magazine. Citing Kara Cooney, Egyptologist, University of California, Los Angeles.

25. "A Local Church Living for Dialogue: Muslim-Christian Relations in Mindanao-Sulu (Philippines), 1965-2000." By William Larousse. 2001. p. 35.

26. "The First Voyage Round the World by Antonio Pigafetta." 1522, translated by Lord Stanley of Alderley. p. 94.

27. "The South China Sea Dispute: Philippines Sovereign Rights and Jurisdiction in the West Philippine Sea" By Philippine Supreme Court Justice Antonio T. Carpio. 2017. The Institute for Maritime and Ocean Affairs. p.3.

28. "Suvarnadvipa and the Chryse Chersonesos." W. J. van der Meulen. Cornell University. p. 3.

29. "Mesha." Abarim-Publications.com.

30. "Antiquities of the Jews." Josephus, Flavius. 93 A.D. Book 1, Section 143.

31. "Mesha." Strong's Concordance #H4852. Blue Letter Bible.

32. "Meysha." Strong's Concordance #H4338. Blue Letter Bible.

33. "The Mesha Stele." c. 800 B.C. Discovered 1868 Dhiban, Jordan. Department of Near Eastern Antiquities: Levant. The Louvre Museum, Paris.

34. 'Antiquities of the Jews" Flavius Josephus. Book 1, Chapter 6:4.

35. "Sephar." Easton's Bible Dictionary. International Standard Bible Encyclopedia. BibleHub.com.

36. "The Earthly Inheritance Series of Bible Subjects . Oriental Origins in the Bible." By Paul Phelps. 2000.

37. "Two thirds of the world lives in Asia and 12 other things you need to know." By Alex Vinci. Nov. 7, 2014. globalcitizen.org.

38. "Sefirot." Wikipedia. "What You Need to Know about Kabbalah. Jerusalem: Gal Einai Institute." Rabbi Yitzchak Ginsburgh. 2006. Strong's Concordance #H5611.

39. "Qedem." Strong's Concordance #H6924. Blue Letter Bible.

40. "Mt. Qatar." "Developing and Establishing Effective Leadership for a Prosperous Edenic Hebrew Civilization. A Manual and Manifest for Laying the Foundations to the Eternal Kingdom of Yahwah." By Rabi-Kohan Shalomim Y. HaLevi, Ph. D, D. Div., O.R. Thrpst. S.A.C. 2004. p. 32.

41. "Havilah." Hitchcock's Dictionary of Bible Names from BibleHub.org and KingJamesBibleDictionary.com, Strong's Concordance #H2341. Blue Letter Bible.

42. "Eve - Havah." Strong's Concordance #H2332. Blue Letter Bible.

43. "This $100 Million Pearl Is The Largest and Most Expensive in the World." By Roberta Naas. Forbes Magazine. Aug 23, 2016.

44. "Pinoy in Canada Discovers Strange Family Heirloom is Actually a Giant Pearl Worth $90 Million." Buzzooks.com. May 23, 2019.

45. 1. "ROMBLON: 8 Awesome Places You Should Visit in Romblon!" Our Awesome Planet. Sept. 7, 2016. 2. "The Romblon Marble." Ellaneto Tiger Marble Trader, Romblon. 2010.

46. "Marvelous Marble" By Robert A. Evora. Manila Standard. Jan. 16, 2014.

47. "Parvaim." Smith's Bible Dictionary, International Standard Bible Encyclopedia, ATS Bible Dictionary, Easton's Bible Dictionary, Strong's #H6516. BibleHub.com.

48. "The Complete Dead Sea Scrolls." By Geza Vermes, Penguin Classics. p. 481-482, Column II.

49. "Uphaz." Hitchcock's Bible Names Dictionary, ATS Bible Dictionary, Easton's Bible Dictionary, International Standard Bible Encyclopedia, Strong's #H210, #H211. BibleHub.com.

50. "19th-century reconstruction of Eratosthenes' map of the (for the Greeks) known world," c. 194 BC. Public Domain.

51. "Kephiyr." Strong's Concordance #3715 and #3722. Blue Letter Bible.

52. "Havilah." Wikipedia citing Kitab al-Magall (Clementine literature) and the Cave of Treasures.

53. "The Queen Of Sheba." By Michael Wood. BBC News. Last updated 2011-02-17.

54. "Archeologists strike gold in quest to find Queen of Sheba's wealth," By Dalya Alberge. The Guardian. Feb. 12, 2012.

55. "The Wealth of Africa. The Kingdom of Aksum. Student's Worksheet." The British Museum.

56. Netherlands Map. 1893 Nederlandsch Indie Map. Public Domain.

57. Dated and copyrighted to J. H. Colton, 1855. Published from Colton's 172 William Street Office in New York City. Issued as page no. 31 in volume 2 of the first edition of George Washington Colton's 1855 Atlas of the World.

58. "A New Map of the Philippine Islands Drawn from the Best Authorities", Thomas Kitchin. 1769.

59. "Shebua." Strong's Concordance #H7620. Blue Letter Bible. Exodus 34:22 KJV.

60. "Sebu, Sebuyim." Abarim-Publications.com, Strong's Concordance #H6640. Blue Letter Bible. "From Tradition to Commentary. Torah and Its Interpretation in the Midrash Sifre to Deuteronomy." By Steven D. Fraade. Dec. 15, 2016. pp. 168 & 211.

61. "Sheba." Abarim-Publication.com.

62. "Philippine Map by Dudley's Dell Arcano del Mare, 1646" [Detail with Cebu Island as Isle of Sebat. Public Domain.

63. "How Many Islands Are There In The Philippines?" By Vic Lang'at Junior. Oct. 19, 2018. WorldAtlas.com.

64. "Oil and Gas History." Republic of the Philippines Department of Energy, doe.gov.ph. Retrieved Nov. 26, 2019.

65. "Ayit." Strong's Concordance #H5861 and #H376. Blue Letter Bible.

66. "The Largest Eagle in the World." By Blas R. Tabaranza Jr. The Haribon Foundation. July 22, 2019.

67. "The First Voyage Round the World by Antonio Pigafetta." 1522, translated by Lord Stanley of Alderley. p. 80.

68. "The Philippine Islands, 1493-1898, Volume XXXIII, 1519-1522, by Antonio Pigafetta." Editor: Emma H. Blair. Translator: James Alexander Robertson. p.123.

69. "The Datu Who Became A Tortoise." ChoosePhilippines.com. Ancient Philippines Stories Reality Myths. Published July 2016.

70. "Pearls of Mindanao." Ancient Philippines Stories Reality Myths. Published Aug. 3, 2016.

71. "The Book of the Cave of Treasures." By Sir Ernest Alfred Wallis Budge. 2005. Cosimo, Inc., New York. Originally published by Religious Tract Society. 1927. p. 69.

72. "700,000-year-old Butchered Rhino Pushes Back Ancient Human Arrival in the Philippines." By Jason Daley, May 4, 2018, Smithsonian.com.

73. "List of extinct animals of the Philippines." Wikipedia. Last edited 14 October 2019.

74. "Elephants in the Philippines." By Ligaya Caballes, February 11, 2015, Pinoy-Culture.com.

75. "Jesuit Elephant in 17th-century Manila." By Ambeth R. Ocampo. Retrieved March 26, 2019, Philippine Daily Inquirer. Original June 4, 2014.

76. "Elephas Beyeri." Wikipedia citing: "Evolution of Island Mammals: Adaptation and Extinction of Placental Mammals on Islands." Alexandra van der Geer; George Lyras; John de Vos; Michael Dermitzakis. 2011. John Wiley & Sons. p. 223.

77. "State of Archaeological Research in Cagayan Valley, Northern Luzon, Philippines." By Wilfredo P. Ronquillo. The Journal of History, Vol. 46. No. 1 - 4 (2000). Philippine E-Journals.

78. "A Sultan's gift?" By Bob Grant. Jul 1, 2008. the-scientist.com.

79. "The First Voyage Round the World by Antonio Pigafetta." 1522, translated by Lord Stanley of Alderley. p. 112.

80. "The Philippine Islands, 1493-1898: Volume XVI, 1609." By H.E. Blair. Chapter 8. ebook: p. 81 and note 65. Citing Antonio De Morga, 1609.

81. "Philippine progress prior to 1898." "Rizal's Note to de Morga." By Austin Craig and Conrado Benitez. 1872. p.8.

82. "Qowph." Strong's Concordance #6971. Gesenius' Hebrew-Chaldee Lexicon. Blue Letter Bible.

83. Phoenician Sailors Bringing Monkeys from Ophir. From court D, panel 7, the north-west palace of the Assyrian king Ashurnasirpal II at Nimrud (ancient Kalhu; Biblical Calah). From Mesopotamia, modern-day Iraq. Neo-Assyrian period, 865-860 BCE. The British Museum, London. Public Domain.

84. 1. Wikipedia citing: "Palaeogeography, Palaeoclimatology, Palaeoecology." Piper, P. J.; Ochoa, J.; Lewis, H.; Paz, V.; Ronquillo, W. P. (2008). 264: 123–127. Ochoa, J.; Piper, P. J. (2017). "Tiger". In Monks, G. (ed.). Climate Change and Human Responses: A Zooarchaeological Perspective. Springer. pp. 79–80. 2. Philippine Long-Tailed Macaque (Macaca fascicularis philippensis). Project Noah.

85. "The First Voyage Round the World by Antonio Pigafetta." 1522, translated by Lord Stanley of Alderley. p. 110 & 114.

86. "Palawan peacock-pheasant." Wikipedia. Updated Feb. 25 2020.

87. "In The Know: The Philippines' mining industry." Compiled by Kate Pedroso, Inquirer Research. Philippine Daily Inquirer. July 10, 2012.

88. "Port of Manila and other Philippine ports year book. [1936]." pp.5 and 17. The United States and its Territories. 1870-1925: The Age of Imperialism. Manila (Philippines), Manila Harbor Board. Philippines. Manila Arrastre Service. Philippines. Bureau of Customs.

89. "Mineral Resources." Republic of the Philippines. Philippine Statistics Authority. 2018.

90. "Lone Philippine iron ore miner suspended in gov't crackdown." By Manolo Serapio, Jr. and Enrico Dela Cruz. ABS-CBN News, Reuters. Aug. 8, 2016.

91. "Science in the Philippines. A review by James J. Walsh, Ih.D., M.D." Walsh, James Joseph, 1865-1942. The United States and its Territories. 1870-1925: The Age of Imperialism. Manila (Philippines). Manila Harbor Board. Philippines. Manila Arrastre Service., Philippines. Bureau of Customs. p.8.

92. "Tin sources and trade in ancient times." Wikipedia citing "Tin in the Mediterranean area: history and geology." Valera, R.G.; Valera, P.G. (2003). Giumlia-Mair, A.; Lo Schiavo, F. (eds.), The Problem of Early Tin, Oxford: Archaeopress, pp. 3–14.

93. "Tin Mining in Mindanao." World Encyclopedia 2005, originally published by Oxford University Press 2005., The Columbia Encyclopedia, 6th ed. Also, The American Desk Encyclopedia. Edited by Steve Luck. p. 533.

94. "Development of the Jewelry Industry." Board of Investments. DTI Business Development Manager for Fashion and Jewelry. Bureau of Export Trade Promotion. p. 1.

95. "Lead: `owphereth." Strong's Concordance #H5777. Blue Letter Bible.

96. "Philippines Resources and Power." By Michael Cullinane, Carolina G. Hernandez and Gregorio C. Borlaza. Last Updated: Sept. 13, 2019. Encyclopaedia Britannica.

97. "Mining & Natural Resources: Primer on the Philippine Minerals Industry." By Quisumbing Torres. p. 4.

98. "Poor Man's Frankincense" Manila Elemi. "Young Living sees growing demand for essential oils." By Zsarlene B. Chua. Business World. Apr. 22, 2019.

99. "List of Gemstones and Non-Metallic Minerals Found in the Philippines." okd2.com, Feb. 12, 2018.

100. "The Philippines at a Glance." Permanent Mission of the Republic of the Philippines to the United Nations. United Nations. Retrieved Feb. 2019.

101. 1. pealim.com#3811. 2. The Name Book, Over 10,000 Names – Their Meanings, Origins, and Spiritual Significance. By Dorothy Astoria, Bethany House Publishers, 1982. p. 217. 3. "Naara." The Name List.

102. 1. "Narra." Godofredo Stuart. StuartXchange. 2. "Narra." The Wood Database.

103. "Tirzah." Strong's Concordance #H8645. BibleHub.com.

104. "Gopher Wood." Strong's Concordance #H1613. Blue Letter Bible.

105. "Opher Wood." studylight.org citing Noah Webster's American Dictionary 1828.

106. "Opher Wood." A Poetic Descant on the Primeval and Present State of Mankind; or The Pilgrim's Muse, Published 1816 by J. Foster Printing, Winchester, VA, Rev. Joseph Thomas, p.47.

107. "Cargoes" Salt-Water Poems & Ballads by John Masefield. Published 1903.

108. "A History of The Holy Bible From The Beginning Of The World To The Establishment Of Christianity; Vol. II" By The Rev. Thomas Stackhouse, M.A., Late Vicar of Beenham in Berkshire. Blackie & Son, 1846. Book VI. p. 430.

109. "Quinquireme." Collins English Dictionary – Complete and Unabridged, 12th Edition, 2014.

110. Mark Cartwright, "The Phoenicians - Master Mariners," Ancient History Encyclopedia. Last modified Apr. 28, 2016.

111. "Antiquities of the Jews." Flavius Josephus. Book VIII . Chapter 6:4.

112. "History of the Phoenician Civilization." By George Rawlinson. Chapter IX. 2018.

113. "Phoenician Ships of Mazarron. Puerto de Mazarron, Spain." By Dr. Alan P Newman. atlasobscura.com.

114. "How Much Of The Ocean Have We Explored?" By Oishimaya Sen Nag. WorldAtlas.com.

115. "CoinWeek Ancient Coin Series – Coinage of the Phoenicians." By Mike Markowitz. Feb. 29, 2016.

116. "The death of gold in early Visayan societies: Ethnohistoric accounts and archaeological evidences." By Victor P. Estrella. Archaeological Studies Program. University of the Philippines Diliman. Aug. 15, 2014. p. 234. Citing Villegas, R. N. (2004). Ginto: history wrought in gold. Manila: Bangko Sentral ng Pilipinas. pp. 15-16.

117. "The First Voyage Round the World by Antonio Pigafetta." 1522. translated by Lord Stanley of Alderley. ebook: pp. 76, 78, 100, 108, 115, 118, and 120.

118. "The Butuan Two boat known as a balangay in the National Museum, Manila, Philippines". Paul Clark, Jeremy Green; Rey Santiago, Tom Vosmer. The International Journal of Nautical Archaeology 22. 1993. pp. 143-159.

119. "Balangay bill passage seen before Victory in Mactan revelry". By Filane Mikee Cervantes. Republic of the Philippines, Philippine News Agency. Dec. 5, 2019.

120. "Butuan's ancient Balangay boat replicas sail to start 500-day countdown to Mactan quincentennial celebrations." By The Good News Pilipinas Team. Nov. 8, 2019.

121. "The Adventurers at the Helm of the Last Voyage of the Balangay" By Angelica Gutierrez. Esquire Magazine Philippines. Mar. 21, 2018.

122. "פה." Abarim-Publications.com. "PY (פי)."

123. "'Game-changing' study suggests first Polynesians voyaged all the way from East Asia." By Ann Gibbons. Science Magazine. American Association for the Advancement of Science. Oct. 3, 2016.

124. "The Voyages and Adventures of Fernando Mendez Pinto, The Portuguese." Done Into English By Henry Cogan. London: T. Fisher Unwin. New York: Macmillan & Co.. 1888. p. 77.

125. "The Philippine Islands, 1493-1898: Volume XVI, 1609." H.E. Blair. Citing "Sucesos de las Islas Filipinas." Antonio de Morga; Mexico, 1609. ebook: p. 35.

126. Rizal's note to Morga. "The Philippine Islands, 1493-1898: Volume XVI, 1609." H.E. Blair. Citing "Sucesos de las Islas Filipinas." Antonio de Morga; Mexico, 1609. ebook: p. 158. Print: p. 84.

127. 17th-century depiction of a Visayan karakoa from Historia de las islas e indios de Bisayas (1668) by Francisco Ignacio Alcina. Public Domain.

128. Barangay. Sixteenth-Century Philippine Culture and Society. By William Henry Scott. Ateneo de Manila University Press. 1994. p. 63.

129. 1. "Pre-Hispanic Era." "Piloncitos." Bangko Sentral Ng Pilipinas. 2. Photos: Barnaby's Auctions. 3. "History of the Philippines." Wikipedia.

130. "Karakoa" Wikipedia. Last Edited on Nov. 10, 2019.

131. "Filipino Seaman Still Rule The Seas, For Now." By Perla Aragon Choudhury. Department of Labor and Employment of the Philippines and Philippine Overseas Employment Administration (POEA). Feb. 2, 2010.

132. "Protect seafarers from pirates - solon." By Eduardo A. Galvez. Media Relations Service-PRIB. Republic of the Philippines House of Representatives. May 27, 2013.

133. "Sebastian Cabot, British Navigator." Encyclopaedia Britannica. Last Updated Nov. 5, 2018.

134. "History of the Philippine Islands From their discovery by Magellan in 1521 to the beginning of the XVII Century; with descriptions of Japan, China and adjacent countries." By Dr. Antonio de Morga. Alcalde of Criminal Causes, in the Royal Audiencia of Nueva Espana, and Counsel for the Holy Office of the Inquisition. Completely translated into English, edited and annotated by E. H. Blair and J.A. Robertson. "Sucesos De Las Islas Filipinas." By Dr. Antonio de Morga. Mexico: at the shop of Geronymo Balli in the year 1609; printed by Cornelio Adriano Cesar. Source: The translation is made from the Harvard copy of the original printed work. TRANSLATION: This is made by Alfonso de Salvio, Norman F. Hall, and James Alexander Robertson..- The Philippine Islands, 1493-1803, 1569-1576 by Edward Bourne, E.H. Blair, and J.A. Robertson. Vol. 16, pp. 76-77, 101-103. ebook: Chapter 8. p. 2064, 2086, 2087, 2088.

135. "Reply to Fray Rada's 'Opinion.' Guido de Lavezaris and others;" Manila, June 1574. The Philippine Islands, 1493-1803 — 1569-1576 by Edward Bourne, E.H. Blair, and J.A. Robertson Vol. 3. p. 241.

136. "Philippine Progress Prior to 1898." By Austin Craig and Conrado Benitez. Of the College of Liberal Arts Faculty of the University of the Philippines. Philippine Education Co., Inc. Manila. 1916. p. 38.

137. "The First Voyage Round the World by Antonio Pigafetta." 1522, translated by Lord Stanley of Alderley. p. 14.

138. "A Golden Discovery in the Philippines," Asian Society. Sept. 11, 2015.

139. "Las nueas quescriven de las yslas del Poniente, Hernando Riquel y otros. Mexico, News from the Western Islands by Hernando Riquel and Others." January 11, 1574. The Philippine Islands, 1493-1803 —1569-1576 by Edward Bourne, E.H. Blair, and J.A. Robertson. Vol. 3, p. 217.

140. "Two Letters from Guido de Lavezaris to Felipe II." Manila, July 17, 1574.- The Philippine Islands, 1493-1803 — Volume III, 1569-1576." by Edward Bourne, E.H. Blair, and J.A. Robertson. Vol. 3. p. 247.

141. "Philippine Progress Prior to 1898." By Austin Craig and Conrado Benitez. Of the College of Liberal Arts Faculty of the University of the Philippines. Philippine Education Co., Inc. Manila. 1916. p. 27.

142. "A History of the Philippines." By Dr. D. P. Barrows. Chapter 5. pp. 101-102.

143. "The Philippine Islands, 1493-1898." Translated from the Originals. Edward Bourne, E.H. Blair, and J.A. Robertson. Vol. 36, p. 201. Vol. XXXVI 1649-1666. The Arthur H. Clark Company. 144. "Christopher Columbus and the participation of the Jews in the Spanish and Portuguese discoveries." By Meyer Kayserling. 1829-1905; Gross, Charles.

145. "King Solomon: Stanford Scholar considers how the man who had everything ended with nothing." By Cynthia Haven. Stanford Report, July 14, 2011.

146. "Columbus' Confusion About the New World." By Edmund S. Morgan. Smithsonian Magazine. Oct. 2009.

147. "The Jews and the Expansion of Europe to the West, 1450 to 1800." Edited by Paolo Bernardini and Norman Fiering. Berghahn Book. 2001. Chapter 1. p. 30.

148. "Magellan's voyage around the world; three contemporary accounts [by] Antonio Pigafetta, Maximilian of Transylvania [and] Gaspar Correa." Charles E. Nowell. 1962, Northwestern University Press. p. 20. Citing Livro de Duarte Barbosa, 1516.

149. "Colleccion General De Documentos Relativos A Las Islas Filipinas Existentes En El Archivo De Indias, De Sevilla." p. 54-55.

150. "Magellan's voyage around the world; three contemporary accounts [by] Antonio Pigafetta, Maximilian of Transylvania [and] Gaspar Correa." Charles E. Nowell, Northwestern University Press, 1962. p. 21-22.

151. "Scythians." The Editors of Encyclopaedia Britannica. Last update Nov. 5, 2019.

152. "Collecion General de Documentos Relativos a las Islas Filipinas" 1519-1522, p. 112-138, Doc. # 98. Directions: Entire Chapter. Tarsis and Lequios/Ofir on P.137-138.

153. "The Discoveries of the World, from Their First Originall Unto the Yeere of our Lord 1555." By Antonio Galvao. Corrected, Quoted and Now Published in English. By Richard Hakluyt. Londini. 1601. p. 8.

154. 1. "The surueye of the vvorld..." Dionysius, Periegetes. By Thomas Twyne. 1543-1613. Chap. Of the Ilandes in the Oceane. Parts 4 and 5. 2. "Monsoon Winds to the "Land of Gold." Authoring Institution: California University, Berkeley. Office of Resources for International and Area Studies." p. 38. citing "The Golden Khersonese." Paul Wheatley, p. 131-133.

155. "Origen de los indios de el Nuevo Mundo e Indias Occidentales." By Gregorio Garcia. Con Priveligio. p. 37.

156. 'The Philippine Islands, 1493-1898 - Volume 40 of 55, 1690-1691." By Francisco Colin, Francisco Combos, Gaspar de San Aguston and Dominican Gregorio Garcia locating Ophir in Moluccas and the Philippines. Edited By: E.H. Blair J.A. Robertson. Appendix: Ethnological Description of the Filipinos. Chapter IV. ebook: p. 38.

157. "Philippine Progress Prior to 1898." By Austin Craig and Conrado Benitez. Of the College of Liberal Arts Faculty of the University of the Philippines. Philippine Education Co., Inc., Manila, 1916. p. 92. Citing Works on Conjectural Anthropology, Former Prime Minister Pedro A. Paterno. Mojares 2006. p. 85.

158. "Impresion al offset de la Edicion Anatada por Rizal, Paris 1890." By Prof. Fernando Blumentritt. Manila: Historico Nacional, 1891.

159. Ruddock, Alwyn A. (1974). "The Reputation of Sebastian Cabot". Historical Research. University of London. 47: 95–99.

160. "The giant undersea rivers we know very little about" By Richard Gray. BBC News. July 6, 2017.

161. "The Suma Oriental of Tome Pires, Vol. I." Compiled by Tome Pires. Works Issued By The Hakluyt Society. Second Series. No. LXXXIX. Issued 1944. Digitized By McGill University Library. p. 162.

162. Strong's Concordance "Leqach" #H3948. "Laqach" #H3947, "Liqchiy" #H3949. Blue Letter Bible.

163. "Leukos." Strong's Concordance #G3022. Blue Letter Bible.

164. "Hiram." tagalog-dictionary.com.

165. "Ilokano." tagaloglang.com.

166. "The Suma Oriental of Tome Pires." "Which Goes From The Red Sea To China." Compiled by Tome Pires. Works Issued By The Hakluyt Society. Second Series. No. LXXXIX. Issued 1944. Digitized By McGill University Library. pp. 131 and 133.

167. "Ancient chicken DNA reveals Philippines home to Polynesians." By Rosalinda L. Orosa. The Philippine Star. Mar. 18, 2014.

168. "Researchers discover fossil of human older than Tabon Man." By Howie Severino. GMA News. Aug. 1, 2010.

169. "A History of the Philippines." By Dr. D. P. Barrows. Chapter 5. pp. 91.

170. Contextualising the Teaching of Biblical Hebrew." Stephen H. Levinsohn, Ph.D. SIL International. p. 1.

171. "Pulag." pealim.com#1635.

172. "Eber." Strong's Concordance #H5677. Blue Letter Bible.

173. "Hebrew." Strong's Concordance #H5680. Blue Letter Bible.

174. "The Antiquities of the Jews." Flavius Josephus. Book I. Chapter 6:4.

175. "Samar." pealim.com#1380. "Bristle." By Angus Stevenson, Maurice Waite. 2011. Concise Oxford English Dictionary: Luxury Edition. p. 176.

176. Strong's Concordance "Pala" #H6381 and "Awan" #H5770. Blue Letter Bible.

177. "Bin" and "Alvah." Abarim-Publications.com.

178. "Al Panay." pealim.com#6015. "Panayim." pealim.com#6011. "Pana." Abarim-Publications.

179. 1. Batangas Provincial Information Office. Province of Batangas. 2. Strong's Concordance "Ba'ah" #H1158 and "Tan" #H8565. Blue Letter Bible.

180. "Davah." Strong's Concordance #H1738. Blue Letter Bible.

181. "Prophetic Warning To Davao, Philippines and the Whole World! Why on All Saints Day?" Oct. 13, 2019. The God Culture YouTube Channel.

182. "Samal." By David Curwin. Balashon. Parashat Vaetchanan. 1-10-11.

183. "The NKJV, Charles F. Stanley Life Principles Bible, 2nd Edition." By Thomas Nelson. Charles F. Stanley, General Editor. 2009. The Book of Haggai. p. 1445.

184. Strong's Concordance #H935. Blue Letter Bible.

185. "Female Hebrew Names – Abra." FineJudaica.com, Retrieved Nov. 26, 2019.

186. "The Origins of English Words: A Discursive Dictionary of Indo-European Roots." By Joseph Twadell Shipley. Section D. The Johns Hopkins University Press. 1984.

187. "Bacolod." The Concise Dictionary of World Place Names. By John Everett-Heath. Oxford University Press. 2017.

188. "Baka." pealim.com#250.

189. "Lod." Strong's Concordance #3850. BibleStudyTools.com.

190. Old map of Cagayan Province, Philippines during 1918 Census. Public Domain.

191. "Chaggiyah." Strong's Concordance #2282 and 2291. BibleStudyTools.com.

192. 1. "History of Cagayan de Oro." By Antonio J. Montalvan II, Ph.D., Mindanao anthropologist and ethnohistorian. 2. "A Cagayan de Oro Ethnohistory Reader." March 8, 2004. Cagayandeoro.gov.ph.

193. "Oros." Strong's Concordance #3735. Blue Letter Bible.

194. "Ancient Israel in Sinai: The Evidence for the Authenticity of the Wilderness." By James K. Hoffmeier. Oxford University Press. 2011. Chapter IV - Archaeological Exploration in North Sinai: 1970s to the Present.

195. "Cilla." Collins Complete Spanish Electronic Dictionary. Harper Collins Publishers 2011.

196. "Sarai." abarim-publications.com.

197. "Gaal." Strong's Concordance #1350. BibleStudyTools.com.

198. "Historia do descobrimento e conqvista da India pelos Portvgveses, Volumes 4-5." By Fernao Lopes de Castanheda. Ch. 40. pp. 91-92. Lisbon. Na Typographia Rollandiana. 1883.

199. "Yan." babynames.merchant.com#70864. "Yan – God's Grace." Babynames.ch. "Chanan." Strong's Concordance #2605. "Yah." Strong's Concordance #3050. Blue Letter Bible.

200. "Saga." Strong's Concordance #H7679. Blue Letter Bible.

201. "Yada." Strong's Concordance #H3045. Blue Letter Bible.

202. "Da'at." pealim.com#4189.

203. "Encyclopedia Judaica: Sambatyon." 2008 The Gale Group. JewishVirtualLibrary.org.

204. "Tub." Strong's Concordance #2898. BibleHub.com.

205. "Gat" and "Mattan." abarim-publications.com.

206. "Bo." abarim-publications.com. "Chol." Strong's Concordance #2344. Brown-Driver-Briggs Hebrew and English Lexicon. BibleHub.com.

207. "Ara." Strong's Concordance #H772. Blue Letter Bible.

208. "Yaat." Strong's Concordance #H3271. Blue Letter Bible.

209. "Pena: Tree planting at Mt. Arayat." By Rox Pena, Sept. 4, 2014, Sun Star Philippines.

210. "Banah." Strong's Concordance #H1129. Blue Letter Bible.

211. "The Voyages and Adventures of Fernando Mendez Pinto, The Portuguese." Done Into English By Henry Cogan. London: T. Fisher Unwin. New York: Macmillan & Co.. 1888. pp. 61, 77, 259, 262, 265 and 308.

212. "An Explanation (Part Two)." "Tahal." by Kenneth Fortier. Ken Fortier Ministries. p.2.

213. Strong's Concordance #4131. BibleHub.com.

214. "Balut." Pealim.com #3309.

215. "Naga." Pealim.com#1140.

216. "Min." pealim.com#5053. pealim.com#6051.

217. "Min." Strong's Concordance #4327. BibleHub.com.

218. "Dor/Dorot." pealim.com#4339.

219. "Mt. Cabalian(the hidden mountain)" To Climbers and locals: Nov. 1, 2014. lagataw.com.

220. "Chaba." Strong's Concordance #H2244. Blue Letter Bible.

221. "Lian." Strong's Concordance #G3029. BibleHub.com.

222. "Kana." pealim.com#1913.

223. "Kan." Strong's Concordance #2579. BibleHub.com.

224. "Laon." HEBREW AND GREEK WORD-STUDY FALLACIES. By Benjamin J. Baxter. McMaster Journal of Theology and Ministry 12. p. 15. Citing Cf. Barr, Semantics, 234–35; Cotterell and Turner, Linguistics, 122.

225. Strong's Concordance #1588. Blue Letter Bible.

226. "Iggereth, Igorowt." Strong's Concordance #H107. Blue Letter Bible and BibleHub.com.

227. University of California Publications in American Archaeology and Ethnology. "Ifugao Law" By R.F. Barton, Vol. 15, No. 1, pp. 1-186, plates 1-33, February 15, 1919. P. 16.

228. "Apo." Strong's Concordance #G575. Thayer's Greek Lexicon. Blue Letter Bible. "Apo." Dictionary.com By Random House Unabridged Dictionary. Collins English Dictionary - Complete and Unabridged 2012. The American Heritage Stedman's Medical Dictionary. 2002.

229. pealim.com#6051.

230. Strong's Concordance #4327. BibleHub.com.

231. "Danot/ Dana." pealim.com#417.

232. "Saba." Strong's Concordance #7646. BibleStudyTools.com.

233. "Buka/ Buk'u." pealim.com#250.

234. "Bath." Strong's Concordance #H1324. Blue Letter Bible.

235. "Ala." Strong's Concordance #H5967. Blue Letter Bible.

236. "Goyim." Strong's Concordance #H1471. Blue Letter Bible.

237. "Aras." Strong's Concordance #H781. Blue Letter Bible.

238. "Mahar." Strong's Concordance #H4117. Blue Letter Bible.

239. "Lecha." Pealim.com#6014.

240. "Pili." Strong's Concordance #6383. BibleHub.com. "Hebrew Names and Meanings. "Pili." Finejudaica.com.

241. "Pinnah." Strong's Concordance #H6438. Blue Letter Bible.

242. "Malak." Strong's Concordance #H4397. Blue Letter Bible.

243. "Achyan." Strong's Concordance #H291. BibleHub.com.

244. "Anan." Strong's Concordance #033. BibleHub.com.

245. "Eskaya." Wikipedia citing Tirol, Jes B. (1991). "Eskaya of Bohol: Traces of Hebrew Influence Paving the Way For Easy Christianization of Bohol". Bohol's Pride: 50–51, 53. Tirol, Jes B. (1990a). "Bohol and Its System of Writing". UB Update (July–September): 4, 7.

246. "Purchas his Pilgrimage; or, Relations of the World and the Religions observed in all ages and places discovered, from the Creation unto this present." By Samuel Purchas. Book 1. Printed by William Stansby for Henrie Fetherstone. 1626. All of Chapter IX. pp. 47-51.

247. "Hakluytus Posthumus, or Purchas his Pilgrimes, Contayning a History of the World, in Sea Voyages, & Lande Travels." By Dr James Robert Wood, Trinity College Dublin.

248. "Controller Houses Of The East India Company: EIC Series Part IV." Great Game India Magazine. East India Company Series (Apr-June 2016 Issue). June 26, 2016.

249. "Ophir." Wikipedia citing Smith, William, A dictionary of the Bible, Hurd and Houghton, 1863 (1870), p. 1441. Smith's Bible Dictionary. Ramaswami, Sastri, The Tamils and their culture, Annamalai University, 1967, pp.16. Gregory, James, Tamil lexicography, M. Niemeyer, 1991, pp.10. Fernandes, Edna, The last Jews of Kerala, Portobello, 2008, pp.98. Encyclopaedia Britannica and Fourteenth-century biblical commentator, Nathanel ben Isaiah.

250. "Parrots." Chabad.org.

251. "Peacocks." Strong's Concordance #H8500. Blue Letter Bible.

252. "Unearthing the golden days of Ilocos Sur." By Michael Armand P. Canilao. Rappler, July 5, 2015. Citing "Mountains and Sea: Case Studies in Coastal, Riverine, and Upland Archeology of Ilocos Sur." Published by UST Publishing House. 2015. Analysis of Archeological Data Unearthed Through the Ilocos Sur Archaeology Project.

253. "Hoduw/ India." Strong's Concordance #H1912. Blue Letter Bible.

254. "The Dispersal of Austronesian boat forms in the Indian Ocean." By Waruno Mahdi . Roger Blench & Matthew Spriggs (editors). Archaeology and Language III: Artefacts, languages and texts, One World Archaeology 34. pp. 144–179. London & New York: Routledge. 1999. p. 154.

255. The Statue of Darius exhibited at the National Museum of Iran Archives de la Maison Archeologie & Ethnologie, Rene-Ginouves, JP_V03. Mission de Suse. Delegation archeologique francaise en Iran / Jean Perrot. India is rendered in Egyptian.

256. "Chrysion." Strong's Concordance #G5553. Blue Letter Bible.

257. Gen. 10: 29-30. LXX Greek Septuagint in Greek. Blue Letter Bible.

258. "Gunung Ledang (Mt. Ophir)". Johor Malaysia Tourism. Nov. 27, 2019.

259. 1862 British Map of Malaysian Peninsula. T. Moniot. Showing Mt. Ophir. National Archive of Singapore. Public Domain. For educational and research purposes per photo terms and Fair Use Act.

260. "The Alchemist" by SIR FRANCIS Bacon's friend Ben Jonson. 1610.

261. "The Biblical Land of Ophir (Peru), Frances Bacon, Ben Johnson, King Solomon, and Gene Savoy." Apr. 2, 2010. genesavoy.blogspot.com.

262. "Purchas his Pilgrimage; or, Relations of the World and the Religions observed in all ages and places discovered, from the Creation unto this present." By Samuel Purchas. Book 1. Printed by William Stansby for Henrie Fetherstone. 1626. Chap. VIII. p. 27.

263. "Tartessus, Ancient Region and Town, Spain." By The Editors of Encyclopaedia Britannica. Last Updated Apr. 17, 2016.

264. "Tartessus." By Simon J. Kaey. Oxford Classical Dicionary. Mar. 2016.

265. "We Three Kings of Orient Are (Del oriente venimos tres)." John H. Hopkins, Jr., 1820-1891. Hymn #107. Santo, Santo, Santo. p. 169. "When from the East the wise men came." John H. Hopkins, Jr., 1820-1891. Hymn #64. The Church Hymnal. p. 134. hymnary.org.

266. "Libanos." Strong's Concordance #G3030. Blue Letter Bible.

267. "Lebownah." Strong's Concordance #H3828. Blue Letter Bible.

268. "Hebrew Word Study – Violence – Chaman – חמן " by Chaim & Laura, Jun. 6, 2018, ChaimBenTorah.com.

269. "Chaman." Strong's Concordance #H2555. Blue Letter Bible.

270. "Young Living sees growing demand for essential oils." By Zsarlene B. Chua. Apr. 22, 2019. Business World. bworldonline.com. Confirmed by numerous distributor sites such as: theoildropper.com, essentialoilexchange.com, mountainroseherbs.com, bmvfragrances.com, butterflyexpress.com. "Reference Guide for Essential Oils." By Connie and Alan Higley. Abundant Health. Ninth Edition. Revised Oct. 2005. p. 66.

271. "Canarium luzonicum. Manila Elemi." Stuart Xchange. Godofredo U. Stuart Jr., M.D. Updated June 2017.

272. Cephisodotus the Elder, Eirene, daughter of Fallen Angel Poseidon, bearing the infant Ploutos, a Nephilim, 380-370 BC. Plaster cast. Gallery of Classical Art in Hostinne. (Roman point copy exists at the Glyptothek in Munich and fragments in various collections.) Wikimedia Commons. Public Domain.

273. "Magos." Strong's Exhaustive Concordance #G3097. Blue Letter Bible.

274. "Chakkiym ." Strong's Concordance #H2445. Blue Letter Bible.

275. "Sophos." Strong's Concordance #G4680. Blue Letter Bible.

276. Strong's Concordance "Mizrach" #H4217 and "Tsedeq" #H6664. Blue Letter Bible.

277. Cebu's historical landmark Santo Nino religious vested statue of the infant Child Jesus. It is permanently encased within bulletproof glass at the Basilica Minore del Santo Nino. Wikimedia Commons.

278. Mineral-laden water emerging from a hydrothermal vent on the Niua underwater volcano in the Lau Basin, southwest Pacific Ocean. As the water cools, minerals precipitate to form tower-like "chimneys." Image taken during 2016 cruise "Virtual Vents." By Schmidt Ocean Institute. ROV ROPOS.

279. 'History of the Philippine Islands, by Antonio de Morga, 1559–1636." ebook: P. 2070.

280. "Kedar." Strong's Concordance #H6938. Blue Letter Bible.

281. "Kephiyr." Strong's Concordance #3715. BibleHub.com.

282. "The First Voyage Round the World by Antonio Pigafetta." 1522. translated by Lord Stanley of Alderley. pp. 82, 103 and 104.

283. Yam." Strong's Concordance #H3220. Blue Letter Bible.

284. "Nahar." Strong's Concordance #H5104. 1. Blue Letter Bible. 2. Brown Driver Briggs Hebrew and English Lexicon. BibleHub.com.

285. NASA/Goddard Space Flight Center Scientific Visualization Studio U.S. Department of Commerce, National Oceanic and Atmospheric Administration, National Geophysical Data Center, 2006, 2-minute Gridded Global Relief Data (ETOPO2v2). Horace Mitchell (NASA/GSFC): Lead Animator.

286. 1. "Oceanic Trenches." The Editors of Encyclopaedia Britannica. Last Updated July 25, 2016. 2. "Oceanic trench." Wikipedia.

287. "Cabab." Strong's Concordance #H5437. Blue Letter Bible.

288. "Kuwsh." Strong's Concordance #H3568. Blue Letter Bible.

289. Herodotus' Map of the World. 450 B.C. Library of Congress, Washington, D.C. Public Domain.

290. Ptolemy Cosmographia 1467 - North Africa translated by Jacobus Angelus. Public Domain.

291. "Eden," "Ararat," and "Hell." geotargit.com.

292. "What Is The Source Of The Tigris River?" By Joseph Kiprop. World Atlas. May 15, 2018.

293. "Tigris-Euphrates river system." By Lewis Owen, McGuire Gibson, Seton H.F. Lloyd. Encyclopaedia Britannica Last edited Jan. 20, 2016.

294. "What Is The Source Of The River Nile?" By John Miaschi. June 2017. World Atlas.com.

295. Book of Tobit 6:1 in Hebrew. Sefaria.org.

296. 1. "The Project Gutenberg EBook of Mi Ultimo Adios, by Jose Rizal." pp. 3-14. 2. "My Last Farewell ("Mi Ultimo adios")." By Dr. Jose Rizal, Dec. 30, 1896 (Eve of his execution). Original in Spanish. English translation by Encarnacion Alzona & Isidro Escare Abeto. Wikipedia.

297. "Pison." Tagalog Lang Dictionary.

298. "Gan." Strong's Concordance #H1588. Gesenius' Hebrew-Chaldee Lexicon. Blue Letter Bible.

299. 1595 Boxer Codex. Lilly Library, Indiana University, Bloomington, Indiana (U.S.A.), Catalogue Record of the Boxer Codex. p. 119, 115, 23, 70, 123. C.R. Boxer.

300. "Indonesia's Mountains of Fire." By Daniel Quinn. Indonesia Expat. June 30, 2014. Indonesia's Volcanological Survey. Laporan Kebencanaan Geologi. Apr. 2, 2019.

301. "Ham." Strong's Concordance #H2526. Blue Letter Bible.

302. "Hereford Mappa Mundi." circa 1300. By Richard of Haldingham. Scanned by Scott Ehardt from Decorative Maps by Roderick Barron. ISBN 1851702989. Wikimedia Commons. Public Domain.

303. "Hereford Mappa Mundi 1300.jpg, edited, some details explained." By Richard of Haldingham. Scanned by Scott Ehardt from Decorative Maps by Roderick Barron. Annotations by WolfgangW. Wikimedia Commons. Public Domain.

304. "Lanzones, Fruit for the Gods." By Renzelle Ann Palma. Choose Philippines, ABS-CBN Corporation. May 23, 2013.

305. "Ta." Strong's Concordance #H8372. Blue Letter Bible.

306. "Ha." "Heblish – Hebrew lessons: Day 7, Lesson 3." By Yaron. free-hebrew.com. Jan. 25,2010.

307. "Rom." Strong's Concordance #7315. Brown-Driver-Briggs Hebrew and English Lexicon. Strong's Exhaustive Concordance. BibleHub.com.

308. "Ybl." Strong's Concordance #2988. BibleHub.com.

309. "Beth Biri." Abarim-Publications.com.

310. "N: Nun." By Jeff A. Benner. Ancient Hebrew Research Center.

311. "Lanzones: the sweetest gift to the Island Born of Fire." By Julius D. Ranoa. SunStar Philippines. Dec. 31, 2015.

312. "Why The Pina Has A Hundred Eyes And Other Philippines Folk Tales About Fruits. Makati, Philippines: Ilaw ng Tahanan Publishing." Sta. Romana-Cruz, N. philippinature.com. 1993.

313. Matthew 23:37-38 showing as anchored to 2 Esdras 1:30." The Geneva Bible. 1560 Edition. Photos of Physical Copy with Highlighted Emphasis Added.

314. "Qatar." Strong's Concordance #6999. BibleStudyTools.com.

315. "Hiboch!" pealim.com #3963-lehiboch.

316. "Ma'an." Strong's Concordance #4616. BibleStudyTools.com.

317. "Kam, Kama." pealim.com#1876.

318. "Agon." Strong's Concordance #73. BibleHub.com.

319. "Mabo." Strong's Concordance #3996. BibleHub.com.

320. "Lo." Strong's Concordance #03808. BibleStudyTools.com.

321. "Mai: Maon or Main ." abarim-publications.com.

322. ""Thummim, Tom" Strong's Concordance #8550 and #8537. BibleHub.com.

323. "Enoch and Qumran Origins: New Light on a Forgotten Connection." Gabriele Boccaccini, Editor. William B. Erdemans Publishing Co. Grand Rapids, MI and Cambridge, UK. 2005. p. 137.

324. "The Complete Dead Sea Scrolls In English Revised Edition." "The Damascus Document." Translated By Geza Vermes, 2004, Penguin Classics Books. London, England. First Published 1962. Revised Edition 2004. p. 139.

325. "Book of Jubilees." Wikipedia.

326. Matthew 23:37-38 KJV. Original Authorized 1611 King James Version. Emphasis added.

327. "What's baffling about recent Mindanao quakes." By Mario A. Aurelio. Philippine Daily Inquirer. Nov. 10, 2019.

328. Prophetic Warning To The Philippines" The God Culture. 2: Pattern of Earthquake History, The God Culture YouTube Channel Citing USGS, Wikipedia, Philippines Institute of Volcanology and Seismology, Philippine Daily Inquirer.

329. "The Spaniards' first 50 years in the Philippines, 1565-1615: A sourcebook." VOL. II, pp. 210-216. Blair & Robertson, The Philippine Islands, Vol. 2, pp. 174-182; Vol. 34, pp.195-213.

330. "The First Voyage Round the World by Antonio Pigafetta." 1522. translated by Lord Stanley of Alderley. p. 103.

331. "The First Voyage Round the World by Antonio Pigafetta." 1522. translated by Lord Stanley of Alderley. p. 105.

332. Abirim-Publications, NOBSE Study Bible Name List, Jones' Dictionary of Old Testament Proper Names, BDB Theological Dictionary.

333. balashan.com, June 26, 2006.

334. HebrewName.org.

335. "Filipinos In China Before 1500." By William Henry Scott. Asian Studies Journal. (Manila: De La Salle University China Studies Program, 1989), pp. 1 and 3.

336. "Mindoro." Wikipedia. No source indicated for "Mina de Oro."

337. "Han Nationality." Travel China Guide. Last Modified Jan. 24, 2019.

338. "Mai Mandarin." dictionary.hantrainerpro.com. Last updated: Feb. 11, 2020.

339. GlobalSecurity.org. Citing "The Philippines in the 6th to 16th centuries." By E. P. Patanne. Quezon City. LSA Press, Inc., 1996.

340. "Ma-i / Ma-Yi- / Mindoro." GlobalSecurity.org.

341. "The Philippine Islands, 1493-1803 — Volume III, 1569-1576." By Edward Bourne, E.H. Blair, and J.A. Robertson. Vol. 3. p. 58.

342. "Contact And Ethnogenesis In Mindoro Up To The End Of The Spanish Rule." By Violeta B. Lopez.

343. The God Culture YouTube Channel Comments on Miraculous Mindoro: Part 12H: Solomon's Gold Series.

344. "The book Chu Fan Chi (Zhu Fan Zhi or Description of Various Foreigners)" written by customs official Zhao Rukuo (Chao Ju-kua) in 1225, which narrates pre-Hispanic Philippine history during the Song dynasty (960-1279).

346. 1. "History of Batangas." Batangas Provincial Information Office. Province of Batangas. 2. Strong's Concordance "Ba'ah" #H1158, "Tan" #H8565, and "Gan" #H1588. Blue Letter Bible.

347. 1. "Romblon Triangle." Mar. 1, 2012. PhilUrbanLegends.blogspot.com. 2. "Ang Pinaka: Ten popular Pinoy urban legends." GMA News Online. Oct. 17, 2014.

348. "Ancient Jewish History: The Ten Lost Tribes." 2008 The Gale Group. Jewish VirtualLibrary. org. Citing Babylonian Talmud, Shabbat 147b, and Numbers Rabba 9:7. The legend is also mentioned by Josephus Flavius (Wars: 7:96-97) and the Greek author Pliny the Elder (Historia Naturalis 31:24).

349. Strong's Concordance #6376 and #6335. Blue Letter Bible.

350. Tagalog-Dictionary.com.

351. "Environmental Biology of Fishes." K.E. Carpenter and V.G. Springer. 2005. 72: 467-480.

352. "Center of the Center of Marine Diversity." CNN. Apr. 30, 2012.

353. "100 Scientists Declare RP as World's 'Center of Marine Biodiversity." By Katherine Adraneda. June 8, 2006. The Philippine Star reporting on "Philippines Environmental Monitor, 2005" by the World Bank.

354. "Chabayah." Strong's Concordance #2252. BibleHub.com.

355. "Ba." pealim.com#28.

356. "Yah." Strong's Concordance #H3050. Blue Letter Bible.

357. 1. "Antiquities of the Jews." Flavius Josephus. Book 1, Chapter 6. 2. "Kabul River." Wikipedia. 3. "Ariya." Old Iranian Online.

358. "UFEI - SelecTree: A Tree Selection Guide." selectree.calpoly.edu. Retrieved Apr. 29, 2018.

359. "Rainbow Gums". Double Helix. CSIRO. Retrieved Aug. 8, 2017.

360. "Eucalyptus deglupta." World of Forestry. Retrieved May 28, 2019.

361. Strong's Concordance "Cala" #5537 and "Maya'an." #4599. BibleStudyTools.com.

362. "Mas." Strong's Concordance #4522. BibleHub.com. "Batem." pealim.com#28.

363. "The Philippines is the ancient Ophir" By Joseph F. Dumond affirming much of the Hebrew used in this book in his blog. Apr. 1, 2018. Sighted Moon.

364. "Paga." Strong's Concordance #H6293. Blue Letter Bible.

365. "Dayyan." Abirim-Publications.com.

366. "Davao City 75th Anniversary Commemorative Stamps." Philippine Postal Corporation. Mar. 14, 2012.

367. 1. "Pope at General Audience: You Have an 'Idol'? Take It and Throw It Out the Window." By Deborah Castellano Lubovpope. Pope Francis To General Audience at Vatican. Aug. 1, 2018. Zenit.org. 2. 'False idols always let you down,' says Pope at general audience ." Pope Francis To General Audience at Vatican. By Catholic News Service. Catholic Herald. Jan. 11, 2017. 3. "Do Catholic's Worship Statues? ." By Graham Osborne. Catholic Education Resource Center. The B.C. Catholic (2012).

368. Sugar Regulatory Administration. Republic of the Philippines. Department of Agriculture. Retrieved Dec. 17, 2019.

369. "Research Article: Sugarcane Landraces of Ethiopia: Germplasm Collection and Analysis of Regional Diversity and Distribution." Hindawi Advances In Agriculture, Aug. 14, 2018. Vol. 2018, Article ID 7920724, 18 pages.

370. "Acorus calamus L." By Joseph Khangela Baloyi & Linette Ferreira. South African National Biodiversity Institute. Pretoria National Botanical Garden. Mar. 2005.

371. "Lubigan." Stuart Xchange. Godofredo U. Stuart Jr., M.D.

372. "Shachah." Strong's Concordance #7812. BibleHub.com.

373. "Perfumery Material: Elemi." By Elena Vosnaki. Perfume Shrine. Dec. 18, 2012.

374. "Bicol-grown 'pili' has the fragrance world over a barrel." By Alma P. Gamil. Philippine Daily Inquirer. May 18, 2011.

375. "The World Leaders In Coconut Production." By James Burton. World Atlas. Apr. 19, 2018.

376. "Which Country Has The Most Islands?" By Mark Owuor Otieno. World Atlas. Sept. 11, 2018.

377. 1. "Almug Wood." By E. W. G. Masterman. BibleStudyTools.com. 2. Wikipedia citing Elwell, Walter A.; Beitzel, Barry J. (1988). "Plants of the Bible". Baker Encyclopedia of the Bible. Grand Rapids, Michigan: Baker Book House. p. 1702. 3. dictionary.com. Based on the Random House Unabridged Dictionary, Random House. 2020. 4. "Praising God – Almug Wood." By Carolyn A. Roth. Carolyn Roth Ministry. Oct. 22, 2016.
378. "Aqua Facts." Hawai'i Pacific University Oceanic Institute.
379. "Hindu Kush." By Ervin Grotzbach. Encyclopaedia Iranica. Vol. XII, Fasc. 3. 2012 Edition, Original: 2003. pp. 312-315.
380. "Hindu Kush." By Nigel John Roger Allan, Fosco Maraini and Lewis Owen. Encyclopaedia Britannica. Last Updated Sep. 2, 2014.
381. "Letter from Royal Officials of the Filipinas from Cubu, 1665." The Philippine Islands, 1493-1803 — Vol. 02 of 55, 1569-1576 by Edward Bourne, E.H. Blair, and J.A. Robertson. ebook: pp. 240-241. Also, Child Jesus found on pp. 7, 17, 150, 152, 163, 202, 241, 291, 304.
382. 1. Lupang Hinirang." In Tagalog, English and Spanish.
2. "O Land Beloved (1919)." Wikipedia.
383. "Enrique, 1st Filipino to Circumnavigate the World?" By: Ambeth R. Ocampo. Philippine Daily Inquirer. July 10, 2019.
384. "Duarte Barbosa." encyclopdeia.com. Oct. 2, 2019.
385. Villarroel 2009, pp. 93–133.
386. "Is Allah the Name of God?" Let Us Reason Ministries. 2014.
387. "Origin of Babuyan Islands." filipiknow.net. Mar. 9, 2019.
388. Basalt Tel Dan Stele affirms the "House of David" dated Iron Age II, 9th century BCE. Israel Antiquities Authority. The Israel Museum, Publisher: Harry N. Abrams, Inc. 2005. IAA: 1996-125, 1993-3162. H: 34; W: 32 cm.
389. "The World's 17 Megadiverse Countries." worldatlas.com, July 25, 2018; rankred.com, Dec. 22, 2018. Data from Conservation International 1998.
390. "World's greatest concentration of unique mammal species is on Philippine island." The Field Museum Press Release. Chicago. July 15, 2016. Published in Frontiers of Biogeography. 15-year Study.
391."Chicken DNA Challenges Theory That Polynesians Beat Europeans to Americas." By Roff Smith, National Geographic. Mar. 19, 2014.
392. Strong's Concordance "Dalal" #H1809 and "Nuwa" # H5128 with Gesenius' Hebrew-Chaldee Lexicon. Blue Letter Bible.
393. 1. "Where Are Most of Earth's Volcanoes?" By Live Science Staff January 18, 2013. 2. "Deep Ocean Volcanoes?" Ocean Today. NOAA. Retrieved Feb. 9, 2020.
394. A modern facsimile of Martin Behaim's 1492 Erdapfel map. Behaim Globe (1492–1493) Ernst Ravenstein: Martin Behaim. His Life and his Globe. London 1908. Public Domain.
395. "Alabaster, Mineral." and "Marble, Rock." By Editors of Encyclopaedia Britannica. Encyclopaedia Britannica. Updated Jan. 24, 2018 and Jan. 24, 2020.
396. "Nineveh." Wikipedia. Citing 1. Mieroop, Marc van de (1997). The Ancient Mesopotamian City. Oxford: Oxford University Press. p. 95. 2. Geoffrey Turner, "Tell Nebi Yunus: The ekal masarti of Nineveh," Iraq, vol. 32, no. 1, pp. 68–85, 1970.
397. "Second Book of Adam and Eve." By Rutherford H. Platt, Jr. The Forgotten Books of Eden. 1926. Chapter VIII. V. 16-19. p. 66.
398. "Phoenicians in the Lands of Gold." By J.G. Cheock. P.11. Citing Rebecca Catz, trans. The Travels of Mendes Pinto by Fernao Mendes Pinto. University of Chicago Press. 1989.
399. "Ben Jonson's Alchemist and Early Modern Laboratory Space." By John Shanahan. The Journal For Early Modern Cultural Studies. Vol. 8, No. 1. Spring/Summer 2008. p. 42. Citing "The Alchemist." By Ben Johnson. 2.1.1–5.
400. "What is the mid-ocean ridge?" Office of Ocean Exploration and Research, National Oceanic and Atmospheric Administration and U.S. Department of Commerce. Retrieved Aug. 16, 2019.

401. World map, shaded relief with shaded ocean floor. High Resolution map from Alamy based on National Geographic's "Atlas of World: 8th Ed. Physical Map of Ocean Floor." By National Geographic Society. First published 1974. Compare the two and you will find them the same.

402. "Mining for Gold: The Niche Concept and the Survival of Traditional Small-Scale Miners." By Evelyn J. Caballero. Philippine Sociological Review. Vol. 39, No. 1/4, 1991 PSS CONVENTION (January-December 1991), pp. 17-23. Philippine Sociological Society. p. 17.

403. "A thousand years of Philippine history before the coming of the Spaniards." By Austin Craig. Associate Professor of History. University of the Philippines. 1914. p. 1. Citing "Europe and the Far East." By Sir Robert K. Douglas. Cambridge University Press. 1904. Chap. 1. pp. 2-3.

404. "The Butuan Archaeological Finds: Profound Implications for Philippines and Southeast Asian Prehistory." By Wilfredo P. Ronquillo. Man and Culture in Oceania. 3 Special Issue: 71 – 78, 1987. p. 6.

405. "Good, Towb." Strong's Concordance #2896. BibleHub.com.

406. "FactChecker: Does 'Abba' Mean 'Daddy'?" By Glenn T. Stanton, Focus On The Family. The Gospel Coalition. May 13, 2013.

407. "The Austronesians: Historical and Comparative Perspectives." By Edited by Peter Bellwood, James J. Fox and Darrell Tryon. (Professor Adrian Horridge). A publication of the Department of Anthropology as part of the Comparative Austronesian Project, Research School of Pacific Studies. The Australian National University Canberra ACT Australia. 2006. p. 146.

408. Hsiao-chun Hung , Kim Dung Nguyen , Peter Bellwood & Mike T. Carson (2013) Coastal Connectivity: Long-Term Trading Networks Across the South China Sea, The Journal of Island and Coastal Archaeology, 8:3, pp. 384-404.

409. 1. "AELANA or AILA (Tell el-Khuleifa) Israel." The Princeton Encyclopedia of Classical Sites. By Richard Stillwell, William L. MacDonald, Marian Holland McAllister, Stillwell, Richard, MacDonald, William L., McAlister, Marian Holland, Ed. 2. "Aelana." Dictionary of Greek and Roman Geography (1854). William Smith, LLD, Ed.

410. "Lashon." Strong's Exhaustive Concordance #3956. BibleHub.com. 2. "Lason." Tagalog Dictionary. Pinoy Dictionary.

411. 1. "Baths in 16th Century Philippines." By Beth Ocampo. Philippine Daily Inquirer. July 30, 2013. 2. "When Did Philippine History Begin? " American Historical Association.

412. 1. "Ancient Trade Routes: Santa Cruz Junk." Underwater Archaeologist Franck Goddio. The Hilti Foundation. https://www.franckgoddio.org/projects/ancient-trade-routes/santa-cruz.html. 2. "Maritime Trade in the Philippines During the 15th Century CE." By Bobby C. Orillaneda. Moussons. 27 | 2016, 83-100.

413. "99 Names of Allah (Al Asma Ul Husna)." Never Abba. https://99namesofallah.name/

414. "The Thanksgiving Hymns (iQH, 1Q36,4Q427-32). Hymn 14." The Complete Dead Sea Scrolls. By Geza Vermes. Penguin Classics. P. 278.

415. "Solomonic Gate" in Megiddo. Similar walls dated to the 10th century B.C. found in Hazor, Megiddo and Gezer. AdobeStock image.

416. "Bul." Abarim-Publications.

417. "Gold in early Southeast Asia." By Anna T. N. Bennett. ArcheoSciences, 33. 2009, 99-107.

CHECK OUT OUR YOUTUBE CHANNEL:
Over 250 teaching videos and 10 million views

ORIGINAL SOLOMON'S GOLD SERIES:

Join millions of views with our original series from 2017 which went viral documenting our journey to Ophir, Sheba, Tarshish and the Garden of Eden. English and Tagalog.
www.OphirInstitute.com.
YouTube: The God Culture

ORIGINAL CANON SERIES:

Find the home fo John the Baptist and the Temple Levite priests who were exiled. What scripture did they keep? Were they Essenes? Is Jubilees scripture?
www.OphirInstitute.com.
YouTube: The God Culture

FLOOD SERIES:

Restore the Biblical version of the worldwide deluge including the landing of Noah's Ark and Noah's Division of Territories to his sons.
www.OphirInstitute.com.
YouTube: The God Culture

READ OUR OTHER BOOKS:

REVIEW OUR SOURCES:

Our complete, comprehensive
Sourcebook of our sources includes
the origin source document with link
in most cases, additional commentary,
maps, complete attribution, etc. is
available for free download
as an electronic file at:
www.OphirInstitute.com.

COFFEE TABLE BOOK:

A high quality pictorial view touring
the Philippines with an abbreviated
case as the ancient land of gold.
Available for purchase at:
www.OphirInstitute.com.

TEST THE BOOK OF JUBILEES:

Apply the Torah Test to this book found
in the Dead Sea Scrolls and viewed
as scripture since at least 150 B.C. by
Levites Temple Priests. 50 Chapters,
Full color maps, Torah Calendar, Cross-
references, etc.
Available for purchase at :
www.OphirInstitute.com.

Printed in Great Britain
by Amazon

27308337R00215